DRAMA, PLAY, AND GAME

DRAMA, PLAY, AND GAME

English Festive Culture in the Medieval and Early Modern Period

LAWRENCE M. CLOPPER

The University of Chicago Press   Chicago & London

LAWRENCE M. CLOPPER is professor of English at Indiana University. He is
the author of *Songes of Rechelesnesse: Langland and the Franciscans* (1997)
and *The Dramatic Records of Chester, 1399–1642* (1979) and a coeditor of
The Performance of Middle English Culture (1998).

The University of Chicago Press gratefully acknowledges the assistance
of the John Simon Guggenheim Memorial Foundation
in the publication of this book.

The University of Chicago Press, Chicago 60637
The University of Chicago Press, Ltd., London
© 2001 by The University of Chicago
All rights reserved. Published 2001
Printed in the United States of America

10 09 08 07 06 05 04 03 02 01   1 2 3 4 5

ISBN: 0-226-11030-3 (cloth)

Frontispiece: "A Dancer before the Ark of the Lord." From Helena M.
Gamer, "Mimes, Musicians, and the Origin of the Mediaeval Religious
Play," *Deutsche Beiträge zur geistigen Überlieferung* 5 (1955).

Library of Congress Cataloging-in-Publication Data

Clopper, Lawrence M., 1941–
    Drama, play, and game : English festive culture in the medieval and early
modern period / Lawrence M. Clopper.
        p.   cm.
    Includes bibliographical references and index.
    ISBN 0-226-11030-3 (alk. paper)
    1. English drama—To 1500—History and criticism.   2. English
drama—Early modern and Elizabethan, 1500–1600—History and
crictism.   3. Theater—England—History—Medieval, 500–1500.
4. Medievalism—England—History—16th century.   5. England—
Social life and customs—1066–1485.   6. Recreation—England—
History—To 1500.   7. Festivals—England—History—To 1500.
8. Games—England—History—To 1500.   I. Title.
    PR641 .C58   2001
    822'.109—dc21   00-011851

FOR MARTIN STEVENS

CONTENTS

❧ ACKNOWLEDGMENTS ❧

In some respects this book began more than thirty years ago when I first read the Brome *Abraham and Isaac* and thought it undramatic and boring. My response also created a puzzle: if my reaction were somehow right, then why did the play have a two-hundred-year performance record? My quandary, at first a subconscious nagging, led me to Martin Stevens, with whom I wrote my M.A. thesis and Ph.D. dissertation. In hindsight the events that followed seem fated. To revise my dissertation I went to England to look at manuscripts containing the Chester records in order to ascertain that the published transcriptions were accurate. The first manuscript I examined, British Library Harley 2054, contained records that I did not recall having seen before. I found more unpublished records; threw away my dissertation because it was obsolete; discovered that other scholars were locating unpublished records in the archives at York, Norwich, and elsewhere; and met G. R. Proudfoot, who was general editor for the Malone Society, and Arthur Cawley, who was encouraging publication of new essays on the medieval drama in *Leeds Studies in English* and who, coincidentally, was coeditor with Martin Stevens of the Early English Text Society edition of *The Towneley Plays.* It was Alexandra Johnston who had the vision to try to coordinate the work in which many of us were engaged. After a preliminary meeting at Toronto, she established the Records of Early English Drama (REED) project, which was to oversee the collecting and publication of all extant references to drama, ceremony, and spectacle from the earliest records until 1642. The beginning of the REED project was a significant moment in the revisionist assessment of the drama already under way. My own research underwent considerable change over the years. My first project was an edition of the records of Chester; however, I subsequently moved from editor and historian to cultural historian. The precipitating event was the very search for the records themselves, for I discovered that I had developed a detailed understanding of the city of Chester through looking at its records. The experience changed the way I looked at the city's drama—not in isolation but in a rich context of religious and political interrelationships. My interest in Chester broadened to other cities; that in drama grew into other arenas of play and game. And hence this book on festive culture: drama, play and game.

My greatest debt is to Martin Stevens. He survived my dissertation and has been a source of inspiration and support throughout my professional life. He is a mentor in the deepest sense of that term: he is an excellent teacher, a remarkable scholar, an able administrator, a political force in working toward the good of our profession, and a great friend to a great many people. We all ought to try to emulate him.

My debt to David Bevington is of a different kind, but what I have said of Martin Stevens is true of David as well. I first met David in the Modern Language Association seminar devoted to early drama, a group that eventually became the Medieval and Renaissance Drama Society. The seminar provided an important venue for sharing new work in the drama. But, perhaps most important, it was a place where younger and older scholars met to talk and share information. It is the conversation that I recall most because it was from this talking together that I and others got many ideas and new information. Happily, that sharing continues whenever the members of MRDS get together at conferences. David helped me in various other ways in my career, but he was particularly generous in his support of this manuscript when it was under consideration at the University of Chicago Press.

Most of this book was written while I held a Guggenheim Fellowship, and I would like to thank the John Simon Guggenheim Memorial Foundation for giving me the time to undertake the project. I am also grateful to the foundation for its contribution toward the publication of this book. The book was completed while I was on sabbatical from Indiana University.

I would like to thank Richard K. Emmerson for reading the manuscript and suggesting ways to improve it, but also for all the helpful support for and comment on my work over the last two decades.

Many of the data in the central chapters come from documents published by Records of Early English Drama or ones stored at REED. I would like to thank Alexandra Johnston, the director, and Sally-Beth MacLean, the executive editor, for their kindness and help when I worked at the archives and on many other occasions. I also want to thank Abigail Young, REED's paleographer and Latin expert, and the other members of the staff over the years for their help. I have benefited from the access to yet-unpublished transcriptions made by Anne Brannen, John Coldewey, Mary Erler, James Gibson, Alice B. Hamilton, Anne Lancashire, Alexandra Johnston, Sally-Beth MacLean, John McKinnell, and Diana Wyatt. I have cited few unpublished records but benefited greatly from being able to look at collections because they helped me formulate my ideas about practice in different ludic venues. Many of these editors, as well as many editors of published collections, kindly responded to inquiries. They are responsible for neither my errors nor the judgments I have made about the records.

It has been a great pleasure to work with the University of Chicago Press. Thanks to my editors, Alan Thomas and Randy Petilos, and to Leslie Keros and Jane Zanichkowsky for helping to bring my text to its final form.

Although I quote from and use portions of essays that have appeared in print, I do not use any previously printed material in its entirety. I would like to thank the following publishers for permission to use or quote from my earlier publications: "Lay and Clerical Impact on Civic Religious Drama and Ceremony," in *Contexts of Early English Drama,* ed. John Coldewey and Marianne Briscoe (Bloomington: Indiana University Press, 1989): 103–36; "*Miracula* and *The Tretise of Miraclis Pleyinge*," *Speculum* 65 (1990): 878–905; "*Communitas:* The Play of Saints in Late Medieval and Tudor England," in *Medieval and Early Renaissance Drama: Reconsiderations,* ed. Martin Stevens and Milla Riggio, for a special issue of *Mediaevalia* (gen. ed. Sandro Sticca) 18 (1995): 81–109; "English Drama: From Ungodly *Ludi* to Sacred Play," in *The Cambridge History of Medieval English Literature,* ed. David Wallace (Cambridge: Cambridge University Press, 1998), 739–66; and "Why Are There So Few English Saint Plays?" *Early Theatre* 2 (1999): 107–12.

Finally, I would like to thank my wife, Pegram, for having survived yet another project of mine. Fortunately, this one was not quite as trying as the one on Langland. My work would have been less happy had it not been for the companionship of Gabriella.

❧ INTRODUCTION ❧

Late nineteenth- and early twentieth-century scholars imagined that a dramatic tradition that had virtually disappeared with the fall of the late Roman Empire was reintroduced into the West as an embellishment of the liturgy.[1] Initially the interpolations were sung responses—*Quem quaeritis*—but by accretion they gathered dramatic attributes such as impersonation, costume, and imitative gesture. These burgeoning scenes gradually evolved into more complex organisms, one result of which was that the choirs could no longer contain the action and the dramas moved first into the nave, then onto the steps, and finally into the streets and onto pageant wagons. As these dramas were emerging from the church—the best example being the *Jeu d'Adam,* which was performed on the steps—they passed into the hands of the laity, one consequence of which was that vernacular religious drama became increasingly contaminated by comic intrusions and base scenes. Some scholars who promoted this history expressed puzzlement that the drama should have (re-)originated in the monastic choirs given the thunderbolts directed against the theater in the late empire and early Middle Ages. Equally puzzling was the almost total absence of an antitheatrical polemic in the late Middle Ages after the reinvention of the drama. Gerhoh of Reichersberg and Herrad of Landsberg, both from the twelfth century, were cited by everyone as representative of what little antitheatrical senti-

---

1. Chambers, *Mediaeval Stage,* and K. Young, *Drama of the Medieval Church,* are the two older, standard references. Hardison exposed the evolutionist thinking of earlier scholars in *Christian Rite and Christian Drama in the Middle Ages.*

I

ment remained, and the Middle English *Tretise of Miraclis Pleyinge* (early fifteenth century) was given as the only sustained polemic between the late empire and the Puritan attacks of the late sixteenth century.[2]

Behind this set of problems and issues lay another more fundamental question: How could this phenomenon, the emergence of a dramatic tradition, have occurred a second time in Western history? There are a number of cultural prejudices hidden in the question. There seems to have been skepticism that medieval culture could duplicate the art forms of the great civilizations of Greece and Rome. Given the considerable decline since the Age of Gold, as well as the general superstitious nature of religion and society in the Middle Ages (a Renaissance and Protestant construct), it seemed difficult to locate the cultural initiative that could have produced a new Aeschylus or Sophocles. One solution was to assert the continuance of the classical tradition no matter how small that great river had become.[3] Some proposed that the dramatic tradition never died; we simply do not have the documents to substantiate its presence. Others argued that the tradition narrowed to that of the mimes, but their activity was sufficient to spark the rebirth of the theater in liturgical drama when the mimes showed the monks how to impersonate historical figures. The desire for origins, especially the need to place those origins in the classical tradition, resulted in a history of the drama that was continuous. The Middle Ages did not have to take on the burden of the rebirth of the theater; rather, that renewal could be attributed to the descendants of the *mimi* of the ancient world.[4]

To account for the appearance of drama in the later Middle Ages by positing the transmission of the ancient tradition over six to ten centuries by mimes is to construct an overly elaborate and unnecessary sequence of causes. There is a simpler answer to the two questions posed: Christian Europe in the later Middle Ages was able to develop a drama—an enacted and staged script—because most persons did not associate such dramas with the *theatrum* either in mode or in content. When clerics begin to represent Rachel and the *Quem quaeritis* within the church and at the altar, there would have been no reason to identify these liturgical responses with the *theatrum* because the church was a sacred place and the action cultic and symbolic. The clerics' actions did not re-

---

2. Henshaw, "Attitude of the Church"; Barish, *Antitheatrical Prejudice* ; and Woolf, *English Mystery Plays*, 77–101.

3. Chambers, *Mediaeval Stage;* Nicoll, *Masks, Mimes, and Miracles;* Hunningher, *Origin of the Theater;* Ogilvy, "*Mimi, Scurrae, Histriones*"; and Axton, *European Drama of the Early Middle Ages.* For a critique, see Mann, "Roman Mime and Medieval Theatre."

4. There were, of course, other solutions, the most important being the anthropological argument that the mimetic necessarily and inevitably arises from cultic ritual.

semble what they understood actors and mimes to have done in the *theatrum*. Similarly, when English Christians in the fourteenth and fifteenth centuries began to present biblical and moral dramas in the streets and on village greens, they did not associate their plays with the ancient *theatrum* because the mode and content were pious. I believe we have misrepresented Western stage history because we have assumed that *theatrum* designated what we moderns mean by "theater," a place for dramas. But though the Middle Ages retained the idea that the *theatrum* was a place for spectacle, it was also a place of obscenities: the commonest words connected with *theatrum* in the Middle Ages are *impudicitia, spurcitia, impuritas, turpitudo, licentia, luxuria, foeditas, obscenitas.*[5] Second, we have come to recognize that liturgical representations not only differ from drama in most, perhaps all, ways but that liturgical and vernacular traditions developed separately; indeed, I would argue that not only did most clerics fail to conceive of what they were doing as theatrical but that, insofar as they were enjoined not to attend upon *spectacula,* they were not particularly involved in establishing or encouraging a vernacular dramatic tradition.[6] On the other hand, the evidence suggests that clerical attempts to suppress and constrain the *spectacula* and *ludi inhonesti* of the laity resulted in some places in the invention of a lay vernacular drama. I believe that in the late Middle Ages as lay people began to institutionalize themselves—as civic corporations or trade or religious guilds—they increasingly contested clerical attempts at domination. Although the stronger groups made some concessions to clerical initiatives with regard to appropriate behavior and recreation, they also seem to have tried to find acceptable entertainments that reflected their concerns for their own spiritual welfare.

The Problem of Terms

This broad statement of my argument must be refined in a number of ways, as subsequent chapters will illustrate; however, here at the beginning we have to confront the terminological difficulties before us. These are of several kinds. First, whether we are talking about modern or medieval usage, there is the general slipperiness in terms such as "drama" and "theater." Second, the slipperiness in modern usage has contaminated our reading of medieval texts and documents. When we attempt to construct a history of the "theater," we put

---

5. Bigongiari, "Were There Theatres?"

6. For the separate development of the liturgical and the vernacular traditions, see Hardison, *Christian Rite,* 253–83. For the lack of clerical involvement in vernacular drama, see my essay "Lay and Clerical Impact."

the theater at the center of the discussion and force the documents to operate within that arena. When we look for the emergence of drama from the liturgy—the problem of origins—we not only evoke an evolutionary model but may ignore how medieval writers imagined the liturgy to relate to the *theatrum*. We have often, I think, attempted a history of the theater without bringing to bear the importance of how medieval writers used theatrical language. Much of my discussion, therefore, but especially in the first chapters, will center on terms: What is the *theatrum?* What are *miracula?* What are "saint plays"? My thesis is—not surprisingly—that we have applied modern senses of theatrical terms to medieval texts and documents with the result that we have "theatricalized"—made into theater—activities that do not properly belong in that category as we understand it. But even this formulation has its problems because on one hand I wish to argue that our literary critical language has proved inadequate in dealing with the medieval phenomena—an anthropological language might be more useful—at the same time that I recognize that medieval rhetorical discourse ("literary theory") is more systematic and useful than we might think and, yet, medieval vocabulary, as we will see, is often inadequate to verbalize a theory of the phenomena we would regard as dramas. Before we get into this study I want to advertise some of the terminological problems, then give some instances of the medieval treatment of theatrical terms, and finally set—somewhat arbitrarily—the definitions I will use for "drama," "theater," and "*theatrum.*"

Words such as "drama" and "theater," "dramatic" and "theatrical" are troublesome even though in modern usage we normally can distinguish meaning according to circumstance. If we say that we are going to the theater to see a drama, most listeners would understand the statement: we are going to a place, the theater, which is where the genre of drama is enacted, in order to see a play, which is a generic type. Technically, our statement could have meant that we were going to the theater where there was a drama in order to watch the drama of the audience's reception of the play. We might not even have ventured beyond the lobby because we became intrigued by the social dramas of self-display and some carefully staged opportunities for persons to exhibit their sophistication by being overheard. But the genre "drama" itself has complications because even though we have a sense of the category, we are also aware that there are phenomena on the edges that we might put into the category even if they do not totally conform to our sense of the genre. Further complications arise—but can usually be resolved—when a term with fairly specific generic expectations is used metaphorically. When we say that someone is "dramatic," we may compliment or criticize, but it is normally clear that we mean that the person is acting in some overblown fashion. Similarly, "theatrical" can mean "staged" without indicating that the event is a play within a proscenium arch and we will understand the difference.

Despite their broad semantic range, we live comfortably with these terms and ably discern their usage. We have relatively clear notions of "theater" and "drama" and can readily grasp the use of metaphor: "the world is a stage"; "he's a bit theatrical." People in the Middle Ages could use theatrical metaphor in what appears to be the same way.[7] But the basic difference between our and the medieval usage of theatrical terms is that we have a strong generic sense of the terms, even when they are deployed as metaphors. Medievals had a location for theatrical terminology, but it was not primarily generic in our sense. As the phrasing of the preceding sentence suggests, there were even greater problems in talking about the *theatrum* in the Middle Ages than there are now. Medieval people had some historical knowledge of the *theatrum,* which coincidentally enabled theatrical metaphor; however, in the initial periods when dramas begin to appear in the medieval west, medievals did not have an adequate vocabulary to describe the phenomena because the theatrical vocabulary that we would recognize as such had been preempted. One of my basic premises is that we—that is, modern scholars and readers—have looked at medieval documents and texts with our notions of "theater" and "drama" fairly well sorted-out generically and metaphorically and have assumed that medieval terminology points to the same phenomena, that is, that the language and its usage are consistent and continuous over time. In general, the assumption is accurate, but it is also fundamentally flawed insofar as the object of study, the *theatrum,* is not the same. If we extrapolate from there, then it can be argued that where the vehicles of metaphor, here medieval *theatrum* and modern "theater," differ, then the tenor will as well even should they look alike.

Because the early Middle Ages did not have a theater for dramas in its midst, it did two things with theatrical terminology and language: drawing on ancient polemic against spectacle and the *theatrum,* it created a rhetoric of abuse to direct at activities having nothing to do with the stage, and, partially under the influence of the rhetoricians, the terms lost some generic concepts or were translated into poetic modes. For example, what happens to the word "drama" or its equivalents in European languages over the millennia? In Greek, the word could mean "deed," "action," or "play," especially "tragedy." In late

---

7. See chapter 1 below.

and medieval Latin rhetorical texts, as we will see, it describes a mode of presenting a narrative. It does not appear at all in the *Middle English Dictionary*. The *Oxford English Dictionary* gives the first recorded usage as occurring in 1515 in Barclay's *Eclogues,* where it refers to plays in honor of the ancient gods and thus not to current practice. In English the word does not develop—nor recapture—its generic sense of an enacted text for contemporary theater until much later.

For medieval rhetoricians and commentators, "dramatic" is one of three modes of narrative. As Nicholas Trevet says, "The poets wrote in three modes *(modi),* either in the narrative mode, in which only the poet speaks, as in the *Georgics;* or the dramatic mode, wherein the poet nowhere speaks [sc. in his own person] but only the characters *(personae)* who have been introduced— and this mode is particularly well suited to tragic and comic writers—while the third mode is a mixture of the other two . . . [in which] sometimes the poet speaks in his own person, and sometimes the characters who have been introduced. This is Virgil's method in the *Aeneid.*"[8] The "dramatic" mode is that in which the author or narrator is not represented in his own or narrative voice; instead, there are speakers alone.

The quintessential Christian "dramatic" text was the *Song of Songs.*[9] From the time of Origen, commentators treated *Song of Songs* as a dramatic piece. According to Joseph Jones, Origen gives a particularly vivid account of the text in "acts" with fully imagined scenes, perhaps influenced by the theater, though, Jones acknowledges, we have next to no information about drama in Alexandria at the time.

Later medieval commentators understood the *Song* to be in the dramatic mode and to have a relation to the dramas of the ancients; however, in their denigration of ancient drama, they separated sacred song from pagan plays and rituals. Isidore says that "Epithalamia are the songs of persons getting married which are sung by scholars in honor of the bride-groom and bride. Solomon first composed these in praise of Christ and the Church. The pagans

---

8. Nicholas Trevet's introduction to Seneca's tragedies (Minnis and Scott, *Medieval Literary Theory and Criticism c. 1100–c. 1375,* 344). And see Isidore of Seville, *Etymologiarum* 8.7.11, and the other instances cited in Minnis, *Medieval Theory of Authorship,* 22, 57, 58. Whenever possible I have used translations from the Latin by others; unascribed translations are my own.

9. J. Jones, "The *Song of Songs* as a Drama." I think Jones's essay is extremely valuable and revealing, and I have relied on it quite a lot; however, I also think Jones reads "dramatic" too much as we use it and without regard for what these commentators knew and thought of the theater. Where, for Jones, "dramatic" conjures up notions of the theater in these writings, I would argue that the commentators make a sharp distinction between the "dramatic" and the "theatrical."

appropriated the epithalamium. . . . This genre was first celebrated by the pagans on the stage."[10] The *Song of Songs* is made up of sung exchanges between the bridegroom and his bride, not choruses sung by scholars, as Isidore has it here. Later commentators point out this difference in the genre, but Isidore's remark is revealing because it implicitly opposes a choir of monks singing sacred hymns to the choruses of the *theatrum* that he later describes and thus further debases the pagan practice.

The relation of the sacred epithalamia to ancient drama is a commonplace, and, concomitantly, the discussion of that relation provides a clear picture of the distance medieval commentators put between themselves and the *theatrum*. In illustrating this example, I want to show not only what the commentators say but also how easy it is in translating from Latin to English to create an element of the *theatrum* that does not exist in the original. For example, Philip of Harvengt (d. 1183) says that before the Incarnation actually took place, some foresaw it in the spirit and set it down in writings: "One of these is found to have described explicitly the mutual affection of the Bridegroom and Bride and to have composed a delicate, chaste, spiritual, modest play, as it were."[11] Philip goes on to describe the musical instruments and other parts that belong to the epithalamium, then he says that

> our writer . . . has composed this novel and previously unknown drama in the fashion of the later comic poets, who bring on stage different persons or players speaking their parts [novum et inauditum drama instar composuit comicorum, qui loquentes, introducunt personas varias scenicorum] . . . Antiquity certainly did not know this kind of writing before his [the composer of the *Song*'s] time, but it appears that posterity took it from him much later. Afterwards, the disciples of the Greeks, because they were unable quite to understand what he wrote about in mystical fashion, transferred the same kind of writing to their frivolous and inept works [Quod nimirum scribendi genus ante illum non novit antiquitas, sed ab illo, ut videtur, longe infra sumpsit posteritas: dum post sequentes Graecorum scholae quid de quibus mystice scriberet, quia non satis capere potuerunt, ipsum saltem scribendi modum ad suas vanitates et ineptias transtulerunt].

---

10. Isidore of Seville, *Etymologiarum*, I.39.18, cited by J. Jones, "*Song of Songs*," 38. Radbertus Paschasius's book on Psalm 44, the other epithalamium in the Bible, makes a similar link between epithalamia and the dramas of worldly men, but he attributes the invention of the form to David (Jones, 39–40).

11. Jones's translation; the Latin is "Quorum unus mutuos Sponsi et Sponsae affectus invenitur expressius descripsisse, subtilem et honestam, spiritualem et modestem velut fabulam texuisse." J. Jones, "*Song of Songs*," 42; the Latin is from PL 203.185A.

The larger concerns of the passage are to ascribe the invention of the epithalamia to writers before the Incarnation and to contrast the chastity and delicacy of the Hebrew ones with those made by the Greeks. We should also note that where Jones reads "play," it would be more accurate to say that the writer "wove a fable," my point being that this is not a true story but a mystic composition that the Greeks could not understand. Because they did not understand the text to be mystical, they debased the dramatic narrative mode by treating the content literally and then having it acted out by persons. This latter detail indicates that Philip did not understand Solomon's epithalamium to be enacted; rather, it was sung by two or more voices in turns (that is, it is choral). Similarly, Gerhoh of Reichersberg understands the *Song* to be dramatic but not theatrical: "We should observe with what variety the psalms were sung in those days and may be sung now, and how the persons singing or speaking in the psalms are varied, so that we may join our emotion as we sing with the emotion of the psalms. For if this principle, when observed, has been successful in comedies and tragedies—that an actor in frivolous shows *[theatricis nugis]*, who recited *[repraesentaret]* the words of a character rejoicing or mourning, simulated the emotions of the person rejoicing or mourning—how much more should we, in the praises of the True Christ, not in simulated fashion but with true devotion adopt the emotions of those whose words we echo."[12] There is a formal similarity between the dramatic and the theatrical— persons sing or speak in response (without the intervention of the poet)—but there are also distinctions: psalms are not frivolous, as are comedies and tragedies; psalm singers do not simulate but express true devotion. Gerhoh, like others, identifies comedies and tragedies as dramas of the past.[13] He also distinguishes between liturgy, a sacred choral drama, and a drama for the *theatrum:* the latter inevitably involves simulation, a disjunction between what is represented and the person who represents it. Gerhoh's distinction is based in ancient polemic that the actor is a hypocrite, a feigner of emotion.[14]

Although it may not always be easy for us to see the distinctions between "dramatic" and "theatrical" in medieval texts, I think it is clear that medieval commentators and rhetoricians had such a distinction. In speaking of the difficulties of the *Song of Songs,* the commentators seem rather obsessed with the

---

12. Jones's translation from PL 193.632–33 ("*Song of Songs,*" 41).

13. For example, Honorius of Autun, speaking of the *Songs,* says that in this "canticle of the play" *[Cantico dramatis]* there is alternation of persons, as in pagan comedies *[in comoediis gentilium];* in J. Jones, "*Song of Songs,*" 40–41.

14. Lewis and Short, *Latin Dictionary: hypocrita* sb[1].

absence of identifying markers for the speakers—though these were often pro-vided in manuscripts—at the same time as they identify the "dramatic" as a mode in which there are only speakers. This obsession, it seems to me, reveals that they think of the dramatic not just as a poetic mode but in terms of manu-script presentation. The *Song of Songs,* being a mystical text, lacks the visual signs of a dramatic text, yet it is a text on the page that can be rubricated to con-form to other liturgical manuscripts (responsories, for example). Liturgical manuscripts, among other things, may, therefore, serve as memorial cues to an-cient dramatic texts such as Terence, for both have visual rubrics for responses. Textually and formally, the liturgy is a drama in the medieval sense; it is not a drama in our or the ancient one. When we see the word "drama" in a medieval text, therefore, we ought not to think of a script for enactment by persons as-suming roles; rather, we should think of it as a formal and visual presentation of responding voices.

Just as the term "drama," as *theatrical genre,* was absent from medieval lan-guages, so too were the Aristotelian categories of tragedy and comedy.[15] As we have seen above, "tragedy" and "comedy" do continue to exist as designators of certain kinds of dramas for the ancient *theatrum;* however, they no longer function as terms for similar phenomena in medieval culture. That is not to say that medievals did not recognize and use "tragedy" and "comedy" to refer to certain kinds of content or style (as Chaucer's monk does) but that the terms were not used to denote liturgical *representationes* or vernacular dramas. This point is decisively revealed in Averroes' commentary on Aristotle's *Poetics,* which was transmitted to the West through Herman the German's Latin trans-lation (1256).[16] When Averroes came to the *Poetics,* he was confronted by an insuperable problem: his culture did not have a theatrical tradition, as a conse-quence of which it was not clear to what literary forms Aristotle was referring when he used the words "tragedy" and "comedy." Jorge Luis Borges has imag-ined this situation in his tale "Averroes' Search."[17] Borges presents The Com-mentator, as Averroes was known in the Middle Ages, at work on his treatise on universals but at the same time in a puzzle about certain words in Aristotle's *Poetics.* During the course of an evening he is joined by some friends, including one who has just returned from a journey and tells a marvelous story in which he says he was taken to a painted wooden structure where there was a perfor-

---

15. Allen, *Ethical Poetic of the Later Middle Ages* ; and Kelly, *Ideas and Forms of Tragedy.*

16. See the introduction and partial translation of Herman's translation in Minnis and Scott, *Medieval Literary Theory,* 277–307.

17. Borges, *Labyrinths.*

mance in which there were speakers who personated others. Everyone is skeptical. Farach, one of the listeners in the garden, concludes that twenty persons are unnecessary to relate such a story since one single speaker is capable of telling all that is necessary no matter how complicated the tale might be. The others approve his words. As Averroes retires, he makes his decisive comment: "Aristu (Aristotle) gives the name of tragedy to panegyrics and that of comedy to satires and anathemas. Admirable tragedies and comedies abound in the pages of the Koran and in the *mohalacas* of the sanctuary."[18]

When Herman the German translated the commentary, he did not rectify Averroes' error despite the fact that liturgical *representationes* had been in existence for several hundred years, the preceding century had produced the great musical dramas like those in the Fleury playbook, and Herman's own age had begun to produce vernacular dramatic texts. Herman simply did not associate current phenomena with what Aristotle was talking about. Influenced by the Arab commentators, Herman understood poetry to be either praise or blame, an Averroistic reorientation of Aristotle's discussion of the origins of poetry. Furthermore, the crucial concept of imitation *(mimesis)* is replaced with imagination *(imaginatio)* or "likening" *(assimilatio),* a kind of representation that arouses the emotions of the audience so that they are encouraged to pursue virtue and flee vice. Rather than representation through personation, which we have in Aristotle's discussion of tragedy and comedy, we have a displacement in the Arabic texts to a poetry that is ethically motivated through "likenings" or the imagination. Thus, tragedy becomes defined as "the art of praise" and comedy as "the art of blame." The characteristics that Aristotle assigns to tragedy —catharsis, the six parts of tragedy, and so forth—are reoriented to support an ethical notion of narrative rather than dramatic forms.

It might be objected that Herman appeared on the scene too early to make the connection between Aristotle's descriptions of tragedy and comedy and the relatively recent appearance of works that seem to us to be dramatic or semidramatic. If we move to the early fourteenth century, however, we do not find that matters have appreciably changed. In his commentary on the tragedies of Seneca, Nicholas Trevet understands that they are represented by *personae* who spoke in the poet's place, and then he gives a picture of ancient dramatic practice that is dependent on Isidore of Seville.[19] Yet he also speaks of the tragedies as being in the "dramatic mode," so when he comes to the conclusion

---

18. Ibid., 155.
19. Minnis and Scott, *Medieval Literary Theory,* 344.

of his prologue, it is not surprising that he speaks more in terms of "mode" and content than mimesis: "Seneca, in the book under discussion, not only wrote about tragic subjects but also employed the tragic mode of writing. So, his book is rightly called 'the book of tragedies.' For it contains sorrowful verses on the misfortunes of great men, in which the poet never speaks in his own person, but only the characters who have been introduced."[20] Trevet has placed Seneca within a rhetorical rather than a theatrical tradition, and I think he does so because the rhetorical tradition is more meaningful and present to him than the theatrical past preserved by Isidore. Trevet's discussion reveals that for him Seneca's plays are stories "As olde bookes maken us memorie / Of hym that stood in greet prosperitee, / And is yfallen out of heigh degree / Into myserie, and endeth wrecchedly."[21] They are texts in which the persons speak in their own voices without the intervention of the poet.

This preliminary study of terms has revealed that "drama," "tragedy," and "comedy" were generally restricted to historical contexts: they refer to literary products of the ancient pagan world. When the terms or their derivatives are used in medieval texts to denote contemporary phenomena or literary categories, they refer to modes, style, or content, not theatrical genre. Most important, despite the potential for theatrical language to be reapplied to phenomena that we recognize as dramas, medieval writers did not make such a move (in England, before the sixteenth century). Although the *Song* commentaries describe a dialogic relation between speakers that would seem readily applicable to liturgical or vernacular dramas, no medieval writer to my knowledge made such a connection. The words "drama" and "dramatic" do not exist in Middle English. Similarly, although the words "tragedy" and "comedy" conceivably could have been applied to enacted vernacular scripts in the medieval period, they are not so used until the sixteenth century, when they designate staged ancient plays or dramas modeled on them. When medieval writers refer to enacted scripts or liturgical *representationes,* they are much more likely to call them "pleys," "jeux," or *ludi.*

In order to keep ourselves aware of the semantic disjunctions I wish to discuss, I will observe the following usages to avoid awkward and repetitious phraseology. When I use the term "drama," I mean an enacted script that contains, or, if it is a fragment, at one time contained, an entire narrative; that is, it is a text and a performance. There are obvious deficiencies in this usage. A text

---

20. Ibid.
21. *Canterbury Tales* VII.193–97, in Chaucer, *Riverside Chaucer.*

can formally be a drama without being performed; an enactment need not have a script to be a dramatic representation. Certain kinds of events—royal entries, for example—may have pageants with speeches, and the whole sequence can be understood as an enacted script or drama. I do not wish to separate "dramas," that is, enacted scripts of a whole action, from these other kinds of "dramas"; nevertheless, I think a study of this sort requires at times a restricted vocabulary for the purposes of clarification. My major purpose in adopting this usage, as will be apparent in subsequent discussion, is to distinguish a drama from a social event. The context will, I hope, indicate specific usage.

I will consistently separate "theater" from *"theatrum."* I will use "theater" most narrowly to indicate our modern sense of dramatic genre and the place in which dramas are enacted. But I will also use it with all the semantic range that it has and that it at times shares with the Latin term. I will use *"theatrum"* whenever I want to indicate that we are talking about ancient or medieval usage; *"theatrum,"* therefore, will function not only as a word with meaning but as a sign that we should not read the term in the modern senses of "theater."

The terms "comedy" and "tragedy" will not be given much attention in themselves, but it is important to note that some medieval writers used them to refer to ancient dramatic scripts, texts that they associated with the past rather than the present. The terms designate genres that are no longer actively present: Terence manuscripts contain comedies that were once acted but that remain only as reading texts; texts written in the Middle Ages are called comedies if they are versified narratives of a certain sort.[22] The category "enacted script" has been removed from the medieval genre "comedy."

The most vexed medieval usage is *ludus,* or "pley," for it is tempting in many cases to read these terms as "drama" when there is insufficient evidence for that understanding. As John Coldewey has shown, the "word 'play' is historically and conceptually a philological subset of the word 'game,' not the other way around."[23] Both *ludus* and "play" include all kinds of games and sports; in addition, a "player" may not only be a participant in any of these activities but a musician or even a player at dice and cards. Coldewey's most instructive example of how such terms can mislead is his record of the Dunmow Corpus Christi play. The surviving receipts prove that this is not a religious drama but a series of games. They read in part:

---

22. Raby, *History of Secular Latin Poetry,* 2:54.
23. Coldewey, "Plays and 'Play' in Early English Drama," 182.

Receved at our playe fyrste the games of the bysshope of Seynth Andrewe
and for the shotyng . . .
Rc for the games of our runnyng . . .
Rc . . . at the games at the leapyng . . . [24]

The receipts go on to list three similar contests. This "pley" of Saint Andrew is
not an enactment of his vita but a parish Olympics.

There is also the possibility that the phrase "a play" and related usages may
refer to a musical performance rather than an enacted script. I first began to
think about this when looking at the references to "ludi" at Beaurepaire, the
prior of Durham's manor.[25] It is difficult to know what a payment such as this
from 1430–32 means: "Pro quatuor ludis Prioris, 40s" (1:142). Such payments were regular until at least 1528–29. In the latter year there was also an
additional payment of 3s. 4d. "cantoribus ad ludum suum ex curilietate" (to
the chorister [or precentor] for his play from the court [presumably the clerical
household], 1:163). In 1324–25 the chamberlain paid 20s. to the prior "ludenti" at Beaurepaire on Saint James's Day (1:166). Here undoubtedly "ludenti" means "playing" in the sense of "recreating." And a payment made in
1361–62, "In precentori et sociis ludentibus apud Bewrpayr ante Natale, 5s"
(1:127), undoubtedly means that the choirmaster and his fellows sang—perhaps with the boy bishop—at Christmas. So what are the "quatuor ludis Prioris"? It seems probable that these were "plays" in the sense of "musical
entertainments" since other records from Durham routinely rewarded musicians, both those who traveled to the priory as well as those within it, and
the four "plays" may refer to four occasions during the Christmas season.
Durham's monastic records are much like those Sheila Lindenbaum describes
for Westminster Abbey: numerous references to musicians but little that would
suggest dramatic performance.[26]

---

24. Ibid., 184–85.

25. Fowler, *Extracts from the Account Rolls of the Abbey of Durham*. Chambers published selected entries, *Mediaeval Stage*, 2.240–44 (further references appear in the text). John McKinnell,
the REED editor for Durham, has told me that it is not possible to say exactly what went on at
Beaurepaire, but he thinks the term is used for the prior's holidays (as it certainly is for the choristers' annual holiday and for the monks who relaxed at Finchale). McKinnell notes that the few daily
accounts at Beaurepaire during *ludi* are costs for large amounts of food and drink, so if there were
dramatic or musical entertainments on these occasions, the prior did not pay anything for them,
which is surprising, given his generosity at Durham (partly quoted and partly paraphrased from
McKinnell's private communication).

26. Lindenbaum, "Entertainment in English Monasteries." See chapter 3 for my discussion of
monastic practice.

There is a related odd locution at Shrewsbury. The bailiffs made frequent payments to *histriones* and *interlusores* of a variety of noble companies (the King's, the Lady Princess's, Arundel's, Suffolk's).[27] The terminology in some of these entries suggests the citizens are looking at the interluders ("Intuidentibus Interluda" [175], "ad visum Interlusorum suorum," [180]), but there are other records that suggest that the audience is listening to songs: in 1530–31 the king's *histriones* are paid 20s. and more is spent on wine while hearing their melody ("audientibus melodiam eorundem histrionum" [189–90]). This phrase is often used of other traveling groups. To complicate matters further, some entries link the viewing with the hearing: "audientes melodiam & ludentes inspicientes" (1525–26, 182), and "lusoribus & Interlusoribus . . . ostendentibus & offerentibus Ioca sua" (191).

The Shrewsbury records suggest that an "interlude" is a musical performance that includes something to look at—perhaps a pageant—or perhaps the audience simply looks at the performers. These may be similar to the "plays" that John English and Slye provided for the Drapers in London in the early sixteenth century: in 1515 "to Iohn Slye & his company for ij plays, Monday & Tuysday," payment of 13s. 4d.; in 1517 "to Iohn Slye & his company for ij plays for monday & tuysday & for a mery conseyt for the Bachillers Brekefast the same tuysday,"payment of 13s. 8d.; in 1520 "to Iohn Englishe. Slee & ther fellos for ij plays for monday & tuysday," payment of 13s.[28] English was one of Henry VII's players by 1494; Slye was one of the "olde" players when the company was divided circa 1515.[29] The activity may be clarified by later references among the expenses for the company dinner in August.[30] In 1529 there are payments for three of the king's minstrels for playing in the first course on Monday and others for "playing" on Monday and Tuesday. In 1530 there is payment to Slye for "a play" on Monday. These records suggest that "a play" may be a musical performance or a musical performance in conjunction with a pageant like those presented at other times in Henry's court (see below for my discussion of the London aesthetic) or similar to the pageants that the Drapers had in the Midsummer Show. Some records from Sandwich suggest similar us-

---

27. Somerset, *Shropshire*. Further references appear in the text.

28. Robertson and Gordon, *Calendar of Dramatic Records*, 136–37.

29. Streitberger, *Court Revels, 1485–1559;* for English, 38–40, 424 and passim; for Slye, 424.

30. This and the following item from the Drapers' court minutes were not printed by Robertson et al. I wish to thank Anne Lancashire, the REED editor for London, for permission to print them here.

age. In 1502–3, 3s. 4d. was paid for "a play a fore Mr Mayre at the freers." This same sum was also paid "for a player a fore the mayer at Cristmas" as well as a bearward in 1505–6.[31] These records suggest that payments at this level were for musicians and that "players," who appear in other entries and were paid the same or less, were also musicians.

If "a play" may be a musical entertainment, then a "play book" may be a musical manuscript and a "book bearer" someone who holds the manuscript for the minstrels. For a related usage, see the payment in 1559 at Beverley of 3s. 4d. "for making the mynstrelles reginall."[32] We have assumed in the past that a "reginall" is a register or codex containing a text of a drama; here it would appear to be a musical manuscript.

When we see the term "stage play" we tend to think of enacted dramas presented on a stage, and when we see references in churchwardens' accounts to stage plays in the churchyard, we might conclude that these are religious dramas. It is clear in some records, however, that these stage plays are king games and other folk activities that were not always decorous but satirical and parodic.[33]

Given this understanding of "stage play," how are we to interpret interventions on behalf of Saint Katherine Cree and All Hallows in the Wall? In 1529 the city granted Saint Katharine's a license to "make & Sette vp a Stage pley for the profight of their Chirche & the ornamentes of the same from this day vn to mighelmas nexte. And that no graunte or licence be made or graunted by this Courte to eny other parysshe within this Citie or liberties of the same of & for eny other Stage pley duryng the seyd tyme."[34] Saint Katharine's had made a similar petition the previous year for a stage play in the summer, as had All Hallows in the Wall, which was granted a license a year earlier to have a stage play beginning at Easter and continuing to Michaelmas. These exceptions—made during the summer, when such gatherings were normally prohibited—were made because of the decay of the parish churches. None of the records specify that the parishioners performed a religious drama or saint play; instead, they may have had a church ale with a king game or some other kind of *ludus*.

---

31. Dawson, *Plays and Players in Kent*, 149–50.
32. Governor's Minute Book 2, f. 22v, in Wyatt, *Performance and Ceremonial*.
33. The *OED* lists the reference in More's *History of Richard III* (1513), 80–81, 258–59, as the earliest usage (see chapter 8). For the temper of these plays and games, see Billington, *Mock Kings in Medieval Society*.
34. Mill and Chambers, "Dramatic Records of the City of London," 287–88.

Not all references to stage plays suggest that the term is understood pejoratively, even though in some instances there may linger negative connotations. In his prologue to Leviticus, William Tyndale (1530) makes the case that Christians can learn something from the rituals of the Old Testament even though they have been superseded by those instituted by Christ. He says that once Christ is known, Christians can find allegories and similitudes in the earlier practices and that similitudes have more virtue and power than bare words in leading a man into the path and spiritual understanding of things: "And though also that all the ceremonies and sacrifices have as it were a starlight of Christ, yet some there be that have as it were the light of the broad day a little before the sun rising, and express him, and the circumstances and virtue of his death so plainly as if we should play his passion on a scaffold or in a stage play openly before the eyes of the people."[35] The passage suggests that Tyndale does not oppose the representation of Christ's Passion in play, but the context also implies that this similitude is not the full light of day but somewhere between the darkness of the Old Testament and the revelation of the New. A later reformer, looking at the same text, seems to rebut Tyndale: Henry Bullinger says that God is pleased by the representation of his Passion in the sacrifices described in Leviticus, and in the sacraments, but not "by stage-plays; which are at this day greatly set by, although scarce godly, by no small number of trifling and fantastical heads."[36]

Other records suggest that a stage play may be respectable fare. At the entrance of King Henry and his queen into Coventry in 1511, there were three pageants, the latter of which is called a "goodly Stage Play."[37] Nicholas Udall (1542) defines "tragedies" as "sadde entreludes which wee calle staige plaies."[38] Henry Machyn refers to a "stage play" of the Passion of Christ that began at the Grey Friars and another stage play "of a goodly matter" at Saint Olave's.[39] In 1555 a stage play was planned at New Romney that was to run for three days. From the extant accounts it is clear that this was an elaborate production of Christ's Passion.[40]

The term "stage play" continues to have negative associations throughout

---

35. Tyndale, *Tyndale's Old Testament*, 146.

36. Bullinger, *Decades of Henry Bullinger*, 2:194.

37. Ingram, *Coventry*, 107. The notice appears in an antiquarian compilation and so the usage may be later than the date.

38. From Udall's commentary and annotations on Erasmus' *Apophthegmes*. Cited in Lancashire, *Dramatic Texts*, item 292.

39. Machyn, *Diary of Henry Machyn*, 138, 145.

40. Dawson, *Plays and Players in Kent*, 136–37, 202–4.

the sixteenth century, especially when it is used to refer to popular entertainments and the theater, but it also is used to refer to performances that were approved by authorities who produced them. My point is that when one sees a reference to a stage play, one cannot assume that it is to a licensed drama or to a religious drama even if it is being produced in a churchyard, since these precincts were also often the places where games were held.[41] A stage play is not necessarily a scripted drama; it may be a king game or some other rowdy entertainment used to raise money, which may account for the persistence of orders against *ludi* in churchyards.

"Interlude" as a generic term is more diffuse than even modern drama scholars have allowed. It has been noted that in the early Tudor period playwrights attached the term to a wide variety of usually short play texts and that as the century continued, especially in royal proclamations, the phrase "plays and interludes" was used as a catch-all expression for every kind of drama.[42] But prior to this the term could refer to musical performances or a variety of entertainments or simply to amusements. Fabyan's *Chronicle* reports, on the authority of William de Regibus, that King Alfred put on the habit of a minstrel and with his instruments of music entered the tents of the Danes in order to spy on them while performing his "enterludes & songes."[43] *Sir Gawain and the Green Knight* puts interludes in a musical context, and Robert Mannyng of Brunne in *Handlyng Synne* puts interludes with singing and playing on the tabor or pipes rather than with carols (dances), wrestling, and summergames.[44] But the word can refer to games and entertainments as well. A preacher, circa 1400, charged his parishioners whether in the church or the churchyard to make "ne dauncys, ne werdly songys, no interlodyes, ne castynges of the stonne, steraclys, ne pleying at the balle, ne other ydell iapys and pleyis."[45] Similarly, in 1348 John de Trillek, bishop of Hereford, issued a decree against *ludi theatrales*, which were raucous games, and which he refers to as "ludos

---

41. In addition, we should note that references to stages may be to scaffolding erected for the spectators, not the players, a distant evocation of Isidore's *theatrum*, where the spectators stood in the amphitheatres in order to witness the games.

42. Craik, *Tudor Interlude*, 1; Bevington, *From "Mankind" to Marlowe*, 8–9; Wilson, *English Drama 1485–1585*, 10–11; and Nicholas Davis, "Meaning of the Word 'Interlude'" and "Allusions . . . (4): Interludes," 5–15, 61–91. Alan Dessen, in *Shakespeare and the Late Moral Plays*, 10–16, discusses the terminological problems of the word "interlude."

43. Nicholas Davis, "Allusions . . . (4): Interludes," item B34.

44. Ibid., items B10 and B02, respectively.

45. Ibid., item B15. As we shall see, such games and amusements were commonly forbidden in early synodal decrees.

sive interludia" at the end of the decree.[46] Henry Knighton uses the term to refer to a mock tournament, and a 1518 record from Shrewsbury uses it to describe a riding of the Three Kings.[47] My point is that "interlude" denotes a wide variety of activities, some of which are not dramas at all.

My discussion thus far has focused on generic terminology—*theatrum, drama, play, ludus,* stage play, interlude—but I should note also the frequently impenetrable terminology used to refer to performers.[48] Many of the records that remain to us use terms that are not fixed: *histrio,* minstrel, *joculator, mimus,* player, and the like. When is a "player" an actor who performs a text, and when is he a musician? There are times when *mimi,* which we might think of as actors or pantomimes, are actually musicians.[49] Is a *histrio* or an *interlusor* an actor or a musician or one in some cases and the other in others?

Given the difficulty of the language, how do we know when the touring companies of noble patrons began to perform texts rather than provide music? Peter Meredith doubts the existence of traveling professional players in the fifteenth century or earlier, placing the development of such troupes sometime after 1500.[50] Suzanne Westfall has noted that of the eighty-eight references to players in the Selby Abbey accounts between 1431 and 1532, thirty-five specify the size of the group, but more than 60 percent of these are for three or fewer "players," groups too small to man the dramatic interludes we have assumed they played.[51] In a list of royal and noble troupes, Westfall cites groups of four or slightly more, most of which enter the records in 1519–20, the exceptions being the troupes of Richard III and Henry VII.[52] Rather than performing texts as we imagine them to have done, might they not have exported noble and court culture, musical entertainments perhaps with pageant scenes at times, that is, spectacular presentations without dialogue? But many of these

---

46. Ibid., item B03. Trillek is quoting Innocent III's decree, which I will discuss in more detail below, but it is Trillek, not Innocent, who equates the *ludi* with interludes.

47. Ibid., items B12 and B53.

48. My discussion is based on A. Young's "Plays and Players."

49. James Gibson, the REED editor for the records of Kent, communicated to me that in Lydd and New Romney in the fifteenth century the records invariably use *mimici,* whereas other towns in the area use *ministralli* (private communication).

50. Meredith, "Professional Travelling Players of the Fifteenth Century." See also A. Young, "Minstrels and Minstrelsy."

51. Westfall, *Patrons and Performance,* 210. Of the plays David Bevington cites in his appendix on role doubling, none calls for fewer than four players (*From "Mankind" to Marlowe,* 265–73). *Mundus and Infans* is the only play I can think of that would fall below this minimum.

52. Westfall, *Patrons and Performance,* 211–12. The royal troupes were engaged in court pageantry, not the production of vernacular moral or educational dramas. See my discussion of the London aesthetic below.

records of noble players must be of musical performers who provided concerts. This study will not address the issues concerning traveling players; rather, I will leave the matter to those now engaged in the investigation of touring companies and noble patronage. Nevertheless, I think we must proceed with the same caution I have suggested above when reading the records of noblemen's "players" as we should when reading town and church documents.

My intent is to err on the side of caution and not to use either "pley" or "*ludus*" as a generic term for "drama" because it is demonstrable that in the medieval languages and early modern English both are used to designate a whole range of sports, games, and recreations. It is because a drama is recreational, given to delight, that it is called a play, not because it is a drama (meaning "play"). When we look at documents that refer to "pley" or "*ludus*," we must be skeptical; we ought not hastily conclude that the term points to the existence of a drama. We should certainly not read "theater" or "*theatrum*" in medieval and early modern records as a reference to a place for the performance of dramas before the sixteenth century.

From *Ludi Inhonesti* to Sacred Play

In the past thirty years the study of English medieval drama has undergone a revolution thanks to the reedition of most of the texts and to an enormous amount of archival work by English, Canadian, and U.S. scholars. Equally important has been the reexamination—and repudiation—of early twentieth-century theories of the development of the drama. In 1965, O. B. Hardison Jr. was the first to show that E. K. Chambers's monumental work *The Mediaeval Stage* (1903) and the works of other early scholars were culturally conditioned by Darwinian theories of evolution; as a consequence, scholars now deliberately avoid speaking of the evolution of dramatic forms. Nor do we any longer subscribe to Chambers's thesis of "secularization": that drama was born in the liturgy and gradually moved out of the church into the streets where the drama fell into the hands of the laity with the consequence that pure liturgical forms were contaminated by vulgarities that resulted in the mixed styles of the English Renaissance theater. In addition, early drama courses and texts have traditionally treated the field as if it had a single chronology and linearity that is historically incorrect: we begin with liturgical dramas and move on to the northern biblical cycles and then to morality plays and finally to the development of secular, commercial drama. Although no one would argue the point, the implication is often that biblical plays replace liturgical dramas, moralities replace biblical plays, and the commercial theater replaces all the preceding.

Remarkable as the rethinking of early drama has been, we continue to use schemes of organizing material in our histories that imply the theories that we dismiss. For example, a couple of recent introductions to early drama (or parts thereof) follow the same pattern as older ones did in devoting a chapter to liturgical drama, one to the cycles of biblical plays, and a third to moralities and interludes.[53] Not only does this organization imply evolution, it also suggests that the more highly evolved forms replace earlier ones, that the history of the drama is unilinear and the forms distinct and separate.

The history that I provide focuses less on chronology than on communities —lay and clerical; national and regional; cities, towns, and rural areas. The larger question I wish to answer is: How was it possible for drama, especially biblical representation, to appear in the Christian West given the early church's aversion toward and condemnation of the *theatrum* of the ancient world? To address such a question I propose to discuss the drama within the larger ludic arena in which it took place, for I think it can be shown that the appearance of vernacular drama in the late Middle Ages coincides with attempts of the clergy to suppress a variety of games and other *ludi* that they regarded as unholy or immoral. Before we can begin to make this argument, however, we must have a more rigorous examination of the language of *theatrum* and *ludus* than we have had in the past. This kind of philological study is essential since many of us now believe that the history of the drama has been plagued by the impreciseness of the theatrical vocabulary in the sources and by modern scholars' assumptions that words such as *ludus* and "pley" signify enacted scripts. My study, therefore, begins in philology in order to move to cultural history.

Although it is difficult if not impossible to escape the tyranny of chronology, in my discussion I will not adhere to a unilinear timeline; rather, I will try to describe successively smaller arenas that exist within larger ones in order to show how communities conceived of unholy and sacred play in the period from the late Middle Ages until the early years of Elizabeth's reign. This study is divided into the following chapters:

---

53. See Beadle, *Cambridge Companion*, which is divided according to traditional categories. Sanders et al., in *Revels History of Drama in English*, continue the evolutionary thesis by its silences; there are no references to biblical and allegorical plays in the medieval traditions in its calendar of plays, 1495–1575 (38–67), though they do note the demise of the Chester, York, and Coventry plays in the 1560s and 1570s. See Ian Lancashire's review, "History of a Transition." Cox and Kastan's *New History of Early English Drama* also has gaps. Despite saying that its "primary aim is to provide the most comprehensive account yet available of early English drama" (1) and "to erase the sharp distinction between *Medieval* and *Renaissance* that has traditionally been used to mark a period boundary" (3), the *History* primarily concerns sixteenth-century drama.

Chapter 1, "The *Theatrum* and the Rhetoric of Abuse in the Middle Ages," attempts to describe the largest arena, the notion of *theatrum* in late antique culture and the Middle Ages. My chief point is that the *theatrum* came to be associated with obscene pagan practices and with the games of the Roman circus; it was not primarily understood as a place where "dramas" were enacted. In a real sense, medieval clerics lost the concept of "drama." When the tenth-century liturgical embellishments began to appear that included representations of biblical story—the shepherds, the Marys at the tomb—clerics did not understand themselves to be creating dramas, and these liturgical pieces were certainly not associated in their minds with the *theatrum* because they were performed at the altar, not in the arena. There were, however, scandalous activities within churches and monasteries at certain times of the year that Innocent III labeled *ludi theatrales* because the term *theatrum* and its related forms had pejorative connotations. One purpose of this chapter is to get beyond the modern terminological assumption that "theater" is synonymous with "drama" in order to show that dramatic representation could occur in the Middle Ages without any associations to the *theatrum* of the ancient world. In terms of my larger argument, the chapter defines the basic *clerical* distinction between unholy and sacred play throughout the medieval period.

The next two chapters describe the antitheatrical traditions of the Middle Ages: those in opposition not to religious dramas but to immoral practices, *ludi inhonesti*, and games. Modern scholars from the nineteenth century to the present have believed that the term *miracula* was a generic designation for miracle or saint plays or religious dramas in general. My examination of all examples of the use of the term in England, whether in Latin, Anglo-Norman, or English, has led me to conclude that the term was used in monastic and cathedral records and in preaching manuals to refer to activities like those Innocent labeled *ludi theatrales*. This usage derives from the Old Latin sense of *miracula,* which meant "monstrosity," or something wondrously hideous. The word is preserved in the Old Testament where it indicates derision or sacrilegious offense, and this specialized sense was retained in the commentaries of Jerome, Bede, Hugh of St. Cher, Nicholas of Lyra, and others. My conclusion is that there is little opposition to vernacular religious dramas in the late Middle Ages in part because the latter were not understood to be associated with the *theatrum;* they were not *miracula,* as I define it here. There is, however, an antitheatrical or antiludic tradition focused on lay activities such as the summergames and other *ludi* held within sacred precincts. I read the *Tretise of Miraclis Pleyinge* as an attack not on religious drama but on these various forms of *ludi inhonesti.* This antitheatrical tradition, which differs from the Puritan assault on the stage, can be traced into the seventeenth century.

Ludic practice varied widely in England depending on participants' clerical or lay status and location; it also differed at the level of parish, village, or town. In "*Communitas:* The *Ludi* of Monasteries and Cathedrals, Towns and Parishes" I provide profiles of ludic practice in these different venues before turning to the matter of "saint plays." The prototypical *ludus* of late medieval and early modern England was the parish ale held on a saint's feast day. Often mistaken as occasions for the performance of the *vitae* of saints—saint plays— these *ludi* involved games, wrestling matches, tilts, or the like, but some are the lay equivalent of clerical *miracula.* That some clerics saw a danger in these assemblages is apparent in their attempts to suppress them throughout the period from the thirteenth through the seventeenth centuries. The efforts at suppression, as I argue more fully in the following chapter, "*Civitas:* Drama and the City," were often met with successful resistance and things continued as usual. On the other hand, the confrontation in some instances seems to have encouraged lay groups to circumvent clerical opposition to "play" by substituting biblical and moral dramas for "unholy" festivities, a solution apparently satisfactory to both groups. In light of late-sixteenth-century developments, when the theater came to be centered at London, it is interesting that fully enacted vernacular scripts tend to be provincial and are the productions of lay corporations or groups. The "London Aesthetic," as epitomized in the work of John Lydgate, privileges pageant presentations with little interactive dialogue. This preference continues well into the reign of Henry VIII when new factors—both religious and educational—shape dramatic possibilities in the city and elsewhere.

The next two chapters, "Texts and Performances" and "The Matter of These Plays," move from consideration of why dramas should have developed in some cities and towns and not others, to an analysis of the surviving texts and who produced and used them, to the content of the surviving plays and questions about for whom they speak. My argument is that in the political contest between clergy and the laity, a space was opened in cities, where civil authority held sway, for the governors to take on one of the duties formerly left to the clergy: concern for the citizens' spiritual welfare. The motives for the productions of dramas, however, are not simply pious; drama was also a remarkable display of urban prestige and power (not to mention commercial opportunity). "Texts and Performances" assesses what scholars currently believe the extant play texts to be and attempts to describe the venues of performance of those texts about which we have information. The following chapter assesses the "matter" of the biblical plays: the kind of information that gets into them, the anxieties the texts display, and the effect performance styles may have had on the reception of the texts. I also address issues of how we read and use these texts. It has been the practice to treat medieval and early modern dramatic texts as if they were fixed at the time of their writing and that the meaning we attach to them remained with them through their performance histories. These assumptions are simplistic in several ways. First, we know that some of the oldest texts were periodically revised. Equally important, however, is that even if the texts were not revised, their reception might change, especially as England moved through the Reformation period. The chapter considers texts written to meet the needs of the reformers as well as texts written under Catholicism—the biblical cycles—that continued to be performed well after the Reformation began.

Traditionally, allegorical and moral dramas have been treated separately from the biblical plays, a practice to which I object. Nevertheless, in "Variety in the Dramas of East Anglia," I have segregated my discussion of *Mary Magdalene, The Castle of Perseverance,* and *Wisdom* from that of the cycle plays in order better to focus on issues of genre (saint play), mode (allegory), and auspices (monastic production), respectively. My thesis is twofold: by approaching these plays from assumptions about genre, mode and auspices, we have created impediments to reading what the playwrights were attempting to do and we have failed to see how these plays, no matter what genre we imagine them to be, form part of a broader dramatic tradition that includes biblical plays, romance narratives, and other forms of pageantry. My discussion of these three plays is ultimately intended to show how they fit within the larger traditions of provincial drama, whether from the north or East Anglia or the southeast.

I conclude with a chapter called "The Persistence of 'Medieval Drama' in the Tudor and Elizabethan Periods." Although scholars are well aware that the biblical cycles continued to be performed into the 1570s, standard histories ignore this part of the record by treating these dramas under the rubric "medieval" rather than "Renaissance" or "early modern." The argument has been that these plays became debilitated or were in decline as a consequence of the Crown's attempts to control the drama beginning in the latter part of Henry VIII's reign.[54] The production records suggest this not to be the case, and a

---

54. Gardiner, *Mysteries' End;* Wickham, *Early English Stages.*

rereading of royal proclamations with regard to dramatic activities indicates that the target was polemical drama, not the biblical and moral plays produced in the provinces. Indeed, it was not until well into Elizabeth's reign that we find action against the traditional drama. My argument is that historians of the later Elizabethan stage have read Puritan attacks on the stage as the culmination of an anticipatory antitheatricalism from earlier in the century. Such an argument confuses the Puritan attack on the stage with the antiludic medieval tradition. During the crucial period, from about the 1530s to the 1560s, there is little or no evidence that producers of traditional biblical and moral drama understood royal proclamations against seditious plays to be directed at them. Indeed, one reason that traditional drama survived so late into the sixteenth century is that there was not an antitheatrical tradition that could be used to formulate a position against dramatic representation.

⁂

This study is not a traditional history of medieval and early modern drama, nor is it an exhaustive one for a variety of reasons. Except for my discussion of the *theatrum,* I have largely confined my inquiries to English documents and texts; thus, I exclude materials from Cornwall, Wales, Ireland, and Scotland. I have not commented on the Anglo-Norman vernacular dramas, the *Jeu d'Adam* and *La seinte resurreccioun,* nor Latin musical dramas, nor medieval Terentian imitations, which, I believe, like the medieval Terence, were reading texts. I would have liked to have discussed more of the vernacular texts from the first half of the sixteenth century, but limitations of space prohibited it. Nevertheless, I have intruded my discussion of the English dramatic traditions well into the sixteenth century because I do not believe that we have a simple, linear dramatic history: medieval, early Tudor, and then Renaissance.

The figure I have chosen for the cover and frontispiece was once thought to be a representation of the descendants of the ancient mimes; however, it is now understood as that of a liturgical dancer.[55] I identify the person as "a dancer before the Ark of the Lord." Although it is not a picture of David, it is linked with his dance before the Ark, an action that is referred to on several occasions in my discussion below. I take the current understanding of the figure as emblematic of the revisionist work of *Drama, Play and Game.*

---

55. Gamer, "Mimes, Musicians, and the Origin of the Mediaeval Religious Play."

The *Theatrum* and the Rhetoric of Abuse
in the Middle Ages

The urbane and learned John of Salisbury devotes book 1 of his *Policraticus* to courtiers' frivolities, among which he counts hunting, gaming, the support of *histriones, mimi,* and other entertainers, and, with some careful distinctions, playing and listening to music.[1] His two icons for appropriate and inappropriate behavior are Augustus, who, when rebuked for playing on a tambourine at a feast, abandoned the practice, and Nero, who pandered to *histriones* and who became the more disreputable the more he became a singer and entertainer himself.[2] Even though John uses biblical texts to underpin moral examples, his discussion of the wise and honorable man, or the philosopher, is heavily influenced by a sense of Roman decorum. Such a person is grave, dignified, and restrained in gesture, all external indications of his inward reserve and attention to that which has moral significance and intellectual value. After denouncing most recreational activities, John pulls back a bit to state that moderate and reasonable use of music, sports, and entertainment is acceptable, even to be valued, but he is unable to specify the difference between the decorous and the immoderate except to say that that which is good appeals to virtue and does not destroy consciousness of the thing on which it ought properly to reflect. If it attracts attention to itself for itself, then it is excessive, shameful, and defiling.

---

1. John of Salisbury, *Policraticus.* Unless otherwise noted, translations are from the Pike translation of John of Salisbury, *Frivolities* On the humanist critique of entertainers, see Baldwin, *Masters, Princes, and Merchants,* 1:198–204.

2. Book 1, chap. 7 (*Policraticus,* 1:44–45); *Frivolities,* 35–36.

Later in the *Policraticus* John seems to banish some of the arts of entertainment from the court of a righteous prince: "Concerning actors and mimes, buffoons and harlots, panders and other like human monsters [histrionibus et
mimis, scurris et meretricibus, lenonibus et huiusmodi prodigiis hominum],
which the prince ought rather to exterminate entirely than to foster, there
needed no mention to be made in the [Old Testament] law [which John has just
cited]; which indeed not only excludes all such abominations from the court of
the prince, but totally banishes them from among the people of God."[3] John's
apparently unequivocal assertion here is moderated in his earlier account of entertainers in book 1, chapter 8.[4] There, continuing his discussion of Nero, John
complains that some still imitate the emperor as far as they can by currying favor with "actors" and "mimes" *(histriones et mimi)* even though—and here he
quotes Macrobius' complaint—Nero's age possessed more respectable "actors" than did John's own. Once there were actors —contemporaries of Plautus and Menander and those intimate "with our favorite Terence"—who by
the magic of gestures, of language, and of voice reproduced vividly for the audience both fact and fiction. Subsequently, comedy and tragedy disappeared,
since frivolity *(leuitas)* held universal sway and the actors of the legitimate
drama were consequently forced into retirement. "Our own age," John continues, evidences an even greater degeneration:

> descending to *[gestes]* and similar folly *[fabulas et quaevis inania]*, [it]
> prostitutes not only the ear and heart to vanity but also delights in idleness
> with the pleasures of eye and ear. It inflames its own wantonness, seeking
> everywhere incentives to vice. Does not the shiftless man divert his idleness
> and court slumber with the sweet tones of instruments and vocal melody,
> with gaiety inspired by musicians and the pleasure he finds in the narrator
> of tales *[sompnos . . . intrumentorum suauitate aut uocum modulis, hila-
> ritate canentium aut fabulantium gratia]* or, and this is more disgraceful
> still, in drunken revels? . . . Hence the procession of *mimi*, jumping or leap-
> ing priests *[salii uel saliares,* which DuCange defines as priests of Mars],
> buffoons *[balatrones]*, Aemilian *[emiliani]* and other gladiators *[gladia-
> tores]*, wrestlers *[palestritae]*, sorcerers *[gignadii]*, jugglers *[praestigia-
> tores]*, magicians *[malefici]*, and a whole army of jesters *[et tota ioculato-
> rum scena]*.[5]

---

3. Book 4, chap. 4 (*Policraticus*, 1:245). The translation is John Dickinson's in John of Salisbury, *Statesman's Book of John of Salisbury*; 16.

4. *De histrionibus et mimis et praestigiatoribus* (*Policraticus*, 1:46–49; *Frivolities*, 36–39).

5. *Frivolities*, 37, and *Policraticus*, 46–47; *Frivolities*, 38, and *Policraticus*, 48.

This well-known passage has proved tricky for modern translators and commentators alike.[6] First, John uses *histriones* to refer to performers in Nero's, Macrobius', and his own day. Modern translators gloss *histriones* as "actors" even when it is quite apparent that John distinguishes, as we will see below, the legitimate actor of Plautus and Terence from the buffoons of Macrobius' era and from the further degenerated species of his own day. John's *histriones* are not "actors of texts" but reciters of *fabulae* and other inanities, one suggestion being that not only are their tales false but that the *fabulae* have no moral content.

Second, in the passage immediately above John provides a lengthy list of terms for entertainers, a list that was mined by Roger Sherman Loomis and Gustave Cohen in their attempt to establish the existence of a *theatrum* in the twelfth century.[7] But as Dino Bigongiari demonstrated, when John uses such technical vocabulary, he is usually quoting ancient sources; indeed, John quotes Macrobius' lament about the degeneration of the theater in his own day in order to imitate him: "At nostra etas prolapsa ad fabulas."[8] It is reasonably clear that John's targets are not "actors of texts," yet these few passages illustrate the difficulty of determining the precise connotations of theatrical language in late medieval contexts.

John seems caught between his approval of Terence and his disdain for entertainers; he allows that it is not unbecoming to a man of honor to indulge occasionally in "reasonable mirth" but finds it disgraceful to lower one's dignity by "excessive indulgence in it."[9] The wise man's mind examines individual instances; he does not shun fables, stories, or spectacles in general "providing that they possess the requirements of virtue and honorable utility." John idealizes the period of Roman moral supremacy between the first and second Punic wars and deplores the subsequent degeneration, which he associates with late antiquity and his own day. For example, he says, "I do not . . . assert that the actor is dishonorable when he follows his profession, although it is undoubtedly dishonorable to be an actor."[10] He concludes his chapter by reminding his audience that the Fathers forbade the sacrament to actors and mimes as long as they persisted in their careers and draws the moral that the supporters of such creatures occupy a similar perilous position and are likely to suffer a like penalty, the impli-

---

6. On the difficulties of translating the last sentence, see Bigongiari, "Were There Theatres?" 204–5.

7. Loomis, "Some Evidence for Secular Theatres"; Loomis and Cohen, "Were There Theatres?"

8. *Policraticus*, 46–47.

9. *Frivolities*, 38; *Policraticus*, 48.

10. Book 8, chap. 12; bk. 1, chap. 8.

cation being that the supporter invalidates his taking of the sacrament and thus risks his own salvation. The status of the actor was like that of the slave, yet, John concedes, the actor has some usefulness in teaching the art of poetry.

These conflicts arise anew in a later passage in which he attempts to negotiate between his sense that entertainments are debilitating and immoral and his knowledge that ancient philosophers and moralists indulged in them to some extent.[11] In this passage he seems to be trying to develop the notion from the first book that activities in themselves need not be immoral but can easily become immoderate. He points to Cicero, a hero in John's pantheon, who lent respectability to (some) actors, specifically, Roscius and Aesop; indeed, the philosopher is said to have looked after their property and other interests.[12] Cicero berated the Romans for rioting while Roscius was acting *(agente)*, and the orator used to contest with the actor "to see whether the latter with his gestures could express more often the same idea, or he himself with his flow of eloquence and command of words."[13] Given Cicero's patronage—as well as the financial success of the actors—John concludes that actors are to be admitted into the company of sages, but, if so, they should be men like Roscius and Aesop because they would be patrons rather than assailants of literature. The implicit point is that Roscius and Aesop are associated with Terence and Plautus and thus are upholders of literature; however, they were succeeded by degenerates who ridiculed such literature. Yet John never entirely approves the *histrio:* he says that he cannot readily believe that any man of letters could be induced to take up histrionics as a profession even though "it is easy enough to find many who are not ashamed to act *[agere]* and to fill *[implere]* the actor's sordid role since they do employ the technique *[gestus siquidem exprimunt]* without however deriving any advantage from it. . . . As regards acting, there is to be sure some pleasure of the eye connected with it, but it can scarcely be practiced or accepted without degradation."[14] The first statement suggests that it is common for men to take on roles, to become *like* actors, but they get no profit from it, alluding to Roscius and Aesop, who were said to have amassed great fortunes; therefore, John's modern "actor," the misguided courtier, gains only the disgrace. John is willing to concede, in the second sentence, that one might gain pleasure from watching entertainers; nevertheless, to be one is degrading.

I have summarized and quoted John at length because he registers common

---

11. Book 8, chap. 12 (*Frivolities*, 369–70).

12. Here John is quoting Macrobius, *Saturnalia*, III.xiv.11.

13. Macrobius, from whom the quotation comes, understands the actor to be a pantomimist.

14. *Frivolities*, 370.

medieval anxieties about the usefulness of the ancient world—which claims admiration but also should be kept at a distance—and because he focuses many of the issues we need to assess. Like his predecessors, he labels the denizens of the theater degenerates and panders, yet he cannot finally condemn Terence or the actors who presented his works. Augustine took a more austere view of the matter. Amidst his attack on the mystic rites of the temples, which he called obscenities, Augustine says that comedies and tragedies written for the stage were less offensive because they did not use the filthy language of the mystic rites; indeed—though he seems to find it regrettable—these dramas remain part of the training of gentlemen.[15] Here we must understand precisely what Augustine is saying. He is not defending the theater of his day—which elsewhere he says contains the same obscenities as do the rites of the temples (*City* 2.26)—rather, he concedes some moral value to "comedies and tragedies," terms that have technical specificity, that is, the plays written by Terence and Plautus. His remark would seem to sanction these playwrights for the later Middle Ages *as reading texts.*[16] Jerome thought the opposite, and his protest against priests reading comedies passed into canon law.[17]

But John of Salisbury is not intent on mounting a defense for the study of the classics; it is obvious that he has resolved that issue for himself since he is as learned in the literature of antiquity as he is in that of the Christian period. Instead, he holds up to his audience the ideal of Augustus, an ideal that has authority in antique texts but which is authorized by the Old and New Testaments as well and, as we will see, is manifested in decorous clerics. To John and his contemporaries, not only the prince but the clergy should shun the indecencies of the *theatrum;* hence, John's comparison of the degenerate theater of antiquity with practice in his own day.

I believe that John's evocation of a golden age of actors that was supplanted by a dissolute array of pimps and panders, a troupe that monopolizes the "theater" of John's own day, provides a paradigm for late nineteenth- and early twentieth-century theories that the Western dramatic tradition was continued by mimes from late antiquity, though John's notion of "devolution" was characterized as "evolution" by modern scholars. To put John's remarks in this critical context is to misread them, however, for John talks about neither theaters

---

15. Augustine, *City of God* 2.8. Translations are from Marcus Dods.

16. Theiner, "Medieval Terence." Hrotswitha of Gandersheim, of course, used Terence as a model to create her own Christian texts.

17. Friedberg, *Corpus iuris canonici* pt. 1, quaest. 37, cap. 2 (hereafter, e.g., 1.37.2; 1:135 in Friedberg).

in his day nor the continuity of a dramatic tradition. It is quite clear that come-dies and tragedies, like the actors Roscius and Aesop, are things of the past. The plays no longer existed as enacted scripts in what we call late antiquity when Augustine and Macrobius were writing, nor do they exist in John's day.[18] Instead, the "legitimate drama was forced into retirement," John says, and its presenters were replaced by undesirable persons who inflamed the eyes and ears of their beholders. Similarly, in John's day entertainers are given to las-civious actions and inanities. One could easily mistake some of John's charac-terizations of ancient entertainers as descriptions of ones in his own day were it not for the fact that frequently he is quoting or ventriloquizing Macrobius' *Sa-turnalia.* This kind of quotation establishes the likeness between the degener-acy and frivolities of the two ages, but if we want to know the kinds of persons John attacks in his own, then we must look to the passages in which he does not quote ancient authorities.

He gives a few examples that might come from contemporary practice, such as readers or singers of tales, but he chiefly concerns himself with the vulgarity of *joculatores:*

> They are in such vogue that even they whose exposures are so indecent that they make a cynic blush are not barred from distinguished houses. Then too, a surprising fact, they are not even turned out when with more hellish tu-mult they defile the air and more shamelessly disclose that which in shame they had concealed. Does he appear to be a man of wisdom who has eye or ear for such as these? Who would, however, not be glad to see and laugh when a juggler is drenched with urine, his tricks disclosed, and when eyes that have been blinded with his magic find their power restored?[19]

John of Salisbury's characterization of the *histriones* of his day corresponds roughly with those in the anatomy of Thomas de Chobham, Bishop of Salis-bury (d. 1313):

> There are three kinds of *histriones.* Some transform and transfigure their bod-ies through foul movement and gesture or by baring themselves lewdly or by

---

18. Barnes, "Christians and the Theater."

19. John of Salisbury, *Frivolities,* 38, *Policraticus,* 48. The notoriety of minstrels continues into the later Middle Ages. Langland's Haukyn complains that he gets no rewards "amonges lordes Mynstrals. / Ac for I kan neiþer taboure ne trompe ne telle no gestes, / Farten ne fiþelen at festes ne harpen, / Iape ne Iogele ne gentilliche pipe, / Ne neiþer saille [=dance] ne [sautrie] ne synge wiþ þe gyterne" (13:229–33 in Langland, *Piers Plowman: The B Version.* The first interpolation is mine; the second is that of Langland's translators, Kane and Donaldson. On the disreputability of min-strels and *Piers,* see Craun, *Lies, Slander, and Obscenity,* 157–86.

wearing horrible masks. All such are damnable unless they relinquish their office. Others, having no permanent abode, follow the courts of the great and amuse by satire and raillery. These are damnable because the Apostle prohibited communion with such and called them *scurrae vagi* because they are useless except to devour and revile. The third use musical instruments and are of two kinds. Some of these sing wanton songs at public drinkings and lascivious congregations; they sing *cantilenas* that move men to wontonness, and these are damnable like the others. There are others who are called *ioculatores* who sing the deeds of princes and the lives of saints and give solace to men either in grief or anguish and do not make innumerable base [things] such as male and female dancers and others do who play out indecent fantasies. According to Pope Alexander, the [second category] is to be sustained in its profession if its members abstain from wantonness and baseness.[20]

Because John's remarks on *histriones* derive primarily from ancient authorities—as opposed to reportage of a theatrical tradition in his own time—he reveals that he has no firm grasp of theatrical practice in the Terentian theater. This point will require further development below, but for the moment, let us contrast John's statement about actors in the "legitimate theater" (book 1, chapter 8) with that about Roscius' contest with Cicero. In the first John says there were once "actors who by the magic of gesture, of language, and *of voice* reproduced vividly for the audience both fact and fiction,"[21] but when he talks of Roscius and Cicero, his point seems to be that Roscius conveys *without words* the same meaning that Cicero does with his oratory (otherwise there would not be a contest). All of this is being appropriated from Macrobius and other ancient authorities, but the fact remains that two different theatrical traditions are being confused. Ancient writers were aware of the difference between the stagings of Terence and those in the late antique theater in which mimes enacted words spoken by someone else, but it was the latter tradition that scholars in the Middle Ages, through Isidore of Seville, thought to be characteristic of the *theatrum*. Although John seems to be aware of the difference between the Terentian and late antique theaters, he associates the difference with moral content rather than mode of representation. In reporting the story about Roscius and Cicero, John has made the Terentian actor into a late an-

---

20. Thomas de Chobham, *Summa confessorum*, 291–93; the text is also in Chambers, *Mediaeval Stage*, 2:262–63. Chobham elaborates a division that becomes a commonplace; see Baldwin, *Masters*, 1.199–204; Briscoe, "Some Clerical Notions of Dramatic Decorum"; and Olson, "Plays as Play," 197–205, 218–21.

21. John of Salisbury, *Frivolities*, 36, emphasis added.

tique mime: Roscius does not speak but only gestures. To push a bit further, the mixing together of the two modes suggests to me John's reliance on ancient authority—which he apparently did not feel required rationalizing in order to remove inconsistencies—but it also suggests that he had no experience of performed Terentian drama, only a bookish knowledge of the *theatrum* as filtered through Isidore and, perhaps, the illustrated Terence manuscripts that depict dramatic action according to the Isidorean tradition.[22]

⁂

The purpose of the present chapter is to pull out of texts such as John of Salisbury's *Policraticus* what medieval theologians, scholars, and preachers understood the *theatrum* to be. Part of the task is philological and historical, but I am not content to provide a list of usages of theatrical terms. I am interested in discovering how medievals applied what they thought they knew about the *theatrum* in order to stigmatize and ultimately to control social practice.

The chapter will first consider why the *theatrum* was perceived to be such an enemy to the early church that it became necessary to enact conciliar legislation to separate Christians from it. As the empire collapsed, so did the theaters, yet the early medieval period not only retained a memory of them, largely through Isidore of Seville, but also continued to anathematize the *theatrum*. There is a collection of texts, mostly from the twelfth century, that uses theatrical metaphor to stigmatize as "theatrical" certain kinds of liturgical practice as well as liturgical parody and exaggerated clerical gesture. Some of these documents have been read as statements that compare improper clerical activity inside the church with a theatrical tradition in the twelfth century and thus take theatrical metaphor as proof of the existence, first, of a theatrical tradition in the simple sense, and, second, of the continuity of medieval drama from the ancient *theatrum*. Yet many of these same scholars express puzzlement at the absence of an antitheatrical tradition given the fact that there is authority in the Fathers (and canon law) for opposition to dramatic imitation. By this time in the twelfth century, we must bear in mind, monasteries and secular cathedrals had had *representationes* of visits to the sepulchre and the manger for several

---

22. From library catalogues we know that Terence manuscripts existed in many monastic and cathedral libraries (see Lancashire, *Dramatic Texts*, items 421, 491, 498, 607, 619, 825, 830, 1246, 1248, 1249, 1297, 1311, 1341, 1350, 1352, 1526, 1558). The twelfth-century copy owned by the Benedictine abbey of St. Albans, now Bodley MS Auct. F.2.13, contains ink drawings of masked actors and representations of the stage as medieval scholars understood it (Lancashire 1350). See Jones and Morey, *Miniatures of the Manuscripts of Terence*.

centuries and were then engaged in rather elaborate presentations such as the *Ordo repraesentationis Adae* (the *Mystère d'Adam*), the Beauvais *Daniel,* and the Benediktbeuern Christmas and Passion plays.

Hardison and others have shown us how our desire for origins and our thinking in evolutionary terms have in some respects distorted our understanding of the phenomena we seek to study.[23] By questioning how, given the early church's antagonism to the *theatrum,* a dramatic tradition could have arisen anew in the Christian West, I do not intend to present a quest for origins in a new guise. Rather, I wish to pursue further the point that the forms of the questions we ask, and have asked, have distorted our perceptions of the materials we study. In this chapter I argue that there is indeed an antitheatrical tradition in the West in the Middle Ages but that it is not directed against enacted scripts of biblical and moral content. This thesis will have to be modified in a few instances, but I remain confident of its general accuracy.

The major impediment in our assessment of medieval "theatrical" documents is that we know more than medieval people did. We have a history of the drama that runs from the first yearnings in Greece to the present. We have reconstructed, as best we can, the traditions of the theaters of Greece and Rome. Aware as we are of gaps in our knowledge, we nevertheless have a concrete sense—perhaps even actual experience—of how the texts remaining to us might be performed. When we read Isidore of Seville's description of the *theatrum,* we gain little sense of theatrical representation. We may say that Isidore got matters essentially right, but we believe that only because we have a lot of documents that flesh out Isidore's pared down, inconsistent and incomplete depiction of the theater. We may thank him for his testimony, but let us at the same time try to imagine what our understanding of the *theatrum* might be if he were our principal authority. To be sure, there were other writers to whom a medieval person might appeal for information, but again we should keep in mind that if those authorities were Christian, they were hostile and hence not entirely trustworthy witnesses to practice, and even among pagan authors we find more often than not models for the abuses of the theater to which Christians could readily say "amen."

If we try to read medieval references to the *theatrum* with Isidore's analysis in mind and if we read medieval theatrical metaphor as the polemical rhetoric that it is, then it is easy enough to understand both that there is an antitheatrical tradition in the medieval West and that it is (largely) directed against other

---

23. Hardison, *Christian Rite,* 1–34.

activities than scripted biblical and moral texts. I ask that we read *theatrum* not as we have with our superior historical sense and our collection of Greek and Roman documents and texts in mind but as medieval readers did: not in terms of genre but of gesture, not as a place for the performance of edifying scripts but as the locus of the lubricious and the lascivious.[24]

Theatrum

The first part of my thesis may seem paradoxical: A dramatic tradition could be reestablished in the Christian West because neither liturgical *representationes* nor vernacular religious dramas had associations with the *theatrum* for their participants; nevertheless, there was a strong antitheatrical tradition throughout the Middle Ages, a tradition that we have not recognized as such because it was directed against other activities and *ludi* than dramas.

In the late empire, as Christianity was defining itself and disentangling its adherents from the surrounding pagan culture, prominent members of the church mounted insistent attacks on the *theatrum* and related phenomena.[25] I shall confine my discussion to Augustine and Isidore of Seville because it can be shown that their comments shaped the discussion throughout the Middle Ages.[26]

In his *Confessions* (3.2.2) Augustine says that when he first went to Carthage he was ravished by spectacles of the theater *(spectacula theatrica),* by which he means recitations by actors of events in the ancient past or of fictions *(vel antiquae vel falsae).*[27] On reflection he is perturbed by the fact that the success of these feigned actions depends on the ability of the actor to evoke strong emotion in the spectator; he is bothered that actions do not ask the spectator to relieve the suffering he sees (that is, take moral action) but, rather, to revel in the suffering.

---

24. A very useful index to comments on the *theatrum* is M. Marshall, "*Theatre* in the Middle Ages."

25. The Christian attacks were not new; indeed, they often drew on pagan assaults on actors and the theater and on the low legal status of performers. See Barnes, "Christians and the Theater," 161–80. For the early Christian materials, see Henshaw, "Attitude of the Church"; Barish, *Antitheatrical Prejudice,* 38–43; and Schnusenberg, *Relationship Between the Church and the Theatre.*

26. I do not discuss Tertullian's *De spectaculis* here because it is my understanding that this important antitheatrical tract was not known in the Middle Ages except through excerpts incorporated into Augustine, Isidore, and church canons.

27. Augustine, *Confessions,* 1:23.

Although Augustine indicates that he was attracted to theatrical story and imitation, he reveals his sense of the typology of *spectacula* when he reports that his friend Alypius was more attracted than he to the circus (6.7.11–12) and to the gladiatorial games (6.8.13).[28] Augustine distinguishes these two activities from those one would find in the *theatrum*, where one would see the mime, the *histrio*, and the pantomime.[29] The passage suggests Augustine's preoccupation with the way one can be perversely moved by seeing, or, as O'Donnell puts it, with his wariness of *curiositates* and his belief that *spectacula* were the occasions of *concupiscentia oculorum*.

When Augustine turns to the theater in *City of God,* he mounts an attack not just on the institution and its occasioning of sin but on the whole theological foundation for the use of *spectacula* within the empire.[30] His condemnation of the theaters takes place within his larger contention that Rome is threatened not because it abandoned the old gods for Christ but because of its immoralities past and present. And the games at the theaters and the rites within the temples of the mystery cults provide the most immediate examples of this immorality. The defenders of *spectacula,* he says, claim that the theatrical entertainments were instituted by the gods as the price for successfully quelling a pestilence that was ravaging Rome (1.32).[31]

In an earlier age Scipio had prohibited the construction of theaters because he feared they would wreck virtue and honor; he saw how easily prosperity would corrupt and destroy the Romans (1.33). Nevertheless, the "voluptuous madness of stage-plays" took possession of a warlike people hitherto accustomed only to the games of the circus, which were used to promote training in

---

28. Ibid., 2:52. Tertullian had also made this tripartite distinction in his *De spectaculis.*

29. Sermon 198.3: "delectantur nugatorio spectaculo et turpitudinibus variis theatrorum, insania circi, crudelitate amphitheatri, certaminibus animosis eorum qui pro pestilentibus hominibus lites et contentiones usque ad inimicitias suscipiunt, pro mimo, pro histrione, pro pantomimo [these three from the *theatra*], pro auriga [charioteers from the circus], pro venatore [hunters or sportsmen from the gladiatorial amphitheatre]." Cited by O'Donnell, 2:152, in his comment on *Confessions* 3.2.2. Augustine's three types of theatrical performers are echoed elsewhere: the pantomime performed excerpts from tragedy that included the dance of the pantomime, a song sung by others to which he danced, and accompanying music; excerpts from tragedy performed by tragic actors (here *histriones*); and the mime (see Barnes, "Christians and the Theater," 168–69).

30. Augustine, *City of God,* 1.32–33, throughout much of bk. 2, and 4.26. Further references appear in the text.

31. Throughout this discussion I have incorporated Dods's translation into my paraphrase of *City of God.*

martial combat and athleticism. And even when some fled to Carthage, they continued the madness: contending with one another to see who should most madly run after the actors in the theater (1.32).[32] Such immoralities were not instituted by gods but by demons.

Augustine claims that the theaters had turned to the same obscenities that one observes in the temples, the enactment of the immoralities of the gods. His point is that the pagan gods do not instruct their followers in the moral life; rather, they provide them with sacrilegious entertainments and spectacles (2.4–2.7). Citing the games in honor of the virgin Coelestis (especially worshipped in Africa) and Berecynthia (= Rhea, Cybele), mother of the gods, Augustine gives a description of the lewd actions played and sung before the mother of the gods —so base, he says, they would shame a chaste matron. He emphasizes that these are the kinds of words no one would say before one's mother. Later he asks whether Scipio Nascia, who prevented the building of a theater in Rome, would wish his mother immortalized, as great leaders' were, if she were to have such rites performed before her. The gods never inculcated the holiness of life. He asks to be shown those "assemblages in which, instead of the obscene songs and licentious acting of players, instead of the celebration of those most filthy and shameless Fugalia, people were commanded to restrain avarice" and other immoral behavior (2.6). Adherents to these cults prefer to witness the deeds of Jupiter than to listen to the philosophers. Then he gives an instance of a young profligate in Terence who sees a wall painting of Jupiter portrayed as gold coins falling into the lap of Danaë and concludes that this justifies his own licentiousness.[33] To the objection that these mystic rites are the fables of poets, not the deliverances of the gods themselves, he replies that he does not intend to arbitrate between the lewdness of theatrical entertainments and mystic rites (which indicates that he recognizes a distinction of form and place of performance).

Turning to the content of the theater, the fables about the gods, Augustine asks how "true" gods could have wished to have their own crimes made public, especially when Rome condemned the satire of living persons in the theater

---

32. Pagan writers also associated the degeneracy of the empire with actors and the theater; see Henshaw, "Attitude of the Church," 3 n. 3.

33. This scene was the focus of considerable discussion about the worthiness of the *theatrum* and Terence. Some instanced it, as Augustine does here, as proof that representations of immoral actions led to immorality. Proponents of Terence argued that the play in which the scene appears shows the bad consequences of the young man's bad judgment and hence that Terence was an instructor of morality.

(2.8–2.14). He attacks indecent skits that vilify public officials who should be honored, quoting Cicero's condemnation of libelous comedy and approval of the measure that would sentence to death those who write satires that defame others. Cicero had said that ancient Romans did not allow any living man to be praised or blamed on stage. Augustine compares this more sober stance with the lesser restraint of the Greek comedy, which used both scurrilous language and personal invective in order to point to the irrationality of the whole system of rewards within the theater. The Greeks, he says, elevated the actors and the playwrights who wrote dramas that ridiculed the gods because they imagined that the dramas were pleasing to their gods, but why should the gods be pleased to have their immoralities displayed? According to Cicero, the ancient Romans were unlike the Greeks insofar as they forbade comedy and theatrical performances and made stage players outcasts. Indeed, all players continue to be barred from all honors and offices. But this is illogical: if the plays are demanded by the gods, then why are the performers stigmatized and refused citizenship and position? Augustine concludes with a syllogism that reasons that such gods ought not to be worshipped: "The Greeks give us the major premise: If such gods are to be worshipped, then certainly such men may be honoured. The Romans add the minor: But such men must by no means be honoured. The Christians draw the conclusion: Therefore such gods must by no means be worshipped" (2.13). Augustine approves Plato's banishment of the poets so that the citizens will not be depraved by their fictions. He also understands the banishment to be in the interest of preserving the people's religious faith.

In building his case Augustine points out that persons associated with the theater could not be Roman citizens; consequently, it is not surprising that the ancient stigma of the theater and persons associated with *spectacula* was carried over into early church canons.[34] Actors and other denizens of the theater were not allowed to be baptized as Christians unless they abandoned their professions (Council of Elvira 306, cap. 62, cited in Henshaw). Although the early church councils did not prohibit converts from going to the games, except on Sundays and church festivals, it condemned associations with actors and those who performed in the *theatrum* (Carthage 399, caps. 86, 88). Priests or clerics were not to be present at *spectacula* at feasts or weddings *(in cenis aut in nuptiis)* but were to leave before the performers *(thymelici)* entered (Laodicea, 343–81, cap. 54). These canons tell us that the early church wished to separate its priesthood entirely—and its laity as far as possible—from the *theatrum* and

---

34. Henshaw, "Attitude of the Church," 5–6.

certain kinds of secular entertainments. Although it was willing to concede what it could not entirely control—allowing the laity to go to the games (with restrictions)—it could deny association to those who participated in the games and the theater.

After the theaters were closed, sometime in the early sixth century, the canons against the *theatrum* would seem to have no objects, but they subsequently were put to new use to help define clerical decorum in the later Middle Ages. For example, in Gratian's *Decretum* and the various continuations of it (together, the *Corpus iuris canonici*), clerics were forbidden to be amidst *spectacula* and other pomps (dist. 23, cap. 3); all clerics, and the laity, were to avoid games of chance (which might include everything from gambling to martial contests), and the clergy were not to attend on or observe *mimi, ioculatores, et histriones* (dist. 35, cap. 1); and clerics were not to go to taverns or engage in feasts or entertainments with the laity or in activities that involved singing or the wearing of distorted masks (*larvae;* dist. 44, cap. 2).[35] The clergy were not to give things to *histriones* (dist. 86, cap. 7).[36]

Because some of the canons contained archaic or puzzling vocabulary, they had to be glossed. *Decretum* III, dist. 5, cap. 37, is the Laodicean canon referred to above: "Non oportet ministros altaris vel quoslibet clericos spectaculis aliquibus quae in *nuptiis* aut in *scenis* exhibentur interesse sed antequam thymelici ingrediantur surgere eos de convivio et abire debere."[37] [Neither ministers of the altar nor clerics should be present at *spectacula* either at weddings or *in scenis* but should withdraw from the feast before the *thymelici* come in.] The decretal is first cross-referenced to dist. 35 ("Episcopus"), forbidding clerical attendance on *spectacula*.[38] The archaic word *thymelici* is glossed: "*a thymele, quod est pulpitum,*" referring to the platform, according to Isidore, on which the *thymelicus,* a musician, performed. Further, *thymelici* are said to be those who wait on players or are *histriones et cantatores,* and *Thymele* is a Greek word. Dino Bigongiari believes the *in scenis* crept into the decree in the tenth century as an attempted scribal correction of what in the Greek should have been translated as Latin *in caenis.*[39] I suspect the scribe was motivated to correct the text because he knew that Isidore had called *thymelici musici scenici*

35. Friedberg, *Corpus Iuris Canonici,* 1:80, 1:131, and 1:157, respectively.
36. Ibid., 1:299.
37. Ibid., 1:1422.
38. *Decretum Gratiani* , fol. 691.
39. Bigongiari, "Were There Theatres?" 207–8.

who sang on a *pulpitum*.[40] The decretist is correct in identifying *thymelici* as singers, not actors, hence, the importance of the decree to the later Middle Ages: Although these persons no longer exist—the word is Greek and refers to early practice—there are contemporary counterparts—*histriones* and *cantatores*—and these are to be avoided by priests and clerics because, according to dist. 35, they are not to attend on *spectacula*. To make this even more obvious, our scribal corrector has intruded the theater into the text *(in scenis)* because he associates entertainment of this sort with the *theatrum*. The decree does not testify to the existence of a theater but to the association of certain kinds of music with the *theatrum;* a wedding feast, after all, is likely to appeal to the senses, and the music is likely to be indecorous or to lead to inappropriate behavior.

In this legislation we can see the desire to separate physically both laity and clergy from pagan culture; however, within this impulse we can also discern an interest in clerical decorum per se. The clergy are to absent themselves from all *ludi* and amusements; they are to be sober in action and dress.

Isidore

For the Middle Ages the most important source for the traditions of the ancient *theatrum* was Isidore of Seville's *Etymologies*.[41] Cap. 18 is devoted to war and *ludi,* and the agonistic element is apparent in most of the descriptions that follow. Beginning with war, Isidore moves toward *ludi* and *theatrum* by means of a segue from warriors to gymnastic games to games in the circus and from the circus to the theater and from there to the amphitheaters where gladitorial contests occurred before ending with games of chance. This last part of the discussion stands as a kind of emblem of the element of chance within both war and the games of arenas. *Agon* and *fortuna* are his central themes.

The Isidorean tradition describes the theater as a round or semicircular structure in which the audience stands to watch the show. The *scena* was a place within the theater, in a kind of building that had a pulpit *(pulpitum)*, which is called the orchestra, where comedians and tragedians sing and *histriones* and mimes dance.[42] The orchestra was the platform of the *scena* where a dancer could perform *(agere posset)* or two persons dispute between them-

---

40. Isidore of Seville, *Elymologiarum* 18.47.

41. Ibid., 18.42–53; and see J. Jones, "Isidore and the Theatre."

42. J. Jones translates "pulpitum" as "platform"; for discussion, see "Isidore," 34–35. The remainder of this paragraph is an editing down of Jones's translation.

selves. There are several forms of *officia scenica,* those of the tragedians, the comedians, the thymelicians, the *histriones,* the mimes and the dancers *(saltatores).* Tragedians declaimed *(concinebant)* the ancient deeds and crimes of wicked kings in mournful poetry before the watching populace. Comic poets sang *(cantabant)* the acts of private men with spoken acts and gestures, and the senselessness of young virgins and the loves of harlots are portrayed *(exprimebant).* *Thymelici* were musicians who sounded organs, lyres and cytheras. Their name derives from the fact that once they stood singing in the orchestra on the platform called a *thymele.* *Histriones* portrayed *(exprimebant)* women and used impudent movements; they also, through song, showed *(demonstrabant) historias et res gestas.* Isidore derives this point from the fact that *histriones* were so called either because they were from (H)Istria in Illyria or because they expressed perplexing fables in stories *(historiis).* Mimes are imitators of human affairs. Their leader recited *(pronuntiarent)* the story before they mimed it, for the *fabulae* thus composed by poets were particularly suited to bodily movement. *Saltatores* comes from the name of theArcadian Salius, who first taught noble Roman youths to dance.

As for Augustine, so for Isidore: the *theatrum* was a place of obscenities. He described the continued tradition that following performances the theater acted as a house of prostitution (XLII), called a *lupanar* because the women who worked there were as rapacious as wolves. At the conclusion of his discussion of the theater (LI) he points out that the scenic arts were in honor of Libera (= Proserpina) and Venus, as a consequence of which they contained gestures and movements of the body of a dissolute sort. Later, as a conclusion to the whole section on the circus, the theater, and the amphitheater, he makes a comment that is repeated in many other writings: "These spectacles of cruelty and displays of vanity were created not only by the vices of men but also by the commands of devils. Hence the Christian should have nothing to do with the foolishness of the Circus, the immorality of the theater, the cruelty of the amphitheater, the atrocity of the arena, the lust of the show. He who attends such things is denying God, and he becomes a traitor to the Christian faith who again longs for what he has already renounced at his baptism, namely, the devil, his pomps, and his works."[43] The Christian who attends on such *spectacula* renounces his baptism; he is no longer Christian.

Isidore was a learned scholar who reported what he could glean from earlier

---

43. J. Jones, "Isidore," 39; Jones thinks Tertullian is probably the source of the oft-repeated idea that baptism is an implicit repudiation of the theater and all the games of the pagans.

authorities. That his discussion of the theater comes from report, not experience, is indicated by his sources (Eusebius, Augustine, and others) and by his use of the imperfect tense as if he were talking of that which is past and gone.[44] His vocabulary does not suggest that he understands the theater to be a place for enacted dialogues, as in a performance of Terence, for example. Rather, there are soli performances of tragedians in which sorrowful events are declaimed or of comic poets who sing of human folly. Both, it is true, use histrionic gesture. Isidore's *histriones* look more like actors impersonating figures in a drama, though even they are said to sing *res gestae* and *historias,* which suggests solo performance of poetic texts. But, for the later Middle Ages, the most profound description is that of the mimes: they are imagined to act out in mime what their leader narrates. Indeed, the allusions to the *pupitum* and the *scena* on which the participants danced and sang gave rise to the belief that in the theater of the ancient world the poet sat at a lectern or in a chair to read the text while mimes acted out the stories with gestures.[45]

Although Isidore's technical vocabulary is cited in bits and pieces in many kinds of writings, there is ample evidence in later writings of confusion about the theatrical structures as well as a tendency to foreground the immoral connotations of the *theatrum.* These developments suggest that for the Middle Ages the *theatrum* as a structure was so much a thing of the past that it was no longer necessary to try to have much of a consistent picture of it; more important, the vocabulary of the theater could be used to stigmatize activities thought to be immoral and worldly.

There can be no question that Isidore's entries on the ancient theater had an authoritative grip on subsequent references to the theater; indeed, most comments of more than a sentence allude to, incorporate phrases from, or echo some part of Isidore's description. Nevertheless, there is early evidence of a drift from particulars to generalities and especially to moral condemnation. For example, there are only two instances of *theatrum* in the Bible (Acts 19:29, 31), both of which concern a confrontation at Ephesus. Paul has decided to preach in Asia Minor for a while with the result that the silversmiths of Ephesus fear that he will undermine their trade in images of Diana. The mob is outraged and rushes into the theater *(in theatrum)* with Paul's two fellow

---

44. Chambers, *Mediaeval Stage,* 1:22.

45. Important transmitters of this tradition are canonists such as Hugutio, Nicholas Trevet in his marginalia on Augustine's *City of God,* commentators on Boethius's *Consolation* (the strumpet muses who "comfort" Boethius), and many others. And see M. Marshall, "*Theatre* in the Middle Ages."

travelers, Gaius and Aristarchus. Followers beg Paul not to go into the theater. In the meantime the assembly is in an uproar until the town clerk reminds the crowd that they can settle any charges of blasphemy against the goddess in the appropriate courts. Bede's comment on the passage combines that of Isidore with a reference from Arator, a sixth-century Christian poet who retold the acts of the apostles: "A theater is a place with a semicircular shape, in which people stand and watch *ludos scenicos* inside. Hence it takes the name theater from the Greek word for a *spectaculum* [Isidore, *Etymologiarum* 15, 2, 34–35]. Accordingly, as Arator says: "It was fitting that lascivious men dealt with the claims and the worth of Diana nowhere else than in the marketplace *[in foro]*."[46] Arator apparently understood *theatrum* to be equivalent to *forum*, and this equation seems untroubling to Bede even though Bede has just quoted Isidore with fidelity. As we shall see, this generalizing of *theatrum* as the central marketplace is common in later medieval texts.

Mary Marshall has cited numerous examples of this kind of expansion of the semantic meaning of *theatrum*, of which Papias the Lombard's comment from his *Elementarium doctrinae rudimentum* or *Vocabulista*, compiled in 1053, might serve as an example.[47] Papias begins with a description of the theater's structure, including the *scena*, according to Isidore and the *liber Glossarum*. Then he equates *theatrum* with *spectaculum*, which he says is a place *(locus)* in the city for royal games and the public execution of prisoners.[48] More generally, *theatrum* is a *spectaculum* wherever it is said to be made, called so from the Greek *a theoro* . . . that is, the Latin *video*. Papias repeats the range of definitions for *theatrum* that exists in classical Latin, but his assertion that *theatrum* is *spectaculum* gives evidence that, despite the citation of Isidore, *theatrum* has come to be less a physical structure than a locus (not a building presumably) for certain urban activities, but also anywhere at all that *spectacula* may be seen.

From this analysis, we may conclude that there were competing definitions of *theatrum*. From Isidore and others, there was the picture of the *theatrum* as a structure that contained a platform on which mimes and others imitated the

---

46. Bede, *Expositio actuum apostolorum et retractatio*, 73. The translation is Martin's in Bede, *Commentary on the Acts of the Apostles*, 157.

47. M. Marshall, "*Theatre* in the Middle Ages," 20–22.

48. The common belief that the *theatrum* was a place of punishment probably comes from Tertullian's *De spectaculis*. See, e.g., the comments on the passage in Acts of Hugh of St. Cher, *Opera omnia*, and Nicholas of Lyra, *Postillae perpetuae*.

actions read out by the poet who was seated at a lectern while the audience stood to watch. The *theatrum* also contained a *scena,* most frequently understood to be a tent in which the mimes could change costume and from which they came into the theater to perform. The *theatrum* was a *lupanar,* a house of prostitution. But there need not be a structure; the *theatrum* could be the marketplace or any place in which *spectacula* might be seen. *Spectaculum,* the more common word, seems to be less pejorative than *theatrum;* nevertheless, it too has connotations of immorality, idleness, and worldliness.

The Antitheatrical Tradition in the Twelfth Century: Gerhoh and Herrad

Before we can pursue my central point about theatrical metaphor as a rhetoric of abuse, we must consider Gerhoh of Reichersberg's and Herrad of Landsberg's assaults on inappropriate *ludi* within the church because Gerhoh and Herrad are often cited as the only two voices in the antitheatrical tradition between late antiquity and the *Tretise of Miraclis Pleyinge.* I believe this characterization to be partially misleading, especially in the case of Herrad; instead of saying that Gerhoh and Herrad were opposed to drama, I think it would be more accurate to say that they regarded certain activities within the church to be inappropriate and indecorous and that they—especially Gerhoh—associated these activities with the *theatrum.* This revisionist view of the two puts them much closer to the other employers of theatrical metaphor whom I discuss below. But there is a distinction to be made: Gerhoh deployed a theatrical rhetoric of abuse against liturgical representations that scholars have thought were precursors to a renewed Western drama, whereas the other figures I will treat labeled nondramatic activities as theatrical in order to stigmatize them.

Gerhoh (d. 1169) was for most of his career provost of the Augustinian monastery at Reichersberg.[49] He was deeply involved in the Gregorian reform movement in Germany, a consequence of which he came into conflict with powerful political figures such as Frederick Barbarossa. After his decision to become an observer of the rule of Saint Augustine (a canon regular), he made several attempts to reform religious instutions such as the cathedral at Augsburg, where he had been a secular canon, to the more strict *vita communis.* In his *De investigatione Antichristi* (1161–62), a lengthy polemic, Gerhoh includes a chapter titled "De spectaculis theatricis in ecclesia Dei exhibitis" in

---

49. Viller et al., *Dictionnaire de spiritualité,* 6:303–8; Chambers, *Mediaeval Stage,* 2:98–99.

which he charges that a dissolute clergy has turned churches into *theatra* where Antichrist or Herod is represented.[50] His accusation is that by simulation ("lieing" is his other verb), the clergy intend to present a true picture of Antichrist and Herod, but by their exhibition of these figures the participants become the lies, the Antichrist, they would represent, Gerhoh's point being that this wanton clergy inverts the ritual and symbols of the Christian cultus. As evidence that their lies become truth, he cites the instance of the person who took the part of a dead man to be resurrected by Elisha only to be found dead. Similarly, their Antichrist, who was buried and raised again, was found seven days later to have died. Thus their "lies," that is, their representations, become truths. Further, they show the child in his cradle, the weeping of the little one, the childbirth of the Virgin, the star, the death of the innocents, and the weeping of Rachel, all apparently from the Christmas liturgy.[51] But the church, he goes on, abhors theatrical spectacle *(spectacula theatralia)* and vanities and false (actually true) insanities in which men change themselves into women to their shame, and clerics into knights, and in which men transform themselves by wearing demonic masks *(daemonum larvas)*. This last charge against *spectacula theatralia* may be in reference to raucous activities of the choirboys and lower clergy on the eves of Holy Innocents, Saint Stephen's, and Saint John's (see below).

Theater historians have understood Gerhoh's to be an attack on liturgical drama, specifically the Tegernsee *Ludus de Antichristo,* a polemical retort on the part of the empire, but also Christmas celebrations (and presumably other liturgical dramas not mentioned).[52] I am willing to concede the general point but remain puzzled by some of the details and the purpose of the passage. First, the incidents in the *ludus* of Antichrist to which Gerhoh refers—for example, the raising of the dead by Elisha, Antichrist's death and resurrection—simply do not occur in the Tegernsee *Antichrist.* I am also puzzled by Gerhoh's segue from the Antichrist *ludus* to the Christmas plays in the quotation above and then immediately to the charge about men becoming women and men wearing

---

50. K. Young, *Drama of the Medieval Church,* 2:524–25.

51. "Exhibent . . . imaginaliter et Salvatoris infantiae cunabula, parvuli vagitum, puerperae Virginis matronalem habitum, stellae quasi sidus flammigerum, infantum necem, maternum Rachelis ploratum." Ibid.

52. Scholars have argued that Gerhoh attacked the *Ludus* because it characterized him and other reformers as *hypocritae.* Chambers, *Mediaeval Stage* 2:62–64, 98–99; K. Young, *Drama of the Medieval Church* 2:393; J. Wright, *The Play of Antichrist;* and Aichele, *Antichristdrama,* 33–34.

masks, because the first and third of these charges are not descriptive of the Christmas liturgies that we have (nor, for that matter, do persons in the Tegernsee *Ludus* wear demonic masks). In liturgical *representationes* participants are usually described as wearing liturgical garments; they are not costumed. On the other hand, the Tegernsee *Ludus* has props—crowns, for example—and there is a mock battle. So what is Gerhoh complaining about? Because we have assumed a link between the Tegernsee *Ludus* and Gerhoh's remarks, we have pictured liturgical performance in Gerhoh's comments. But what is a *ludus* of Antichrist, and why does Gerhoh associate it with a raging Herod? Again, we might say that these are two types of liturgical drama common in the period and the region. But it is also possible that these are two figures in liturgical parody or intruders on the liturgical scene. For example, Gerhoh might have in mind something like the later *Representatio Herodis in Nocte Epyphanie* in the thirteenth-century *ordinarium* of the cathedral of Padua.[53] During the concluding parts of Matins, Herod and his chaplain, clad in untidy tunics and carrying wooden spears, erupt into the choir, where Herod throws his spear into the choir and then, in a rage, reads the ninth lesson. During the reading Herod's ministers attack the bishop and other members of the choir with an inflated bladder before attacking the lay men and women in the nave. Herod joins in these antics until the reading of the Genealogy, at which point he apparently ceases to disrupt the services. Although we do not have any Antichrist *ludi* from the period except for the Tegernsee *Ludus*,[54] we might imagine such *ludi* to be common enough because there would be opportunity for spectacular illusion: turning trees upside down, and, according to Gerhoh, raising the dead, a contest between Elisha and Antichrist, and the resurrection of Antichrist himself. These actions have in common the potential for spectacle; more important, they are by the very nature of the Antichrist legend inversions and thus might have occasioned the raucous kinds of activity we see in the period from Saint Stephen's day (Dec. 26) to the Octave of Epiphany (Jan. 13). Perhaps it was the notion of the way the Antichrist legend (and *ludus*) parodies the events of Christ's life that led Gerhoh to attack liturgical *representationes* at Christmas, not because they in themselves were wanton

---

53. K. Young, *Drama of the Medieval Church*, 2:99–100.

54. Aichele, *Antichristdrama*, 27–34. It remains puzzling to me that Gerhoh speaks as if Antichrist plays were common and yet we have no records of any of the type he describes or, for that matter, any other one than the Tegernsee. Bernd Neumann lists no Antichrist drama nor any figure in a procession or tableau before 1468 (*Geistliches Schauspiel im Zeugnis der Zeit*, 1:312).

but because they were a part of a larger arena of license. Furthermore, during these festivities, choirboys and members of the lower clergy take over the liturgy from persons whom, I suspect, Gerhoh would find the only appropriate celebrants. Behind Gerhoh's objection to the *Rachel,* therefore, may lie a more profound objection to the usurpation of liturgical practice by inappropriate persons.

The motive for Gerhoh's antagonism toward "theatrical" *ludi* is clarified in his commentary on Psalms 133:3: "May the Lord bless you from Zion, he who made heaven and earth!"[55] There he confesses that when he was master of the school at Augsburg Cathedral *(Magister scholarum et doctor juvenum),* he was a producer of similar insanities and vanities, but, he adds, when he was called to a higher and more strict condition of the common life, he no longer found comfort in activities of this kind. Gerhoh had been a secular canon at Augsburg, but, forced to flee from there, he found refuge with the canons regular of Rottenbuch, where, under the influence of a hermit, he converted to the severity of the *vita communis.* After the Concordat of Worms, he returned to Augsburg, where he attempted to reform the cathedral clergy without success. It is his failure there that occasions his complaint that they no longer observe a communal life: they do not sleep in the dormitory, nor do they eat together in refectory except on rare feasts, especially, when they represent Herod, the persecutor of Christ, the slaughter of the children, or other "theatrical" plays or spectacles.[56] Then the canons come together to make the symbol of *convivium* in a refectory otherwise left empty. We might note that Gerhoh places these activities not in the church, but in the refectory; thus, they are extraliturgical. Gerhoh associates the representation of Herod and the Innocents with a lapse in communal discipline; the only occasion on which the canons function communally is a perverse one, that is, when they can be entertained. I suspect that Gerhoh is complaining about two kinds of phenomena in the two passages I

---

55. Gerhoh, *Commentarium in Psalmos,* PL 194.891: "Cogor hic reminisci propriae stultitiae in amaritudine animae meae dolens et poenitens, quod non semel talibus insaniis non solum interfui; sed etiam praefui utpote Magister scholarum et doctor juvenum, quibus ad istas vanitates non solummodo frenum laxavi, sed etiam stimulum addidi pro affectu stultitiae, quo tunc infectus eram, et in quo supra multos coaetaneos meos profeceram."

56. Ibid., col. 890–91: "Cohaerebat ipsi Ecclesiae claustrum satis honestum, sed a claustrali religione omnino vacuum, cum neque in dormitorio fratres dormirent, neque in refectorio comederent, exceptis rarissimis festis, maxime, in quibus Herodem repraesentarent Christi persecutorem, parvulorum interfectorem seu ludis aliis aut spectaculis quasi theatralibus exhibendis comportaretur symbolum ad faciendum convivium in refectorio aliis pene omnibus temporibus vacuo."

have cited—spectacular liturgical representations that strike him as inappropriate for cultic sites and inappropriate games and parodies that involve not necessarily personation in a scripted text but the assumption of disguise for festive license. From the austere view of the converted canon regular—and from his remote and harsh monastery at Reichersberg—the community at Augsburg can only seem lapsed and worldly. They are denizens of a new *theatrum*.

Herrad of Landsberg (1167–95) also expressed concern that the liturgy and churches were suffering from neglect or being contaminated by transformation of the *exempla* instituted to remind the faithful of Christ.[57] The old fathers of the *religio,* she says, instituted certain rituals and offices to excite the unbeliever *(incredulus)* to faith in the cult: symbolic representations *(imaginaria)* of the star leading the Magi to the newborn Christ, of Herod's rage and his deceitful malice, of the soldiers sent to cut down the children, of the lying-in of the Virgin, of the angel warning the Magi not to return, and of other events. Now, she complains, these rituals are turned into occasions of irreligious dissoluteness and youthful wantonness. The habits of clerics are changed with those of knights so that no difference is to be seen between them. The house of God is confounded by a mixture of lay people and the clergy, feasts, inebriations, scurrility, hateful jokes, plays, the clang of arms, the concourse of bawdy women, vanities, and a riot of indiscipline. Would it not be better, she asks, that the older ritual *(exemplum)* be wholly broken off than such offenses be permitted to continue? As she comes to the end of her diatribe, Herrad insists that this kind of feasting desecrates the *cena* of the Lord because it merely satisfies the body, whereas the ritual was instituted that men would recall and imitate the *religio* according to the form of Christ.

This passage has been read as an attack on liturgical drama. Karl Young says that she advises those in spiritual authority to prohibit liturgical plays, admirable though they may be in themselves.[58] Rosemary Woolf describes Herrad's as a measured attack on liturgical plays; her comment "both states and admits the force of the traditional justification of the plays . . . but nevertheless forbids them for bad things can come of good."[59] Chambers seems more accurate in his view that her objection is not to liturgical dramas like the *Stella* but to the Feast of Fools.[60] Herrad does not condemn liturgical dramas; rather, she

---

57. K. Young, *Drama of the Medieval Church,* 2:412–14. For other details of Herrad's life, see Viller et al., *Dictionnaire de spiritualité,* 7:366–69.

58. K. Young, *Drama of the Medieval Church,* 2:414.

59. Woolf, *English Mystery Plays,* 78–79.

60. Chambers, *Mediaeval Stage,* 1:318–19, 2.98.

objects to their transformation or replacement. She says that certain rituals were instituted by old fathers of the cult, and gives her list of *representationes,* but she objects that the observation of the Feast of the Epiphany and the Octave have become occasions of wantonness and irreligiosity. When she says that these representations were aimed at the unbelieving, she cannot be referring to veteran monks, who presumably are *adepti;* and when she says that they are now occasions of youthful wantonness, she perhaps implies that the *increduli* are the young choirboys who took a part and who also during the Christmas season were given license to engage in other *ludi.* But, as she continues, it becomes clear that she sees this dissolute behavior not only in the choir but in the nave. She is offended by the mixing together of laity and clergy, of the inability to distinguish the clergy from the laity because clerics have abandoned their habits for knights' armor. The first of these complaints suggests that rituals are destroyed when the clergy fails to maintain its distance from the laity, that it cannot remind and educate and excite to the faith when it indiscriminately mixes itself with those it should instruct.[61] The second charge makes a distinction between liturgical representation and whatever is going on at present. In liturgical representation the clergy do not costume themselves in worldly garb but wear liturgical garments. Although it is true that liturgical texts may say that participants "signify" the angel or the *obstetrices* of the *Pastores,* they frequently indicate that the participants are wearing albs or amices. They are *not* costumed to represent a figure; rather, they are *said* to represent a figure in the liturgical responses. Herrad's objection, by contrast, is to costume that misrepresents a clerical person.

To a proponent of the evolutionary theory of drama, it would appear that Herrad is complaining that participants in liturgical representation have taken the further step of using costumes to signify identity; to the contrary, it seems to me that she objects to the substitution of a different activity for liturgical representation. The liturgical rituals, which have a spiritual effect, have been replaced by material celebration: an orgiastic feast rather than the mass; uncontrolled, scurrilous, and raucous combat (some kind of parody or game) rather than a decorous remembrance of the slaughter of innocents. The participants are not uplifted in spirit but weighed down in body. When she asks

---

61. Herrad's remarks postdate Gerhoh's, but she seems to be describing the same kinds of things to which Gerhoh objects at the end of his comment. Perhaps for Gerhoh the events that followed the liturgical representations contaminated the approved rites and thus he sees them all as theatrical.

whether it would not be better to put down altogether the appropriate ritual *(exemplum)* than to permit the offenses to the cult to continue, I do not think we are obliged to understand her rhetoric to recommend suspension of the rituals of the fathers of old; rather, she appears to want to reform the clergy so that they no longer scandalize the unbelieving. She reminds them of the effect of visual *imaginaria* on the cult of Christ; these they should foster. The liturgical season to which Herrad refers, Epiphany (January 6) or its Octave (January 13), provides a clue to what is going on, for on these days the subdeacons take control of festivities.[62] The Feast of Fools arose in the twelfth century, hence Herrad would seem to be objecting to novelties that then are contrasted with older practice. The feast gave the subdeacons the opportunity for misrule—bodily feasts as well as liturgical parody.

I think it incorrect to lump Gerhoh and Herrad together as opponents of liturgical drama, as scholars often do, because Herrad does not object to decorous liturgical *imaginaria* that are *exempla* (both exemplifications and reminders). Gerhoh, on the other hand, seems to object even to liturgical *representationes,* perhaps because he associates them with a time of license and misrule. Both seem to be talking about the same period of the year, from after Christmas to the Octave of Epiphany. These were the days during which, by the twelfth century, the lower clergy were licensed to take over liturgical functions not normally given to them and, thus, to provide the potential for parody and misrule. I suspect that the motivation behind Gerhoh's and Herrad's attacks on these festivities is that they regard them as inappropriate intrusions into or disruptions of the liturgy. Herrad was the second abbess of the monastery of Hohenburg, which had been restored under Frederick Barbarossa and which was committed to the rule of Canonnesses of Saint Augustine, the women's version of the rule adopted by Gerhoh. In addition, Herrad entrusted the spiritual direction of the sisters to the Premonstratensians, another reformed order obedient to a rule of Saint Augustine. All of these orders reinstituted monastic labor, which in turn required a reformed and straitened liturgy. I think we can surmise that Gerhoh's and Herrad's objections, therefore, were to activities that they regarded as excrescences to, novelties in, a bloated liturgy (Gerhoh's objection to liturgical *representationes*) or intrusions of the *theatrum* into the church (Gerhoh's language but Herrad's sentiment). Both also seem outraged by the fact that these inappropriate "liturgies" are carried out by clerics who recall

---

62. See K. Young, *Drama of the Medieval Church,* 1:104–6.

neither their office nor the decorum that separates them from the world of ordinary men and women. Such clerics scandalize the *increduli* rather than excite them to devotion.

If we look at Gerhoh's and Herrad's remarks within the context of institutional reform, then they seem directed less against "liturgical dramas" per se than against inappropriate embellishment and lack of decorum. The distinction between the two critics is that Gerhoh includes the *Quem quaeritis* and the like as embellishments, whereas Harrad only objects to the activities that have been added to the *imaginaria*. I believe that Gerhoh labels these activities "theatrical" not so much because they are enacted scripts as that they are gestural; they are given to illusion and lack solemnity.

Theatrical Metaphor

Once the church had replaced the *theatrum* as the center of cultic practice, the *theatrum*, or things "theatrical," are defined as things not associated with the center of the cult (religious structures with their altars), things outside the cult (secular concerns or interests), or things that threaten the cult by an invasion of the outside into the cult center (the devil's pomps). Whatever is indecorous, given to emotion, conducive to sin can be placed under the rubric *theatralis*. The allusion to *theatrum* in later medieval documents is not a sign that the *theatrum* or things associated with it continued to exist in any real way, but that *theatrum* was a ready metaphor for the things perceived by individuals within the church not to be of the church. Theatrical metaphor is a rhetoric of abuse.

Because the ancient theaters were understood to be cultic centers—their *ludi* were required by the gods and represented stories about the gods—one could imagine the church as the victorious "*theatrum,*" the new cultic center. This analogy was frequently made, but it is easy to misread it, for we often look at such passages with *our* deeply researched, historical knowledge of the ancient theater rather than with the limited knowledge of medieval people. One of the better-known examples of this kind of metaphor occurs in the *Gemma animae*, where Honorius of Autun contrasts an actor in a tragedy with the priest at the mass:

> Sciendum quod hi qui tragoedias in theatris recitabant, actus pugnantium gestibus populo repraesentabant. Sic tragicus noster pugnam Christi populo Christiano in theatro Ecclesiae gestibus suis repraesentat, eique victoriam redemptionis suae inculcat. Itaque cum presbyter *Orate* dicit, Christum pro nobis in agonia positum exprimit, cum apostolos orare monuit. Per secretum silentium, significat Christum velut agnum sine voce ad victimam

ductum. Per manuum expansionem, designat Christi in cruce extensionem. Per cantum praefationis, exprimit clamorem Christi in cruce pendentis. Decem namque psalmos, scilicet a *Deus meus respice* usque *In manus tuas commendo spiritum meum* cantavit, et sic exspiravit. Per Canonis secretum innuit Sabbati silentium. Per pacem, et communicationem designat pacem datam post. Christi resurrectionem et gaudii communicationem.[63]

[It is known that those who recited tragedies in theaters represented the actions of opponents by gestures before the people. In the same way our tragic author (i.e., the celebrant) represents by his gestures in the theater of the Church before the Christian people the struggle of Christ and teaches to them the victory of His redemption. Thus when the celebrant (presbyter) says the *Orate (frates)* he expresses Christ placed for us in agony, when he commanded His apostles to pray. By the silence of the *Secreta* he expresses [actually, *significat*] Christ as a lamb without voice being led to the sacrifice. By the extension of his hands he represents [actually, *designat*] the extension of Christ on the Cross. By the chant of the Preface he expresses the cry of Christ hanging on the Cross. For He sang *(cantavit)* ten Psalms, that is, from the *Deus meus respice* to *In manus tuas commendo spiritum meum,* and then died. Through the secret prayers of the Canon he suggests the silence of Holy Saturday.][64]

This passage has been cited as evidence that Honorius—and other medievals—recognized the dramatic element in the mass, knew that the liturgy was a drama. Hardison says:

That there is a close relationship between allegorical interpretation of the liturgy and the history of drama becomes apparent the moment we turn to the Amalarian interpretations. Without exception they present the Mass as an elaborate drama with definite roles. . . . Perhaps the most remarkable expression of this idea is found in the *Gemma animae.* . . . Honorius not only uses the vocabulary of dramatic criticism, he uses it with considerable sophistication. The church is regarded as a theater. The drama enacted has a coherent plot based on conflict *(duellum)* between a champion and an antagonist.[65]

Despite its apparent literal statement, Honorius' passage, I would argue, makes a sharp *distinction* between the *theatrum* and the church, the tragic ac-

---

63. Honorius of Autun, *De Gemma animae,* Liturgica, cap. 83: De tragoediis (PL 172.570).
64. The translation is from Hardison, *Christian Rite,* 39–40.
65. Ibid., 40.

tor and the celebrating priest. The first three sentences assert an analogy; the remainder of the passage makes the distinction.

Note that Honorius uses *representare*, a verb with liturgical significance, to set up the theatrical metaphor: the tragedian and "our tragedian" *represent*. But when he moves into the description, he uses other verbs: *exprimit, significat, designat, innuit*.[66] Honorius is not imagining the mass as a theatrical piece; indeed, he implies that the church has taken over the ritual function that the theaters claimed (note that these tragedies are said to have taken place in the past). Second, he implies, through the verbs that he uses to describe the priest's movements, that the ritual is restrained and signifying rather than mimetic. The verb *representare*, which he uses to set up the analogy, has a nice edge to it: The Herod, Rachel, and other pieces are *representationes*. Honorius uses liturgical vocabulary to approximate what he imagines tragedians did when in solo performance they "represented" ancient stories and fables. The analogy is being made from the twelfth century to the ancient period, not the other way around and not as we would make it with our knowledge of the late antique theater. But, to me, the most significant point of the passage is that the priest's movements are said to be restrained; they are decorous.

The *theatrum* was associated with hypocrisy and effeminancy: hypocrisy because the actor wore a mask (a *persona*) that disguised his true self and because he expressed emotion that was not his (*hypocrita* is Latin for "actor" or "mime"), and effeminacy because the actor's gestures were exaggerated. Gerald of Wales presents a humorous episode in which extravagant gesture is stigmatized as theatrical in his autobiography, circa 1200, and *Speculum ecclesiae*, circa 1216, in which he lampoons a group of monks who observe their rule of silence but who engage in extravagant hand gestures in order to obtain special foods. He says that "all of them [were] gesticulating with fingers, hands and arms, and whistling one to another in lieu of speaking . . . so that [Giraldus] seemed to be seated at a stage play *[ludos scenicos]* or among actors and jesters *[histriones et joculatores]*."[67]

---

66. Hardison's description of Amalarius of Metz's allegorical comentary on the mass ("Mass as Sacred Drama," 35–79 in *Christian Rite*) imposes a dramatic sensibility on the language and actions of the mass and its participants, yet the vocabulary he reports Amalarius to use, like that which Honorius uses here, insists that the action is understood symbolically, not represented mimetically.

67. Gerald of Wales, "Tot etenim prior ad monachos servientes, et illi e contra ad mensas inferiores exenia ferendo, et hi quibus ferebantur gratias referendo, digitorum et manuum ac brachiorum gesticulationibus et sibilis ore pro sermonibus, longe levius atque licentius quam deceret, effluebant; ut quasi ad ludos scenicos aut inter histriones et joculatores sibi videretur constitutus":

Exaggerated bodily movement is labeled histrionic or theatrical because the actor in the ancient theater manipulated the audience's emotions through expressive gesture. This circumstance enables theatrical metaphor to be used to stigmatize and characterize cultic activity to which one objects—in the example I am about to cite, the objection is to expressive singing but may also be directed against polyphonic chant. Aelred of Rievaulx, in his *Speculum caritatis*, circa 1141–42, inveighs against the flamboyantly performed new music, which he compares to the singing and gesticulation of *histriones:*

> In the meanwhile, [the singer's] whole body is violently agitated by histrionic gesticulations *[histrionicis . . . gestibus]*—contorted lips, rolling eyes, hunching shoulders—and drumming fingers keep time with every single note. . . . Meanwhile, ordinary folk *[vulgus]* stand there awestruck, stupefied, marvelling at the din of bellows, the humming of chimes, and the harmony of pipes. But they regard the saucy gestures of the singers *[lascivias cantantium gesticulationes]* and the alluring *[meretricias]* variation and dropping of the voices with considerable jeering and snickering, until you would think they had come, not to an oratory, but to a theater *[ad theatram]* not to pray, but to gawk *[ad spectandum].*[68]

He comes back to the matter of singing when he says that what the holy fathers instituted to awaken the weak to devotion is usurped for illicit pleasure, the implication being that the fathers had instituted a solemn music with meaningful content that is now being rendered as sound without sense in order simply to move people:

> Therefore, after someone has scorned that ridiculous ruinous vanity and has applied himself to the ancient moderation of the Fathers, if the noble gravity cause his itching *[prurientibus]* ears frightful aversion when he remembers such theatrical nonsense *[nugarum theatricarum]*, and if in consequence he despises and condemns as rustic crudeness all the Fathers' gravity in their way of singing (which the Holy Spirit instituted by these holy Fathers, that is, by Augustine, Ambrose, and especially Gregory, as though by his own instrument) and prefers what they call Iberian lullabies *[Hiberas naenias]* . . .[69]

Speculum ecclesie, 2.4 (4:40–41), and *De rebus a se gestis*, 2.5 (1:51). The translationis Butler's, in Gerald of Wales, *Autobiography of Giraldus Cambrensis*, 71.

68. Aelred of Rievaulx, *Speculum charitatis*, pt. 2, cap. 23 (PL 195: 571–72). The translation by Connor is from Aelred, *Mirror of Charity*, 209–12.

69. Aelred of Rievaulx, *Mirror of Charity*, 211–12. Connor says that *hiberas naenias* is

It is remarkable how the theatrical metaphor controls the description and stigmatizes the action of these singers. Before he asserts the comparison to the *theatrum*, Aelred focuses on the histrionic gestures, the dissoluteness of the practi-
tioners. The singers' gesticulations are lascivious and meretricious, the latter
suggesting the feminine, but especially the movements of a harlot *(meretrix)*.
The vulgar are awestruck and stupefied; they jeer and snicker as if they were at
a theater where, rather than praying, they gape *(ad spectandum)*.

The object of Aelred's attack is readily apparent; indeed, there are others
who felt that the new music encouraged singers to pay attention to the musical
sounds rather than the words that were being sung. But why is it Aelred who
makes this complaint, and is he only concerned about musical novelty? We
must begin with the fact that Aelred is a Cistercian; moreover, he was a contemporary of Bernard of Clairvaux, and thus was drawn to the order while it
was in its early fervor. The Cistercian break from Cluniac monasticism was
motivated by the desire to return to a more literal practice of the Benedictine
Rule, and this return required liturgical reform (specifically a reduction of the
liturgy in order to allow time for manual labor). But there was also the desire to
preserve the purity of Gregorian chant. Louis Lekai, the historian of the Cistercian order, says: "Even in the lifetime of Saint Bernard, the General Chapter
had to insist on a virile pitch of recitation *[non more femineo tinnulis]* and to
banish the 'theatrical' effects of falsetto *[falsis vocibus velut histrionicam imi-
tari lasciviam].*"[70]

An even more specific objection may be implied when in the middle of the
passage, Aelred seems to pause to appeal to the singers to "honor that mystical
crib before which they render cult," as if implying that the singing to which he
objects is associated with the Christmas season, specifically, to liturgical *representationes* at Christmas, whether of Herod or of Rachel or of some more raucous liturgical parody. If this is the case, then Aelred would seem to identify the
Cistercian cultus with that of the Fathers, and in so doing Aelred constructs
Benedictine monasteries and cathedral schools as *theatra* because those places
allow an embellished and feminized liturgy to push aside the solemn chants of
Gregory.

The point that I have been trying to make is that theatrical metaphor is a
rhetorical weapon. Its use does not point to the existence of an actual theater or

---

found in the first lesson of the Septuagesima night office in the twelfth century (219 n. 11). Jerome,
who used the expression, considered the *Ibera* prone to following heretical novelties.

70. Lekai, *Cistercians,* 252–53.

even necessarily a mimetic tradition; rather, theatrical metaphor stigmatizes: the activity denounced is not Christian; it threatens the sanctity of the cult. With this rhetoric in mind, it is all the more obvious what Innocent III was condemning—and why—when he forbade *ludi theatrales:*

> Interdum ludi fiunt in eisdem ecclesiis theatrales, et non solum ad ludibriorum spectacula introducuntur in eis monstra larvarum, verum etiam in aliquibus anni festivitatibus, quae continue natalem Christi sequuntur, diaconi, presbyteri ac subdiaconi vicissim insaniae suae ludibria exercere praesumunt, per gesticulationum suarum debacchationes obscoenas in conspectu populi decus faciunt clericale vilescere, quem potius illo tempore verbi Dei deberent praedicatione mulcere.

> [From time to time public spectacles are made in certain churches, and not only are masks of monsters introduced in derisive spectacle, but in truth during other feast days of the year which follow immediately after the birth of Christ, deacons, presbyters and subdeacons in turn presume to exercise their insane mockeries (and) by the gestures of their obscene rages demean their clerical office in the sight of the people when it would be more profitable during that time to soothe (the populace) by teaching the word of God.][71]

Although authorities as grand as E. K. Chambers and Karl Young have asserted that the *ludi theatrales* in this passage are not liturgical pieces, one still finds the phrase translated as "stage plays."[72] It is patently obvious that Innocent objects to the shenanigans of the lower clergy during the Christmas season, and he demonizes these activities as theatrical, of the *theatrum*. But if there is any doubt about what he meant, all we have to do is look at the standard gloss by Bernardo Bottone that distinguished *ludi theatrales* from acceptable *representationes*. Bernardo said that Innocent was not prohibiting *representationes* of the Nativity, Herod, Rachel, and so forth, because these encourage men to worship; rather, he forbade ones that encourage lasciviousness and voluptuousness, such as those on the feasts of Saint Stephen, Saint John, and Holy In-

---

71. Friedberg, *Corpus Iuris Cononici*, 2:452:*Decretals of Gregory IX*, 3.1.12; Chambers, *Mediaeval Stage*, 2:100.

72. For example, Briscoe, "Clerical Notions of Dramatic Decorum," 9; Wasson, *Devon*, 4 (trans. on 318) [Exeter Cathedral Statutes, 1287], 7 (trans. 320) [Bishop John de Grandisson's Register, 1339], and 16 (trans. 329) [Bishop Lacy's Register, 1451]; and Stokes, *Somerset*, 1:236 (trans. 2:830), 1:238–39 (trans 2:832) [Cathedral Statutes of Wells, 1330–31 and 1337–38]. All of these documents quote the language of Innocent's decree.

nocents, with their parodic liturgies and general mayhem.[73] The distinction within Bernardo's gloss, *Cum decorem,* is between liturgical representation that is conducive to devotion as opposed to demonic substitution that is worldly, grotesque, deformed, and derisory, that is, theatrical.

But, one might object, if Innocent's letter is so clear, why did Bottone feel the need to comment on it? First, one could say that Bottone was doing what commentators do: comment. But there may be an additional motive. There were critics of liturgical *representationes*—perhaps Aelred but certainly Gerhoh of Reichersberg. What the Bottone gloss accomplishes, therefore, is the sanction of devotional *representationes.* Opponents cannot cite Innocent's letter as a means of disparaging or suppressing them. Or, to put it more bluntly, Cistercians, Augustinian canons, and other reformed orders could not use Innocent's text in polemical tracts sometimes launched against the Benedictine order or secular clerics.

I would like to conclude this section with one of the more complex—and satisfying—examples of theatrical metaphor: Bernard of Clairvaux's stigmatizing of the perfect. Here Bernard of Clairvaux compares himself to a *joculator* in order to contrast theatrical with Cistercian humiliation. He is writing to rebuke Oger, a canon regular of Mont-Saint-Éloi, for his resignation as superior of his monastery out of a (misguided) desire, according to Bernard, to return to the simple life of a monk. At the end of the letter, in which he has been at some pain to remark on how the wise are foolish and the foolish sometimes wise, Bernard uses a ludic metaphor in which the *joculator dei* is said to be the greater fool because he does *not* play:

> I rightly apply to myself those words of the Prophet: "I have been lifted up only to be cast down and discomforted"; and again "I will play, and make myself more vile" (2 Kings 6:22). I will play that I may be mocked *[illudar].* A good sort of playing this, a playing calculated to enrage Michol and please God. A good sort of playing which is ridiculous to men, but a very beautiful sight *[spectaculum]* to the angels. I say it is a good sort of playing by which we become an object of reproach to the rich and of ridicule to the proud. In fact what else do seculars think we are doing but playing when what they desire most on earth, we fly from; and what they fly from, we desire? Like ac-

---

73. *Decretalium copiosum,* fol. 171r: "non tamen hic prohibetur representare praesepe domini, herodem, magos et qualiter rachel plorauit filios suos, etc., quae tangunt festiuitates illas, de quibus hic fit mentio cum talis potius inducant homines ad conpunctionem quam ad lasciuiam vel voluptatem: sicut in pascha sepulchrum domini et alia representatur ad deuotionem exictandum."

robats and dancers *[joculatores et saltatores]*, who with heads down and feet up, stand or walk on their hands, and thus draw all eyes to themselves. But this is not a game for children or the theater where lust is excited by the effeminate and indecent contortions of the actors, it is a joyous game, decent, grave, and admirable, delighting the gaze of the heavenly onlookers. The pure and holy game he plays who says: "We are become a spectacle to angels and men." And we too play this game that we may be ridiculed *[illudamur]*, discomforted, humbled, until he comes who puts down the mighty from their seat and exalts the humble.[74]

The theatrical metaphor presents the *joculatores et saltatores* as a spectacle of the world turned upside down; they are stigmatized by their effeminate and indecent movements.[75] The similitude with monks is grounded in the fact that these performers are recognized as fools and objects of reproach (insofar as their profession separates them from the society within which they function). The metaphor is complicated by the allusion to Michal's reproach of David for leaping and dancing before the ark of the Lord (2 Sam. 6:14–23). Michal, the daughter of Saul, charged that David had dishonored himself because he uncovered himself like one of the vulgar and shameless. But David responded that the Lord had chosen him above Saul and therefore he would make merry before the Lord. Indeed, he proposes to make himself even more contemptible than he has shown himself to be and thus to abase himself before Michal, yet he will be held in honor by those Michal says were shamed by his dancing. The account ends with the terse statement, "And Michal the daughter of Saul had no child to the day of her death."

David's exuberant dance before the ark of the Lord cannot in any way be imagined to be like the joyous, decent, grave, and admirable *ludus* of Bernard; indeed, David would seem to be more like the *joculatores et saltatores* whom Bernard ridicules. But David ultimately is the appropriate model for Bernard because, having a high status, he humiliates himself before the ark, and, later, after his dance, he enters the tent to make burnt offerings and peace offerings. Both David and Bernard play so that they will be mocked *(illudamur)*, an appropriate sacrifice for their Lord. The second ground for Bernard's theatrical

---

74. The translation, with some modifications, is from Bernard of Clairvaux, *Letters of Bernard of Clairvaux*, 135. The Latin text is in Bernard of Clairvaux, *Lettere*, Letter 87, 1:434–36.

75. The image of the *joculator, histrio*, or *saltator* upside-down is common in representations of acrobatic performers and dancers. See Davidson, *Illustrations of the Stage*, pl. 105, and Salome dancing before Herod, pls. 94–100.

metaphor, then, is that both minstrels and monks turn the world upside down: the first for the amusement of the worldly, the second as a spectacle for angels (and men). The latter sentiment—that the humiliation of monks is a spectacle for angels—is made even more potent because it recalls Saint Paul's comment that the early Christian martyrs in the arena were made spectacles for the angels (1 Cor. 4:9).[76]

The Return of the *Theatrum* to England

Because of the negative connotation of the *theatrum,* the word "theater" in Middle and Early Modern English occurs rarely, and when it is used, it often retains some of its pejorative meaning. The word is most commonly used to refer to ancient structures in which dramas or athletic contests were held, but this notion allowed the association of the *theatrum* with jousts and tilts, though these latter are usually represented as having happened in the past.[77] Isidorean structural details are common,[78] as is the linking of the *theatrum* to the brothels or the immoral.[79] Whether historical, pejorative, or both, the English term "theater" is almost always associated with the ancient past of Greece or Rome.[80]

---

76. Space does not permit discussion of the more complex play on the ludic in Saint Francis's representation of his brothers as *joculatores dei.*

77. Chaucer, The Knight's Tale, A.1885, 2091; Christine de Pisan, *Middle English Translation,* 90, line 9; Hall, *Union,* fol. 2v; and Capgrave, *Life of St. Katharine of Alexandria,* 1:759. Capgrave seems to want to neutralize the reference to *theatrum.* He says that at Katharine's coronation jousts were held in the theater but there was no war—perhaps trying to dissociate the term from its usual connotations in order to keep Katharine saintly. In another work, however, Capgrave links ancient *theatra* with some places in his own area. In the midst of his description of the emperors' palaces in Rome, he says, "These emperoures eke had certeyn places whech þei clepid *theatra* and þat soundith in oure tunge a place in whech men stand to se pleyis or wrestilingis or swech oþir exercises of myth [might, strength] or of solace. Summe of þese places were called ampheatrum þat was a place all round swech as we haue here in þis lond, summe were called *theatrum* & þat was a place was lich half a sercle of whech þere were uii in rome" (*Solace of Pilgrimes,* 17–18). I think for Capgrave the *theatrum* is a place where sports competitions, not dramas, take place.

78. Chaucer, The Knight's Tale, A.1885, 2091; Higden, *Polychronicon,*4:99; and Lydgate, *Lydgate's Troy Book,* 2:863, 900, 943.

79. *Medulla grammatice,* cited in *MED* sub[1c]; Chaucer, *Boece,* bk. 1, prose 1, line 50, which associates Boethius's comforter-muses with the "comune strompettis" of the theater; and Lydgate, *Fall of Princes,* 8:239, in which Commodus's fleshly appetite is linked to his going to the theater.

80. There is one puzzling reference in John Lydgate's *Saint Albon and Saint Amphibalus:* The reader is admonished to be glad now that Albion has been "enbawmyd with the purpil blood" of Albon; "For on *thi* soile of newe ther is descendid / Celestial dewe of grace and al foisoun, / And specially bi revelacioun / Which on thi theatre of newe doth rebounde, / Now blissid Albon is in thi boundis founde" (3:1368–79). Lydgate must be using the word in an expanded sense of market

Latin clerical usage, as we have seen, draws on notions of the immorality of the ancient theater in order to label indecorous behavior theatrical. In order to reinstate the *theatrum,* therefore, there must be some kind of *apologia* for the *theatrum.* Terence is the means for this restoration even though it takes thirty or forty years after the introduction of his texts into the curriculum before the *theatrum* in a physical sense reenters the English scene—this time without pejorative connotations.

Terence was a troubling figure for medieval Christians.[81] As we have seen, Augustine grudgingly acknowledged his usefulness in training gentlemen, whereas Jerome condemned him, as did canon law. Yet Terence continued to be read throughout the Middle Ages, and we find numerous references to Terence manuscripts in English monasteries from as early as the eleventh century.[82] Toward the end of the fifteenth century Terence was introduced into the curriculum of Cambridge University in place of Priscian, and Oxford included Terence in the grammar curriculum sometime between 1505 and 1515.[83] In the early sixteenth century schools followed suit by using him in the third and fourth forms.[84] Along with the introduction of Terence as a study text was a defense of the material often along the lines of the medieval one. The first stage seems to have been the argument that the content of the plays—which might strike some as immoral—had a moral purpose: it warned the young, especially, against the kinds of activities that they read about in the plays.[85] Terence was defended—by Erasmus, for example—because of his accessibility, his colloquial Latin, and his depiction of life as it actually is.[86] These defenses treat the texts rhetorically: they are to be admired for their deftness, wit and moral sen-

---

place or populated center. Two of the six MSS substitute "lande" and a third leaves a blank space, which suggests the scribes were puzzled by the usage.

81. Norland, "Terentian Commentaries," in his *Drama in Early Tudor Britain,* 65–83.

82. Bannister, "Bishop Roger of Worcester," 389–93 (Lancashire, *Dramatic Texts,* item 1526). The Benedictine Abbey of St. Alban's owned a twelfth-century Terence with ink drawings of masked actors (now Bodleian MS Auct. F.2.13); see Ker, *Medieval Libraries of Great Britain,* 94. For the illustrated Terence manuscripts, see Jones and Morey, *Miniatures.*

83. Hackett, *Original Statutes of Cambridge University,* 68, 300–302; McConica, *English Humanists,* 87.

84. These included St. Paul's, London, in 1518 (Lancashire, *Dramatic Texts,* item 985); Cuckfield (Sussex) Free Grammar School in 1520 (item 589); Cardinal Wolsey's College Grammar School in Ipswich (Suffolk) in 1528 (item 794); Eton College in 1529–31 (item 650); and Winchester College in 1529–31 (item 1504).

85. This argument goes back to ancient times in Donatus's essay *De comoedia,* which prefaces all sixteenth-century editions of Terence (Norland, *Drama in Early Tudor Britain,* 70–72).

86. Norland, "Erasmus," in his *Drama in Early Tudor Britain,* 84–94.

timent. For these commentators Terence is a written text to be pondered rather than one to be acted. The argument was carried a step further when school-masters suggested that the texts be "enacted" in order to train students in elo-cution and rhetorical presentation. At first these "plays" may have been nothing more than exercises in reading aloud, but they quickly became much more elaborate presentations—but always with an educational justification at-tached to them.

The earliest unequivocal reference to a drama in the Cambridge records is to the comedy of Terence performed at King's Hall in 1510–11.[87] To be sure, there are references to *ludi* at Christmas from 1455–56 on, but I suspect these are to Christmas Lords of Misrule, though it is uncertain what the college dis-guisings may have been (from 1456–57 on). The move at the Cambridge col-leges from Terence as reading to Terence as performance may have been in part a not entirely successful attempt to contain the rowdyism associated with Christmas and other revels. There are an astonishing number of records of pay-ments for replacing the glass in the halls and chapels after the performances. That this bacchanalian eventuality was expected is indicated by the replace-ment of glass with lesser work before some performances and finally by Trinity College's decision to put nets before the windows in 1578–79 (they still had to replace some glass that year). Nevertheless, it is clear from later records that the performance of Terentian plays were intended to control behavior and to give an educational justification for Christmas revels. Like other clerical insti-tutions, the Cambridge colleges had attempted to control the raucous behavior of these young men during the reformist initiatives implemented earlier in the fourteenth century. The Peterhouse Statues (1343–44) echo the canonical pro-hibitions: "ioculatoribus & hystrionibus publice non intendant. ludis theatral-ibus aut ludibriorum spectaculis publicis in ecclesiis theatro uel stadiis seu locis aliis publicis interesse nisi recreacionis causa honestate seruata fortassis ad modicum tempus intersint / uel ea personaliter exercere."[88] The decrees were intended to restrain the clergy from involvement in *public* amusements, espe-cially ones that were conducive to immorality, and to forbid these raucous aci-

---

87. Nelson, *Cambridge*, 1:84, 88.

88. See ibid., 1:3–4: "not to watch jesters or entertainers in public, nor by any means to pre-sume to be present at stage plays or public shows of mockeries in churches, a theatre, or racecourses or other public places unless they should perhaps be present for a short time for relaxation while de-cency is preserved" (2:1045). I think "stage plays" is incorrect for *ludis theatralibus*, since it clearly refers to Innocent's decree. Similarly, *theatro* should probably be understood in the sense of mar-ketplace or public place.

tivities of clerics in minor orders within churches and monasteries, especially on the eves of Saint Stephen's, Holy Innocents, and Christmas. The statutes for King's College, 1442–43, allow the boys to sing the liturgy on the feast of Saint Nicholas, the usual day for the boy bishop ceremonies, but forbids it on Holy Innocents.[89] The statutes of St. John's College, 1529–30, forbid scholars to attend *spectacula . . . aut ludos* prohibited by ecclesiastical or common law when they are outside the college. At the same time that the university was increasing pressure to put down *ludi* in and around the town, colleges such as Gonville and Caius forbade these same activities to their scholars[90] and incidentally sought to restrict attendance on their comedies and tragedies to the college community. The university officers, therefore, can be seen as following the English bishops who, from the early thirteenth century, began a campaign not only to eradicate obscene *ludi* within ecclesiastical precincts but also *ludi inhonesti* among the laity.

The prohibitions and the rise of interest in the drama may be related. Alan Nelson points out that the colleges tended to stage plays during the festival period between Christmas and Epiphany, and again from Epiphany to the beginning of Lent.[91] It was during the first of these periods that the disruptive behavior of the minor clergy had occurred, so the establishment of drama had the effect of substituting for indecent rowdyism an approved form of recreation that was also educational. In 1559–60 Trinity College justified the plays given during the twelve days of Christmas on the grounds that they enabled the youths to spend the Christmas season with greater profit. According to a Queens' College statute passed a year earlier, the Greek master and the examiner were responsible for the production of plays before the twentieth of December lest the youth "remain crude in pronunciation and gesture and unpolished."[92] In 1546 Queens' College required that all scholars below the master of arts attend and, when appropriate, participate in the dramas on pain of dismissal. Eventually the reforms needed reforming. The Christmas Lord of Misrule, in the fifteenth-century records, may have been an early attempt to rechannel energies away from the activities of the choirboys in the choir and around the altar on Christmas eve. The Lords of Misrule seem to have gotten out of hand as well, however, for in 1548 the university issued the first order

89. Ibid., 1:29.
90. Ibid., 1:267.
91. Ibid., 2:715.
92. Ibid., 2:1130.

that no one should be lord of games at Christmas no matter what name he used.[93] We might also recall the glass-breaking incidents, which suggest that the colleges' efforts at restraint were not entirely successful.

The increasing secularism of the colleges is indicated not only by the introduction of the drama but the reintroduction and approval of a vocabulary once used to describe the forbidden. The first use of *theatrum* in the Cambridge records comes in the Queens' College payments of 1547–48 for setting up the *theatrum* and *screne* (from *skena*?) for Roman comedies.[94] The resurrection of this old vocabulary to describe a performance structure appears a bit earlier at Oxford even though, as John Elliott has argued, the colleges of Oxford University took to the stage later than those at Cambridge.[95] In 1538–39 one Mr. Hammon[d]s was paid 18d. for three days' labor on the *proscaenium*, in later records called a *scena* or *scanna*.[96] It was not until 1553–54 that this structure was referred to as a *theatrum*, and by then the costs had risen considerably. Indeed, by 1559–60 the costs had risen even more substantially—from 11s. 6d. to close to 50s.—and the number of laborers had also increased.[97] Perhaps the first *theatri* were wooden platforms with painted backdrops, whereas the later ones were more fully realized replications of ancient stages.

The ancient Latin terminology seems to have been revived because it described the place, the *theatrum,* in which the old comedies had been played. They are called *spectacula* because that is what they had been called in the late Roman period and in subsequent clerical writings that condemned the late antique stage. The reappearance of these words in nonpejorative usage indicates the distance early English society had moved with regard to dramas on profane subjects. The universities, we might say, prepared the way for a new *theatrum,* the Theatre, built in 1576.

---

93. Ibid., 1:164.

94. Ibid., 1:149–50. In the same year King's College paid for *ludicra spectacula in Aula colegij* and a few years later for *ludicrorum;* this is vocabulary that once designated the forbidden.

95. Elliott, "Drama at the Oxford Colleges," 64–66; "Plays, Players, and Playwrights," 179–94; and "Early Staging in Oxford," 68–76.

96. Alton, "Academic Drama in Oxford," 50.

97. Ibid., 53–55.

❧ T W O ☙

Miracula, Ludi inhonesti, "Somergames," and the Tretise of Miraclis Pleyinge

Scholars have read the *Tretise of Miraclis Pleyinge* as an attack (probably Lollard) on the religious drama of the late Middle Ages and the only sustained antitheatrical piece between late antiquity and the late sixteenth century.[1] The absence of an antitheatrical tradition allows for the possibility that there was wide support for religious dramas, and the *Tretise* can be seen as an anomaly, an extreme position taken by persons who were opposed to images and thus to any kind of simulation of the sacred. But there is an antitheatrical tradition, as I indicated in the preceding chapter: Innocent III objected to *ludi theatrales* in monasteries and cathedrals. His decree was part of a larger reform effort, some of which preceded his action and much of which continued through the medieval period and the Reformation and well into the seventeenth century. This tradition was not directed toward religious drama but *ludi theatrales, miracula,* "somergames," "scotales," and other *ludi inhonesti.* It is not until the earliest years of the sixteenth century, when drama became a potentially dangerous political weapon, that attempts were made to regulate the drama, that is, to determine what could or could not be played. There was, of course, regulation of the great urban cycles of plays and presumably other kinds of town drama, but these controls were intended to ensure that the plays went forward smoothly; they were not attempts to censor the drama.

The antitheatrical or antiludic traditions that I describe in this chapter can

---

1. Barish, *Antitheatrical Prejudice,* 67–68; Woolf, *English Mystery Plays,* 85–86; and for further background and recent commentary, see the introduction to Davidson's revised edition, *Tretise of Miraclis Pleyinge.* Other commentary is cited below.

be seen as part of the reform movements that were codified, as it were, in the Fourth Lateran Council (1215). The legislation of this council was largely devoted to the reformation of the clergy, the regularization of institutions, definitions of the obligations of clerics and bishops, and rulings on the faith (the doctrine of transubstantiation). But there were also important provisions regarding lay people: the requirement of annual confession and injunctions concerning what the clergy were to teach their parishioners. Many of these rules can be read as attempts to instill conformity and morality, to create a sense of one's status and obligations, and to define the elements of the faith and foster a system for their dissemination.

Although reformation of the clergy was founded on different principles and desiderata than that of the laity, over time injunctions directed specifically toward the clergy had an effect on those against similar lay activities. When Innocent issued his decree against *ludi theatrales* within sacred precincts *(Cum decorem)*, he specifically attacked clerical mispractice.[2] The *theatrum* is drawn into this legislation because Innocent made an implicit comparison between the *theatrum* and the church. The *theatrum* was where ancient peoples honored their gods; the church is where Christian people do the same. Practice differs, however, because the *spectacula* and games of the ancient *theatrum* were lewd, gestural, noisy, and held in honor of demons, whereas those of the church are to be devotional and held in honor of the one God. The ones Innocent condemned were theatrical because they were thought to be like ancient pagan practice.

English episcopal statutes and synodalia recognize that engagement in "play" differed for clerics and laypersons. Drawing on an ancient tradition of separating the clergy from the *theatrum*, Lateran IV, capitulum 16, forbade clerics to attend on worldly entertainers and activities: "mimis, ioculatoribus et histrionibus non intendant et tabernas prorsus evitent, nisi forte cause necessitatis in itinere constituti; ad aleas vel taxillos non ludant, nec huiusmodi ludis intersint." [(Clerics) should not watch mimes, entertainers and *histriones*. Let them avoid taverns altogether, unless by chance they are obliged by necessity on a journey. They should not play at games of chance or of dice, nor be present at such games.][3] These few sentences, which I will refer to as *Mimis*, come in

---

2. *Cum decorem* was incorporated into Gregory IX's *Decretals*, published in 1234. It is quoted, for example, in Wells Cathedral Statutes in 1330–31 and 1337–38 (Stokes, *Somerset*, 236, 236–37), and alluded to or partially quoted by Grandisson in 1333 (Wasson, *Devon*, 6–7) and in John Trillek's *Register* (1348) (Klausner, *Herefordshire*, 57–58).

3. Tanner, *Decrees of the Ecumenical Councils*, 1.243. The translation is Tanner's.

the capitulum on the dress of clerics; however, it begins with a prohibition of clerical engagement in commerce and moves to the provisions given above, then to correct tonsure, before going on to details of dress. The chapter as a whole comes amidst a section dealing with clerical decorum. For example, the immediately preceding chapter warns against drunkenness and ends with a prohibition against hunting and the possession of hunting dogs and fowls. Capitulum 16 was later incorporated into Gregory IX's *Decretals* (III, 1, 15), within the larger rubric: *De vita et honestate clericorum.*[4] In English episcopal statutes, *Mimis* often appears under the same rubric, *De vita,* but occasionally under others: *De superbia vitanda in verbo et gestu.*[5] No matter where *Mimis* appears, it is always in conjunction with clerical decorum, especially dress.

Just as *De vita* and related legislation center on the purity of the body of the priest, so is there concern for the purity of sacred precincts. The two are often linked in bans on *choreas* and scotales. Priests are forbidden to proclaim the banns of scotales or to attend them; if they do, they are to be punished according to the canons.[6] Cemeteries are to have ditches or walls about them to keep out animals; "et ne in ipsis in sanctorum festivitatibus aut aleas lucte fiant, coree ducantur, vel alii ludi spectabiles habeantur" [and nor are there to be during holy days wrestling games, dance-songs, or any other spectacles].[7] There is to be no singing or other *ludi::* "Ut nec cantilene seculares quamdiu corpora defunctorum in domibus iacent nec choree nec lucte in eisdem fiant. Ut nec choree nec lucte fiant propre cimiteria quamdiu matutine, missa, et vespere cantentur" [That neither secular songs be made during the time the bodies of deceased lie in the house (= the church?) nor dancing songs nor wrestling in the same. That neither dancing-songs nor wrestlings be made in the churchyard while matins, mass and vespers are sung].[8] These two statutes are typical of attempts to control use of the churchyard, but they also testify to practice. Parish ales, which often included celebratory dances, drinking, and wrestling and other sports,

---

4. Friedberg, *Corpus iuris canonici,* 2:453.

5. Powicke and Cheney, *Councils and Synods,* e.g., Statutes of Salisbury, 1217x1219 (1:63); Statutes of Lincoln, 1239? (1:271).

6. Canterbury I (1213x1214), cap. 60 (Powicke and Cheney, *Councils and Synods,* 1.35–36); Salisbury I (1217x1219), cap. 13 (ibid., 1:64). The relevant canons are *Decretum,* dist. 23, cap. 3; dist. 35, cap. 1; *De Consecratione,* dist. 1, cap. 66; *De consecratione,* dist. 5, cap. 36 (Friedberg, *Corpus iuris canonici,* 1:80, 1:131, 1:1312, and 1:1422, respectively).

7. Winchester III (1262x1265), cap. 35 (Powicke and Cheney, *Councils and Synods,* 1.709). See also Canterbury I, cap. 60; Salisbury I, cap. 103 ; and Exeter II (1287) (ibid., 1:35–36, 1:93, 2:1009, respectively).

8. Worcester II (1229), cap. 22 (ibid., 1.174).

were held in churchyards, often with the consent of the parish priest. Commonly they would be held on the feast days of saints, hence the prohibition of the activity when it would disrupt service. Here the concern for clerical purity impinges on lay practice; such statutes do not restrict what lay people do outside sacred precincts, but some groundwork has been laid for making an analogy between *ludi inhonesti* of the laity and that of the clergy.

Possibly as early as the late thirteenth century the phrase *ludi theatrales* begins to be applied to activities of the laity. In 1287 Bishop Peter Quinel's Statutes for Exeter Cathedral ordered his parish priests to preach that "luctas coreas vel alios ludos inhonestos in cimiterijs exercere presumat precipue in vigilijs & festis sanctorum cum huiusmodi ludos teatrales & ludibriorum spectacula introductos per quos ecclesiarum coinquintur honestas, sacri canones detestentur" [no one should presume to carry on wrestling, dances, or other improper sports/plays in churchyards, especially on the vigils and feasts of the saints since the sacred canons (i.e., canon law statutes) loathe for such stage-plays and spectacles of derision to be introduced, by which the decency of churches is polluted].[9] As I indicated in the preceding chapter, "stage plays" is an inaccurate translation of *ludi theatrales,* but what is interesting in this quotation is that Quinel sees an equation between the *ludi inhonesti* of the laity and what Innocent had designated clerical improprieties.[10] Quinel can make this move because *ludi inhonesti,* lay games and entertainments, are spectacles of the marketplace *(theatrum)* and in this instance are like clerical ones insofar as they are invasions of the *theatrum* into sacred precincts, the cemetery. In 1337–38 the statutes of Dean Walter de London, Wells Cathedral, make the equation between clerical and lay activities even more apparent. The rubric for chapter 26 is: "Prohibicio ludorum theatralium & spectaculorum & ostentacionem laruarum in ecclesia Wellensis" [A prohibition of *ludi theatrales* and spectacles and showings of masks in the church of Wells].[11] The chapter begins "Item cum infra septimanam Pentecostes & etiam in alijs festiuitatibus fiant a laicis ludi theatrales in ecclesia predicta" [Also since during Whitsuntide and

---

9. Wasson, *Devon,* 4. The translation is Wasson's. There is a similar equation in 1312 from Ripon Minster: the charge is that "vicarii, capellani, et caeteri ministri . . . spectaculis publicis, ludibriis et coreis, immo teatricalibus ludis inter laicos frequentius se immiscent." Chambers, *Mediaeval Stage,* 1:40 n. 3, cites this from Fowler, *Memorials of the Church of SS. Peter and Wilfred,* 2:68.

10. John Bromyard makes a similar equation when he compares the clerks' *officia larvarum* with lay *chorea* (*Summa predicantium, Chorea,* art. 3, fol. 152v).

11. Stokes, *Somerset,* 1:238–39. The translation is mine. Stokes translates *ostentacionem laruarum* as "showings of ghosts (*or* spirits *or* demons)," any of which may be correct.

also on other feast days *ludi theatrales* are made in the said church] before going on to quote *Cum decorem* with regard to clerical *ludi theatrales* at Christmas.[12] We can say that the references to the laity's spring games have been inserted into *Cum decorem;* although the activities may differ and come at different times of the year, they are alike in being *ludi* of the *theatrum.*

In 1451 Bishop Lacy spells out the logic of the analogy: he says there should be no "cachinnaciones conclamaciones risus immoderati inhonesti atque indiscreti coree ludibria & ludi inhonesti noxij forenses siue theatrales qui fierent in locis ad speculandum aptis vt in theatro in quo homines ad spectacula venire solebant non in locis sacris" [laughter, shouting, immoderate mirth, indecent and indiscreet dances, indecent mockeries and harmful plays proper to the market-place or the *theatrum* which ought to occur in places apt for viewing such as in the *theatrum* where men are accustomed to come to spectacles, not in sacred places].[13]

These documents may help us understand another that is murkier. In 1339 John de Grandisson wrote to Master Robert Hereward, Canon of Exeter, that he had heard that Robert Lucy maintained a "canopy or balcony" (salarium seu protectum) on posts fixed in sacred ground that hinders the procession around the church.[14] There, before the aforesaid "roof" *(sub domo)* occurs "a gathering of rogues [scurrorum], actors [scenicorum], whores [meretricam], and other vile persons [aliarum turpium personarum]" who hinder the peace of the church by "putting on stage-plays [ludos excercencium theatrales]." John Wasson translates the passage as evidence of play production in the churchyard.[15] But I suspect that Grandisson has theatricalized something to which he objects. His names for the rabble are pejorative—and ancient; indeed, the inclusion of "whores" no doubt is intended to recall the whole Isidorean tradition of the *theatrum.* Rather than using theatrical language to describe a performance, Grandisson is making participants of some festivity into denizens of the *theatrum.* But what is the bishop specifically talking about? Is he really complaining that someone has set up a booth stage for the performance of plays? I think it more likely that he is objecting to the kinds of lay games of which he complains throughout his episcopacy. Here, it is not the *ludi* per se but the structure that is the object of his wrath because the structure impedes the church's processions. Perhaps he is complaining about the construction of

---

12. My translation.

13. Wasson, *Devon,* 16. The translation is Wasson's.

14. Ibid., 7–8. My initial description depends on Wasson's translation (319–20).

15. See also his comments in "English Church as Theatrical Space," 26.

an arbor during festive celebrations when there would have been processions outside the church, and thus the letter indirectly objects to lay festivities in the churchyard.[16] Something of this sort, from a later date but described in some detail, occurred in 1469 when Thomas Barker and Margaret More were chosen king and queen of the village (Wistow, Yorkshire). The game included a procession of the royal couple and the villagers led by a minstrel that went to a barn called a "somer house" next to the parish church where Margaret stayed on the Sunday before the feast of Saint John the Baptist from noon until after sunset.[17]

However we are to interpret Grandisson's references, we can conclude several things about the use of the phrase *ludi theatrales*. First, Innocent used the term to designate inappropriate *clerical* activities. He likened these diversions to those of the *theatrum* because they were "not-Christian" yet occurred within the church. Like *ludi* of the *theatrum*, they were in honor of the devil, not Christ. Clerical reformers extended the meaning of the term. There were lay *ludi* that were also of the *theatrum,* and especially when these occurred within sacred precincts, usually the cemetery, then they also could be called *ludi theatrales*. But this extension of the definition tells us even more than the canonists do that *ludi theatrales* are not "stage plays," as we have often used that term; they are games and amusements, specifically church ales, song-dances *(choreas),* wrestling matches, and other festivities. They are linked to the *theatrum* not because anyone is enacting a script but because the participants are irreverent and immoral; these *ludi* are occasions of lechery, gluttony, anger, and adultery.

This chapter argues that some reforming bishops began in the early thirteenth century to suppress clerical *ludi theatrales* and to require them to avoid *mimi* and their like. Some—Grosseteste is the best example—also moved to extirpate lay *ludi inhonesti,* somergames, and scotales. The reformers, and this would include both bishops and preachers, sometimes indicate that they imagine these lay *ludi* to be what we have called "pagan survivals," but the primary motivation is their belief that these activities lead to anger, drunkenness, and lechery. Although these attacks are heavily moral and thus the proper subject

---

16. For legislation against construction of arbors within church precincts, see the statutes of John Pecham, 1280, the Council of Ripon, 1306, and the Council of London, 1342, in Wilkins, *Concilia Magnae Britanniae et Hiberniae,* 2.49, 286, and 709, respectively. Mary Marshall, "Theatre in the Middle Ages," 5, says that the medieval use of *scena* is *porticus,* a roof shading a place in the theater, such as an arbor of branches or some other form of temporary shelter or porch built onto a more solid surface. And see John Bromyard's description of such activities in *Summa predicantium: Chorea,* fols. 152v–53v.

17. Parker, "Some Records of the 'Somyr Play,'" 20–22.

of a sermon, they are often invoked out of concern that these immoralities pollute sacred precincts, specifically the churchyard but at times the church itself. We can see, then, that the demonization of *ludi* is partially motivated, on one hand, by the clergy's desire to separate themselves and their enclave from contaminations of the world, and, on the other, by the extension of notions of clerical purity to lay activities. These may seem contradictory movements, but they are not if one realizes that the clergy do not intend to make the laity clerics—they recognize the necessary distinction of status—but that the reformation of the laity, making lay people moral Christians, can best be effected by instituting lay practice that is imitative of but does not entirely duplicate clerical practice. This kind of initiative might result in a lay procession on a feast day in place of a gargantuan feast (though such attempts, as we will see, were not entirely successful).

This chapter treats attempts to suppress *miracula*, which are roughly equivalent to Innocent's *ludi theatrales*, and the extension of the antitheatrical argument to lay somergames and *ludi inhonesti* in the *Tretise of Miraclis Pleyinge* and other texts. My larger argument is that we have mistakenly read the term *miracula* as a generic term for saint play or religious drama in general and that we have misread the *Tretise* as a tract directed against biblical drama when in fact it is an attack on *miracula*, somergames, and other *ludi inhonesti*. The *Tretise* is antitheatrical in opposing itself to the games of the world, of the *theatrum*, not to religious dramas. It is a significant document in the antiludic discourse of the later Middle Ages.

Miracula

In his *Gesta abbatum* Matthew Paris says that Geoffrey, a secular cleric, was called to St. Albans about 1100 to head the school but arrived too late and was sent to the one at Dunstable, where he made ("fecit") a certain "ludum de Sancta Katerina—quem 'Miracula' vulgariter appellamus."[18] This annal is often cited as the earliest English record of a saint play. Early scholars assumed that the term *miracula* was a label derived from the content of a drama; hence, a drama about miracles performed by Saint Nicholas, for example, began at some point to be called *miracula*. This assumption formed the basis of John Manly's theory that *miracula* was a generic designation for saint plays.[19] His theory could not

---

18. Paris, *Gesta abbatum*, 1:72–73.
19. Manly, "Miracle Play in Mediaeval England." The best defense of the argument is Coffman's "Miracle Play in England—Nomenclature." The most succinct refutation of the Manly-Coffman thesis is Chambers's *English Literature*, 15–16.

be sustained, however, because other occurrences of the word indicated that no such restrictive definition would hold (for example, items 3 and 4 in appendix 1). Subsequently, Chambers made the case that "miraclis" was a "mere convenient shorthand for *repraesentatio miraculi.*" He cited the *Tretise of Miraclis Pleyinge* as the strongest evidence for his position that, especially in England, "miracle" came "to stand for 'religious play' in general."[20] At issue were twelve pieces of evidence.[21] In the discussion that ensued, most of these records were ruled out of court with the result that Manly's—and George Coffman's— thesis had to stand on the Dunstable reference alone. Chambers allowed that the Dunstable annal concerned a saint play, so his larger argument is reduced to a single piece of evidence, the *Tretise of Miraclis Pleyinge.*[22]

My analysis of the few records we have of *miracula* and "miracles" in English documents demonstrates that until at least the late fourteenth century the term had a quite specific meaning.[23] *Miracula* were not vernacular religious dramas produced by lay people, towns, or guilds; nor were they saints' plays nor the kind of liturgical enactments best known in the editions of Karl Young. Rather, they are activities we have called "pagan survivals" or ones that parody the liturgy or make jest of sacred events. Of the seventeen references to ludic *miracula* or miracles in English sources that I have located up to and including the *Tretise of Miraclis Pleyinge* (late fourteenth or early fifteenth century), a few are too terse or obscure to enable us to attribute specific meaning to their

---

20. Chambers, *Mediaeval Stage*, 2:104, and *English Literature*, 14–16. K. Young agreed but included the liturgical drama within the term as well (*Drama of the Medieval Church*, 2:414).

21. Appendix 1, items 1–5, 7–8, 10, 13, 17, and the two rejected entries. The other seven references to *miracula* never entered the discussion because they were unknown at the time.

22. Manly's argument was based on two pieces of evidence, one of which—William Fitz Stephen's statement—was cited by both sides but ultimately rejected (by Chambers) because *miracula* was not used in a generic sense. Coffman successfully repudiated two pieces of evidence (Chaucer's Wife of Bath's Tale and *Pierce the Ploughmans Crede*) but not a third (Lichfield). For reasons that are not clear, the Lichfield record never had a large role in the discussion. The Sloane MS story was cited by both sides, but no one seems to have read it far enough to realize that it did not refer to a religious drama. Similarly, Bromyard was occasionally cited but no one seems to have realized that his sometimes graphic descriptions were of folk customs and festivals, not dramas. Both sides agreed that Grosseteste and the *Manual* (followed by *Handlynge Synne*) confused the issue when they failed to distinguish properly between unacceptable folk custom or riotous clerical parodies, which they called *miracula*, and acceptable religious dramas, which they called *representationes*. All the remaining pieces of evidence were either successfully repudiated by one side or the other, or were allowed to be dropped from discussion (Lichfield), or could not be used because they quite patently argued against both sides (Grosseteste, the *Manual*, and *Handlynge Synne*).

23. I state my conclusions here; for the analysis on which they are based, see my "*Miracula* and *The Tretise.*"

use.[24] Nevertheless, among the first thirteen items in appendix 1—those prior to 1400—there is not a single document that unequivocally refers to religious dramas such as cycle plays, liturgical plays, or saint plays.[25] By "unequivocal" I mean a document that contains sufficient detail to assure us that *miracula* is being used to refer to a religious drama. On the other hand, items 5 (Sloane MS 2478) and 10 (Bromyard) describe *miracula* that are patently not religious dramas, and both, I might add, equate *miracula* with *spectacula,* a point to which I will return in the discussion of *Dives and Pauper.* The documents to 1400 establish early usage that is consistent in suggesting that *miracula* are neither saint plays nor religious dramas in general. If *miracula* were not vernacular or liturgical religious dramas, as we have assumed in the past, then our traditional reading of the *Tretise of Miraclis Pleyinge* as an attack on all religious drama may be inaccurate.

The evidence from Matthew Paris and Robert Grosseteste, the Lichfield Statutes, the record from Carlisle, the *Manual des Péchiez,* and *Handlyng Synne* all tell us that *miracula* were performed by *clerici,* that is, clerks in minor orders or choirboys, and that these activities were boisterous, sometimes parodic, sometimes involved the use of masks, and occurred during the Christmas season and in the spring from Easter into Whitsuntide.[26] Several of the documents indicate that *miracula* is a specialized term (items 1, 3, 5, and 10 in appendix 1) used by clerics; these records say that the activities are what "we" or "they" call *miracula,* and the pronouns refer to clerical persons. A number of other records that mention *miracula* indicate that they are "clerkes pleis" (for example, items 2, 3, 4, 6, 8, 10, 11, 16, and 26), and we have several records that do not use the term but indicate that clerkes pleis are clerical revels involving the use of masks, torturers, and ragged costumes (for example, Beverley [see below], *The Simonie,* and Wyclif).[27]

---

24. Appendix 1, items 9, 13, 15–16.

25. Item 1, widely thought to refer to a play about Saint Catherine, is, I believe, a clerical game; see my "*Miracula* and *The Tretise,*" 879, 885.

26. Bromyard also associates *miracula* with clerics in the section marked *Audire (Verbum Dei):* "& pauci sunt, quos occupatio impedit a nouis spectaculis, sicut in ludis, quos *miracula* vocant, quare ergo impediuntur ab audientia *miraculorum* clericorum fatuorum" [and they are few whose business keeps them from new spectacles, as in the plays which they call *miracula,* by which means therefore they are prevented by foolish clerics from the hearing of (true) miracles]. (fol. 77; cited by Owst, *Literature and Pulpit,* 480–81; I have altered his translation of the last sentence).

27. T. Wright, *The Simonie,* 323–45 (lines 283–88), 399–401. Nicholas Davis has reprinted the passage along with a variant from Peterhouse MS 104 in "Allusions . . . (3)," 83–84. Wyclif: "plus odiunt videre talia signa ypocritica quam ludum estivum tortorum, quia signa eorum sunt irrisiones dei et voces et mendacia; et talis ludus, cum sit illusioni dei propinquior, est magis abhomi-

Several records, including *Cum decorem,* complain of the use of masks. These masks, it is said, deform. They are not used to aid the representation or portrayal of something sacred. Indeed, a recent discussion of the Latin word for mask, *larva,* argues that it connoted dead spirits or devils and that a *larva* was intended to terrify or horrify.[28] In 1377 in Colchester William Baroun charged in a suit in the hundred court that John Kentyssh had borrowed and not returned a mask *(laruam),* a tunic with tails, and other apparatus for playing miracles (appendix 1, item 12). The use of *larva* in *miracula* ties the practice to *ludi theatrales,* in which *larvae* are also used.[29]

Siegfried Wenzel has discovered a description of a somergame that may tell us what the lay equivalent of some clerical *miracula* may have been.[30] In a sermon exemplum from the late fourteenth century, the preacher announces his theme that man's life in this crucified state is like the experience of men in a somergame in which

> Vnus erat Christus, alius Petrus, alius Andreas, quidam tortores, quidam demones. Christus pretensus crucifixus est, verberatus, derisus, reputatus fatuus; esuriebat, sciciebat, et nemo ei dabat nisi ictus et despectus. Et quis-

nabilis quam ludus aliquis laicorum" (*De novis ordinibus,* 1:334–35; cited by Davis, "Allusions . . . (3)," 84–85). Note the key words: "irrisiones," "mendacia," and "illusioni." The hypocritical sign that makes the link to this allusion to the *clerkes plei* is the garment that those in religious orders wear. The comparison turns on theatrical language: classical Latin *hypocrita* is a mime who gestures and pretends emotions. Wyclif's point would seem to be that the clerical garb of religious is as offensive (and as hypocritical) as the mis-robing of clerics in a summergame since they misrepresent the person beneath. Also see the series of letters from Grandisson, Bishop of Exeter, in Wasson, *Devon,* 6–14, and the directive to the sacrist of Thornton Abbey (1440) not to lend vestments to those engaging in "ludos noxios" and "alia ludibria vel spectacula" among the laity ("inter laicos" or "inter populares") (Thompson, *Visitations of Religious Houses,* 3:372, 381–82).

28. Twycross and Carpenter, "Masks in Medieval English Theatre," esp. 24–29.

29. The use of masks in the *representatio* at Beverley, ca. 1220, during which two boys fell from the tower and were miraculously saved, suggests the *ludus* was a *miracula* rather than a devotional presentation of the Resurrection. We are told that it took place in the summer ("aestivo") in the cemetery of St. John's, on the north side of the church, and that the participants, as usual, wore masks ("larvatorum" ["ut assolet"]; text in K. Young, *Drama of the Medieval Church,* 2:539–40). Since the "personae" are wearing masks, they are probably devils; thus, the *ludus* is more likely to be a raucous Harrowing than the Resurrection. Perhaps it is something like the one that John Bale says he has seen—and also himself had set forth—in which "Christ fought violently with the devils for the souls of the faithful" (Gairdner, *Letters and Papers,* 11:446–47). Patricia Badir has given the most recent analysis of the *ludus* as a Resurrection play; see "Representations of the Resurrection at Beverley Minster."

30. Wenzel, *"Somer Game."* Wenzel concludes that this is a reference to a Corpus Christi play even though the evidence from the period indicates summer games not to be activities of this sort (see the opening part of his essay).

cumque magis torquere et dispicere eum sciuit, melius ludere videbatur. Facto ludo habuerunt colloquium omnes lusores et deliberauerunt inter se iterum ludere, et dixit vnus: "Quis erit Christus?" Alii dixerunt: "S[i]t ille qui hodi fuit, quia bene fecit." Quibus ille dixit: "Ego eram Christus crucifixus, eram verberatus, eram derisus, eram reputatus stultus; esuriebam, sciciebam, et nemo michi dabat. Respexi inferius et vidi tortores et demones in multis solaciis, na[m] bene videbatur sibi qui eos facere poterat bibere vel comedere. Respexi ex parte dextra et vidi Petrum crucifixum, et respexi ex parte sinistra et vidi Andream crucifixum, sic quod omnia tediosa erant michi et apostolis, omnia solaciosa tortoribus et demonibus. Et ideo pro certo dico vobis quod si debeam iterum ludere, nec volo esse Christus nec apostolus set tortor vel demon.

[One person was Christ, another Peter, another Andrew, some were the tormentors, and some the devils Christ was stretched out, crucified, and beaten, mocked, and held a fool; he was hungry and thirsty and no one gave him anything but strokes and scorn. And whoever knew how to torment and scorn him best was reckoned to play the best. When the game was over, all the players talked among themselves and considered playing again; and one of them said, "Who shall be Christ?" The others said, "He who was today, since he played well." That one then said to them: "I was Christ and was crucified, beaten, mocked, held to be a fool; I was hungry and thirsty, and nobody gave me anything. I looked down below and saw tormentors and demons in great joy. For he who could make them drink and eat was well pleased. I looked to the right and saw Peter on the cross, and I looked to the left and saw Andrew on the cross, so that for me and my apostles everything was a pain, but for our tormentors and the demons everything was comfort. And therefore I tell you for sure that if I must play again, I do not want to be Christ nor an apostle but a tormentor or a demon."][31]

Although the description might suggest that this is a Passion play, clearly it is not, because Peter and Andrew, although they were crucified, were not crucified with Christ. The fact that the two disciples are tormented along with Christ suggests to me that they are the patron saints of the church and that the parishioners are engaged in some annual attempt to coerce protection for another year or something of the sort.[32]

---

31. Wenzel's translation, 279–80.

32. That such games were disliked by some is apparent from Sloth's comment that he would "leuere here an harlotrye or a Somer game of Souters, / Or lesynge[s] to lauȝen [of] and bilye my neȝebores, / Than al þat euere Marc made, Mathew, Iohan and Lucas" (Piers, B.5.406–8). Sloth suggests that somergames are not biblical accounts but lies and things that cause laughter.

The somergame is a game, and the contest seems to center on the rewarding of the tormentors and demons with food and drink for being the best tormentors. It appears to be an unscripted event that takes place during the summer, as many *ludi inhonesti* did. The bishops disliked these popular *ludi* because they were inappropriate (in taking place within sacred space) and sacrilegious (in deriding Christ and the saints). Indeed, the author of the *Tretise of Miraclis Pleyinge* utterly rejects the argument that such "pleyinge" is to the honor of the saints, as the supposed defenders of such games tried to claim; instead, he charges, the participants "bourd and jest" with holy things.[33] Such games are *irrisiones*.

The clerical objection in part can be traced to the unscripted quality of the game. Our sermon exemplum suggests that the audience invents enticements to encourage the tormentors and demons to imaginative—and humorous?—kinds of excess. Unlike scripted boy bishop ceremonies, which control license as long as the boys stick to the script, the somergame treats an event—Christ's Crucifixion—unhistorically and raucously, as feasts of fools and other events do once they stray beyond their scripts. That similar parodies existed within religious houses is attested by Bishop Adam of Orleton's condemnation in 1320 of nocturnal travesties of the Crucifixion at the abbey of Abergavenny in which one comes down from the dormitory at night with a rod and with his arms extended as if crucified and with a crown of straw on his head, thereby inflaming and playing to the court of his associates.[34]

My analysis of *miracula* has shown that there is not a single instance up to the late fourteenth century in which *miracula* is used unequivocally to designate a religious drama, that is, a reverential narration of scriptural events. Usage of *miracula* in the Latin documents is consistent from the twelfth century (Lichfield Statutes, 1188–98) to the mid-fourteenth (Bromyard, circa 1325–50; Carlisle, 1345). Vernacular usage (French or English) is consistent with that in Latin from the late thirteenth century (*Manual,* after 1272) to the late fourteenth (Colchester, 1377). Indeed, the principal distinction between *miracula* and acceptable liturgical enactments is that the latter were called *repre-*

---

33. Davidson, *Tretise,* 97–99. Bromyard also responds to this argument. The Beverley annalist alludes to this defense when he says that some come for delectation, some for the wonder of it, and some because it excites devotion.

34. "[A]liquociens ... nudi extensis brachiis cum baculis et ligatis ad modum crucifixi, stramine vel alio aliquo ad modum corone capitibus eorum superposito de ipsorum dormitorio nocturno tempore descendentes, et sic incedentes, ac ludentes coram sociis suis" (Adam of Orleton, *Registrum Ade de Orleton,* 151, 190–94).

sentationes or, in Anglo-Norman, *representementes,* in accordance with the Bottone gloss on Innocent's *ludi theatrales.*[35] *Miracula,* a term used in some records in place of *ludi theatrales,* seem less religious than social; in any event, they are not decorous and worshipful but boisterous and rude.

There is a relatively simple explanation for how these activities came to be called *miracula.* In the Old Testament *miraculum* was used to translate a number of Hebrew words of varying connotation but none of which corresponds to the medieval and modern sense of a supernatural event caused by divine intervention and involving a suspension of the laws of nature.[36] The New Testament uses an entirely different vocabulary to describe occurrences that we normally call miracles. That there was a recognized difference between *miraculum* in medieval and classical Latin (and hence the Vulgate Old Testament) is attested by Paul the Deacon's comment on Festus Paulus: "miracula, quae nunc digna admiratione dicimus, antiqui in rebus turpibus utebantur" [(the word) miracula, which we now say are worthy of awe, in antiquity was used of base things].[37] Of the eight instances of *miraculum* in the Vulgate, I believe that the key to the usage we have been examining lies in two passages from Jeremiah. In one Jerome translates the equivalent of "horror" as *miraculum:*

> Therefore, this is what Yahweh of Hosts, the God of Israel, has said: Ah, but I am determined to bring evil upon you, even to the extent of destroying Judah entirely! I will take those of the remnant of Judah who were determined to come to Egypt to settle, and they shall all perish. In the land of Egypt they shall fall by the sword or perish through starvation; both small and great, they shall die by the sword and of starvation, and become an execration, an object of horror, a curse word and a taunt [et erunt in iusiurandum, et in miraculum, et in maledictionem, et in opprobrium]. (Jer. 44:11–12).[38]

This usage points to the basic meaning of *miraculum:* something that causes wonder, something monstrous or horrible. Indeed, Varro glosses a line from Plautus' *Cistellaria,* "diabolares, schoenecolae, miraculae," as "*miraculae,* "wonder-foul," from *mira,* "wonderful things," that is, monstrosities; from

---

35. The use of *representatio* in the Beverley annal is an exception, if my analysis is correct. But I suspect that usage was not fixed, if ever, until after the publication of the Bottone gloss, which postdates the Beverley annal.

36. German Academic Societies, *Thesaurus linguae latinae, miracula* and *miraculum.* For a discussion of Greek and Latin usage, see Stein, *Furstenwaldensis,* 7–11, 17–19; Grant, *Miracle and Natural Law,* 6–7, 153–220; and Grant, "Vocabulary of Miracle."

37. Sextus Pompeius Festus, *De verborum,* 88 (also PL 95.1605–1704).

38. Bright, *Jeremiah,* 260–61.

which Accius says: Misshapen masks with twisted features, ugly wonders."[39] The gloss recalls the basic meaning—*miracula* cause wonder—but particularizes it by reference to distorted masks *(personae)* and emphasizes the ugliness, the monstrous quality of things that terrify.

The second passage from Jeremiah (23:31–32) concerns false prophets who lead the people astray with pretenses and lies: "Believe me, I am against the prophets—Yahweh's word—who, using their own speech, put forth what purports to be a prophecy. Believe me, I am against the prophets who preach fraudulent dreams—Yahweh's word—and who, by repeating them, mislead my people with their mendacious claptrap."[40] John Bright, whose translation is cited here, notes that "their mendacious claptrap" is literally "their lies and their *pahazut,*" which has the force of "loose talk" or "exaggerated, boastful tales."[41] The Vulgate renders the last part as: "In mendacio suo et in miraculis suis." In the citation of the scriptural passage before his comment, Jerome glosses "in miraculis" as "siue stuporibus atque terroribus"; hence, "in miraculis," to him, means "in astonishment and terror."[42] The scriptural context suggests that these pseudoprophets claim to have visions and then seduce and astound the people with their lies and tales. The significant point is that *miracula* are associated with lies *(mendaciis)*: in some texts of the Vulgate, the phrase "in miraculis suis" is rendered "in inanibus verbis." *Miracula,* therefore, are not wondrous events that are true, like the miracles in Christ's and his saints' lives, but irreverent stories filled with vain words or illusions and false prophecies.

Later medieval commentators preserved the Old Latin meanings of *miracula.*[43] The Jeremiah commentaries demonstrate that an older sense of *miracula* was retained in the late Middle Ages, a sense that differs radically from that of medieval Latin *miraculum* (a supernatural event brought about by the intervention of God or his agents). For late medieval readers, the context

---

39. "Miraculae a miris, id est monstris; quo Accius ait: Personas distortis oribus deformis miriones" (Varro, *On the Latin Language,* 1.322–5). See also Nonius Marcellus, *Compendiosa doctrina,* 521 line 27: "mira et miracula veteres pro monstris vel horrendis ponebant." *Mirio* is the Greek for "cretin," a sense carried over into archaic Latin (Keller, *Lateinische Volksetymologie,* 133).

40. Bright, *Jeremiah,* 150.

41. Ibid., 153.

42. Jerome, *In hieremiam prophetam libri sex,* 228–29.

43. Rabanus Maurus, *Expositio super Jeremiam,* PL 111: 979–90; Nicholas of Lyra, *Postillae perpetuae,* unfoliated (see under Jer. 23); Thomas Aquinas, *Opera omnia,* 14:651–54; Hugh of St. Cher, *Opera omnia,* 4:235v.

would establish the precise meaning the term was to bear. My contention is that when, between the late twelfth and the late fourteenth centuries, monks, canons, bishops, and others used *miracula* in monastic legislation, episcopal prohibitions, and the like, they were using the term with the Old Latin sense. Jerome did not understand the false prophets he was speaking of to be performing miracles or plays about miracles; rather, he understood them to be imitating true prophets except that they were more ostentatious in word and manner and their intent was to evoke terror or awe. Most commentators—Rabanus Maurus, Aquinas, Hugh of St. Cher, Nicholas of Lyra—note that these *miracula* imitate truth or claim to be true but that they mix in lies or fictions. *Miracula* are derisive; they jest with or mock the truth of God's word. The commentators understood the pseudoprophets to be the doctors and preachers of the church who mocked the words of the Lord when they encouraged their flock to evil, calling it good, or when they did not live according to the example they taught, or when they pursued foul lucre instead of spiritual good, or, according to Hugh, when they brought *verba risoria in sermonibus suis.*[44]

In most of the English documents I have cited above the word *miracula* has a pejorative connotation; nevertheless, there are a number of documents that suggest that some clerical institutions used it neutrally to refer to activities of the *clerici*: the Benedictine priory at Dunstable (appendix 1, item 1), the cathedral at Lichfield (item 2), the Benedictine abbey at Gloucester (item 6), the Cistercian abbey at Boxley, Kent (item 15), and the Benedictine cathedral priory of Durham (item 16). Two of these associate the *miracula* with boy bishop ceremonies (Gloucester, Boxley), two with a saint (Dunstable, Durham), and the last (Lichfield) with Easter and Whitsuntide. I think that the designation of boy bishop ceremonies as *miracula* may offer a clue about how Jeremiah and the commentaries on it are connected to this practice. Jeremiah complains that false prophets present themselves as God's by imitating true prophets. They, in effect, disguise themselves by aping the manners of God's prophets with the result that they burden God with their jeering and derision. The last part of my preceding sentence comes from the commentaries, but I wanted to include it here because the word *miracula* is received and used in two ways. I think that the monasteries and cathedrals cited above came to call the activities of the boy bishop on his feast day *miracula* because the *clericus* was not a bishop but a choirboy disguised as a bishop—by analogy, one of Jeremiah's false prophets. This usage is, in itself, not pejorative; rather, it recognizes that a certain kind of

---

44. Hugh of St. Cher, *Opera omnia*, 4:235.

activity that is allowed to take place involves an inappropriate person to act as if he were the proper person. But the Jeremiah commentaries also point to the disruptive, the derisive character of *miracula;* consequently, it would be easy for a reformer or critic to appropriate the Jeremiah passages for the purposes of condemning and even characterizing monastic and cathedral *miracula* as *irrisiones.* In fact, the Lichfield statutes seem to recognize that the allowed *miracula* might become the other kind of *miracula* when it orders the subchanter to make sure the *miracula* are meet and honorable.

Beneath these Jeremiah commentaries, we can read an antitheatrical aesthetic. I do not mean that the commentators understood themselves to be making an antitheatrical statement; rather, the things that they associate with *miracula* are what we would call theatrical. The perpetrators are hypocrites; like the actor, they pretend to be one thing when they are another. They appeal to the crowd through gimmicks that induce horror, through exaggerated gesture and bombastic speech. It would appear, then, that reformist clerics who applied the term *miracula* to the activities of *clerici* did so because they recognized in their disruptive behavior the kind of imitation (actually parody) of the sacred that Jeremiah and others denounced.[45]

Dives and Pauper and *The Tretise of Miraclis Pleyinge*

I believe that the term *miracula,* with the specialized meanings outlined above, came into currency in the early thirteenth century in order to clarify the distinction between *representationes* and certain *spectacula* or *ludi theatrales* and that it went out of currency in the early sixteenth century about the time that the monasteries were suppressed and the boy bishops put down.[46] Although there are a several references to *miracula* in fifteenth-century English sources, only two, the *Tretise of Miraclis Pleyinge* and the Franciscan *Dives and Pauper,* contain enough detail to command our attention.[47] The *Dives* has been understood to defend the playing of miraclis, that is, vernacular religious dramas; the *Tretise* is thought to be an attack on the drama. Since the two are the last medieval works to use the term *miracle,* the question arises whether they pro-

---

45. We might note that both the *Manual* and *Handlyng Synne* equate "miracles" with "bourds."

46. The Lichfield Statutes are one possible exception since they are dated 1188–98; however, the earliest copies are from the thirteenth century, and we cannot tell when the entries about *miracula* were first included.

47. Barnum, *Dives and Pauper.* The date was established by Richardson, "Dives et Pauper," 321–23. The Franciscan authorship of *Dives* has been confirmed by a set of sermons by the same author in MS Longleat 4; see Hudson and Spencer, "Old Author, New Work."

vide evidence for a change in the meaning of the word. But if it can be shown that both continue medieval usage, then we must alter our understanding of what the texts say. The simplest procedure, it seems to me, is to analyze the *Dives* and later usage in order to determine if there has been a change in the meaning of "miracle" and then turn to the more problematical *Tretise*.[48]

The *Dives* defends the performance of devotional "steraclis, pleyys and dauncis," which I believe is equivalent to the Dominican John Bromyard's condemned triad, "spectacula, ludos, & choreas."[49] Pauper says: "Steraclis, pleyys & dauncis þat arn don principaly for deuocioun & honest merthe [to teche men to loue God þe more] & for no rybaudye ne medelyd with no rybaudye [ne lesyngis] arn leful, so þat þe peple be nout lettyd þerby fro Godys seruyce ne fro Godis word herynge and þat þer be non errour medelyd in swyche steraclis & pleyys aȝens þe feyth of holy chirche."[50] The discussion centers on appropriate activities for the Sabbath, and this in turn raises the larger issue of amusements and entertainments, especially those appropriate to religious holidays. Pauper defends activities that are devotional; indeed, he goes on to quote Bottone's canonical gloss that it is "leful" to "representyn in pleyynge" Herod, the Three Kings, and so forth.

Manuscript Y of *Dives* substitutes "miraclis" for all three instances of "steraclis," and MS B, of the same manuscript group, makes the substitution for the last two.[51] The assumption has been that "miraclis" are "pleyys" and that the discussion which follows defends vernacular religious dramas. But the gloss that is cited is relevant only to *representationes;* it says nothing, for example, about "dauncis," the third word in the series. Moreover, both *Dives* and

---

48. The *Tretise* has been dated to the late fourteenth century but survives in a unique early fifteenth-century manuscript (Nicholas Davis, "Another View of the *Tretise of Miraclis Playinge,*" 51). Thus, its composition may well have preceded that of *Dives and Pauper* (between 1405 and 1410). In any event, only two manuscripts of the *Dives* contain "miraclis" rather than "steraclis," and these were probably copied after the *Tretise* was composed.

49. Barnum, *Dives et Pauper,* 1:293–98. Bromyard is discussing the way the devil nullifies the contrition of Lent: "Thus, to the contrite sinner, the devil shows *[spectacula, ludos, & choreas],* and so forth, which, by the devil's procuring, begin around the time of Easter, so that the contrition which they had in Lent is revoked" (Ita diabolus ostendit peccatori contrito spectacula ludos, & choreas, & huiusmodi, quae circa tempus paschae diabolo procuranti, vbique incipiunt, vt contritione, quam in quadragesima habuerunt revocat" [*Summa predicantium,* fol. 117v]).

50. Barnum, *Dives et Pauper,* 1:293.

51. Barnum, in ibid., xiii–xiv, has argued that group A MSS constitute an earlier form of the work than group B (comprised of the three manuscripts B, Y, and L). The general agreement between manuscripts of both groups (all A MSS and MS L) suggests that "steraclis" is the original reading. The variant manuscript for which we have the firmest date, MS Y, was copied in 1456, so the substitution of "miraclis" may have occurred toward mid-century.

Bromyard use two words, "steraclis/pleyys" and "spectacula/ludi," which suggests there might be a distinction between them. We ought not conclude, therefore, just because Pauper cites the canon about appropriate pleyys, that he understands it to defend steraclis or miraclis any more than we would conclude that it defended dauncis. I believe that Pauper defends steraclis/miraclis *and* pleyys *and* dauncis. To put it another way, I think that the original writer understood steraclis to be different from pleyys and that the later scribes preserved that distinction when they substituted miraclis for steraclis. More to the point, he is not concerned with these steraclis, pleyys, and dauncis as activities per se but with whether the intent of the participants is devotional.

Usage of "steraclis," a rare word, supports a distinction between "miraclis" and "pleyys." The first recorded appearance of "steraclis" is in the *Dives*. The *OED* cites only two other instances in the fifteenth century and three from the sixteenth. The word is of obscure origin; it is conjectured that it derives from the verb *stare,* after "spectacle," and thus is a Middle English equivalent of Latin *spectacula,* "worldly sights." The fifteenth-century usages of "steraclis" suggest that it means a "spectacle" of some sort. The Middle English translation of a pseudo-Mapes poem lists sitting on stages at steraclis among the disreputable activities of fickle women.[52] *Jacob's Well* speaks of going to wrestlings, dances, and steracles, a combination that may recall the language of the legislation against *luctas, choree, spectacula,* and *miracula.*[53] Paul Rutledge has recently found a more detailed record, circa 1410–20, in which "diuerse pleyes" are defined as "Schetyng*is* wrestelyng*is* puttyng*is* of þe ston," activities that are later grouped under "Steraclis."[54]

---

52. They rejoice to see and to be seen, to go on pilgrimage, to walk on the plain at great gatherings, and "at staracles to sitte on high stages, / If they be faire to shewe ther visages." The poem, "The Payne and Sorowe of Evyll Maryage," is a fifteenth-century English version of *De conjuge non ducenda,* but the Latin has no exact counterpart to these lines. See Mapes, *Latin Poems Commonly Attributed to Walter Mapes,* 297.

53. The discussion centers on the sin of sloth, which, the commentator says, leads to every kind of vice. After listing idle activities and specifying certain games, he adds that, out of time and measure, people "gon to wakys & to wrestlyng*es,* to dau*n*syng*es* & to steraclys, to tauernys, to reuell, to ryott, to shetinges, to feyrys, to markettys on þe holy-dayes," and so on (Brandeis, *Jacob's Well,* pt. 1, 105). See also a sermon, ca. 1400, against holy day abuses such as "dauncys," "werdly songys," "interlodyes," "castynges of the stonne," "steraclys," and "other ydell iapys and pleyis" (Nicholas Davis, "Allusions . . . (4): Interludes," 65).

54. Rutledge, "Steracles in Norfolk," 15–16. William Boter deposed as follows: he "saugh diuerse times & ofte*n* pleyes pleyed vpon þe fornseyd lyng*is* [the place where the activities occurred] made be þo me*n* of lucham þat is to seyne steraclis Schetyng*is* wrestelyng*is* ren*n*ing for þo spere ren*n*yng at þo fotbal for kak*is.*"

Of the three sixteenth-century usages, only two are defined well enough to permit analysis. In Bale's *Kyng Johan,* Dissimulation, a priest, says that Usurped Power (= the Pope) will put all men under his obedience, create religious orders, and build them places to corrupt cities and towns: "With ymages and rellyckes he shall wurke sterracles" (line 996).[55] It is clear that the pope is not going to work miracles but create some kind of illusion in order to dupe people. We should recall here the passage from Jeremiah, especially as it was interpreted by Jerome to refer to false priests who dupe the populace with the "lies and miracles." Similarly, in his *Acts of Christ,* Becon says, "But to pray at places where the devil worketh steracles, I would say, miracles, thus passeth al."[56] This passage suggests that Becon understood "miracles" to be a synonym of "steracles" and that steracles are illusions of some sort. But why does Becon equate "steracles" with "miracles"? It cannot be that he believes the devil actually capable of miracles; rather, it suggests that the old meaning of *miracula* remained current and that he associated it with "steraclis." We might also note that Becon links these activities with devils, as do the record at Colchester and the frequent injunctions against the wearing of *larvae* in clerical *ludi theatrales.* The consensus of these few usages is that steraclis are shows or sights, and there is the suggestion that they are linked with banned amusements like ancient *spectacula* or have a pejorative connotation that derives from the creation of illusions, especially of a demonic or obviously wicked sort. The Sloane MS story of the friars in Corinth who come upon a pythoness making satirical remarks helps confirm the point. When the friars wondered why there should be such a laughing throng of people in the square, they determined that the populace was frequenting *spectacula* that "we," the friars, were accustomed to call *miracula.* Similarly, John Bromyard complains of *nova spectacula* called *miracula* that keep people from hearing the word of God. In both

---

55. Bale, *Complete Plays,* 1:54. Note also the interesting rhyme in the N-Town *Temptation:* When Christ ascends the pinnacle of the temple, the devil says: "Whan þu art sett upon þe pynnacle, / Þu xalt þer pleyn a qweynt steracle, / Or ellys shewe a grett meracle; / Thysself from hurte þu saue" (23.114–17).

56. Becon, *Worckes of Thomas Becon,* 3:416b (STC 1710). The third sixteenth-century example suggests that steraclis included boisterous activity such as skipping, jumping, and making wild gestures. In John Palsgrave's translation of Fullonius's *Comedy of Acolastus,* Pamphagus, a parasite who has fleeced a guest at dice, enters in an ecstasy over his good fortune. His friend, Pantolabus, overhears him and says: "What Pamphagus, I praye the for goddes sake, why whippest thou it about, or playest thou thy steracles (on this fascion)?" The line is equivalent to the Latin: "Quid Pamphage, Quid gestis obsecro?" See [Gnaphaeus], *Comedy of Acolastus,* 139, l. 20, and 187.

cases *spectacula* is made equivalent to *miracula,* and *spectacula* is the word used to describe the forbidden games of the ancient world or things reminiscent of them. If "steraclis" is Middle English for Latin *spectacula,* then "steraclis" is equivalent to "miraclis," as is confirmed by Becon's gloss of "steraclis" as "miraclis."

The *Dives* copyist very probably understood the two words to be synonyms. I do not think, however, that he was providing support for illicit entertainments; nor do I believe that he understood "miraclis" to refer to vernacular religious dramas. *Dives and Pauper* is a Franciscan work, and this passage is typical of mendicant thinking. The context of the discussion is what is permitted on Sundays and feast days. Pauper argues that steraclis, plays and dances that are done primarily for devotion and honest mirth and to teach men to love God, are acceptable, but there must not be any "rybaudye" in them; moreover, they cannot promote error against the faith, the estate of the church, or good living. All others are forbidden by the canons.[57] He then quotes the gloss that permits liturgical drama. Just before he cites the canons, he reduces what is being defended to "steraclis and pleyys," so the canons would seem to be relevant only to those two, not "dauncis."

When Dives questions whether men may make mirth on holy days, Pauper insists they can because holy days were ordained for rest and relief of body and soul—as long as the recreation is appropriate. English synodalia had forbidden "cantilene seculares," "choree, [et] lucte" in cemeteries and other sacred precincts.[58] Pauper too condemns dauncis and other activities that are undertaken wickedly or that lead to lechery, gluttony, and other sins. His point is that there are legitimate forms of entertainments that are sanctified by Old Testament example (the feast of the tabernacles and David dancing before the ark); therefore, he does not condemn activities merely because they belong to a class of things (games, dances, and so forth). And his argument is not unusual. Owst cites several sermons that make similar distinctions between licit and sinful songs, dances, and other games.[59] In any event, the Franciscan author of

---

57. Barnum, *Dives et Pauper,* 1:293. He cites *De consecratione*s, dist. 3, cap. 2, "Irreligiosa" (*Corpus iuris canonici,* 1:1353) and "Extra[vagantes]," bk. 3, tit. 1 [Quum] decorum (*Corpus iuris canonici,* 2:1255–57).

58. Statutes of Worcester II, cap. 22 (Powicke and Cheney, *Councils and Synods,* 174); similarly, the Statutes of Salisbury I prohibited "choree vel turpes et inhonesti ludi" (ibid., 93). *Chorea* are dances, but they probably involved singing as well. The *Thesaurus lingua latinae* cites Isidore: "chorae ludicrum cantilenae vel saltationes classium sunt."

59. Owst, *Literature and Pulpit,* 483–85.

Dives could not condemn dancing per se when the founder of his order danced before the pope who gave him his rule.[60]

"Sterclis & pleyys" prompts him to think of the canons, and since he cites the Bottone gloss on *Cum decorem*, he does not understand "steraclis" necessarily to be pejorative; he does not understand it to refer simply to *ludi theatrales*, as some writers did. Exactly what it might have meant to him remains obscure, but since he cited the canons, it must include clerical *ludi* of some sort, but specifically the Christmas and Easter rituals. Later he links "pleyys and dauncis" and defines them as minstrelsy, singing and dancing. We may conclude, then, that "pleyys" is a term that he used broadly to refer to many kinds of activity. In any event, he seems to understand that "steraclis" and "pleyys" are not entirely synonymous any more than are "pleyys" and "dauncis."

When the *Dives* copyist substituted "miraclis" for "steraclis," he did not alter the context: he did not defend all miraclis any more than he defended all dauncis or pleyys other than those allowed by the canon. The miraclis he allows, presumably, are those that provided entertainment or amusement without attracting persons to lechery and gluttony. The difference might be that between the women of Boston who belonged to the guild of Saint John the Baptist and who danced together while holding candles, and the cursed dancers of Colbek or the women of Bury who went in procession with a white bull in order to ensure their fertility.[61] Since some establishments of monks and canons permitted *miracula*, his position, as we will see, may be similar to that rebutted by the author of the *Tretise*.

It is obvious that the author of *Dives* is more tolerant of "steraclis, pleyys and dauncis" than is the writer of the *Tretise*. Nevertheless, it does not necessarily follow that the writer of the *Tretise* is expressing opposition to all vernacular religious drama. Scholars have been unanimous in the opinion that the *Tretise* is opposed to saint and scriptural plays (as well as other lay games and recreation). My analysis of medieval and early modern usage of "miracle" sug-

---

60. Thomas of Celano, *First Life of St. Francis*, chap. 27, para. 73.

61. For the guild of Saint John, see the guild return of 1389 (PRO C.47/39/76), cited by Westlake, *Parish Gilds of Mediaeval England*, 155. For the dancers of Colbek, see Mannyng, *Handlyng Synne*, lines 9011–263. The procession of the white bull of Bury continued as late as 1533. Saint Edward was invoked for help in conception and childbirth. The white bull, garlanded with flowers, was led by Benedictine monks from the abbey meadows through the streets. As monks sang and pilgrims and others joined the procession, wives desiring offspring walked alongside the bull stroking its sides (BL Harl. 308, fol. 9v; PRO E/327/252; cited by G. Gibson, *Theater of Devotion*, 45; printed in Dugdale, *Monasticon*, 3:133).

gests that the term does not refer to vernacular religious drama either before or after the date of composition of the *Tretise* (circa 1380–1414). Further, one would be hard pressed to substantiate antagonism to all religious drama by pointing to sentences or words in the text. There is not a single reference to the "representation" of any Old Testament subject. None of the *representationes* allowed in the canons—for example, Herod, the Three Kings, Rachel, the Resurrection or the *Peregrinus*—are mentioned by name. The writer never uses the Middle English equivalent of *representatio*. under the circumstances, it seems rash to conclude that the *Tretise* is a blanket condemnation of religious drama.

As we turn to the *Tretise,* therefore, our first question is whether the tract denounces dramatic representations of sacred subjects or some misrepresentation of them.[62] At one point in his rebuttal the writer makes his substantive objection that "plays" are but signs, not things: "Right therfore as men by feinyd tokenes bygilen and in dede dispisen ther neighboris, so by siche feinyd miraclis men bygilen hemsilf and dispisen God, as the tormentours that bobbiden Crist" (lines 226–29 [263–71]).[63] His most insistent point is that these miraclis are outward shows, "verrey leesinges," and "feinyd tokenes." The usual interpretation has been that they are "signs" by virtue of the fact that they are dramatic enactments, that "miraclis pleyinge" scorns and derides the miracles of Christ and the saints *by* representing them.

The distinction between sign and actuality is one key to our understanding of the tract. The *Tretise,* I believe, objects not to devotional representation but to mockeries, a kind of inappropriate gaming that leads to lechery, gluttony, and pride. The writer's usage, at least in this respect, is consistent with that of the thirteenth and fourteenth centuries. The writer, therefore, may have regarded any activity or *ludus* performed on the saint's day or at Easter as scorning the miracles of Christ and the saints;[64] it is not that people reenact those miracles or the Passion but that they substitute amusements that are undevo-

---

62. My discussion centers on what the author attacks, his logic of demonstration, and his use of canon law and sermon manuals. I choose not to address the issue of Wycliffite provenance here because I think it only complicates the discussion and, more important, because I do not think the case that it is a Wycliffite product is credible. Because the issue is complicated and still alive, I defer discussion of it, but I note that Anne Hudson, who included the *Tretise* in her *Selections from English Wycliffite Writings,* has more recently said that the belief that the *Tretise* "is a product of Wycliffism seems to me doubtful" (*Premature Reformation,* 387).

63. Throughout my discussion the first set of lines numbers is to Davidson's second edition (1993) and those in brackets to the first edition (1981).

64. Much of the synodal legislation implies or makes the same point about *ludi inhonesti,* scotales, and the like.

tional or are conducive to immorality. Indeed, his scriptural citations are routinely glossed as admonitions to avoid certain kinds of recreations and the merrymakers who participate in them. In the broadest sense, then, the writer's
objections are to occasions when *miracula* may have taken place. His attack
encompasses any activity that is inappropriate either to the day—Sunday or
feast day—or in itself—game, dancing, or singing.

Nevertheless, he seems to have a specific target in mind as well, in which
case he may be referring either to *miracula*, as they have been defined above, or
to the inappropriate representation of *some actions* in vernacular drama. If the
writer knew the pejorative connotations of *miracula*, if he knew that the principal features of *miracula* were their jeering parody and ridicule of things sacred, then we ought to consider whether he broadened the traditional objections to *miracula* to the irreverent treatment of the Passion of Christ and his
saints and to making sport of demons in the vernacular drama (specifically, to
the bourding with the Crucifixion, the harrowing of hell, the coming of Antichrist, or the Day of Doom). The distinction that I am making here is between
miracula, that is, clerkes pleis, which use masked performers who parody or
make fun of sacred events, and civic or guild vernacular religious dramas
whose intent was devotional (but which, of course, may have included episodes
reminiscent of *miracula*). If the writer intended to include *civic* or lay religious
drama in his attack, then he used the term "miraclis" idiosyncratically. This is
the position, though different in approach, that Nicholas Davis and Glending
Olson must take in order to found their arguments that the *Tretise* is averse to
vernacular religious drama (see below). My position is that the usage is not
idiosyncratic but philologically, historically, and culturally fixed and deter-
minable.

Although it is difficult to establish conclusively that the writer's usage is not
idiosyncratic, there is cogent evidence that the writer was speaking of clerkes
pleis or *miracula*. Let us turn to what he says about content in order to consider
whether it designates *miracula*, the civic religious drama, or both.

The first three points that supporters of miraclis pleyinge advance suggest
that there is some kind of devotional purpose to and religious content in these
activities. "Miraclis pleyers" claim to play these miraclis in worship of Christ.
They say that often people are converted to good living when they see that the
devils by their array make themselves and others servants to hell (lines 50–61
[177–90]). Often men and women "seinge the passioun of Crist and of his
seintis" are moved to compassion and tears (lines 162–65 [191–95]). Later, at
lines 437–41 [517–21], the writer refers to men who "pleyen or favouren the

pley of the deth" of Christ as "unkinde." Elsewhere, the writer condemns men as heretics who say, "Pley we a pley of Anticrist and of the Day of Dome that sum man may be convertid therby" (295–96 [349–51]). The argument that miraclis pleyinge is like a living image and thus defensible on the same grounds has suggested to modern readers that we are concerned with a recognizable *scriptural* dramatization (lines 179–85 [211–19]).

There are, however, several historical impediments to the argument that the *Tretise* attacks the religious drama of the civic cycles. If the tract is to be dated to the late fourteenth century, then we have only two cycles, York and Coventry, known to be in existence around the time of its composition, and we assume from slightly later evidence that these included representations of the Passion and of Doomsday.[65] Chester, N-Town, and Towneley all come after the date of composition, which gives particular point to Reginald Pecock's statement in his *Repressor* (circa 1449) that "a quyk man . . . sett in a pley to be hangid nakid on a cros and to be in semyng woundid and scourgid . . . *bifallith ful seelde and in fewe placis and cuntrees.*"[66] Even if the *Tretise* were to be dated to the early fifteenth century, there is little evidence that the kind of vernacular drama the preacher may be talking about was very widespread. Not only is there little evidence for passion plays at the time the tract was written, there is little for them in the medieval and early modern periods put together.[67] Moreover, if Paul Johnston's placement of the dialect of the *Tretise* in eastern Northamptonshire and northern Huntingdonshire is correct, then the tract was written in an area with little evidence—so far—of dramatic activity of any kind. Even if one moves out into the surrounding towns and shires, the evidence for dramatic traditions in the period or later is sparse. Yet the tract sounds as if it were concerned with a well-known and common activity. The suggestion that the tract may refer to the Coventry plays is not convincing to me; Coventry is rather far (fifty to fifty-five miles) from the dialect area of the writer(s).[68] Why would someone isolated in the dialect region Johnston describes be so concerned with a play so far away? We might do better to inquire into practices at cathedrals (Ely, Lincoln), monasteries (Peterborough, Ramsey), and parishes that are closer at hand. Although Lincoln Cathedral is rather far away, I include it because the proposed dialect area for the *Tretise* falls

---

65. We have a pageant list ca. 1390 from Beverley, but I am skeptical that it is for a cycle of plays; see chapter 4 below.

66. See Pecock, *Repressor of over Much Blaming of the Clergy,* 1:221, emphasis added.

67. See the discussion in the chapters that follow.

68. Davidson, *Tretise* (1993), 2–3, and 78 (for Paul Johnston's commentary on the dialect).

within the Lincoln diocese. The dating of the manuscript, from about the 1380s to the early fifteenth century, certainly does not rule out the possibility that the object of the tract is vernacular cycle drama, but such a dating ought at least to instill caution in how we interpret the *Tretise*. The writer refers to "religious" (monks), so he may have had in mind the *ludi theatrales* of nearby monastic cathedrals or monasteries; however, since the tract is in English, his more immediate audience may have been the parish clergy.

Moreover, there is a piece of negative evidence in the reference to the "play of Antichrist." There is only one extant Antichrist play in civic religious drama, that at Chester, and it is probable that this play is to be dated to the end of the fifteenth or to the sixteenth century.[69] There is no Antichrist play in the York cycle, nor is there any evidence that there ever was one. The same is true for Coventry. Again, the *Tretise* makes it sound as if the "pley of Antichrist" is commonplace. On the other hand, a *ludus* in which Antichrist and devils take part fits our definition of *miracula* quite well. If "miraclis" is equivalent to "steraclis" and both suggest "illusions" or imitations of supernatural miracles, and if *miracula* often included masked devils who sought to astonish and terrify, then we have the ingredients of an Antichrist *ludus*. In the absence of vernacular dramas on the subject, we may reason that plays of Antichrist fell under the terms "clerkes pleis," *ludi theatrales*, or *miracula*, for an Antichrist *ludus* is inherently parodic.

In addition, there has been little or no attention paid to the inclusion of the references to the clergy and how these might affect our understanding of the *Tretise* as a whole. All of the canons cited in the tract are directed against clerical attendance at *spectacula* and especially the participation of clergy in inappropriate jesting and parodic behavior. Why would the author be so concerned about *clerical* participation if he were talking about *civic* vernacular drama? There is no evidence that the clergy took part in the extant religious cycles.[70] We know that there was frequent legislation against *choree vel turpes et inhonesti ludi* and scotales held in churches *per laicos* or outside the chruch *per sacerdotes vel clericos*.[71] We also know that numerous bishops were opposed to *miracula* because the participants masked themselves. In any event, it seems indisputable that one group the writer had in mind was made up of clerics who

---

69. Clopper, "History and Development of the Chester Cycle." Lumiansky and Mills date the play to 1467–68; however, even this date is much later than that of the *Tretise* (*Chester Mystery Cycle: Essays and Documents*, 76).

70. See my essay "Lay and Clerical Impact," 112–18.

71. For example, Statutes of Salisbury I (Powicke and Cheney, *Councils and Synods*, 93).

participated in prohibited *miracula* and other activities where *ludi inhonesti* occurred. I also think that the writer is particularly concerned that the clergy's *miracula* occasion a reversion to pagan practices among the laity.

The *Tretise* has two fairly distinct parts.[72] In the first the speaker attacks miraclis pleyinge because of its irreverence. He cites the canons against clerical participation in such activities and reasons that lay people engage in similar "pleys" because they see the clergy involved in "bourding and jesting." About halfway through the tract, the speaker addresses a "half frynde" who, he says, remains unconvinced by the argument thus far and who thus is a supporter of miraclis pleyinge: "An half frynde tarriere to soule helthe, redy to excusen the yvil and hard of bileve, with Thomas of Inde, seith that he wil not leevyn the forseid sentense of miraclis pleyinge but and men shewen it him by holy writt opynly and by oure bileve" (lines 386–90 [456–60]). The statement suggests that the "half frynde" has listened to the argument but finds it unconvincing because he still believes that miraclis pleyinge can have a good effect. He will be convinced otherwise only if it can be shown that the highest authority, scripture, repudiates miraclis pleyinge. The scriptural demonstration cites the commandment not to take the Lord's name in vain; the incident in which Sarah, when she saw Ishmael playing *(ludentem)* with Isaac, had Ishmael ejected from the house; the incident at the pool of Gibeon when the soldiers of Abner and of Joab rose up to play *(ludere)* before the court and were killed; and the incident in the desert when the Israelites ate and drank and rose up to play *(ludere)* before the golden calf. His final example concerns Elisha, who was jeered at *(illudebant)* by some small boys because of his bald head, a symbol of Christ's Passion. When the prophet cursed them, two bears came out of the woods and killed forty-two of the boys. The preacher's conclusion is that rather than "pleyinge of miraclis," men should play before the ark of the Lord as David did.[73]

Jonas Barish finds this tract, the only extensive antitheatrical text between those of the early Christian period and those of the Puritan era, a singularly unconvincing and utterly wrongheaded piece of polemic.[74] I agree, if we put the

---

72. I believe the tract to be the work of a single author even though there are two parts to it; however, my analysis would be the same even if the text were shown to be written by two authors.

73. Pauper implies this is Dives's position when he uses the example of David (Barnum, *Dives,* 1:297, and see the context).

74. Despite the purported significance of the *Tretise,* the tract has been more alluded to than discussed (Woolf, Kolve, but also Kendall). Except for a sensitive textual—rather than historical—interpretation by David Mills, the only older extended commentaries on the tract are Jonas Barish's

Tretise in such a context; however, Nicholas Davis and Glending Olson have objected to Barish on this point and I agree with parts of their analyses as well.[75] In order to clarify my position, I think it necessary to proceed from Barish to Davis and Olson. All three believe the *Tretise* to be an attack on religious dramas even though Davis and Olson allow that other forms of *ludi* are drawn into the circle of the author's wrath. My argument is that the *Tretise* attacks *miracula* and consequent sinful revelries.

Barish finds the scriptural commentaries entirely off the mark when they are not obvious misinterpretations at the most literal level. He says the reading of the Ishmael and Isaac story is distorted and without precedent in the commentaries because it is quite clear that "playing" means "fighting," not "enacting." The allusion to the young men who rose up and "played" before Abner and Joab seems to him even further from the point because "the playing refers unmistakably to fighting, as the context makes clear." The most bizarre citation, he thinks, is the story of the children who mocked the prophet Elisha and were slain by the bears, because *illudebant,* the verb used in 2 Kings 2:233, "has to do with direct jeering and flouting, and not at all with theatrical play. . . . So the supposed analogy, instead of clarifying matters merely introduces another equivocation on the term *play,* adding one more to the tissue of tautologies of which the argument is largely composed" (74). Barish claims that at the end "the preacher introduces a use of *ludere* that completely undermines his own case" (74). Unexpectedly, the preacher says that there may be godly playing: "yif we wilen algate pleyen," then "pleyne we as Davith pleyide bifore the harke of God, and as he spac byfor Michol his wif, dispising his pleyinge" (lines 724–26). Michal's reproof, Barish points out, follows the line of argument that the preacher himself has pursued in the tract: that it is *wrong* to "play" before the ark of the lord. Yet suddenly the preacher invokes the best example imag-

---

in his survey of antitheatrical polemic and Nicholas Davis's and Ruth Nissé's readings of it as a Lollard text. D. Mills, *"Tretise of Miraclis Pleyinge,"* 83–91; Barish, *Antitheatrical Prejudice,* 66–79 (further references appear in the text); Kendall, *Drama of Dissent,* 50–55; Nicholas Davis, "'Tretise of Myraclis Pleyinge'"; and Nissé, "Reversing Discipline." Clifford Davidson has talked about some of the important issues in the introduction and notes to his edition, but he is primarily interested in the relations between art and drama, a subject that forms a small part of the work, as Nicholas Davis notes in his review ("Another View," 51–52). Other discussion will be cited below.

75. Nicholas Davis, "Another View," 48–55, and "'Tretise of Myraclis Pleying'"; and Olson, "Plays as Play." Ritchie Kendall, who calls the *Tretise* a minor broadside (*Drama of Dissent,* 50), thinks Barish is preoccupied with overt assaults on the stage and unwilling to explore how both fear of and attraction toward self-transforming theatricality constitutes a larger aesthetic. Since Kendall does not talk about the *Tretise* in any detail, I omit discussion of his chapter here.

inable for why it should be acceptable to engage in "religious play." Barish notes that the *Dives* cites this very reference to David to defend "not only dancing but also miracle plays" (75).

Finally, he wonders why the favorable instances of playing in the Scripture—celebrating, giving thanks, participating in sacred festivities—could not have been or were not advanced as texts and precedents to be emulated: "Clearly David's dancing forms a far more telling precedent in favor of play than all the unfavorable instances [in the *Tretise*] together tell against it, and the homilist's abrupt eleventh-hour endorsement of it merely underscores the fact that the whole case against *ludere* is a house of cards" (75). When Barish compares the *Tretise* with Tertullian's *De spectaculis* and passages from Augustine's *City of God,* he points out that the tract writer has failed to retailor his argument to fit the times. The Fathers had charged the Roman *spectacula* with being idolatrous, and the preacher repeats the charge even though he is dealing with a Christian drama "inspired by the Bible," that is "heavily didactic, moreover, in its emphasis on Christian virtues like obedience, penitence, and piety." The charge of idolatry is not germane, yet the preacher "surprises us by reviving the old accusation in a new form. He devises a fantastic analogy between the playing of miracles and the worship of the golden calf to show that miracle plays, by encouraging gluttony, lechery, and covetise, constitute a dreadful 'maumetrie'" (78). In the final paragraphs of his analysis Barish denonounces the crudity and inadequacy of the preacher's categories because no audience, especially a Christian one, would believe that the theatrical events they saw were real. The argument that enactment of Christ's Passion constitutes an actual torturing of Christ anew would not convince the smallest and dullest child (77).

If the tract is attacking vernacular or liturgical religious drama per se, then, as Barish says, the logic and presentation of the argument are absurd. However, Nicholas Davis and Glending Olson, who agree that the tract opposes religious drama, object that Barish has chosen the wrong contexts for his analysis. In a review of Clifford Davidson's first edition of the *Tretise* Nicholas Davis makes the argument that to read the tract as a continuation of the early Christian tradition distorts it because the author shows little interest in the comments of the early fathers and other critics. Similarly, to read it through the lens of the later Puritans is to take it out of its own historical milieu and to distort it in other ways.[76] Davis insists, and I believe him right, that we must try to reconstruct the historical context of the tract.

---

76. Rosemary Woolf and Clifford Davidson interpret the *Tretise* as the first in a long line of

Glending Olson takes an approach that is much like mine even though we use different resources and ultimately come to a difference of opinion about the object of the tract. Olson thinks we can make sense of the *Tretise* if we place it not in the context of early Christian polemics but in that of the discussion of the ethical content of play in its broadest sense: that is, which kinds of recreative activities are acceptable and which are not? He insists that there was a broad range of notions of "play" and *ludus* and that circumstances determined the ethical valence of a given instance of play. He also emphasizes the indeterminant meanings of the vocabulary of *ludus,* which allows him to suggest that though the commentators may not have the genre "drama" in mind when they analyze recreation, religious dramas may lurk under their terminology because the words referring to play are indeterminate.[77]

Olson believes that the proper context for the *Tretise* is ultimately Aristotle's discussion of the necessity and desirability of certain kinds of healthful recreation in the *Nicomachaean Ethics* and the medieval commentaries on this text.[78] The most widely circulated statement on *ludus,* however, is Aquinas's in the *Summa Theologica,* which he adapted from his commentary on the *Ethics.*[79] The larger context—as in canon law and synodal legislation discussed above—is modesty in bodily actions, one part of the cardinal virtue of temperance. Aquinas's question on play is organized around the Aristotelian categories of mean, excess, and defect. Olson concludes that the "terminology varies but usually maintains at the most general level a distinction between wicked or diabolical play (which is always bad), human or recreational play (which is morally neutral and must be judged circumstantially case by case), and spiritual play (which is always commendable and of course ultimately superior to all other forms of play," 205). Olson insists throughout that scholas-

---

antitheatrical arguments. Since there are no other antitheatrical texts in the period when the *Tretise* was written, they tend to interpret it as an earlier version of Puritan attacks. Woolf, in particular, says that since the other medieval defenses of drama are lost, we have no recourse but to understand the *Tretise* in terms of the later texts. Barish's remark (68) suggests that his interpretation is colored by Puritan attacks even though he says he will—and largely does—read it as a text bridging the early condemnations of Tertullian and Augustine and the later ones of the Puritans.

77. He addresses this issue in the opening paragraphs of his "Plays as Play," 195 and n. 1. Further references appear in the text.

78. See also Olson's *Literature as Recreation in the Later Middle Ages.*

79. Thomas Aquinas, *Summa Theologica* II–II, q. 168, arts. 2–3, 13.295–301. We might note that this discussion of games and recreation comes within the question on modesty in outward movements of the body and thus is similar to the placement of clerical *ludi* in the *Decretum* under *De vita et honestate clericorum.*

tic discussions of play make no distinctions between forms of play—jests, jokes, storytelling, banter, raillery, sports, or the like—therefore, religious drama falls within the conceptual framework of play and would be compartmentalized in one of the three modes of play depending on its ethical intentions and effects.

I accept Olson's observation that *ludi* were categorized into ethical compartments. We can see this not only in the commentaries Olson cites but also in a broad range of other materials that might be more immediate resources for the *Tretise*: sermons, sermon manuals, *distinctiones,* and so forth. However, I do not accept Olson's contention that all medieval theatrical terms are indeterminate. It is true that we do not always know in a given situation what *lusores, histriones, ministrales, mimi,* and other such creatures are, but that does not mean that we have no words that are determinate. The gloss on *Cum decorem* gives us a pretty good idea of what Innocent was complaining about, and I have been arguing that the word *miracula* has specific meaning, as well. Indeed, some of Olson's own examples undermine the foundations he would set up in the opening, conceptual part of his essay. Olson makes the argument that religious drama falls under the term *ludus,* a point with which I would agree in general, but he presents some rather odd examples to make this point. He claims that Nicolas Oresme's treatment of play in his commentary on the *Ethics* "mentions religious drama specifically" (201). I assume that by "religious drama" Olson means a devotional representation, but Oresme's remark suggests he is talking about some kind of *miracula.* Commenting on Aristotle's discussion of comedy—which medieval scholastics placed in the evil category—Oresme (circa 1370) explains that by *comedy* Aristotle means plays like those in which one person represents Saint Paul, another Judas, and another a hermit, the kind of plays in which the characters sometimes use foul and insulting language.[80] Olson continues that earlier in the century Henry of Rimini made a similar comment on "religious drama": in a chapter on modesty in external behavior, he asks whether the profession of acting is licit. He adopts Aquinas's position that it is under certain circumstances, then mentions a local case of a play in Venice about the Virgin, "created originally in honor of her" that could "be accepted as long as it served devotional goals, but now it is subject to many abuses prompted by vanity and shamelessness. Such indecent

---

80. Oresme, *Le Livre de ethiques d'Aristote,* 271: "Il entent ici par comedies aucuns gieux comme sont ceulz ou .i. homme represente Saint Pol, l'autre Judas, l'autre un hermite, et dit chascun son personnage et en ont aucuns roulles et rimes. Et aucunes fois en telz giex l'en dit de laides paroles, ordes injurieuses et deshonestes." Cited by Olson, "Plays as Play," 201 n. 14.

ludus demands elimination or improvement by either clerical or civic authorities" (201). The first of these instances is not about devotional religious drama but about a foul and indecent *ludus* in which Saint Paul appears. This is not a saint play but a *miracula*.[81] The second instance echoes Herrad of Landsberg's complaint about observances that were originally founded for devotional purposes but have been allowed to degenerate into indecency; they should be eliminated or reformed by the appropriate authorities. My point is that neither of these instances does what Olson wishes them to do—to demonstrate that devotional religious drama falls under the category *ludus*—because these are not devotional religious dramas. I do not argue that devotional religious drama could *not* be treated within the scholastic analysis of *ludus* but that these two examples appear to set the stage for Olson's argument that the *Tretise* objects to devotional religious drama on the grounds that Oresme and Henry do. They would better support my argument that the objects of the *Tretise*'s attack are irreverent *miracula*.

Olson is more convincing when in the paragraph that follows he cites John of Freiburg's distinction in the *Summa confessorum* between *ludi theatrales* and acceptable *representationes* (the gloss on *Cum decorem*) to show that both are included within the Aristotelian play framework (201–2). But Olson treats these as if both were examples of religious performance, whereas *Cum decorem* argues they are not. What John of Freiburg says is that there are two forms of play in this instance, *ludi theatrales* and *representationes,* and that the former is evil and the later good or proper. It does *not* say that *ludi theatrales* are devotional religious dramas.

Olson's last example is the Dominican Robert Holcot's discussion of play in his commentary on the Book of Wisdom. Holcot concludes with a three-part categorization of play borrowed from Aquinas: Wicked play is the sort that gentiles performed in temples and theaters before their gods; play meant for human consolation is recreational; and spiritual play is exemplified in David's dancing before the ark and "that which Christians do on the day of Corpus Christi" (qualem faciunt Christiani in die corporis Christi). Siegfried Wenzel, who made the transcription Olson uses, interpreted this last remark to be an early reference (circa 1330) to "some type of religious play" rather than to a procession or some other pious activity.[82] Olson also cites Abigail Young's

---

81. Indeed, the labeling of this "play" as comedy, given its cast, suggest to me the opening line of a joke: "Have you heard the one about St. Paul, Judas, and the Hermit?" We might recall that in the commentaries on Aristotle's *Poetics,* comedy is described as the art of vituperation.

82. Wenzel, "Early Reference to a Corpus Christi Play."

point that there is "no *a priori* reason for assuming that Holcot's *ludus* carries the same performative implications that the term does when it appears several decades later in records distinguishing the Corpus Christi play from the procession, and it may well be that a 'wider interpretation' than Wenzel's is thus safer."[83] Olson sides with neither position: "The reference, in fact, is and will remain indeterminate because of a medieval habit of mind that does not perceive, at least at the level of generality of the passage in question, that dramatic activity demands separate attention from other forms of playing" (203). Holcot's ambiguousness is claimed to be a virtue insofar as it forces modern scholars to recognize that there were no rigid distinctions among medieval notions of playing.[84]

Indeterminancy is crucial to Olson's analysis of *ludus* and ultimately of the *Tretise,* for it allows him to read "religious drama" for a variety of terms including "miraclis pleyinge." Olson's argument is based on the assumption that since many theatrical terms in the Middle Ages are indeterminate, all are. But this is not the case. The term *ludi theatrales* has a specific meaning; even if it covers a range of different activities, these *ludi* share certain characteristics, ones that make them, according to Innocent, *ludi* of the *theatrum.*

Although the positions of Barish, Davis, and Olson are largely incompatible, I think they give direction for ways to form a revisionist analysis. Barish has demonstrated that the *Tretise* makes no sense as an antitheatrical assault when read in conjunction with early Christian polemic; indeed, he has shown that the biblical citations are nonsensical as attacks on dramatic representation. Davis has urged us to read the text as a Wycliffite (rather than a proto-Puritan) document that argues that acting out sacred narratives—the mere representation of them—reduces the ineffable to empty signs. Setting aside the question of Wycliffite auspices, Olson asks us to read the *Tretise* within the scholastic discourse on *ludus* and recreation. There is no question in my mind that this is a proper and informative context. In my analysis I use Barish's impatience with the text to argue that it is not antitheatrical in the way that early Christian and Puritan polemics were. Although I endorse Davis's call for a historical reinterpretation, I find the *Tretise* unique only in that it is in English. I argue that it is not unique in the context of related late medieval antitheatrical and antiludic clerical polemic. I find most of Olson's discussion informative; in-

---

83. I'm quoting Olson (203).

84. We should also remember that the Holcot reference is very early, ca. 1330, and that we have no historical evidence of the kind of religious drama that Olson would like it to cover.

deed, I believe him to be right in suggesting that we approach the *Tretise* within an ethical framework. Where he and I disagree most fundamentally is on the indeterminancy of medieval theatrical terms.

I believe it probable that the writer uses "miraclis" in the historical sense that we have seen in other documents in this chapter: he attacks the pleyinge, the jesting or mockery, of *miracula*. The tract then might be read as an English version of the episcopal legislation and works such as *Manual des Péchiez* against *miracula*. If this is the case, then the writer objects to parodies of divine service, plays in which saints are mocked and jeered at, and perhaps even children's games, like the "bobbing of Christ," which may have been part of May games or the forbidden scotales or any secular *ludi* that occur on feast days. For the moment, I leave aside further consideration of the content of miraclis in favor of an examination of the preacher's reasoning. Then I will examine the commentaries on the biblical passages in order to restore what I believe to be an appropriate context for the preacher's use of them.

When we read, near the beginning of the tract, "sithen miraclis of Crist and of hise seintis weren thus efectuel, as by our bileve we ben in certein, no man shulde usen in bourde and pleye the miraclis and werkis that Crist so ernystfully wroughte to oure helthe" (lines 22–25), we have tended to regard the statement as a blanket condemnation of the enactment of events in the life of Christ and the saints. But this is to ignore the emphasis in the sentence that is sustained throughout lines 23–39 [25–65]: "no man shulde usen *in bourde and pleye* the miraclis and werkis that Crist so ernystfully wroughte to oure helthe." That phrase and variants of it occur six times in the passage, and "bourdith" by itself is used in the statement of the theme of the tract that servants should not jest with their masters:

> A, Lord, sithen an erthely servaunt dar not takun *in pley and in bourde* that that his erthely lord takith in ernest, myche more we shulden not maken *oure pleye and bourde* of tho miraclis and werkis that God so ernestfully wrought to us. For sothely whan we so doun, drede to sinne is takun awey, as a servaunt, whan he *bourdith* with his maister, leesith his drede to offendyn him. . . . Therfore right as *pleyinge and bourdinge* of the most ernestful werkis of God takith aweye the drede of God that men shulden han in the same, so it takith awey oure bileve and so oure most helpe of oure savacion (lines 29–43 [34–51], my emphases).

Since "play" is parallel to "bourde" throughout the passage, and since both terms suggest inappropriate familiarity between persons who are not equal, it does not seem safe to assume that "pley" means "drama" or that the writer is simply talking about acting or portraying a character.

If the preacher's point of reference is irreverent bourding, then the Elisha example and the verb *illudebant* are precisely to the point.[85] Nicholas of Lyra comments that the story illustrates the derision of the unjust.[86] The Elisha story is not relevant to plays or dramas; the boys are torn apart not because they pretend *to be* the prophet but because they jeer at him. Its point is that the prophet was mocked just as Christ was mocked by the Jews. The mockers' relation to Elisha is not the same as that of viewers to devotional religious drama: the audience watches a mocking of Christ; they do not mock him themselves. As Lyra makes clear, the result of this mocking was the destruction of the idolaters (and, later, the Jews). Similarly, the *Tretise*-writer likens the "bourding and jesting" of miraclis pleyinge to the Jews' "bobbing of Christ" (lines 129–46 [153–73]; 226–29 [267–71]) and warns that God will take a greater vengeance on Christians who reverse Christ's work than on those who originally opposed it.

The author's position, and the context within which his discussion proceeds, therefore, is not antitheatrical, as we have understood it in the past; instead, he opposes himself to anything *inappropriate* to the commemoration of sacred events because of the persons involved or because the activity intrudes on sacred time and place. Bromyard makes a similar argument. Among the dangers of attending *ludi inhonesti* is the "blasphemy of Christ and the saints" and "contempt of the church and realm."[87]

Like others opposed to *ludi theatrales* and *ludi inhonesti*, the *Tretise*-author frames his rebuttal to the six points advanced in favor of miraclis pleyinge within the terms of papal and ecclesiastical opposition to indecorous behavior and the sins that accrue from attendance on such affairs. His larger argument is that when clerics "play" with their Lord in miraclis pleyinge, they not only debase themselves but cause the mysteries with which they are entrusted to be

---

85. Note that this is the verb Bernard uses in his theatrical passage on the humiliation of the Cistercians.

86. Nicholas of Lyra, *Postillae perpetua*, 4 Kings 2:23.

87. Bromyard, *Summa Predicantium, Ludus,* art. 5 (fol. 455): "Christi, & sanctorum blasphemia, regum & ecclesiae contemptus"; see also *Summa predicantium, Chorea,* art. 3. See also the Constitutions of Bishop Walter Cantilupe (1240), in which he orders that there shall not "be unsuitable plays *[ludi inhonesti]*/pastimes, especially on the eves of the saints and (on) the (patronal?) feasts of the church, because we know that such things bring shame to the saints rather than honour to those presuming (to take part in them)" (trans. Abigail Young, in Klausner, *Worcestershire,* 347 [trans. 551]).

drained of their awe. As a consequence, lay people who see clerics indulge in miraclis pleyinge are led into gluttony, lechery, drunkenness, and fornication, the sins attendant on such irreverent festivity.

He makes a historical comparison at the beginning of his rebuttal in which he seems to associate inappropriate play with the *spectacula* of the pagans:

> siche miraclis pleyinge is not to the worschipe of God, for they ben don more to ben seen of the worlde and to plesyn to the world thanne to be seen of God or to plesyn to him *as Crist never ensaumplide hem but onely hethene men* that evere more dishonouren God, seyinge that to the worschipe of God, that is to the most veleinye of him. Therfore *as the wickidnesse of the misbileve of hethene men lyith to themsilf, whanne they seyn that the worshiping of theire maumetrie is to the worschipe of God,* so mennus lecherye now on dayes to han ther owne lustus lieth to hemself whanne they seyn that suche miracles pleying is to the worschip of God. (lines 186–97 [220–32]; my emphases)

When the writer first says that miraclis pleyinge were not authorized by Christ but by "hethene men," it might be argued that "hethene men" is figurative, that it refers to immoral men who support miraclis pleyinge. However, the next passage seems even more strongly to make a historical comparison: just as the "hethene men" were wicked when they said that worshipping of their "maumetrie" was the worship of God, so are people nowadays sinful when they say that "suche miracles pleying" is to the worship of God. I think the intent of the passage is: *Ludi theatrales,* here "miraclis pleyinge," were the creation of the pagans in honor of their god; and just as their misbelief was wickedness then, so now is the performance of irreverent miraclis pleyinge even though they are asserted to be to the honor of Christ.[88]

After the author has linked the *ludi* of the *theatrum* and miraclis pleyinge to lechery, an Isidorean move (lines 192–97 [227–32]), he proceeds from lechery to adultery on the unstated premise that clerical involvement in miraclis pleyinge is like abandoning one's true lover, God, for another. The author clearly thinks of *miracula* as akin to the games of the *theatrum;* they are obscenities, not representations of Christ's actual Passion. Because they constitute lust and adultery, fornication with the world, they are a denial of the cleric's celibacy,

---

88. It is clear in legislation like that of Grosseteste that at least some of the forbidden *ludi* were understood to be pagan, so the writer here may have in mind either the *spectacula* of the late Roman period or the *ludi* that now survive but are pagan in origin. The historical argument is developed with more force in the second part of the *Tretise.*

the substance of his withdrawal from the *theatrum*. His engagement with the world is adultery because it is a violation of his vow of celibacy and marriage to the church.

The rebuttal constitutes an assault on clerical participation in these activities. Three of the rebuttal arguments, numbers 1, 2, and 4, are explicitly directed against clerical participation, and numbers 5 and 6 implicitly argue that such participation is an inversion of clerical work and decorum. If the attack is on clerical participation in *ludi*, then the *Tretise* is not an assault on vernacular religious drama (because it is secular). The writer says that because miraclis pleying is an occasion of idleness and lechery, "*to pristis* it is uttirly forbedyn not onely to been miracle pleyere, but also to heren or to seen miraclis pleyinge" (lines 211–12 [40–41]; my emphasis).[89] The importance of the passage is that it cites the canons against clerics engaging in *ludi theatrales* and attending on *ludi inhonesti*. He continues that the Psalter says to all men but especially to priests who read it daily in the service, "*Turne awey min eyen that they se not vanitees* . . . . How thanne may a prist pleyn in entirlodies or give himsilf to the sight of hem sithen it is forbeden him so expresse by the forseide heste of God" (lines 243–47 [288–93]).[90] Again, the logic of the argument is that priests should not play in *miracula* because it is likely to lead men astray. In particular, he says that such playing leads men not to believe in hell or everlasting pain (lines 255–58 [303–5]), going on to cite the instance of Sara, who never mingled with merrymakers *(ludentibus)*. And since she, a young woman of the Old Testament, took such care of her bodily chastity and abstained from idle playing,

> myche more a prist of the Newe Testament, that is passid the time of childehod and that not onely shulde kepe chastite but alle othere vertues, ne onely ministren the sacrament of matrimonye but alle othere sacramentis and namely sithen him owith to ministre to alle the puple the precious body of Crist, awgthe to abstene him fro al idil pleying bothe of miraclis and ellis. (lines 272–78 [322–29])[91]

---

89. See also lines 245–49 [290–93]. The specific references are to *Cum decorem* (if "miraclis pleyinge" is standing for *ludi theatrales*), Lateran IV's canon 16 *(Mimis)*, and Boniface VIII's decree against clerics who make themselves *ioculatores or goliardi* (1298), the latter of which has a long history. The complaint that *ludi inhonesti* invite lasciviousness is also common (see Statutes of Salisbury I [1217–19], in Powicke and Cheney, *Councils and Synods*, 1:93).

90. I think this argument indicates the writer reads the second commandment ("heste") not as one against idolatry in this instance but quite literally as the command not to take the Lord's name in vain, that is, not to bourd and jest with it.

91. Note the qualification: Priests who are past the age of childhood. Is this just a flourish or an

In the context, "play" or "playing" appears to have a sexual meaning, which also connects it with the frequent references to the link between *ludi* and adultery. The logic would seem to be that since the clergy have withdrawn from the world and taken a vow of celibacy, to engage in certain kinds of activities, such as illicit play, is like adultery because it abandons the purity of someone like Sara—and if an Old Testament woman could maintain her purity, then surely a Christian cleric ought to do so. Those who handle the body of Christ ought not to give themselves to play "but to alle siche thing as is most contrarious to pley, as is penaunce and suffring of persecution."

Barish and others have taken *ludentibus* in the Sara passage to refer to actors or performers. He remarks that the "case of Sara happens to be nearly the sole instance among the scriptural citations made by the preacher that supports his own interpretation. Most depend on a strained and unnatural reading of the text, and in particular on a forced glossing of the word *ludere*."[92] However, Barish's reading not only strains the sense of the scriptural text but runs counter to the medieval understanding of the incident and the verse.

Sara, the daughter of Raguel, was reproached by one of her father's maidservants because she had been given to seven husbands, and a devil named Asmodeus had killed them at their first going in to her. Sara asks the Lord to loose her from this bond of reproach or to let her die. She says, "Thou knowest, O Lord, that I never coveted a husband and have kept my soul clean from all lust. Never have I joined myself with them that play" (Douai translation; Vulgate: "nunquam cum ludentibus miscui me"). Aquinas links the Sara reference to Jeremiah 15:17. He says that the passage shows that Jeremiah lived prudently in avoiding the wrong kind of consorts; he never sat in the company of merrymakers *(ludentium)*.[93] Hugh of St. Cher's commentary is more revealing: He glosses *cum ludentibus* in Tobias with the phrase *ut in choreis,* and comments: "Whence it is shown that this is sin. And Jerome says: It is difficult for temptation not to rise up when there is touching of fingers or movement of feet. Whence Jeremiah 15:17: I never sat in the company of merrymakers, etc. Rather, I sat alone because you filled me with bitterness (or sorrow)."[94] It is

---

assertion that priests—as opposed to choirboys and lower clergy—should not participate in miraclis pleyinge?

92. Barish, *Antitheatrical Prejudice,* 72.

93. Aquinas, *Opera omnia,* 14.616–17.

94. Hugh of St. Cher, *Opera Omnia,* 1:376: "cum ludentibus] ut in choreis. Unde patet, hoc esse peccatum. Cujus etiam signum est, quia semper ad sinistram vadunt. Et *Hieronym* dicit: Vix potest esse, quin contactu digiti, vel depressione pedis tentatio surgat. Unde *Jerem.* 15. d. Non sed

clear that neither Aquinas nor Hugh understands *ludentibus* in this passage to refer to "actors" or "dramatic players"; rather, they use the term to refer to those who engage in frivolity, especially the kind in which there is bodily contact or movement that gives rise to lechery. Bromyard's discussion of *ludi* is even closer to the logic of the *Tretise*.[95] He says that illicit *ludi* such as tournaments, jousting, dicing, and amusements that waste time and goods are invented or used for cupidity, voluptuousness, vanity, and other damnable things. According to distinction 35, *Episcopus,* all these are prohibited for lay people as well as clerics.[96] In addition, clerics especially are prohibited not only from engaging in such *ludi* but also from watching them. He concludes that such *ludi* ought to be fled by example of what is said in Tobet: I never mingled *cum ludentibus.* The concern in much of the canonical legislation is that if a priest engages in play or attends on it, then his parishioners will have regard neither for him nor the sacraments.[97]

Early in the tract the author singles out clerics as his target, and he returns to them a number of times in his rebuttal of the six points offered by defenders (who, I suggest, we should imagine to be those who participate in and allow *miracula*—monastic and cathedral personnel). They are examples of servants who play with their Lord. Their playing is dangerous not only to themselves but to others. He says that priests should not engage in miraclis pleyinge because it creates an inappropriate familiarity with their Lord (Christ) before the general populace, as a consequence of which, their servants, the laity, lose respect for their superiors, the clergy, as well as the Lord, and themselves engage in miraclis pleyinge. The passage reads as follows: Miraclis pleyinge takes men from their belief in God since they regress from deeds of the spirit to signs done

---

cum conlicio [sic] ludentium, & gloriatus sum a facie manus tuae. Solutio. Sedebam, quoniam amaritudine impleti me. *Psalm 25.* Non sedi cum concilio vanitatis, &c." In the gloss on Jeremiah 15, he links some of the same verses (Ps. 25 and Tobias) and adds: *Contra euntes ad choreas* (4:220). Similarly, the Franciscan *Liber Exemplorum* cites the Sara reference in an exemplum condemning *cantilenas et choreas* (Little, *Liber Exemplorum* 111).

95. Bromyard, *Summa predicantium, Ludus,* art. 2 (fol. 454).

96. Friedberg, *Corpus iuris canonici,* 1:131.

97. The injunctions against attending on performers and playing at *aleas vel taxillos* or attending scotales and other irregular activities often occur in statutes having to do with the avoidance of *superbia* and specifically fall under admonitions about proper dress. The context for the regulations, therefore, is that the priest ought not to make himself too familiar with his flock or seem too much like them. See, e.g., Bishop Pore's Constitutions, item 11 (p. 134) and the Synodal Statutes for an English Diocese [1222–25], caps. 63–65, which concern the "vita et honestate clericorum" (Powicke and Cheney, *Councils and Synods,* 151; Bromyard also cites this decretal in *Summa predicantium, Ludus,* art. 2).

after the lusts of the flesh; consequently, miraclis pleyinge is apostasy (an Isidorean echo; lines 630–43 [742–58]):

> And therfore we schal nevere findyn that miraclis pleying was usid among Cristene men but sithen religious onely in tokenes shewiden ther religioun and not in dedis, and sithen pristis onely in signes and for money schewiden ther pristhode and not in dedis. And therfore the apostasye of these drawith myche of the puple after hem, as the apostasie of Lucifer the first aungel droowgh myche of hevene after him. (lines 537–44 [635–40])

He attributes the rise of miraclis pleyinge to the apostasy and hypocrisy of monks (the "religious") and clerics (the "pristis") and concludes that just as the apostasy of Lucifer drew other angels to hell, so these clerics draw other men to apostasy.[98]

The passage is significant in several respects. First, it parallels the situation described in Jeremiah 23. The pseudoprophets and preachers claim to speak the word of God and thereby deceive the people with their lies and *miracula.*

Second, the statement is made in the context of the story of Ishmael's playing with Isaac (lines 461–544 [545–642]). Since the ceremonies of the Old Law, even though given by God, are fleshly, and cannot hold with New Testament, because it is ghostly, so "pleyinge," since it is fleshly and not bidden by God, should not be done. For just as the playing of Ishmael with Isaac would have bereft Isaac of his heritage, so the keeping of the ceremonies of the Old Law in the New Testament would have bereft men of their belief in Christ and made men revert from ghostly to fleshly living (lines 521–32 [616–29]).

The relation of this conclusion to the overall logic of the tract is clear: the servant ought not to play with or be too familiar with his lord (see lines 498–505 [590–99]). However, the relevance of the story to drama is obscure. The writer claims that since Ishmael "playide" with his brother Isaac in order to steal his heritage, he was thrown out of the house of Abraham; that because Ishmael was born of the flesh and Isaac of the spirit, the play of the flesh is not helpful to the spirit; and that the Old Testament of the flesh may not be held with the New Testament. Therefore, since the play of Ishmael was not "leveful," much more is fleshly play (that is, miraclis pleyinge) not "leveful" with the ghostly works of Christ. Further, since miraclis pleyinge nowadays is worse

---

98. In his attack on scotales and other pagan *ludi* Grosseteste cites Ecclesiasticus 31:38–40 as the basis of his argument that things that inebriate destroy the image of God in man and, among other things, is the root of apostasy (see Grosseteste, *Epistolae,* 73).

than the playing of Ishmael with Isaac, so it deserves greater vengeance than was visited on Ishmael.[99]

Nicholas of Lyra's comment on the Isaac and Ishmael story gives a meaningful context to the *Tretise*-author's argument.[100] Lyra points out that the Hebrew has an equivocal word, "Messabeth," for the one translated as "ludentem" in the Vulgate. At various places in the Old Testament "ludere" is used to signify idolatry, killing, and coming together or lasciviousness. He cites Exodus 32, in which the people before the golden calf eat and drink and rise up to play ("Vbi nos habemus sedit populus manducare & bibere & surrexerunt ludere"; compare *Tretise,* lines 584–626 [690–782]). For "ludere" the Hebrew has "idolatrare."[101] And for the Abner and Joab episode, where the Vulgate has "surgant pueri & ludant," the Hebrew has "& occidant." In his subsequent commentary on the passage in Kings, Lyra iterates the equivocal nature of the word and says that "surgant pueri & ludere" means that they rose to show their fortitude before the court and that they killed one another (which suggests pride and the subsequent punishment; compare *Tretise,* lines 545–65 [644–68]). In the Genesis commentary he cites other passages for the meanings "coecuntem" and "lasciuientem" before returning to the Isaac and Ishmael incident. He says that we must read the Genesis passage in three ways, the second of which connects Ishmael with the flesh and Isaac with the spirit. There are two points to be made about the commentary: Lyra links three texts, all of

99. Nicholas Davis, "'Tretise of Myraclis Pleyinge,'" 127–30, offers as background to the biblical story the Franciscan John of Wales's treatment of it in his *Communiloquium* under *Ludus.* Davis argues that the interpretation of the story indicates that John is condemning the first category of illicit *ludi (ludus perversae illusionis),* those engaged in by the clergy, specifically the Feast of Fools. Davis then argues that the *Tretise* extends John's condemnation of lay *ludi,* John's second category (scotales and the like), to the first category in order to cover stagings of Christian narrative. As evidence for this he cites a remark by Wyclif about adulterous signs, which Wyclif likens to a summer game of tormentors *(ludum estivum tortorum)* and which he says is "considerably more abominable than the game of certain laypeople." Davis reads the *ludum estivum tortorum as* a lay summergame, but the passage distinguishes clerical from lay *ludi.* Wyclif's point is that these clerical games are worse than lay ones at Midsummer and thus are like hypocritical "signs" affected by new religious orders because they claim piousness when they engage in mockeries. It seems to me that Wyclif's remark supports my definition of *miracula* and clerkes plei, and, if it is to be taken in conjunction with Davis's analysis of John of Wales's categories of play, then it supports my contention that the *Tretise* is directed against the *ludi* of the clergy.

100. Nicholas of Lyra, *Postillae perpetuae,* Gen. 21:9–10.

101. The elaborate analogy between the "pleyinge of miraclis" and the worship of the golden calf is neither an invention of the *Tretise* writer nor an unthinking continuation of the early Church's assault on the *theatrum.* Bromyard (*Summa predicantium, Ludus,* art. 1, fol. 454) links *ludi inhonesti* with idolatry, as does the passage in Jer. 23; moreover, both link the idolatry with adultery and lasciviousness, a connection implicit in the passage from Tobit about Sara.

which play similar roles in the *Tretise;* and he interprets this "playing" as idolatry, which he couples with lechery and lasciviousness, the consequence of which is death.

Hugh of St. Cher says that there are various glosses on the meaning of "ludentem" in this verse.[102] Some say that Ishmael made images of clay and taught Isaac to adore them, on which account Sara was indignant, fearing that Ishmael led Isaac to the cult and rite of idolatry. Others say that Sara understood that the elder would seek to be first by struggling with him. Or that Ishmael taught Isaac to be lubricious and lascivious, as he himself was. And this play the Apostle calls persecution (Gal. 4:21). When he glosses the phrase *surrexerunt ludere* in the Exodus passage, he says: "That is, to adore the calf. Such was the play of Ishmael with Isaac. Thus often priests in days of solemnity, after the great oblation, make a relaxation of penance and give license to eating and drinking, which play is often followed by unwarrantable actions."[103] Hugh's comments on the Ishmael and Isaac story provide a kind of map of the logic of the *Tretise.* According to Hugh, the *ludus* that Ishmael played with Isaac is worldly joy, but Sara, the church, orders the procurers of this joy to be ejected.[104] Then he cites Jeremiah 15:17, the prophet's assertion, "I did not sit in the company of merrymakers," and Tobias 3, Sara's "I did not mingle with merrymakers." This "play" Paul called persecution (Gal. 4:21).[105] This latter text is important because it provides one of the tract writer's themes. In Gal. 4:29, Paul says: "But as at that time he who was born according to the flesh persecuted him who was born according to the spirit, so it is now." Hugh comments: "whence Jeremiah 15: 'Discharge me from those who persecute me.' That is, the Lord ejected from present merit and in future shut away from reward *lusores*"; indeed, Hugh adds, "so that I may speak more truly, [he shut away] *illusores*" (jesters, mockers).[106]

But note, Hugh continues, there is good *ludus,* which consists in following

---

102. Hugh of St. Cher, *Opera omnia,* 1.27. The discussion that follows paraphrases Hugh's comment.

103. Ibid.: Surrexerunt ludere] i.e., vitulum adorare. Talis fuit ludus Ismael cum Isaac, *Genes. vigesimo primo.* a. Sic saepe sacerdotes in solemnibus diebus, post magnam oblationem, faciunt relaxationem poenitentiarum, & dant licentiam comedendi, & bibendi ad libitum, unde saepe ineptus sequitur ludus (1:98).

104. Ibid., 1:27; cf. 1:98.

105. Ibid.: Ludus quo Ismael ludit cum Isaac, est gaudium temporale, sed Sara, i. Ecclesia, procuratorem hujus gaudi jubet eiici. *Jerem.* 15. d. Non sedi in Concilio ludentium. *Tob.* 3. c. Nunquam cum ludentibus miscui me, neque cum his, qui in levitate ambulant, participem me praebui. Hunc ludum vocat Apostolus persecutionem. *Galat.* 4[:23].

106. Ibid., 1:27.

the law and the divine obsequies. Then he cites the story of David, who gloried in his persecution by Michal because God had chosen the house of David over that of Saul. The interesting point is that Hugh does not put the emphasis on David's playing before the ark of the Lord but on the persecution he suffered—gladly—when Michal rebuked him.[107] It is the ridicule that interests Hugh as well as the constraints that are placed on those who would imitate David by following the law and performing the divine obsequies. To some, this kind of play seems labor. Similarly, the *Tretise* writer interprets David's response to Michal's rebuke as describing the appropriate kind of play before the ark of the Lord (lines 724–44 [853–75]). First, people should behold how many things God has given through his grace and thank him by fulfilling his will and trusting in him when they are reproved by their enemies. Second, they should be steadfast in devotion and foul and reprovable to the world as Christ and his apostles were and as David said he ought to be. The third point is that we should be more lowly in our own eyes than in outward appearance because we are aware that we have committed more sins than are known by others. Like Hugh, the *Tretise*-writer describes Davidic playing as a penitential life of firm belief and patient suffering of persecution.

Hugh's commentary is very much like that of the *Tretise;* it not only links the key biblical verses but comes to the same penitential conclusion. The commentary on Isaac is particularly revealing because it focuses on the dire consequences of the servant Ishmael's playing with his lord Isaac—idolatry with a subsequent loss of salvation—but it implies that Isaac is the true spiritual leader, representing the "clergy," who are led astray by Ishmael, representing the superstitious people. The inferior persecutes and corrupts the chosen one. The Exodus passage has a similar configuration. While the proper priest, Moses, is on the mount to receive the law, the people rise up to play with, that is, to adore, the idols of their superstition. I think the *Tretise*-author exploits the two kinds of playing with one's lord—the clergy with God, the laity with the clergy—in order to expose the dire consequences of this inappropriate socialization. The *Tretise* argues that when clerics play with their Lord, they lead the populace into lechery, gluttony, adultery and mis- or disbelief, but the passage concerning Isaac and Ishmael also argues that servants—here the laity—pervert their lords—the clergy—when they "play" with their lords, that is, when they participate in or watch miraclis pleyinge.

It might be objected that my analysis still does not account for references to

---

107. This reading of the passage is not only shared by the *Tretise* and the two Dominicans, Hugh of St. Cher and Bromyard, but is in contrast to that of the Franciscan *Dives and Pauper.*

what appear to be biblical dramas: the Passion of Christ, the play of Antichrist, and Doomsday. To this we might add the Harrowing of Hell since there are occasional references in other records to plays of the Resurrection (at Beverley, for example) that use masks and may have been irreverent. There are no explicit references in the *Tretise* to liturgical *representationes* or vernacular plays on Old Testament subjects, Christ's nativity or ministry, or plays about the Virgin. The *ludi* mentioned are linked by two similarities: the actions involve either torturers or devils. If the *Tretise* is directed against vernacular religious drama in general—that is, the representation of biblical events—why are none of these other topics mentioned? At most, one could argue that the *Tretise* is opposed to the representation of these four topics, not to representation itself. But the material I have brought forward to help illuminate *miracula* and somergame suggests that the *ludi* occasioned laughter and irreverence. *Ludi theatrales* and *miracula* are activities in which *personae* wear horrifying or distorted masks; the participants are indecorous in their movements and behavior. It is "bourding and jesting"—disreputable entertainment—to which the *Tretise* objects. The torturers in extant Passion plays make jokes among themselves, but for the audience the effects are grotesque, not humorous. The devils in the plays of the Harrowing and the Doomsday no doubt took advantage of the situation to be amusing (the Chester Alewife scene; the Wakefield Master's satiric opening scene in the *Judgment*), but the somergame I described above strikes me as much more likely to result in viewers' doubting the existence of hell or the punishment of evil, as the *Tretise* author charges, than the vernacular drama does. The danger of a play of Antichrist—that is, a "miracle"—is that it awes and entertains with illusions. However theatrical the Chester *Antichrist* is—and it is a terrific piece—the audience is in on the illusions. They may appreciate the spectacle but they know it is illusion. The "play of Antichrist" that I described above seems intended to entertain with illusion, to engage the audience as did the pythoness at Corinth or as Herrad complains the choirboys did in the nave of the church. The atmosphere of and the relation of participants within *ludi theatrales* and *miracula* are different from those of devotional religious drama. I am not trying to suggest that there is no festivity at a Corpus Christi play; rather, I want to argue that festiveness during the York, Chester, and Coventry cycles is coincident with, not the effect of, the action of the *ludus*.

※※

My reading of the *Tretise of Miraclis Pleyinge* will undoubtedly strike many scholars as tortured, perhaps even perverse. I acknowledge that it is difficult to stop seeing "play" or "drama" for "pley," and "vernacular mystery cycle" for "miraclis pleyinge." Nevertheless, I believe I have demonstrated that it is untenable to hold that the *Tretise* attacks vernacular religious (and liturgical) drama in itself. In addition, I have shown that in records prior to 1377 that are sufficiently detailed to allow judgment, *miracula* is consistently used to refer to the kinds of activities clerics participated in that were prohibited by Innocent III and some English bishops. These prohibitions were directed not at liturgical dramas but at clerical parodies and *irrisiones*. The *Dives and Pauper* and sixteenth-century usage of "miraclis" and its synonym, "steraclis," suggest that *miracula* were understood to be equivalent to ancient *spectacula*, and thus were not religious but heathen. Sixteenth-century usage suggests that miraclis and steraclis involved illusions—not dramatic illusion but tricks intended to delight and amuse people and that, in many cases, led people to devalue the truth of God's miracles. Finally, I have provided an exegetical tradition for an understanding of the scriptural texts in the *Tretise*, one that makes sense rather than one that is illogical.

It seems to me that the *Tretise*-author chose "miraclis" with full knowledge of the pejorative meaning given to it by reforming clerics. Miraclis and miraclis pleyinge are inappropriate kinds of activity because they parody; they are hateful and obscene because ultimately they entertain and amuse rather than teach. Although participants may claim that these activities are held in honor of Christ and the saints, they profane the feasts of saints and holy days of Christ. These miraclis are utterly different from the miracles performed by Christ and the saints, for not only are they conducive to immorality but they are fables, inventions, and jests full of inane words.

The emphasis in the tract is on behavior that involves "bourding and pleying." The writer seems concerned with the clergy's participation in miraclis pleyinge and the way their foolery has given rise to lay revelry. Clerical participation in miraclis pleyinge leads not only to immorality and idolatry but also apostasy because the participants cease to be awed by the divine mystery. Their familiarity with their lords, the priests, leads to a debasement of their faith. The servant who jests with his lord is likely to forget his lord's lordship and then, like the boys who scorned Elisha, he needs to beware the bear.

The miraclis of saints of which the writer complains might have been *ludi* held on the eve of a saint's day, as apparently was the case with the *miracula* at Dunstable and the revels of choirboys on the eve of Saint Nicholas. A later "play" of Saint Katherine at Shrewsbury (1525–26) was not *about* the saint; rather, it included a lord of misrule, a "dizard's" (jester's) head, and materials for explosions and smoke.[108] The "miracle" at Colchester required a devil's mask and a tunic with tails. Finally, we know that Saint George plays were not always reverent enactments of the life of Saint George. These activities are ones that Innocent and the bishops attacked; these may well be the "clerkes pleis" that *The Simonie,* the *Manual,* and other texts, recalling Innocent's prohibition, condemned.[109]

---

108. Somerset treats the record as evidence of a saint play, but there is no reference to the saint herself in the account of expenditure. See "Local Drama and Playing Places at Shrewsbury," 2, 27.

109. In "*Miracula,*" 903–4, I suggested that modern critical notions of *miracula* derive from an error made in 1798 when Monsieur De la Rue, in a paper containing a discussion of the *Manual des Péchiez,* assumed that *miracula* referred to saint plays. Although it later became apparent that the *Manual* was not referring to religious dramas, De la Rue's authority had been established, with the result that scholars argued about which references to *miracula* could be used to determine whether the term referred to saint plays as a genre or to religious drama in general. Coffman's study, for example, began not with De la Rue but with Wright's 1843 edition of the *Chester Plays* ("Miracle Plays in England—Nomenclature," 448).

Communitas: The Ludi of Monasteries and Cathedrals, Towns and Parishes

My analysis of *theatrum, miracula,* and somergame has argued two larger points: that there was considerable clerical aversion to and an attempt to separate clerics from the *theatrum* coupled with a late medieval agenda to reform clerical and lay *ludi inhonesti.* The material we have examined demonstrates that legists perceived that the life of the clergy was so distinct from that of the laity as to require a distancing of the former from the latter; thus, in the *Decretum* and other documents what is permitted the laity is not what is allowed the clergy. This strong binarism accounts for some of the differences in the forms of entertainment and ritual practice that we find in late medieval and early modern England; however, there is not a simple divorcement of the two spheres. This chapter and the next intend to explore not only the divisions between lay and clerical cultures but what they share, and also the diversity within their own hierarchies. My premise is that groups developed a sense of what was appropriate to their status, time, and place. Practice, in addition, is a function of economic capacity and a desire for display. In attempting to make a taxonomy of medieval *ludi,* we should keep in mind that we are talking about groups, not individuals; we are attempting to describe what was allowed and what was common, not what was individual or idiosyncratic.

Records suggest that regular clergy, the Benedictines, for example, tended to share the aesthetic of their aristocratic supporters. The most common expenditures are for musicians, whether traveling alone or in groups. These musicians may come from nearby towns or be itinerant companies of aristocratic lords and ladies. About half of the seventeen English cathedrals were houses of monastic clergy, the other half being secular (Carlisle was a house of canons regular). The secular episcopal establishments shared the tastes of monastic communities. Although the regular and higher secular clerical establishments privilege an aristocratic aesthetic with regard to musical entertainments, they did not normally indulge in noble sports; indeed, canon law opposed blood sports, and preachers' manuals frequently inveigh against the expense and waste of tournaments and other games. The well-run monastery or cathedral had musical entertainments—primarily for its officers—and its liturgies; there is no direct evidence for the production of dramas until the sixteenth century and then only in unusual circumstances. I am not trying to suggest that regular and upper secular clergy engaged only in pious activities; we know that they wrote satirical Latin verse, read comedies against the canon, and permitted clerics in minor orders to engage in normally forbidden behaviors. Nevertheless, annual accounts suggest that entertainments usually fell within acceptable limits.

A selective survey of parishes, smaller towns, and provincial areas suggests that there is a general distinction between lay and clerical entertainments and that the clerical hierarchy attempted, with some success, to impose decorum on festive behavior through ritual, but especially through the promotion of processions and related ritual acts. Whether in the parish or the town, groups used processions to express religious devotion, social unity, or both.[1] The objective was to identify the group as a body, and this need was sufficient that often the group assessed fines against individuals who shunned their duties.[2] Although processions are very common at these levels of society, they never entirely drove out the practices they were intended to replace. The parish ale with its attendant games flourished into the sixteenth century, and the parish priest was implicated in these activities in a number of ways. In some regions these games were organized by the town rather than the parish, but towns that sought some form of display appropriate to their status often merged procession with spectacle—pageants, dragons, giants—and some produced vernacular dramas, usually of biblical stories.

---

1. Charles Phythian-Adams and Mervyn James have presented the classic statements: "Ceremony and the Citizen" and "Ritual, Drama and Social Body," respectively. Other scholars have pointed to the stratifying or alienating consequences of such rituals: see Lindenbaum, "Smithfield Tournament of 1390" and "Ceremony and Oligarchy," and many of the other essays in *City and Spectacle*. See also Kipling, *Enter the King;* Sponsler, "Culture of the Spectator"; Ashley, "Sponsorship, Reflexivity and Resistance"; and Clopper, "Engaged Spectator."

2. See, e.g., the Weavers' and Smiths' accounts and the Tilers' ordinances at Coventry (Ingram, *Coventry,* 122, 142, 484–85).

This chapter will provide the evidence for ludic practices among these various groups. I do not intend an exhaustive or geographical survey, merely some sampling of the most informative sets of records. These profiles will be of use when we turn to cases in the chapter that follows where the evidence is spotty or partial, for they give us some idea of what we might expect in smaller towns or under a variety of auspices. The description of practice is also intended to lay the groundwork in this chapter for a reassessment of the saint play in England, however, for I believe that we have mistaken as a saint play many a parish ale.

Practice: Monasteries and Cathedrals

Clerics were warned not to attend on lay *spectacula* and *ludi;* they were to leave the feast before the entry of the entertainers. But there was a legitimate realm of recreation for clerics as well as lay people even though the whole notion of recreation was problematical.[3]

Despite the inevitable infringements of clerical decorum, when we look at lengthy runs of monastic and cathedral accounts, we find little evidence of expenditure on inappropriate entertainments except possibly for boy bishop ceremonies.[4] Durham Priory records provide a good illustration of expenditures on *ludi* since it has several series of accounts from different departments within the monastic community that, with occasional gaps, run from the early fourteenth century until dissolution.[5] The house was a cathedral priory, that is, a monastic community under obedience to the prior, the bishop being no longer resident at his seat because of public obligations; when he was in his diocese, he usually stayed at one of his manor estates. The priors were also frequently absent; they seem to have preferred to stay on their estates, one of which, Beaurepaire, was the site of annual entertainments at Christmas.[6] Often the accounts, whether for Beaurepaire or the monastery, simply indicate payment to persons, such as the precentor or succentor, for playing or for *ludi* ("pro tribus ludis Prioris" in 1408–9), but there is sufficient detail in the records citing named individuals or their instruments to indicate that these "plays" are musical performances ("in uno viro ludenti in uno loyt [= lute] et uxori ejus cantanti apud

3. Olson, *Literature as Recreation*, 19–127.

4. Other festivities of the choirboys and lower clergy, such as those condemned by the reforming bishops, would not, of course, appear in the accounts of religious institutions because there was no expenditure associated with them.

5. Fowler, *Extracts*. I also consulted materials deposited by John McKinnell at the office of the Records of Early English Drama; see McKinnell, "Drama and Ceremony in the Last Years of Durham Cathedral Priory."

6. See my introduction.

Bewrpayr" in 1361–62).[7] The records also contain incidental expenditures for *istriones* (from New Castle and other places) at various times of the year and are probably payments to musicians or waits. The principal observances were at Christmas, the feast of Saint Cuthbert (20 March) and of his translation (4 September), and at Pentecost, when there was a procession with the shrine and banners in honor of the saint. The other annual sets of payments consist of alms to the boy bishop; these were made by every officer within the monastery. There are no obvious references to productions of dramas.[8]

Sheila Lindenbaum's analysis of the abbatial accounts of Westminster (1280–1435) shows a similar pattern.[9] Most entertainment took place before the head of the house, in his own hall at home or at one of his manors as part of the hospitality he extended to his many guests. Abbot Colchester of Westminster (active in the time of Richard II) rewarded more than sixty groups of entertainers, about one-third of whom were individual entertainers, including a number of harpers and other string players; nearly another third were small troupes of minstrels from the houses of the nobility; and the remainder were groups of two to four unidentified minstrels, along with two groups of *interlusores*. Lindenbaum argues that the entertainments are those that would be appropriate at court or in a nobleman's house, though adapted to suit the abbot's calling and his level of income.

It might be argued that actors of plays lurked under the Latin names for entertainers, but Selby Abbey, Yorkshire, offers evidence to the contrary. The abbey has sufficient accounts from 1397–1533 to establish that the abbey rewarded entertainers from the great households as well as from nearby towns.[10] As Suzanne Westfall has noted, however, Selby Abbey is unusual in often giving the number of players in a group.[11] Of the thirty-five such references out of a total of eighty-eight, fifteen are to single performers (42.8 percent), two to pairs

---

7. Fowler, *Extracts,* 1:138, 1:127.

8. Thompson, *English Clergy,* 298, prints a program of inquiries for Durham in 1408, the only relevant entry of which is article 63, which inquires whether anyone is engaged in *ludus alearum aut alius quocumque ludus inhonestus.*

9. Lindenbaum, "Entertainment in English Monasteries." The treasurers' accounts of Christ Church Priory, Canterbury, which begin in 1257, list payments to the same sort of entertainers from 1272 to 1391, when there is a gap until the records resume in 1444–45 (from inspection of priory records deposited at the office of the Records of Early English Drama). In addition, Worcester Cathedral has extensive records from various departments within the priory that show expenditures for minstrels but no obvious references to plays.

10. Palmer, "Early English Northern Entertainment."

11. Westfall, *Patrons and Performance,* 210. Extracts, with translations, are printed by Wickham, *Early English Stages,* 1:332–39.

(5.7 percent), five to groups of three (14.3 percent), and four to groups of four. Together, these account for three-fourths of the groups hired, and all fall below the requirement of "four men and a boy" that David Bevington has cited as constituting an acting troupe in the sixteenth century.[12] About half of the thirty-five references come from the accounts for 1527–28 and 1531–32.[13] The abbot in these years generally gave 4d. to each player, whether boy or man. Some of the boys were from the choir and performed at the times associated with clerical *ludi*: Christmas, Saint Stephen's, Holy Innocents. There were players—probably musicians—from Ricall, Doncaster, York, Howden, and Leeds. The King's Players came in each year and were given 6s. 8d., the sum that Lord Northumberland routinely gave to minstrels as opposed to the King's Players.[14] When the records specify type of entertainer, they are the usual harpers, fiddlers, and citharists, but the occasional tumbler also appears. The abbey also rewarded the boy bishop of York, the boys of the bishop of Durham, plowboys on Plough Monday, and the occasional Lord of Misrule, and had their own King of the Kitchen Boys on Shrove Tuesday. The records of Selby Abbey, therefore, suggest that *histriones* and *lusores* in these records are musicians or singers.[15]

I want to emphasize that in these accounts there are no unequivocal references to nonliturgical dramas in English monasteries and cathedrals and their manors up to the Reformation; therefore, we should not expect to find religious institutions as sponsors of vernacular dramas until Cromwell, John Bale, and others began to use drama to further religion.[16] The prevailing view—doc-

---

12. Bevington, *From "Mankind" to Marlowe*, 68–95; and see the chart on 72, where only two plays are listed as requiring fewer than four performers (*Mundus et Infans* and Heywood's *John John*), and the cast requirements in the appendix, 265–73.

13. Wickham, *Early English Stages*, 1:336–39.

14. Westfall, *Patrons and Performance*, 132. This payment seems routine at Selby since one of the earliest references, ca. 1450, is the same (Wickham, *Early English Stages*, 1:332–33). Given the early date, I think it safe to assume that we are talking about musicians.

15. Given the similarly in these accounts, we perhaps should be cautious about concluding, as Galloway and Wasson do, that some of the *ludi* at Thetford Priory (Norfolk), a Cluniac house, were dramas and that *mimi* were actors rather than musicians (Galloway and Wasson, *Plays and Players in Norfolk and Suffolk*, 103–4). Richard Beadle, "Plays and Playing at Thetford," also concludes that payments to *lusores* of various noble companies and to the "pleys" of nearby towns indicate that the "monastic community was accustomed to regular dramatic entertainment towards the close of its career" (8). I think this doubtful. The references to the "pleys" (fund-raisers) of nearby towns are treated below; the labels "*lusores*," "pleyerys," and the like cannot securely be tied to actors rather than musicians.

16. Terence and Plautus had begun to be performed at the universities prior to this, and we have records of performances of their and others' plays in houses belonging to Cromwell and Cranmer in the 1530s; see P. White, *Theatre and Reformation*, 16–18.

umented by regular accounts across centuries—must be that monasteries and cathedrals enjoyed entertainment appropriate to their office —chiefly musical presentations—and that they shared an aesthetic with the nobility with whom they often associated and from whose ranks they often were drawn. Hence, it is not surprising that a Lydgate should be called on to provide court entertainments or to translate or write literature that would appeal to the aristocracy.

Practice: Towns

Small self-governing towns, in part because they were secular corporations, often aspired to greater pomp and display. Many towns hired their own waits to perform music on regular schedules and to attend on civic officials at feasts or in perambulations through the town. These officials also welcomed traveling musicians, bearwards, and other entertainers. One gets the impression that the rewarding of such entertainers was a sign of the town's prestige. When towns welcomed visiting dignitaries, they frequently imitated, as far as possible, the shows one would expect in London or the other great cities.

Most English towns, however, were too small to support large-scale spectacle. If we look at the ranking of towns outside London according to 1377 poll tax returns, we find only seven cities with more than three thousand persons: York (population 7,248), Bristol (6,345), Coventry (4,817), Norwich (3,952), Lincoln (3,569), Salisbury (3,226), and Lynn (3,217).[17] The next ten towns have a population of more than 2,000, and a further twenty-two have more than 1,000. Only a few of these towns mounted religious dramas; most, as far as we know, never produced dramas even though some of them would seem to have had both the population and economic resources to do so. Some thinly populated areas found cooperation to be the means for mounting substantial fund-raising activities. There is no simple means of accounting for why one town produced drama and another did not, but one of the first hurdles was economic, and an obvious secondary consideration was the desire to engage in such activities. To illustrate some of the diversity, I will discuss the kinds of arrangements we see in East Anglia, Essex, and Kent.

New Romney, one of the Cinque Ports, lies on the southeast coast of England, to the south of Sandwich, Dover, and Hythe and northeast of Hastings, the four of these completing the group of five. New Romney has a fairly con-

---

17. Hoskins, *Local History in England,* the appendix, "Ranking of Provincial Towns," and "English Provincial Towns in the Early Sixteenth Century." Chester is not included in the ranking but probably would have been high on the list (Hoskins, *Local History,* 174).

tinuous set of Chamberlains' accounts from 1384 to 1580, Jurats' Record
Books for 1454–82 and 1552–68, and a Book of Note 1548–1612.[18] The most
common reference to ludic and ceremonial activity is payment to banns-criers of
nearby towns or for the showing of *ludi* from those towns. The earliest payment
in the Chamberlains' accounts is in 1387–88 to the men of Hythe ("hominibus
de hethe in ludo").[19] By 1423–24 they are paying the men of Lydd, frequently
called "lusores," for their "ludus"; in 1426–27 the men of "boyghter sham" for
showing their interlude ("monstracione Interludij sui"); in 1429–30 the men of
"hyerne"; in 1430–31the players of the "ludum of Rokynge"; in 1441–42 the
men of "Wyghtsham" for showing their "ludus" on Crook Hill ("ad monstran-
dum ludum suum super le Crok hill").[20] Later payments are made to those who
came to proclaim their banns from Folkstone, Charte, Rye, Brokeland, Halden,
Romany, Bethresden, and Appledore. The town also made payments to noble
and royal companies, bearwards, and other entertainers.

Missing from the New Romney records are references to their boy bishop,
whom they sent to other towns. The accounts of Lydd, from 1449, refer frequently to expenses on Saint Nicholas day for the boy bishop of New Romney.[21] The payments continue to 1484–85, when there is a hiatus in the
records. When the records resume in 1512–13 there are no references to the
Romney bishop, but there are occasional notices of the play at New Romney
dating from 1516–17.

By the mid–fifteenth century New Romney apparently had a biblical drama
of Christ's Passion and Resurrection. In 1456 the Wardens of the "ludi de
resureccione" brought a plea of debt against John Lyly.[22] In 1463–64 the
Chamberlains' accounts include expenses "pro ludo interludii Passionis Domini."[23] At some point the play began to be produced over more than one day:
in 1497–98 Richard Fuller was paid 12d. for "prompting" (*?monicione*) the
players on two days.[24] The accounts for the 1499–1500 production are the
first to provide us with any detail. Apparently, there were two productions, but

---

18. I will refer to the records published by Giles E. Dawson, but I have also had access to materials deposited by James Gibson at the office of the Records of Early English Drama. Dawson's tran-
scripts are in *Plays and Players in Kent*, 118–43, 202–11.
19. The transcription is from James Gibson. This was a Robin Hood *ludus* in 1532–33 (Dawson, *Plays and Players in Kent*, 133).
20. All transcriptions are from Gibson.
21. Dawson, *Plays and Players in Kent*, 91.
22. The transcription is from Gibson.
23. Dawson, *Plays and Players in Kent*, 120.
24. "Pro labore suo pro monicione lusoribus duobus temporibus" (ibid., 126).

if the play included a Passion and a Resurrection, then it is possible that the two actions were separated by several days, the first being acted on Good Friday and the second on Easter Sunday or Monday, as is envisioned in the Bodley e Museo text.[25] The performance was cried at the parishes of Ivychurch, Folkstone, Hythe, Lydd, and Brokeland, and there are also receipts for the banns from six persons who are named in the account.[26] It is not clear whether these are representatives of other parishes or whether they were collectors of some sort. To prepare the space, the playing field was mowed and a hell and a heaven constructed.[27] Thomas Taylor made the Tormenters' garments and William Bukherst their heads.[28] There are occasional references to a *ludus,* presumably the same, in the years that follow.

The New Romney *Passion* apparently underwent several revisions in the sixteenth century. We first hear of "le Pleyboke" in 1516, when we are told that the Jurats and the Commonalty gathered on 14 December to elect wardens for holding the play as they were accustomed from ancient times.[29] The book was entrusted to the clerk of the Commonalty, Robert May, for safekeeping and in the following July was transferred to William Bukherste. During this period there was trouble about the play. On 26 May 1517 the Warden of the Cinque Ports sent a mandate to the Jurats that they ought not to perform the play until they had a license of the king ("quod non debent ludere lusum de passione Christi quoque habuerunt licenciam Regis").[30] In 1528–29 there was "a nother [Commission] concernyng no stage plays."[31] It is by no means clear

25. Baker, Murphy, and Hall, *Late Medieval Religious Plays,* lxxiv–xcix, 141–93. The texts were written ca. 1520 by a Carthusian. The prologue suggests that the text was originally intended as a meditation to be read, but the author then gave directions for its performance: at the foot of the second page, he says, "This is a play to be played, on part on Gud Friday afternone, and þe other part opon Ester Day after the resurrection in the morowe" and adds that lines 1–15 "shuld not be said if it be plaied." The text is not fully realized as a drama since it reports events rather than shows them, reports character's emotions, and emphasizes memory rather than sight.

26. The information is from Gibson.

27. Ibid.: Paid "Thome Bursell pro Campanis pro inferno" [bells for Inferno]; paid the said "Thome pro le garnysshynge de heven & pro le takyng down & pro le lambes [lights]."

28. Transcription from Gibson: "to Thomas Taylor for makyng of the Tormentours garmentes iijs. iiijd."; "payd to that same William [Bukherst] for makyng of the tormentours hedes iiijd."

29. Ibid.

30. Ibid.

31. Dawson, *Plays and Players of Kent,* 133. James Gibson has told me that a search of the Cinque Port records and the Public Record Office did not yield the commission. It is possible that the Jurats acted out of a misunderstanding of a proclamation issued 6 March 1529 against heresy, unlicensed preaching, and heretical books; perhaps they feared that the play contained inappropriate material. See Hughes and Larkin, *Tudor Royal Proclamations,* 1:181–86.

why the Passion was stopped, but at roughly the same time the town began negotiations with Richard Gibson concerning remaking or refurbishing it. Gibson had obtained property in New Romney by 1513–14. He was elected a jurat in 1524, served the Cinque Ports as solicitor to the king and council, and in 1529 represented New Romney in Parliament.[32] In 1525–26 an emissary, sent to London to see Gibson, took "the byll of our arrayment for the play" and, as a gift, a fish. A fish was sent to Gibson in each of the next two years. In 1532–33 Simon Huntington was sent to Gibson in London "to know his mynde of our play," and in 1533–34 there were further expenditures on Gibson.[33]

The Richard Gibson of these records had begun his career as one of Henry VII's players of interludes. This troupe was identified with him by 1505–9, before he turned to the production side of revels. By the time of his death early in 1534 he had been involved with court revels and entertainments for forty years. For much of his later career he was in charge of procuring artists and craftsmen, building materials, costumes, and properties for court festivities, for all of which he kept painstaking accounts. At the Field of Cloth of Gold, according to Sidney Anglo, "he was involved in the production of all the masks and magnificences, including the provision of materials for the Tree of Chivalry."[34] He was a deviser of extravaganzas. In 1512, under the direction of Sir Harry Guildford, he arranged a pageant castle and dungeon, "Le Fortress dangerous," which was assaulted by Henry VIII and five other lords;[35] in 1513 he was involved in preparing a royal pageant called the "Riche Mount" on which were set precious stones, herbs, roses, and a burning beacon with six lords and six ladies, all of which was drawn by wildmen;[36] and during the royal jousts of 1524–25, he arranged a great timber pageant, the Castle of Loyalty, which was equipped with drawbridges, ditches, and bulwarks, for assaults in the tiltyard.[37] Sidney Anglo argues that when Gibson died, Tudor court festivities went into decline because he was the last of the great producers of revels and the one longest involved.

When the citizens of New Romney submitted their applications in 1525–26

---

32. This information was supplied by James Gibson.

33. From Dawson, *Plays and Players of Kent,* 132–33, and Gibson.

34. Anglo, *Spectacle, Pageantry, and Early Tudor Policy,* 164–65, 179, 261–62;

35. Lancashire, *Dramatic Texts,* xxii, xxvii, item 100.

36. Streitberger, "Development of Henry VIII's Revels Establishment," with frequent references in his *Court Revels.*

37. Lancashire, *Dramatic Texts,* item 718.

and the early 1530s, Richard Gibson was the finest producer of theatrical extravaganzas in England, yet he was not known for producing dramas, and one wonders whether he was engaged simply to enhance the technical side of the New Romney spectacle. Or was the mission in 1532–33 intended to get Gibson's support for the revival of the play after the commission forbidding stage plays in 1528? We do not know, but the records tell us that in 1540 there was a rehearsal in Lent in and other expenditures "when the ground and stage for our pley was appointed."[38]

Nor do we know what happened between the early 1540s and the accession of Mary, but there was a performance in 1555 and subsequently a "new play" in 1560. Having in mind earlier prohibitions, the Jurats for the first version sent someone "to [the] lorde warden to have his good wyll touchyng o^r playe." John Forcett was hired to write out the parts of the play. Three recognizances survive that list the players and their parts for the "stage play" at the feast of Pentecost.[39] Although there is one curious omission—no mention of Christ—the cast lists are sufficiently detailed to indicate that the play began with the raising of Lazarus and the healing of the blind man. The twelve disciples attend Christ. All the characters for the appearances before Pilate, Caiaphas, and Annas—and Herod, for the trials, flagellation, and scourging—are named. The Tormentors have allegorical names: Mischance, False-at-Need, Untrust, Faintheart, Unhappe, and Evil Grace. The third list includes Malcus, so there must have been a capture. Simon of Cyrene adds the road to Calvary, and presumably there is a Passion (with the Virgin, Mary Salome—and Mary Magdalene?). Although only two are cited, there are three devils, perhaps indicating a Harrowing and thus, presumably a Resurrection. There is also a Doctor, perhaps an expositor.[40]

The 1560 *Passion* was apparently revised or corrected in some way, since it is called a "new play"; there are also several large sums paid out for copying both the text and the parts.[41] Gover Martin, the deviser, was paid 26s. 8d. in wages and an additional 20s. for his labor at the fourth play. Again John Forcett wrote out the parts and then was paid 20s. for writing the book on parchment. To advertise, the town sent out four banns-criers and a fool (they

---

38. Gibson also aided Lydd with its Saint George play.

39. Dawson, *Plays and Players of Kent,* 137, 202–4.

40. The play may have faltered again at Mary's death; there is a payment in 1556–57: "Item payd to Rychard Owton for his paynes in goyng to Rye to speke to the waytes for our playe yat shulde have byn played xijd" (ibid., 137).

41. Ibid., 204–11.

bought beards and wigs for the five in London). We get a peek at the preparations from a memorandum that lists the inhabitants of New Romney who were in church on 28 February 1560, to arrange for the play at Whitsuntide. The bailiff, Simon Padyham, was to provide his own stage; Mr. Cheseman 20s., if he incurred no further obligations; and the others, labor, money, or a combination. There was at least one rehearsal, on 31 March, when beer was brought to the church for the players. The set included Pilate's and the Princes' stage, Anna's stage and the Tormentors', the Pharisees' stage (presumably Caiaphas'), Herod's stage, heaven, the cave (the tomb?), and hell, and there is a subsequent reference to the city of Samaria. The stages suggest an action something like that for 1555; however, there are few references to roles or costumes in the 1560 account. Unlike the earlier performance, there was a Baptism play, as is indicated by payment for John's coat. There are also coats for the First and Second Godhede and for Judas. Presumably there was a now-missing set of recognizances that assigned roles.[42]

The play seems to have been intended to have three performances, but the town must have felt that their success deserved a fourth. The account gives the following receipts: £12 15s. 6d., for the Monday after Whitsun; £7 11s. 3d. ob., for the play on 14 July, a Sunday; and £4 9s. 1d. ob., for the play on 3 August, a Sunday.[43] There is a second set of expenditures for writing out the play book and the parts of the last play and a payment to the scribe for fourteen quires of paper lent to the diviser. Once again there is payment for Judas' coat, sheepskins for the Godhead's coat, and a paschal lamb for the play. There is no date given for this fourth play, and the duplication of some of the costs is puzzling; nevertheless, the record suggests that the town produced the same play four times rather than stretching the action out over four days. The play apparently continued to be performed into the early 1560s, but when it ceased is unknown.[44]

The records for three of the other four ports in Kent, Dover, Hythe, and Sandwich, as well as for some of the neighboring towns, are scattered and often late, but none seems to have had a spectacle as elaborate as that of the New

---

42. This is Gibson's suggestion.

43. The accounting for expenditures on plays in the Middle Ages is notoriously inaccurate; my addition for the Chester records revealed that the accounts rarely balanced. At New Romney there is a similar discrepancy in the accounting for the first play: Receipts for the first day are £14 5s. 6d. Expenses listed at bottom of p. 22 are £8 14s. 1d. (these are difficult to read, so they may not be exact).

44. See the decree, dated 1568, in Dawson, *Plays and Players in Kent*, 211.

Romney *Passion*. New Romney was the center of the Cinque Ports—the Brod-hull usually met there—and perhaps their centrality created the desire to an-nounce the town's prestige with a play of Christ's Passion. But the play was also clearly a financial venture: leading citizens of the town were willing to lend money for the production; many of the citizens pledged money and time. De-spite the vagaries of medieval accounting, it appears that the play in the six-teenth century was a successful commercial venture.[45]

New Romney was a small town in itself but had a network of nearby towns on which it could rely in its fund-raising activities. If we look to a more promi-nent town, Exeter, in a rather sparsely populated area, Devon, we find a more subdued pattern of activity. Exeter, an important market town with a popula-tion in 1377 of about 2,340, was governed by a mayor and a council of twenty-four, almost exclusively wealthy merchants engaged in the wool industry, the wine trade, and other shipping. After 1537 Exeter was a county and ranked fifth or so outside London in wealth and population.[46] Yet there is little evi-dence of drama or other very elaborate ceremonial tradition in the city. Exeter is also a cathedral city; indeed, it was the seat of the reforming bishop, John de Grandisson, and others. Except for prohibitions and warnings in the bishops' registers, the extensive cathedral records produce disappointingly few refer-ences to early drama. John Wasson, the editor of the Exeter records, concludes: "What seems clear is that the bishops were eager to suppress profane and scur-rilous plays and that neither dean and chapter nor vicars choral [who ran day-to-day operations] were fundamentally interested in religious drama. The emphasis was always on processions."[47]

The city seems to have had some kind of Corpus Christi play early in the fif-teenth century, a tradition that was continued in some form by the Skinners' Guild in the late fifteenth century.[48] By the end of the fifteenth century the city

---

45. In 1562 Chelmsford mounted an elaborate series of four plays; however, it was a financial failure and the town seems not to have ventured into drama again. The investment of more than £21 resulted in a loss of £11. See Coldewey, "Digby Plays."

46. Wasson, *Devon*, xviii; Hoskins, "Ranking of Provincial Towns," in *Local History*, 177.

47. Wasson, *Devon*, xvi.

48. The Skinners were cited in a court case in 1414 for not performing their sections of the Cor-pus Christi play along with the other guilds (Wasson, *Devon*, 82–83). The instructions from the mayor indicate there were speeches in each of the pageants, but the scanty evidence allows that these were pageants in procession rather than biblical dramas. The *ludus* was called a *solempnitate* in 1489–90. It is impossible to know why the Skinners were so angry in 1414 that they refused to participate in the play, but since they ended up with full responsibility in the late fifteenth century, perhaps they had initiated the custom and were annoyed when the city extended participation to other guilds.

was making a gift of 10s. to the Skinners for maintenance of the Corpus Christi guild and their play *(lusum; pro lusione facta)*.[49] We do not know what this "lusum" was, but it was presumably smaller than that of the procession earlier in the century.

Otherwise the city's entertainments were much like those one might find elsewhere. There was a procession of the mayor and the guilds on the night of the feast of Saint John Baptist with pipers and a harper.[50] Although the city welcomed the usual traveling companies, fools, and other entertainers, it had its own three waits who were engaged, according to an order of 1544–45, to play before the Watch at midsummer and Saint Peter's Night and at the election of the new mayor and when he took his oath.[51] Among the churchwardens' accounts, some of which are early, we find payments for feasts on Saint George's day, church ales, processions, archery contests, and Robin Hood games. John Wasson has shown that Saint George and Robin Hood *ludi* and games were common throughout Devon, but it is not clear that any of these were dramas.[52]

If one looks at a town in a relatively strategic but somewhat isolated place, the situation does not differ that much from Exeter's. Bristol (Gloucestershire), which had been made a county in 1373, ranked second among the provincial towns in 1377 and second in amount of subsidy paid in 1523–27, yet in the surviving records, there is little to attest to ceremonial activity other than processions and the occasional pageant for a royal welcome.[53] Guilds went in procession with relatively simple pageants at midsummer, Corpus Christi, or Saint Peter's, but Mark Pilkington has speculated that these pageants were small enough to be borne by one person, though the Wiredrawers and Pinmakers

---

49. Wasson, *Devon*, 106–10. The payments begin 1481 and end in 1497. We should note the small amount of subsidy; this sum is less than that paid to earl's and king's players. The guild ordinances for the Merchant Tailors (from 1466–67), the Cordwainers (1481), and the Bakers (1483) do not indicate responsibility for the Corpus Christi play (Smith, *English Gilds*, 312–16, 324–30, 331–34, 334–35.

50. See Wasson, *Devon*, 84, for 1415–16.

51. Ibid., 139.

52. Wasson, "*St. George* and *Robin Hood Plays* in Devon," 66–69. Robin Hood, his band of followers, and sometimes Little John, Friar Tuck, and the Maid Marion appear at parish ales and games in the Thames and Severn Valleys as well, but, oddly, not in Nottinghamshire (according to John Coldewey, the editor of the Nottinghamshire records). Maid Marion, as well as Friar Tuck at times, seems to have been associated with Morris dancers rather than with Robin Hood games. See MacLean, "King Games and Robin Hood"; and Johnston, "Robin Hood of the Records."

53. Pilkinton, "Pageants in Bristol"; Pilkington, *Bristol*. Bristol was a major center for trade with Ireland, Spain, and France, as well as being an important regional economic center (*Bristol*, xvi–xx).

seem to have enhanced theirs by 1530 to include an image that required two bearers.[54] The pageants were accompanied by torchbearers.

These records tell us that even wealthy and important towns did not always elect to indulge in extravagant ceremonial, being content instead with processions with relatively simple accoutrements. They do not give us their reasons for their choices. Some were undoubtedly economic; others political. Perhaps the civic government was weak. Perhaps there was not the critical mass of population necessary to larger enterprises. I will return to these matters in chapter 4, where we will look at the activities of some of the larger cities.

Practice: Parishes

If we move down the ecclesiastical hierarchy and from the regular to the secular clergy, we find that despite canon law, synodal legislation, and reformist directives, clerical authorities were least successful in maintaining decorum and controlling *ludi* at the parish level even though we can see over time the institution of more decorous observance in parishes.[55] Robert Grosseteste had exhorted his clergy that they were not to attend on *"mimi, joculatores, aut histriones,"* to play at dice or archery contests, nor assist *"histriones,"* all forbidden, he says, by the doctrines of the holy fathers.[56] Furthermore, his archdeacons were to prohibit wrestling, tilting at quintains, scotales, and other *ludi inhonesti* of the laity in the churchyard and cemetery. Grosseteste was not alone in trying to protect sacred precincts and to impose an aura of sanctity on clerical and lay recreations, yet many of these activities continued well into the sixteenth century and necessarily had the support of the parish clergy. The resistance to reform at this level no doubt had a variety of reasons: ales were fun and were used quite widely as the means to raise funds for church ornaments and repairs. I also suspect that the parish priest, who helped promote the ales by calling the banns, was less inclined to separate himself from lay *spectacula* than the higher or monastic clergy because he was very much a part of the village or parish, perhaps even from one of the local families, and certainly economically bound to the fortunes of the community. If he lived in a rural parish, he had his glebe land to farm, thus making him both a parson and a plowman.

---

54. Pilkinton, *Bristol*, xxix, 39. The records for the processions are at 15–16, 48, 63–64.

55. There has been some excellent work on English parish life of late: Haigh, *English Reformations*, 25–39; Duffy, *Stripping of the Altars*, 131–54, 478–503; French et al., *Parish in English Life*.

56. Grosseteste, *Epistolae*, letter 52, 159.

Parish ales or related activities were commercial ventures intended to bring money to the parish church for the purchase of ornaments and ritual objects or the sustentation of the fabric.[57] Although these were common throughout England, the accounts of the churchwardens of Henley, Oxfordshire, provide one example of the annual cycle of parish activities. There were three gatherings of money: On Hock Monday by the women, on Hock Tuesday by the men, and at Pentecost.[58] From elsewhere we know that the Hock Monday custom allowed women to capture and bind men, holding them for ransom. The Tuesday event reversed the situation: the bachelors in the towns captured the women. Proceeds from Hock Monday tend to be much larger than those for Hock Tuesday. At Henley the Hock Tuesday gathering came from the "ludi de Robyn hode," probably not a play but a disguising of the young men as Robin and his fellows, who then went about gathering their alms. The Pentecost *ludus* is variously called the "Kinge pley," the "King Game," the "Regia lusione," or the "king ale." We learn that in 1531–32 Richard Numan played the "diser" (disour, a jester or entertainer) at Whitsuntide, which suggests the king at times may have been a fool figure (see the 1550–51 account). Elsewhere king games or *ludi* of the king and queen of May seem to have been occasions on which the locals chose their royal couple to preside over feasts and entertainments for which they constructed bowers, often in the fields, as at Shrewsbury.[59] Sally-Beth MacLean and Alexandra Johnston have shown that these activities are typical throughout the Thames Valley region.[60]

Hocktide gatherings and Robin Hood games fall into the category of the carnivalesque; they have in common overindulgence and (temporary and non-

---

57. Bennett, "Conviviality and Charity"; Hutton, *Rise and Fall;* and Johnston, "Summer Festivals."

58. The items cited from Henley are from Alexandra Johnston's transcriptions at the Record of Early English Drama office. In Henley there was also a Corpus Christi procession, which had four torchbearers about the sacrament and an unknown number of "payantes." In 1511 the borough agreed to make annual payment to Thomas Shelbourne, chaplain, for his labor concerning the Resurrection play and the procession ("circa lusum resurreccionis \ & processionem") on the Sunday in the Octave of Easter, the day before Hock Monday. See MacLean's "Hocktide."

59. The first notice of this practice at Shrewsbury is in 1445–6: "Item pro expensis domine de Talbot vsoris Magistri Iohannis Talbot ad iantaculum suum & in vino expendito dictam dominam in Mansione sua ad lusum, extra Muros in septimana pentecostes duobus diebus" (Somerset, *Shropshire*, 1:134). Somerset reads this as a reference to a two-day stage play (2:387), but I think it's a May game or feast in the fields outside the town. On summer kings and queens, see Billington, *Mock Kings*, 55–85.

60. MacLean, "Festive Liturgy"; Johnston, "Summer Festivals"; and Johnston and MacLean, "Reformation and Resistance."

threatening) inversions of the social and patriarchal orders. We get one cleric's view of hockings in a letter of 1450 from John Carpenter, bishop of Worcester, to John Lawern, almoner of the cathedral church and to every rector, vicar, or chaplain in the diocese.[61] The bishop complains of "Hock days," after the solemn feast of Easter has ended, in which women bind men one day and men women on another (or next) day "and to do worse things . . . in full view of passers-by, even pretending to increase church profit but earning a loss for the soul under false pretences." Many scandals, adulteries, and other outrageous crimes arise from the occasion of these activities and are a clear offense to God and a very serious danger to the souls of those committing them. Carpenter orders them to cease and desist from these bindings and other unsuitable pastimes *(ludis inhonestis),* to instruct the populace in sermons, and to report delinquents to the consistory court before the feast of Pentecost following.[62] The most revealing phrase is "in full view of passers-by"; it is not just that women capture men but that they do it in public, undoubtedly in Carpenter's mind a threat to social hierarchy.

Some scholars have read such Bakhtinian celebrations as situations in which ruling authorities relax their control only that they might reinstate it.[63] We must observe, however, that these *ludi* are not only instigated by the local populace but they are also in defiance of reforming bishops and the regular clergy. John Carpenter, it is clear, sees no virtue in allowing relaxations of this kind. Here we have an instance in which modern theoretical models clash with the realities of the medieval situation.[64]

An alternative to suppression was the substitution of practices thought appropriate to Christian communities. Bishop Grandisson, who acted vigorously against clerical and lay *ludi inhonesti,* promoted processions as more appropriate forms of lay religious observance.[65] The general theory seems to have been that the laity should have practices that had the decorum of religious observances without necessarily duplicating liturgical practice. Simultaneously, there seems to be lay co-option of clerical practice. The most obvious example

---

61. Klausner, *Herefordshire /Worcestershire,* 553–54. Klausner's translation follows.

62. Similarly, in article 4, under *Chorea,* John Bromyard, rather more graphically, warns that just as the arms are tied in play, so will be tied together the fasci for burning; just as the participants sinned together, so they will be punished together *(Summa predicantium,* fol. 153b).

63. Stallybrass and White, *Politics and Poetics,* 13.

64. Alexandra Johnston has pointed out that these were communal celebrations that cut across various barriers of class, age and sex; see "Summer Festivals," 54.

65. Wasson, *Devon,* xxix–xxx.

of the latter is the ubiquitous celebration of the Deposition and Resurrection of Christ at Easter.[66] Originally begun as a monastic observance, the Deposition and Resurrection was embedded in the Sarum Use and thus became common throughout England. However, a practice that was once largely hidden from the laity—until the cloth of the resurrected Lord was shown in the nave—became very much a part of lay worship. In churchwardens' accounts of the late fifteenth and the sixteenth century we find expenditures for the preparation of the sepulchre, for watching the sepulchre, and for lights during the vigil. Testators frequently provide for sepulchres or sepulchre cloths or ask to be buried near the Easter sepulchre. Margery Kempe testifies to the emotional impact of the ceremony, an impact no doubt exaggerated in her case but not unlike the descriptions we get of the intense pressure to see the host at its elevation:[67]

> On a Good Fryday, as þe sayd creatur behelde preystys knelyng on her kneys & oþer worschepful men wyth torchys brennyng in her handys be-for þe Sepulcre, deuowtly representyng þe lamentabyl deth and doolful berying of owr Lord Ihesu Crist aftyr þe good custom of Holy Cherch, þe mende of owr Ladijs sorwys whech sche suffryd whan sche behelde hys precyows body hangyng on þe Crosse & sithyn berijd be-for hir syght sodeynly ocupijd þe hert of þis creatur, drawyng hir mende al holy in-to þe Passyon of owr Lord Crist Ihesu, whom sche behelde wyth hir gostly eye in þe syght of hir sowle as verily as þei sche had seyn hys precyows body betyn, scorgyd, & crucifyed wyth hir bodily eye, whech syght & gostly beheldyng wrowt be grace so feruently in her mende, wowndyng hir wyth pite & compassyon, þat sche sobbyde, roryd, & cryed.[68]

Margery's account comes to focus on the great emotional disturbance caused by her participation in this celebration, but she also testifies, in this "good custom of Holy Cherch," to the participation of priests and other worshipful people, all of whom kneel with burning candles in their hands. This moving ritual, the anticipation of the resurrection of the body, well might induce in the participants memories of Mary's sorrows and Christ's flagellation, scourging, and crucifixion.

It also would appear that parishes—and towns—borrowed the boy bishop from ceremonies at monasteries, cathedrals and schools.[69] Many parishes in-

---

66. Sheingorn, *Easter Sepulchre in England.*

67. Rubin, *Corpus Christi,* 54–63.

68. Kempe, *Book of Margery Kempe,* 139–40.

69. Chambers, *Mediaeval Stage,* 1:336–71; K. Young, *Drama of the Medieval Church,* 1:106–10. For example, the boy bishop appears in London parish records at Saint Mary at Hill (from

clude inventories of garments for boy bishops, either Saint Nicholas or Saint Thomas Becket; churchwardens accounts list costs and income from their appearances. In East Anglia, Essex, Kent, Selby Abbey in Yorkshire, and other places, it is apparent that the local boy bishop traveled from his residence to other towns and institutions. Within his own milieu he often circulated through the parish or town. For monasteries and cathedrals we have a liturgy in which the boy selected for the year replaced the usual celebrant.[70] The practice at the parish or town level seems to require the child to ride or walk; there are no indications in the records that he performed a script. In both venues, however, we have a situation in which the boy bishop collects money; thus, his activities are like those of mummers, disguisers, plow boys, and others who embark on their *quête,* a practice that lies somewhere between seeking donations and holding people to ransom. The liturgy for the clerical boy bishops, usually Saint Nicholas, seems to have been intended to allow license within restrictions but apparently often erupted into disorder. We might see the parish and civic adaptation of the boy bishop as a regularization of or substitution for a less obviously Christian practice.

All of these activities at the parish level—the various *ludi,* scotales, and somergames—bring together groups of people in an untypical relationship that fits, in general, Turner's sense of *communitas,* that is, one of those antistructural situations in which there is a greater degree of equality than usual and that has the effect of renewing the society that it temporarily abandons.[71] The parish ales seem to be fairly simple relaxations of social structures for recreational purposes and economic gain. They create a sense of *communitas* in several ways: first, they temporarily suspend the hierarchy within the parish; and, second, they invite others into the parish from outside. Although I doubt that the parish hierarchy was ever entirely annihilated (would the Wife of Bath

---

1432), the inventory of Saint Peter Westcheap (1431), the inventories of Saint Nicholas Shambles (1469 and 1499), the records of Saint Andrew Hubbard (1487–88), and even more frequently in parish records of the sixteenth century. This information comes from Mary Erler's transcriptions at the REED office. Boy bishops were prohibited by royal proclamation in 1541: "children be strange-lye decked and apparelid to counterfaite priestes, bysshopps, and women; and so ledde with songes and daunces from house to house, bleassing the people and gatherynge of monye; and boyes doo singe masse, and preache in the pulpitt, with suche other unfittinge and inconvenyent usages, rather to the derision than to any true glory of God" (Wilkins, *Concilia Magnae Britanniae,* 3:860; Hughes and Larkin, *Tudor Royal Proclamations,* 1:302).

70. Chambers, *Mediaeval Stage,* 2:282–87, prints the Sarum office; and see Bailey, *Processions of Sarum,* 19.

71. Turner, *Ritual Process.* See also McRee, "Unity or Division?"

give up her need to be first?), the competition of the games and the sharing of food and drink would tend to dissolve or at least temporarily redirect social tension. Opening the parish up to outsiders—even though motivated by the desire for money—acknowledges that there is a larger Christian community. Presumably many clerics supported these efforts or at least did not find them totally offensive since they survived for several centuries. Indeed, I suspect that the reformist clergy objected not so much to the activities per se as to the fact that they took place within sacred precincts, especially cemeteries. Not only might drinking and dancing lead to lechery, and thus pollution of the sacred area, but these activities could be construed as threats to clerical supremacy and hierarchy, hence the inclination to construct them as demonic imitations of God's liturgy, as John Bromyard does in his *Summa predicantium*.[72]

Practice: Parish Religious Guilds

When we dip below the parish level to consider religious guilds, we find that most of them are too small to organize festive occasions or ceremonial activities of any grandeur.[73] If we consider the 471 parish guild returns of 1389 analyzed by Westlake, we see that their most common purpose was to provide a large candle for the altar or image of the saint on his or her feast day, though some, for example, Corpus Christi, All Saints, or Holy Trinity guilds, may simply have placed the candle in the chapel associated with the guild.[74] Only 74 (15.7 percent) of the guilds specify that they participate in processions, either on their own or as groups within larger processions, such as Corpus Christi. Of the fifty-two guilds associated with Lynn (Norfolk), only seven list processions; similarly, of the nineteen guilds of Norwich (Norfolk), only seven specify that they go in procession. Sixteen Lincoln guilds—some of crafts, others religious—assembled at various locations to process with their candles to the cathedral church or the mother church of their guild, though the Guild of the Blessed Virgin Mary, the Cordwainers' guild, had in their assembly Mary, Joseph, Saint Blaise, and two angels. Within seven other towns of Lincolnshire, sixteen guilds went in procession, all on the feast of Corpus Christi. Some of these had fairly substantial commitments; for example, the guilds of Boston

---

72. See Bromyard's descriptions under *Bellum* and *Chorea*.

73. There are some religious guilds that are quite large, both ones that constitute the governing bodies of cities (for which, see chapter 4, below) and ones that have the more usual spiritual functions. In this section, I consider only smaller religious guilds within the parish.

74. Westlake, *Parish Gilds*, appendix, 137–238; Barron and Wright, "London Middle English Guild Certificates"; and McRee, "Unity or Division?"

carried either twelve or sixteen torches each; the twelve guildsmen in the Guild of the Apostles at Louth were dressed as the apostles. Processions seem quite common in Lincolnshire; by contrast, only one of the thirty-one guilds of London specifies that it goes in procession. There are only a few guilds that suggest that they have quasi-dramatic or ceremonial activities. The Pater Noster Guild at York was responsible for the Pater Noster play. The Corpus Christi Guild of Bury St. Edmund's provided lights in the church and an (unspecified) *interludum* on Corpus Christi. The Guild of Saint Helen and Saint Mary, at the church of the Friars Minor in Beverley, processed on Saint Helen's Day with an old man with a cross and another with a spade and a youth dressed as Queen Helen in tokening of the finding of the Cross. Rather more representational were the activities of the Guild of the Purification of the Blessed Virgin Mary. The members assembled at a set place in order to process to the church with a person clad as the Virgin with the "appearance" of her son in her arms and with Joseph, Simeon, and two angels. The Virgin is followed by the sisters and then the brothers, each with a light. At the church the Virgin offers her son to Simeon at the altar and all the brothers make an offering.

The guild inventories of 1547 suggest that activities at this level remained modest (boy bishops, prophets, costumed processors and the like).[75]

Communitas: The Play of Saints in Late Medieval and Tudor England

In my discussion of practice thus far,[76] there have been few references to saint plays, yet the standard histories of medieval drama are nearly uninamous in the opinion that though we have only a few texts of saint plays, the documentary records indicate that there were many more. The list includes dramatizations of events in the lives of Saints George, Thomas Becket, Mary Magdalene, Cuthbert, Nicholas, Rosemont, Swithin, Andrew, Eustace, Margaret, Lucy, Martin, Catherine, Christina, Feliciana, Sabina, Francis, James the Apostle, Thomas the Apostle, Agnes, Edmund, Elizabeth, Julian the Apostate, Paul, Denis, Christian, Fabianus, Sebastianus, Blythe, John the Evangelist, Meriasek, John the Baptist, Lawrence, Susanna, Clare, Holy John of Bowre, and Saint Trin-

---

75. See chapter 4 below for a summary of London practice. Other guild inventories are to be found scattered through the REED volumes.

76. The following section contains excerpts from and the conclusions in my essay of the same title in *Mediaevalia*. I have not repeated all the analysis in that essay. Responses to my conclusions are in Davidson, "British Saint Play Records," and MacLean, "Saints on Stage." See also Davidson, "Saints in Play."

ity.[77] I remain skeptical that there were many saint plays in England from the later medieval period to the Reformation or during the reign of Mary; consequently, my principal argument will be that we have lumped together a variety of lay and clerical activities held on saints' feast days as saint plays when the records cannot support the contention that they are enactments of the vita of a saint.[78]

I believe that we have misread records of the *miracula* of young *clerici* as well as lay parish ales and somergames, all of which took place on saints' or other feast days, as saint plays. These misreadings have resulted in our imposing a pious structure of devotion to saints (through enactment of their lives) onto antistructure, that free play allowed outside the constraints of society. The culprits here are the words *ludus* and "pley," neither of which necessarily denotes dramatic representation.

The impreciseness of this terminology creates difficulties for interpreting a record of the type *"Ludus de sancta Katerina"* from the Dunstable annals (circa 1100–1119).[79] The assumption might be that this is a play *about* Saint Catherine; however, as I argued above, this *ludus* was a *miracula* (a raucous celebration by choirboys) that was to have taken place on the eve of the feast of Saint Catherine. Two other illustrations will demonstrate the possible flaws in the assumption that *"ludus de* [saint's name]" refers to a scripted play of a saint's life. In the churchwardens' accounts at Lincoln in the year 1323–24, there is an expenditure at Easter *"in Ludo de Sancto Thoma didimo."* The formula might suggest that this is a saint play, but accounts later in the sequence

---

77. The list has been compiled from the standard histories of Chambers, *Mediaeval Drama;* K. Young, *Drama of the Medieval Church;* Craig, *English Religious Drama of the Middle Ages,* and Cawley et al., *Medieval Drama;* from the Records of Early English Drama volumes for York, Chester, Coventry, Norwich, Newcastle, Devon, Gloucestershire, Cumberland, Westmoreland, Herefordshire, Cambridge, Worcestershire, Lancashire, Shropshire, Somerset, Bristol, Dorset, and Cornwall; from the Malone Society *Collections* for Lincoln, Sherbourne, Suffolk, Norfolk, Kent, and London; from Lanchashire's *Dramatic Texts* and his annual bibliographies, published in the *Records of Early English Drama Newsletter* for 1976–83 (5 [1980], 1–34; 7 [1982], 1–40; and 9 [1984], 1–56), and continued by Mary Blackstone for 1984–88 (15 [1990], 1–104); from Stratman's *Bibliography of Medieval Drama;* from essays in *Medieval English Theatre* and *Records of Early English Newsletter* cited below; from Davidson, *Saint Play in Medieval Europe;* and from Davidson's Web site, "Saint Plays and Pageants of Medieval Britain": http://www.wmich.edu/medieval/research/edam/saint.html. I should note that my criteria are narrower than Davidson's; see the headnote to my Appendix 2.

78. I use the term "saint play" to refer to enactments that depict the vita of a saint or some momentous event in the saint's life. The distinction is not wholly satisfactory: Saint George fighting a dragon at the end of a procession would not fall within my usage. Most "saint plays" would presumably have a spoken script based on the vita.

79. Paris, *Gesta abbatum,* 1:72–73.

make clear that the *ludus* is a liturgical *representatio,* in this case, some form of the *Peregrinus,* performed at Easter.[80] The second difficulty in records of this sort is that the *ludus* or "play" might not be an acted script at all. In 1505 the Mildenhall Guild of Saint Thomas had "a play off Sent Thom*as,*" for which Thetford Priory made payment to the "pley of Myldenale."[81] The phrasing of the churchwardens' account—"*a* play" rather than "the play"—opens the possibility that it may have been a Becket drama; however, the priory's other contributions that year were to "games" at Berdeswell, Walsham, and Gyslingham and to the "ludu*m* s*an*cti trinita*tis,*" which surely is not a play about a Saint Trinity but the *ludus* or game of St. Trinity's. In the Mildenhall accounts of 1540–41 the "pley" is glossed as a "chyrchall" (church ale).

Such entries provide evidence that the formulae "*Ludus de*" or "*Play of*" (1) cannot be assumed to be the name of a scripted play about the saint named but may be the name of a guild or church that produced the game or *ludus;* and (2) the "play" may be some kind of dramatic enactment but it may also be a festival. A *ludus,* "play," or "game," therefore, is first of all a civic, or more likely, a parish entertainment, a *spectaculum,* whose purpose is to raise funds. Such entertainments might include scripted plays about the patron saint or some other saint; however, they might simply be sports, contests, amusements, pageants, or any combination of these.

Some of the *ludi* that have been thought to be saint plays seem more nearly related to clerical *miracula.* The "play" of Saint Catherine at Shrewsbury (1525–26) included a lord of misrule and payments for heads of hair and beards, a dizard's (jester's) head, and materials for explosions and smoke. There is no expenditure for the saint herself.[82]

Some *ludi* are said "to be shown," suggesting that they are objects, either pageants or mechanical devices, which are displayed but in which there is little or no acted representation. Perhaps the most fully documented of these is the Assumption *visus* at Lincoln, which appears to have been a clockwork.[83]

---

80. Kahrl, *Plays and Players in Lincolnshire,* 24–25. See K. Young, *Drama of the Medieval Church,* 1:449, 464–66 (a *Peregrinus* text that includes Saint Thomas), and 689; and Davidson, "Middle English Saint Plays," 37–38.

81. Galloway and Wasson, *Plays and Players in Norfolk and Suffolk,* 106, 110 (Thetford Priory); 190, 192 (Mildenhall).

82. J. A. B. Somerset treats the record as evidence of a saint play; see "Local Drama," 2, 27. Sally-Beth MacLean does as well; see "Saints on Stage."

83. Kahrl, *Plays and Players in Lincolnshire,* 36–37. In subsequent years (e.g., 1485–86) there are payments for showing the *visus:* "pro ostencione Coronacionis beate Marie in festo sancte Anne."

Some *spectacula* are simply called pageants. Initially *pageant* meant "show," but even more specifically something that was painted or ornamented; the use of *pageant* to designate drama is a derived meaning. Consequently, in the records of the period, the word *pageant* may refer to a decorated mobile object (hence, "pageant wagon") that could function as a dramatic set (an extended meaning of "pageant") or it might be a tableau vivante in a painted set or a decorated object that could be carried but that had effigies or a portable shrine or tabernacle or even a painted cloth.[84] Saints appear frequently in pageants in procession, some of which have been erroneously cited as saint plays. For example, the London records of livery companies contain references to pageants, not saint plays, of Saint Blythe (1512), Thomas Becket (1519), the Virgin Mary and Elizabeth (1519), Saint John the Evangelist (1521, 1529, 1525, 1535), Saint Elizabeth (1536), and Saint Margaret (1541).[85]

The difficulty of establishing the kind of activity that occurred can be illustrated by the cases of the two most popular saints in England, Saint George and Saint Thomas Becket.[86] Of the claimants advanced as saint plays of Saint George, we have one possible instance of a representation of the saint's vita over a number of years (at Lydd) and perhaps another unique production (at York in 1554).[87] The 1511 accounts from Bassingbourne, Cambridgeshire, suggest some kind of event centered on the saint, but it is far from clear that it was a drama of the saint's life.[88] Most of our records imply that Saint George *ludi* were not enacted vitae; rather, the saint appeared in tableaux or pageants, where he may have presented a speech, or in the street, where he fought a

---

84. For the latter, see the payment for a vellum roll of "pagentes," "paynted and lemenyd with gold," in Basing, *Fraternity of the Holy Trinity,* 56. Also see Edwards, "Middle English Pageant 'Picture,'" 25–26. There is a curious usage in the Lincoln records in which a pageant is a place or area for selling (Kahrl, *Plays and Players of Lincolnshire,* 87–88); the guardians for the guilds are divided up to oversee "pagentes," groups of craftsmen.

85. These references are routinely cited as evidence of saint plays. Robertson and Gordon, *Calendar of Dramatic Records,* say there is little indication that the pageants even included speeches (xxi–xxii).

86. See Clopper, "*Communitas,*" 90–94, for analysis of the data on which these conclusions are based.

87. Ibid., 90–91; E. White, "'Bryngyng Forth of Saynt George.'"

88. There are no references to actors in the accounts. In 1500 there is payment of two pence for a "playe Book" and two pence for the "berer theroff," identified as John Best, clerk and taberer, and three pence for the minstrel. Since the 1511 event is clearly a unique occasion, these earlier references do not support the contention that this play book was a script for a Saint George play; rather, it suggests to me that the book was a musical compilation. I surveyed the documents deposited by Anne Brannen at the REED office. She has made the case that the accounts record a Saint George play in 1511; see her "Parish Play Accounts in Context."

dragon, or in folk plays, in which the champion of England fought a motley crew of clowns and Turks.[89]

The evidence for Saint Thomas Becket plays is equally sparse. William Fitz Stephen's description of London, which forms a prologue to his life of Becket, has often been cited as evidence for the earliness of saint plays, that is, dramas that depict the life of a saint, in this case of Thomas Becket:

> Londonia pro spectaculis theatralibus, pro ludis scenicis, ludos habet sanctiores, repraesentationes miraculorum quae sancti confessores operati sunt, seu repraesentationes passionum quibus claruit constantia martyrum.

> [Instead of spectacles of the theatre (public spectacles) or theatrical plays, London has holier *ludi*, representations of miracles made by holy confessors or representations of the passion which illuminate the constancy of martyrs.][90]

Note the careful distinction: Rather than *spectacula theatrales* or *ludi scenici*, London has *representationes* of the miracles of saints or their martyrdoms. The statement seems straightforward, but with what is London being compared? This section of the description is concerned with the *ludi*, games and sports of London, and not at all with Becket. Not only does London have these *representationes*, they also have ice skating, wrestling, and other sports. The unstated comparison is with ancient Rome, the implication being that London is superior in part because it has *representationes*, not *ludi scenici*, a phrase that probably derives from Isidore's description of the ancient *theatrum*. Are *representationes* saint plays? In this instance, I think not: Liturgical pieces such as the Nativity, Herod, and Rachel were rubricated as *ordo* or *ordo ad repraesentandum* because they ritually (re)present a historical event within liturgical time and space. These *representationes* are not enactments; rather, they are recreations and commemorations in which there is no audience but only participants. Indeed, Fitz Stephen may be referring to liturgies for saints like those for Becket that were eventually "razed" from every book in England.[91] Fitz

---

89. Davidson's Web site lists five references to Saint George other than those I have analyzed, of which three are to tableaux in royal entries or processions (Coventry, 1417, Hereford, 1486, and London, 1547) and two are to effigies in processions (Ipswich and Thame). Saint George also appears in folk "Hero-Combat" plays (see Cawley, *Medieval Drama*, 142–46).

90. Fitz Stephen, *Vita S. Thomae*, 3:9. Although Fitz Stephen does not specify that these are about Thomas, K. Young, *Drama in the Medieval Church*, 2:542, and Chambers, *Mediaeval Stage*, 2:379–80, assume that they are because the statement occurs in the *Vita*.

91. See Appendix 2, item 14.

Stephen perceives that Rome differs from London in cultic practice; liturgy has replaced obscenity.

There are not a great many references to Becket dramas. There is an expenditure of 3s. 4d. for persons playing the *interludium* of Saint Thomas the Martyr at Kyng's Lynn in 1385.[92] *Interludium* is a more specific term than *ludus,* so the Kyng's Lynn record may well be to a Becket play; nevertheless, it should be noted that in later entries, from he 1440s to the 1460s, the *ludus* is shown at a variety of times—Epiphany, in March, and at Corpus Christi—and that there are references to a tabernacle and to a Corpus Christi procession. There may be a variety of activities here, but the possibility remains that the *interludium* of 1385 was a singular occurrence of a saint play or that it was an activity of the guild members of Saint Thomas who carried a pageant or tabernacle in procession. Similarly, during the years 1501–38 there are fairly extensive records of a show or pageant at Canterbury that Dawson has said is certainly a debased survival of an old Saint Thomas play. The earlier records consistently called it a "pageant." The 1542–43 account refers to a "pley," for which there was a stage. Dawson regards this as evidence that there was a revival of an old Becket play.[93] The details in the earlier accounts make it quite clear that the pageant, which was transported by four knights, contained an effigy of the saint and a mechanical angel, called the "vice." The evidence that there was a Canterbury drama on the life of Saint Thomas seems thin.

None of the citations for Becket plays in the literature is secure; indeed, the analysis of the evidence for saint plays about these two most famous English saints does not yield very positive results. They are more show than tell. George is more likely to appear in a procession or tableau than a saint play; Becket is more likely to be a boy bishop than the focus of a drama. Most of the remaining "saint plays" can be shown to fall into one of two categories: they are things—objects, shrines, mechanical devices—to be seen rather than dramas enacted by performers, or they are activities reminiscent of the old *miracula* or somergames.

At the beginning of this section, I suggested that a saint play that enacted the vita of the saint was scripted and that other activities traveling under the title *"ludus de sancto X,"* such as parish ales and somergames, were largely unscripted. We must now take up the question whether there can be a *"Liber de sancto X"* that is not a script for a saint play. Although the general rule might

---

92. Galloway and Wasson, *Plays and Players in Norfolk and Suffolk,* 38.
93. Dawson, *Plays and Players in Kent,* 188–98.

appear to be that where there is a book, there is a scripted drama, some of the records are rather cryptic at times about what a "book" is. Both Lydd and New Romney had a book that was taken to Mr. Gibson in London for his perusal, and we know that the citizens of New Romney went to Lydd once in order to see their *"originalem,"* perhaps their book, since *"originalis"* is, according to Latham, an authentic and original or a complete document.[94] Lydd appears to have had a scripted saint play and New Romney a Passion play.

On the other hand, there are records that there were "books" for Corpus Christi and other celebrations that do not appear to be texts of scripted dramas. At Hereford, circa 1440, two men sued Thomas Sporyour over a book *"de lusionibus,"* but we have no other records to elucidate the case.[95] Nevertheless, the Register of the Corporation contains a list of the "paiantes for the procession of corpus christi," about which Chambers comments: "The 1503 list seems to concern a dumb-show only, and it cannot be positively assumed that the 'lusiones' of 1440 were a Corpus Christi play."[96] If the "vni libri de lusionibus" is synonymous with the list of 1503, then the "book" might simply be one that contains the order of the procession or other details of the *ludus* or game; such books might also contain the set speeches that figures sometimes gave in pageant processions and royal entries. Such an explanation seems more obvious for a 1492 order at Ipswich in which one John Regnerer is admitted to freedom on condition that he aid the "pagent *de Corpore Christi"* and correct the book of Corpus Christi.[97] There was no Corpus Christi drama at Ipswich; instead, there were tableaux in procession. Several copies of the procession were entered in the *Little Domesday and Book of Usages.*[98] Similarly, there are references to the "bokes off corpus Christi playe" at Sherbourne, and there was a "playe book" at Bassingbourne, but in neither case is it clear that the *ludus* was a scripted saint's vita.[99]

94. Latham, *Revised Medieval Latin Word-List,* 325.

95. Chambers, *Mediaeval Stage,* 2:368; Klausner, *Herefordshire,* 112, 278 n. *"Lusus"* connotes game or sport more than drama; the Henley *"Regia lusione"* is a king game.

96. Chambers, *Mediaeval Stage,* 2:369; David Klausner, the editor of the REED volume for Hereford, concurs (10–11).

97. "& scilicet erit auxiliator in omnibus pro le pagent de Corpore xpi' secundum suum Ingenium infaciendo & emendando librum Corporis xpi'" (Galloway and Wasson, *Plays and Players in Norfolk and Suffolk,* 175).

98. Ibid., 170, 171, 173–74.

99. A. Mills, "Corpus Christi Play," 1–15. The references to the "bokes" appear in inventories in 1545–48, and Mills believes that these indicate a drama of some sort. The most revealing records from Sherborne come from the 1570s (from another set of church accounts) where there are payments for meal for making Lot's Wife, "for gilting of a face for the playe," for "staynynge of Sodom

Given the ambiguity about what constitutes a "book," how are we to inter-pret the following two intriguing references from York? Robert Lasingby left to the parish of Saint Denis a cloth and "ludum oreginale Sancti Dionisij." The *York* editors translate this as a reference to a book of the play about Saint De-nis.[100] It would be more cautious to say that it was a book for the *ludus* of the parish and that we do not know what the *ludus* might have been. Similarly, in a will dated 1446 William Revetour left to the Guild of Saint Christopher "quemdam ludum de sancto Iacobo Apostolo in sex paginis compilatum" [a certain play of Saint James the Apostle compiled in six pages].[101] Because Revetour also gave the fraternity of Corpus Christi a "librum vocatum le Crede Play cum libris & vexillis eidem pertinentibus" [a book called the Creed Play with books and flags pertaining to the same], the editors concluded that the preceding reference was to a play about Saint James.[102] First, we must allow the possibility that the *ludus* is not about Saint James but a *ludus* of the chapel of Saint James on the Mount.[103] The chapel was not an insignificant place, for it was there that the procession for the coronation of a new archbishop began. But the *ludus* was given to the guild of Saint Christopher. This important guild had been amalgamated with that of Saint George around 1470.[104] The Saint Christopher's guild was involved in the Saint George riding, as is attested by the amalgamation of the two companies and the presence of the Saint Christo-pher effigy in the riding. I suspect that the *ludus de sancto Iacobo Apostolo* may be the book containing the orders for the riding. Although the evidence is indecisive, I do not think we may safely conclude that where there is a book, there is a scripted drama.

This analysis of *ludi* and plays containing saints' names suggests that the as-sumption that there were many saint plays in England is erroneous. We have certain evidence from extant texts or reliable references that there were Marian plays in the civic cycles. We have the Digby *Saint Paul* and *Mary Magdalen* and

---

clothes," and "for clothe and making of the vyse coote." For Bassingbourne, see my essay "*Com-munitas*," 91–92, and the note above.

100. Johnston and Rogerson, *York*, xvi, 88; note the city's payment in 1449 to the "ludentibus de parochia Sancti Dionisij," which suggests that the parish had musicians. Lasingby's will was pro-bated in 1456.

101. Ibid., 68.

102. Ibid., xvi.

103. The chapel of Saint James was in the Church of the Holy Trinity; see Tillott, *History of Yorkshire* 376.

104. E. White, "'Bryngyng Forth of Saynt George.'"

the Cornish *Life of Saint Meriasek*. Steven K. Wright has argued that the Ashmole Fragment may be from a Saint Lawrence play.[105] As noted above, Fitz Stephen says that there were "repraesentationes miraculorum quae sancti confessores operati sunt, seu repraesentationes passionum quibus claruit constantia martyrum" near the end of the twelfth century, but these may have been liturgical *representationes* rather than vernacular saint plays. There may have been a Saint George play at Lydd in the sixteenth century, one at York in 1554 in which the saint, a king, a queen, and a maid appeared, and a third at Bassingbourne. There may have been a play *(interludium)* of Saint Thomas at King's Lynn in 1385; the 1505 "play off Sent Thomas" at Mildenhall seems more doubtful to me. We have an alleged letter from Henry VIII concerning a religious interlude of Saint Thomas the Apostle, which was produced by papists and caused an uprising, but this may well have been a polemical drama like those Bale and others authored.[106] The remainder of the references sort themselves into categories ranging from uncertain to extremely unlikely. This uncertainty is compounded by the fact that the formula *"ludus de"* or *"play of"* may not be an indication of a drama about the saint at all but the entertainment, especially a church ale, of the guild or parish of that saint. It is much more likely that the average English person would have seen Robin Hood or the George, a dragon or the Margaret, or a boy bishop than a saint play.

I do not believe that the incomplete historical record can account for this paucity of evidence. To be sure, if we had more records, we would have more instances of saint plays, but we have enough representative records to indicate that there was not the widespread phenomenon that has been posited in the past. For example, the 1389 guild returns show no evidence of saint plays and only a few quasi-ceremonial representations of saints. Perhaps these returns are too early to register saint play activity, but if we turn to the Edwardian inventories, we do not find a significantly different situation. Many of the London inventories and the parish accounts, several of which go well back into the fifteenth century, contain records of Saint Nicholas bishops and other quasi-dramatic presentations (readings of the Passion or Palm Sunday prophets, for example) but no saint plays. If we look to areas that have extensive records of dramatic activity, East Anglia, Essex, and Kent (as opposed to the west of England), and if we focus on the late Middle Ages and early sixteenth century,

---

105. S. Wright, "Is the Ashmole Fragment a Remnant of a Middle English Saint Play?"
106. Johnston and Rogerson, *York*, 2:649–50.

when we would expect to find evidence of saint play activity, we do not find it.[107] Again, it is not that we do not have fairly extensive records of town expenditure on ceremony and spectacle but that there is little evidence of the performance of saint plays. Instead, we find processions on saints' feasts, church ales, and other games. If we had more records, we might come up with a few more saint plays, but the records we have indicate that there is not a tradition of saint plays in this dramatically rich area.[108]

My analysis may seem to some to have taken a great deal of the fun out of "merrye olde Englande," but I do not think that is the case, nor is it my intent. Rather, I have tried to suggest that the fun usually took a different form than a drama of a saint's vita. Most of the *ludi* I have described took place on the saint's feast day and thus—willy-nilly—honored the saint when the parishioners prepared a feast in the churchyard. Reformers countered that these *ludi inhonesti* defamed Christ and the saints because they were occasions of gluttony, which led to lechery, and that physical contests and games resulted in anger and quarreling. Nevertheless, promoters of parish *ludi*, "pleys," and games seem to have persisted in their endeavors at least until their saints themselves were put down.[109]

If we recall Gregory's model for the conversion of the pagan Anglo-Saxons, it is difficult not to see activities in the churchyard and around the church at spring or in the harvest months as continuations of pagan practice.[110] This is not to say that these festivities contained anything consciously pagan; nevertheless, many clerics, especially the upper hierarchy, maintained that they were profane and sacrilegious if not pagan, despite the laity's claim that these festivities were to the honor of Christ and his saints.

The church tried a dual approach to control: suppression and replacement;

---

107. Galloway and Wasson, *Plays and Players in Norfolk and Suffolk;* and Dawson, *Plays and Players in Kent.* I have also consulted James Gibson's more extensive transcriptions of Kent records at the office of the Records of Early English Drama and John Coldewey's of Essex (in his possession).

108. For further analysis, see my essay "Why Are There So Few English Saint Plays?"

109. Nevertheless, festive games seem to have continued, for well into the seventeenth century we find articles of inquiry whether there be "playes, feasts banquets Church-ales, drinkings, or any other prophane vsages to be kept in your church" (Somerset, *Shropshire,* 1:3 [for 1609], and see those for 1610, 1620, and 1632 that follow). These inquiries are not unique to Shropshire.

110. Bede, *History of the English Church,* bk. 1, cap. 30.

condemnation of current practice and substitution of appropriate behavior. Since local parishioners quite obviously resisted the clerical agenda, the resultant behavior was a mix—apparently quite satisfactory to local populaces—of traditional folk festivity and behavior deemed more appropriate. Among the folk festivities are parish ales, the various Robin Hood games, hockings, and so forth. On the Christian side are Corpus Christi and saints' feast-day processions and Easter sepulchres. Processions on Rogation days appear to be displacements of formerly pagan spring rituals, and the parish boy bishops may have been co-opted from monastic and cathedral practice but tolerated because they replaced the *quêtes* of older rituals. When boy bishops were put down in the early Reformation, there is evidence that parishes and communities were reluctant to let them go; consequently, it is not surprising to find them quickly reinstated when Mary came to the throne. No matter what the community— monastery or cathedral, royal or aristocratic court, town or parish—the *ludi* not only bound the community together but gave it an individual identity.

FOUR

Civitas: Drama and the City

The second part of my thesis is that attempts to suppress or rechannel lay festive behavior opened a space for the establishment of biblical and moral drama in late medieval England; indeed, we might say that vernacular religious drama to some extent countered the clerical attempt to sequester and restrain lay festivity. The reformers seem to have been successful in suppressing activities like the somer-game in the sermon discussed in chapter 2 and clerical *ludi* and *miracula* (but not boy bishops) by the early fifteenth century; they were less successful in abolishing parish ales with their attendant games, but then probably many clerics at the parish level tolerated them for economic reasons. Nevertheless, there seems to have been a gradual movement toward more legitimate Christian play as we go from the fifteenth into the sixteenth century. One form this move took was the increasing use of biblical and moral dramas. Civic oligarchies seem to have felt that they had some religious and moral responsibilities for their fellow citizens and, prompted perhaps by the affective piety of the late Middle Ages, chose to enact biblical scenes in their streets. In the preceding chapter, I described such religious impulses and actions in the smaller towns; in this chapter, I consider the economics, politics, and religious desire that resulted in large-scale dramatic production in some of the northern cities before addressing the issue of why London did not develop a similar dramatic tradition.

Late medieval reforming clerics seem to have understood the principle that in order to extirpate *ludi inhonesti,* one had to allow licit recreation or find appropriate *ludi* to occupy the laity during the same season of the year in which the unholy *ludi* took place. We can see the promotion of the feast of Corpus Christi, especially of the Corpus Christi procession, then, as having two complementary objectives: giving the laity greater participation in the religious life and providing an appropriate form of festive expression. The procession is an obvious solution: it is modeled on clerical ritual and so extends to the laity a similar observance, yet insofar as it is centered on the body of Christ rather than the mass or the wine of the sacrament, it also continues to mark a distinction between clerical and lay celebration. A procession presumably is also reverent; its outward expression can be controlled or controlling. The Rogation Day procession, which marked the bounds of the city or town and its fields, for example, was a way of giving Christian meaning to an originally pagan ritual of fertility.

We can find Corpus Christi and other processions throughout the towns of England, but some of these towns began to present religious and moral dramas along with or in addition to these processions beginning circa 1375. The York cycle, which is believed to have originated sometime in the late fourteenth century, was performed at the conclusion of the Corpus Christi procession until circa 1468, when the procession was moved to the day following the feast.[1] Coventry, whose plays date to the same period as York's, and Chester, which had a play by 1422, also had processions that preceded their plays; however, Chester, sometime in the 1520s or early 1530s, moved its plays to Whitsun week. Other major cities, Lincoln, Norwich, and Ipswich, had only guild processions (on various saint and feast days) in the medieval period except that Norwich, circa 1527, substituted for its procession of pageants and painted images a collection of Old and New Testament plays.

The period during which vernacular dramas begin to emerge is fraught with political and religious tension. Not only were there monarchic disruptions with the deposition of Richard II, the Wars of the Roses, and the revolt against Richard III, but political loyalty was often purchased through the granting of liberties to lay corporations, an action that at times enabled town corporations to gain political supremacy over their clerical competitors. Moreover, the growing literacy of the late Middle Ages in itself constituted a challenge to the clerical elite. The clergy, for its part, could no longer simply claim privilege because it was lettered—although it still insisted that it was the final arbiter of doctrinal meaning—with the result that greater emphasis falls on the clerics' performance of the rituals of the cult and more latitude is given to the laity to develop its own spirituality.

The appearance of vernacular biblical and moral drama can be seen as a consequence of clerical initiatives even though the latter group apparently was

---

1. Johnston, "Procession and Play of Corpus Christi."

little engaged in the production of vernacular dramas.[2] The clergy had taken an active interest, programatically, since Lateran IV (1215) in educating the laity in matters of faith. This initiative produced an enormous body of instructional literature in Latin for the clergy, but by the beginning of the fourteenth century, some of these texts appeared in or were beginning to be translated into the vernacular. In addition, there was a growing body of vernacular renditions of biblical history, both Old and New Testament (for example, *Cursor Mundi, The Northern Passion,* and the *Meditations on the Life of Our Lord* in its various redactions). Not only did these texts answer the layperson's desire to know about scriptural events, but they also, at least initially, one supposes, lessened the demand for biblical translation. These histories were, so to speak, the Bible cleansed of the problematical incidents that could confuse a Wife of Bath or be misread by untrained laypeople. One effect of this increasing body of vernacular religious literature was the desire on the part of the laity to have more of it, and, having more of it, to participate more completely and individually in cultic practice. The clerical response seems to have been to regulate as much as possible the public expression of lay piety and to countenance or tolerate what it could not control.

It is the clergy's inability to completely control lay activities that allowed an opening for dramatization of vernacular biblical texts, for drama appeared in cities and towns where the laity had political dominance or equality. I wish to argue that the development of local governance and the presence of power groups other than craft guilds affected not only the elaboration of established ceremonials but also the kinds of drama and ceremonial that were created. Many of the larger cities, for example, had monasteries or cathedral churches that had been granted privileges before the secular part of the city sought incorporation. Both Lincoln and Norwich had lay governance through religious guilds, but in both cases, until the sixteenth century lay power was subordinate to that of ecclesiastical institutions within the town. The major focus of civic corporate celebration was a procession on Corpus Christi, Saint George's, Saint Anne's or some other feast day. In some cases—Chester, Newcastle, and York, for example—the Crown retained significant powers as a consequence of granting the city the status of county palatine. In the case of Chester the

---

2. My argument runs counter to the general assumption that clerics were the authors and producers of vernacular dramas; see chapter 6 and my essays "Lay and Clerical Impact" and "Framing Medieval Drama."

abbey and the Crown dominated the city until the Crown aided the civic authorities in gaining primacy early in the sixteenth century. By contrast, Coventry and York were given strong secular authority early in the period with the result that they had effective governance of their cities, though, in the case of York, it might be more accurate to say that it had effective governance of precincts within the larger space shared with the minster and other religious institutions. At York civic authorities were able to establish a strong secular government much earlier than at Chester, and, at Coventry, the city gained dominance over its powerful Benedictine abbey almost 200 years before Chester did over its abbey.

These few examples indicate that we cannot expect that social, political, and economic forces, nor the responses to these, would have been the same in all boroughs throughout the period; nevertheless, an examination of these factors might help us determine why some cities and towns produced plays and why others only had processions or other kinds of spectacle. A brief overview of the northern cities for which we now have sets of dramatic records or new social histories suggests that the kind of government in place had an effect on the type of drama or ceremonial that occurred in a given city or town.[3] We know that Coventry and York had cycles of plays early in their histories, and both cities document regular annual production through the fifteenth century and much of the sixteenth. Both cities had strong civic governing bodies and important civic freedoms before the institution of their plays in the late fourteenth century. The situations in Newcastle and Beverley are similar, but the evidence suggests they never developed a comparable cycle of plays. Chester and Norwich, both of which had dramatic and ceremonial activities in the fifteenth century, seem not to have created the cycles we know them to have until the sixteenth century, when there were marked changes in civic governance and responsibilities. Lincoln provides the case of a city that never developed an extensive cycle of religious drama, and it is a city that had to share its power with its secular cathedral and in which the ruling classes were identical with religious guild membership.

Cycles of religious dramas, therefore, seem to have appeared in northern England in the cities that established strong governments centered in the trade

---

3. Two northern cities, Kendal and Beverley, are thought to have had plays, but there is insufficient data about the first. See Douglas and Greenfield, *Cumberland / Westmoreland / Gloucestershire,* 17–19, 168–71, 218–19. Beverley is discussed below.

guilds.[4] In the cities and towns where civic government had to compete against powerful ecclesiastical establishments or where religious rather than trade guilds dominated, cyclic drama does not seem to have appeared; instead, processions, fairly unelaborate dramas, and other quasi-dramatic activities seem to have been the norm. We may tentatively conclude that cycles of drama are to be identified with the secular or lay guild government, perhaps as an expression of civic control, civic pride, and civic concern for the religious education of the townspeople.

Thus far, I have only spoken of collections of biblical plays associated with cities in the north and Norwich in northern East Anglia. Biblical and moral dramas were performed elsewhere; nevertheless, the general thesis outlined above seems to hold true for university towns and significant towns in the south, southwest, and the west midlands (for example, Exeter and Bristol). East Anglia and the counties in the southeast provide the greatest contrast to most of the rest of England, because in these areas relatively small towns discovered ways to transform the fund-raising initiative of parish ales and games into commercial theater. London occupies an anomalous position: wealthy and influential, having a powerful, centralized oligarchic government, it might be expected to be the center of the English dramatic tradition, but it was not until after the period with which we are concerned that London became a center for drama. There are a number of reasons for the absence of drama from Albion's premier city, the most obvious being London's ambivalent relationship with the court.

Whether we are talking about northern cycles or commercial ventures, vernacular drama seems to be the product of and under the control of laymen. This observation may not seem very startling until one recognizes the implications: that there is no continuous development from liturgical to vernacular drama, and that the clergy seem to have been little involved in the production, presentation, or oversight of vernacular drama once it appeared.[5] For many years scholars imagined the growth of cycles and the drama to have been a consequence in some way of the transference of clerical religious plays to civic governments and of the subsequent growth of the craft guilds that constituted the

---

4. Some cities and towns, Coventry, for example, were governed through religious guilds, but these guilds were, in fact, made up of trade groups.

5. O. B. Hardison Jr. has provided the classic rebuttal to the evolutionary theory of the drama and has presented the case for the separate development of liturgical and vernacular drama (*Christian Rite*, 253–83). Not all scholars have accepted the argument. For a restatement of the connection between the two dramas, see Dunn, "Popular Devotion," and Woolf, *English Mystery Plays*, 3–76.

ruling body. But the precise details of these events have often been sacrificed to the evolutionary theory of the secularization of the drama: the transfer, for whatever reasons, was said to have been made, though the details are lacking. Furthermore, the discussion of origins was focused on the northern biblical dramas because they exhibited the best evidence for an evolutionary theory. The texts of the moral plays in this scheme were neglected or pushed to the side except when they were imagined to be transitional pieces between medieval (that is, biblical) drama and secular dramas of the Elizabethan era.

The origins of civic vernacular drama are obscured by time. We have no decrees establishing a cycle of plays; in most cases, the initial references to civic drama tend to be casual ones embedded in a guild dispute or some other record. The earliest ones are from the late fourteenth and early fifteenth centuries, long after the invention of liturgical drama. Cycles of civic plays, therefore, are not likely to be earlier than the 1370s and very probably did not reach the scale suggested by the extant texts until well into the fifteenth century or, as in the cases of Chester and Norwich, until the early decades of the sixteenth. It is a little more difficult to say when smaller towns began to experiment with play production; however, there is a noticeable flurry of dramatic activity in the early sixteenth century, especially around the 1520s, which is also when many smaller towns were first being incorporated.[6]

From this introduction, it should be clear that my argument is not deterministic; that is, we cannot say that where there is a strong, established civic government, there is drama. We can say, however, that certain kinds of economic and political conditions must be in place for drama to be a possibility. Once those are in place, other considerations come into play: whether the corporate body desires to display itself through drama or other spectacle; whether the body perceives itself to have an obligation for religious and moral instruction; and so forth.

Using important northern cities, I will first consider the effects that local governance and relations between competing institutions of power have on enabling the production of dramas. I will conclude with a focus on London.

Power, Politics, Devotion, and Money

Cities that were governed by trade guilds tended to be oligarchies centered in the oldest or most prestigious guilds.[7] This kind of stratification is seen most

---

6. Clopper, "The 1520s." See also the other essays in Coldewey, "English Drama in the 1520s."
7. The discussion in this section draws on my earlier essay, "Lay and Clerical Impact," without reproducing it in its entirety.

obviously in York, with its inner ruling body of the Twelve, from which mayors were selected, and the Twenty-four, which was made up of former sheriffs and was the pool from which members of the Twelve were selected.[8] The Twelve and the Twenty-four were drawn mainly from the trading crafts. The third governing body, the Forty-eight, was drawn from the manufacturing crafts. In 1517 it became the common council of the Forty-one, made up of two members of the thirteen major crafts and one member of the fifteen minor crafts. Effective power lay with the mayor and the inner councils. Chester's guild government was more egalitarian, perhaps because it did not receive full powers to govern until late in its history, after the guilds had developed independently into major companies.

But many cities were not governed by trade guilds on the simple model of Chester; nor were all ceremonial activities undertaken by those who practiced crafts. In some cities religious guilds were synonymous with the civic governing body. Thus, the Guild of Saint George constituted the ruling class of Norwich, but it is not known to have engaged in any dramatic activity.[9] In Coventry, on the other hand, religious guilds combined important roles in both ceremony and governance. Charles Phythian-Adams has shown that the numerous ceremonies in Coventry helped define corporate bodies within the city at the same time that they helped designate social strata.[10] Many of the processions, for example, were made up of the male freemen of the city, but this body was subdivided into craft and religious guilds. The two religious guilds constituted two ranks within the city and were tied closely to city government: The master of the Corpus Christi guild became mayor and then, upon leaving office, master of Holy Trinity. The order of march in the Corpus Christi procession and at midsummer also reflected a guild's status with regard to the governing body; the order was not based on economic class divisions but on occupational groupings according to the quantity and ancientness of their contribution to office-holding.[11] The procession began with the victuallers, who by parliamentary statute were banned from holding civic offices. These were followed by the

---

8. There are several relevant essays in Stacpoole et al., *Noble City of York;* otherwise, see the introduction to Johnston and Rogerson, *York,* x–xiii, and Palliser, *Tudor York.* On the value and importance of examining local government situations, see Kahrl, "Learning About Local Control," 101–18, and John Coldewey's response in the same volume, 118–27.

9. Dutka, "Mystery Plays at Norwich." The guild apparently did sponsor a riding of Saint George (Nelson, *Medieval English Stage,* 121–22).

10. Phythian-Adams, "Ceremony and the Citizen."

11. Ibid., 63.

leather and metal trades and then the wool and textile trades, the latter culmi-
nating with the most prestigious Dyers, Drapers, and Mercers, in that order.

The Corpus Christi plays were regulated by the city government, as is the
case elsewhere; however, individual pageants seem to have been controlled and
dominated by the oldest and therefore most prestigious guilds.[12] This coterie
seems to have been able to sustain its dominance, with a few exceptions, even
after other guilds were forced to contribute to the costs of the play. Thus, in
1494–95, at the end of the long fifteenth-century economic decline, the city
ordered all guilds not contributory to the plays to become associated with
them.[13] In most cases, this simply resulted in the lesser guilds' paying money to
the old guilds; that is, they shared the costs of the pageants but apparently were
not as directly involved in the production of the play as were the old guilds. In
the 1530s, during a short-term decline, guilds that had not complied with the
earlier order were pressed to become contributors, and there was a major
reshuffling occasioned by the decay of the Cardmakers and the emergence of
the Cappers as the largest industry in Coventry.[14] Except for the case of the
Cappers, therefore, the plays were produced and controlled from their inception to their demise by the oldest and most powerful crafts in the city. I think
there is little doubt that the establishment of a strong secular government in the
mid–fourteenth century, a government that had gained dominance earlier over
its Benedictine abbey, partially accounts for the fact that Coventry's play was
controlled by the oldest guilds and that the city had an almost unbroken record
of annual performance of its play through the fifteenth century until its final
production in 1579. The date of the last performance is a significant indicator
of the secular government's identification with its play because it suggests that
this city felt it could perform the cycle despite the actions of Archbishop
Grindal against Chester, York. and Wakefield.[15]

Chester has a more complicated history and politics. Until the granting of

---

12. The following discussion is based on the records and Reginald W. Ingram's essay "'To find
the players.'"

13. Ingram, *Coventry,* 78–80.

14. Ibid., 136, 128–33.

15. One might note that Coventry was not a Catholic survivalist stronghold but had early links
with Lollardy; in fact, John Careles, who had been imprisoned for his religion in 1556, asked to be
released on his own recognizance for one day that he might appear in the Weavers' play with his fellows. He voluntarily returned to jail and afterwards was sent to London, where he thought to die in
the fire for the profession of his faith except that his martyrdom was prevented by his death in
prison (ibid., 207–8). See Luxton, "Reformation and Popular Culture," especially 67–68; Thomson, *Later Lollards;* and Fines, "Heresy Trials."

the Great Charter in 1506, the lay corporation's powers of self-governance were limited and the lay body was overshadowed by the Abbey of Saint Werburg.[16] Perhaps it is for this reason that the Corpus Christi play in the fifteenth century began with a procession from the church of Saint Mary's, the most important parish in the city, to the cathedral of Saint John's outside the walls, where the guilds participated in a Passion play. It is probable that the procession went to Saint John's because that church was believed to have a piece of the True Cross and thus was an important local shrine.[17] It is also the obvious center for the celebration of Corpus Christi, and, if my speculation is right that the old Corpus Christi play was primarily a Passion play, then Saint John's is even more appropriate.[18] The entire activity, in any event, seems expressive of the trade guilds' desire to assert some authority within the political arena while it simultaneously acknowledges its relative lack of power within the city. The key point is that the trade guilds process *outside* the city walls to Saint John's, a cathedral that had been abandoned by its bishop shortly after the conquest, when the bishop came to realize that he could exercise no real power while resident in Chester. The cathedral seems to have provided a space sufficiently beyond the purview of the abbot where the lay people could make their play of the Passion.

In 1506 the relations between the city and the abbey changed in favor of the city with the result that we see in the decades following an enormous expansion of the Chester plays and their removal to Whitsun week. Economic considerations may have had a part in the decision to make the move. Coventry's plays had gained a national reputation and succeeded in attracting royalty on several

---

16. Clopper, "Lay and Clerical Impact," 104–5.

17. D. Jones, *Church in Chester*, 50–51.

18. In my discussion in "Lay and Clerical Impact," I noted that in the Early Banns, which describe the new Whitsun play, we are told that the colleges and priests of Saint John's continued to bring forth a play on Corpus Christi—possibly as late as Edward VI's reign (Clopper, *Chester*, 38). The location of the play at Saint John's and the prominence of the colleges and priests might suggest that the earlier Corpus Christi play resulted from clerical initiative and remained under their auspices despite the fact that the guilds were involved in and probably paid for the production (e.g., ibid., 6–7; 10, line 20; 12, line 15; 13–15). However, I've grown increasingly puzzled by what this reference might mean. Why would—and could—the clergy continue their play without the guilds when there was a more elaborate cycle of plays at Whitsun? And what was the play? The erased section of the Early Banns says that the mayor and his brethren shall go in procession on Corpus Christi with the Blessed Sacrament and "A play [will be] sett forth by the clergye / In honour of the fest" (ibid., 38, lines 31 ff.). The clerk's "play," therefore, may not have been a dramatization but a liturgical representation or some other kind of celebration.

occasions.[19] The city of Chester may have felt that a move to Whitsuntide would result in less competition for merchants and playgoers and would increase the city's commerce during the time of the plays. Still, noneconomic motives seem the more important, for the rejection of Corpus Christi and performance at Saint John's has symbolic significance: it suggests that the city, by having the plays completely within its walls, announced its control of civic space; the plays were to be an expression of civic—and hence lay—piety. We can see the assertion of lay dominance first in the riding of the Banns on Saint George's day, for the route that the procession took touched all the bases of secular power; it, in effect, announced its jurisdiction. But the plays too are processional: they gathered at the barrs outside the principal gate of the city, proceeded to the Cornmarket, which was before the abbey gates, then to the Pentice, where the mayor and aldermen were seated, and then through the streets, the principal thoroughfares, and lanes to Watergate, the west gate, and Bridgegate, the southern gate. The Cornmarket is an equivocal space for performance: the market is one of the largest spaces within the city, which is the reason that it is the market and a convenient place for large gatherings, but it is also before the gates of the abbey. The Cornmarket is under the jurisdiction of the city, yet we are told that the abbey supplied beer to the players. Is the first performance in the Cornmarket intended to express lay authorization of the plays to the monks within the abbey? Or is it a tacit acknowledgment that the laity is ready to be corrected should the abbot find anything objectionable in the performance? Did the abbot send the beer out of a tradition of hospitality or as a sign that he accepts the plays as an appropriate form of lay recreation? Did the monks even attend the plays?

The Banns and the Proclamation admit that there are economic motives behind the production of the plays, but they also claim that the plays are produced "for the Augmentac*i*on & incresse of the holy and catholyk ffaith . . . to exhort the myndes of the comen peple to gud deuoc*i*on and holsom doctryne."[20] We could argue that the latter reason is simply a mask for the true, the economic, motives, but if I am correct in believing that the development of these plays during a period of economic stress occurred as a consequence of the

---

19. Royalty came to see the Coventry plays in 1485, 1487, 1493, and 1511 (Ingram, *Coventry*, 66, 67–68, 77, 106–7, 114). The fame of the plays is also attested by the references in Heywood's *Foure PP*, lines 829–32 (Heywood, *Plays of John Heywood*) and Rastell's *Hundred Merry Tales*, 115–16.

20. Clopper, *Chester*, 33.

city's coming to supremacy in the local power arena, then I think that we ought to concede that the city had gained a sense of responsibility for the moral and religious welfare of the citizenry as well. The lay decision to perform biblical dramas is not so much an illustration of "secularization" in Chambers's sense as it is a redefinition of corporate lay responsibility. We need to consider the possibility, therefore, that the development and maintenance of customs were not just expressions of civic pride—or that the city could afford to do it—but also that the customs were signs of the city's free status. There is not just an economic motive here; there is, in addition, an assertion of political identity and of the city's concern for the welfare of its citizens.

A strong guild government does not guarantee that large-scale dramatic production will develop. Newcastle-upon-Tyne seems to fit the profile of other cities that produced cycles of scriptural plays: It was a fairly prosperous trading center, had a secular government from an early period, and was made a county in 1400.[21] There was no monastery or cathedral in the town to compete for power.[22] There was a hierarchy of guilds: The highest were the Twelve, through whom the mayor was chosen, and there were fifteen second-ranked "by-guilds" as well as assorted others not named as either.[23] But Newcastle apparently did not create an extensive cycle of plays.[24] Instead, I suspect, they had a procession of guilds on Corpus Christi, and some of these guilds, perhaps annually before 1550 and from time to time after 1559, performed a group of plays. There is insufficient evidence to indicate that there was ever a complete cycle of plays from the Fall to Doomsday; in any event, the evidence argues against the traditional estimate of a cycle of twenty-five plays. Nevertheless, the fact remains that a secular government was involved in the production of scriptural dramas.

We have one extant play, *Noah's Dirge,* associated with Newscastle, and a

---

21. Anderson, *Newcastle,* ix.

22. Knowles and Hadcock, *Medieval Religious Houses,* 72, 355. By contrast, all of the mendicant orders had houses there.

23. Anderson, *Newcastle,* x.

24. Historians of the drama have concluded that there were possibly as many as twenty-five plays in the cycle at Newcastle, but I think the evidence unconvincing because it is arrived at by the simple addition of references scattered over a period of 150 years. This method of achieving a total overlooks changes brought about by internal and external forces and fails to comment on the significance of absent data. See my analysis in "Lay and Clerical Impact," 120–21. For arguments that there was a cycle of plays, see Holthausen, *Das Noahspiel,* 16; Chambers, *Mediaeval Stage,* 2:424; Craig, *English Religious Drama,* 305; Norman Davis, *Non-Cycle Plays,* xliii; Nelson, *Medieval English Stage,* 204–6; and Anderson and Cawley, "The Newcastle Play of *Noah's Ark,*" 11.

brief analysis of it might indicate the modest aspirations of the city's playmakers.[25] Like the other Noah plays, Newscastle's opens with God's speech of regret about man's shortcomings. He sends an angel to direct Noah to build the ark, even though Noah is not a shipwright—thus offering an opportunity for shipping humor in this seaport. God intends to save Noah, his wife, and their children and their wives; he directs the angel what to say about saving the animals. The angel does as he is told, repeating to Noah everything that God said to him. Noah complains of his age and says that he is not a shipwright; he concludes that Christ will be the maker of the ship. The Devil enters lamenting; he's heard that a ship will be made to save Noah and his household. The Devil decides to destroy them by approaching Noah's wife to tell her of her danger: if she does as Noah says, she and her children will die (an echo of Satan's reasoning with Eve). She is to get Noah drunk so that he will reveal his plan. She succeeds in making Noah drunk, and when she learns he's building a ship, she exclaims, "Who made thee a wright?" Noah goes back to the ship, where he prays for divine help and finally concludes that the ship is well made. He exits to call his household as the devil speaks the last lines. If we compare this with other Noah plays, we see that the action only concerns events up to the entry into the ark. It is not clear that Noah constructs the ark before the audience, as he and his family do at Chester, because he only has a few lines at the construction scene before going off to Mrs. Noah. More important, Noah's children and their wives do not appear, there is no loading of the animals (as at Chester), there is no flood, no dove and raven scene, no landing with a thanksgiving sacrifice, and no covenant with its allusion to the final destruction by fire. The cast is small; the productions requirements are minimal. If the *Noah* is representative of the other Newcastle plays, then we might conclude that they focused on a single action within a larger narrative but that they did not fully carry out those narratives as do the plays at Chester, Coventry, Wakefield, and York.

Newcastle is about the same size as Beverley; it ranked eleventh, just behind Beverley, in the 1377 assessment but was ranked third in the subsidy paid in 1523.[26] Since both Newcastle and Beverley have been thought to have had cy-

---

25. In Norman Davis, *Non-Cycle Plays*, 19–31.

26. Hoskins, *Local History*, 176–77. My references here and in the discussion below are based on Hoskins's studies of the census and subsidies of 1377 and 1523–27. Hoskins notes that these are not entirely equivalent standards of measures and should be used with that reservation in mind. Also, some cities and counties were exempt, the most important of which for our purposes was Chester. See his appendix, "Ranking of Provincial Towns," in *Local History;* and his "English Provincial Towns."

cles of biblical dramas, our analysis of Newcastle may help us sort out the situation at Beverley.

Arthur F. Leach, the principal authority on Beverley practice until Diana Wyatt wrote her thesis, believed that there was a cycle of biblical plays in the city from circa 1377 until the early sixteenth century.[27] The most informative document is the "Gubernacio Ludi *Corporis Christi*," an undated list of guilds and their thirty-six pageants placed on the first folio of the Great Guild Book, 1409–1589.[28] Leach dated the list circa 1520. The list of pageants makes the Beverley production look more like the cycle of plays at nearby York than those at Coventry or Chester. Because there is a 1390 document for the order of the guilds in the Corpus Christi procession that contains many of the guilds in the 1520 list, and because there are guild ordinances as early as 1392 that specify the subject of guild pageants, Leach concluded that we could assume that the Corpus Christi cycle described in the 1520 document existed from the late fourteenth and throughout the fifteenth century. There are, however, a number of puzzling features in the record, ones that must cause us to wonder exactly what the Corpus Christi *ludus* was.

The city engaged in three kinds of civic activity: the construction of elaborate castles for the Rogation Monday procession of the relics of Saint John of Beverley from the minster to Saint Mary's; the Corpus Christi procession and *ludus;* and the Pater Noster play. Individual guilds had ordinances that required members to contribute toward the first two of these (there's little information about the Pater Noster play), but the city's twelve governors or keepers seem to have overseen all activities. Of the three activities, the castles seem to have been the most important and the most prestigious, for they were places for the prominent guilds to sit to watch the procession. Members were required to wear livery; members of lesser guilds were sometimes affiliated with the greater ones and joined their betters in the castle, which seems to have been not only a viewing stand but a place where ample refreshment was available. One can tell the prominence given to the castles from guild ordinances and other documents. Most ordinances begin with the provisions for the castle and lights. Often there are schedules of fines for misconduct, entrance fees, and requirements of contributions to the castle and lights before one comes to any clause about the Corpus Christi pageant. The city's order for the plays suggests that

---

27. Leach, *Beverley Town Documents*, and "Some English Plays and Players." I have also drawn on Diana Wyatt's dissertation, "Performance and Ceremonial in Beverley Before 1642." And see Nelson, *Medieval English Stage*, 88–99.

28. Chambers, *Mediaeval Stage*, 2:340–41, prints the text.

they are to be produced every year, but it is clear from the guild ordinances and other documents that they were not given every year, whereas the castles are always there for the procession of the relics. Given the prominence allotted the castles, and given that some guild ordinances refer only to castles, it would appear that the castles and lights predated the pageants and constituted the more prestigious activity.

The Corpus Christi procession was instituted by a guild of that name in 1355. According to the 1389 guild return, the priests *(presbyteri)* of Beverley entered into a guild to better support the feast of Corpus Christi with the distribution of alms and so that the solemnity and service might be upheld. Every year on the Thursday after the feast of Holy Trinity, each brother who was a chaplain *(capellanus)* was to walk in procession in albs with a stole and mansiple with the rest of the brethren, literate and lay (defined as chaplains and persons of an honest way of life and a respectable craft). Although the guild seems to have been the originator of the procession, the governors intervened in 1431 when, because of disagreements among the crafts about precedence, the keepers set the order for the procession: the procession would begin with the Host next to the clergy, then the Corpus Christi guild, the guilds of the Blessed Virgin Mary and of Saint John of Beverley, then the trade guilds (twenty trades are named), and finally the guilds of Saint Helen, Pater Noster, Saint John the Baptist, Saint John in May, and Saint Peter of Milan.[29] The Tailors' ordinance of 1377, however, indicates that some of the trade guilds had pageants in the procession, for the Tailors were required to be present for drawing up of expenses for the pageant of the play of Corpus Christi ("expensis pagine ludi corporis christi factis"). In 1390 there is a civic ordinance that requires every craftsman (forty trades are listed) to have their plays and pageants ready "on every day in the feast" of Corpus Christi under penalty of 40s., and in the years that follow we find numerous guild ordinances that require payment toward the pageant.[30]

All of this seems fairly straightforward, but a closer look at the documents raises some questions. Leach—and Chambers followed him in this—assumed that since the 1390 order for precedence in the Corpus Christi procession and

---

29. In a later order of 1498 only the craft guilds are named, but since there is some reordering of precedence, the city may have only been trying to regulate the secular part of the procession.

30. The phrase "on every day in the feast" of Corpus Christi is puzzling since it suggests either that the pageants were available for viewing over a period of several days or that they were processed more than once, whereas the majority of records suggest that the pageants went in procession on Corpus Christi day.

the 1520 list of guilds and their pageants were roughly the same in number and at places in parallel sequence, then the 1520 document described the situation in the late fourteenth century. Some of the fifteenth-century guild ordinances do not refer to pageants, however, even though they are represented in the 1390 Corpus Christi procession and the 1520 list of pageants.[31] For example, the Weavers have "the Stanginge" (probably the Longinus episode, according to Wyatt) in 1520, but their 1406 ordinance makes no reference to a pageant; it is only in 1445 that its members are obliged to pay 6d. when the pageant is played. Similarly, the Tanners' ordinance of 1416, the Dyers' of 1431 (reaffirmed in 1460), and the Shermen's of 1432 do not contain references to pageants. The Drapers did not petition for a play of their own until 1493. The 1520 list cannot accurately reflect the situation in the purported 1390 list. Moreover, the 1431 order for the precedence of guilds within the Corpus Christi procession contains only twenty trades and a 1498 order for the same contains only twenty-three, not the thirty-eight of the 1390 list nor the thirty-six of the 1520 list. This suggests that the 1390 list is not for thirty-eight plays but for thirty-eight trades, some of which may have been amalgamated into one guild (for example, the Coopers, the Bowers, and the Fletchers, a common union here and elsewhere). There is some evidence that an increasing number of guilds took on the responsibility for pageants as the fifteenth century progressed, so we might imagine the 1520 list to constitute the culmination of the process, one in which lesser guilds wished to join the practice—much as lesser guilds affiliated themselves with guilds holding castles—or in which amalgamated guilds—Merchants and Drapers, and Bowers, Fletchers, and Coopers—wished to separate themselves for greater identity. In the 1520 list, for example, the Bowers and the Fletchers have the *Abraham and Isaac* and the Coopers the *Flight into Egypt,* and the Merchants have *Black Herod* and the Drapers *Deeming Pilate.*

Although the 1520 document looks like a list of contents for a cycle of plays like those at York, there is reason to believe that they are more modest productions. First, the city of Beverley had only about one-third the taxpaying population of York in 1377, and the provisions for the castles and the overseeing of the pageants, not to mention the frequent defaults, imply that the guilds were

---

31. I should say that there are some difficulties in putting these two lists together because some trades could go under more than one name, and trade terminology changed between the fourteenth and the sixteenth centuries. I have been unable to match up the two lists completely or with assurance in every instance.

neither large nor very rich.[32] Guildsmen were assessed between four and eight pence when the plays were played. By contrast, the Smiths of Chester in 1561 assessed most of their members 2s. 4d., though the master contributed 13s. 4d., for their Purification, and in 1549–50 the Chester Shoemakers spent a total of 21s. 4d. on their Jerusalem Carriage.[33] We might suspect that the Beverley pageants were spectacles rather than dramas if it were not for the fact that some of the fines are for not playing well; consequently, there must have been speeches or action of some sort. The weight of the evidence implies that many of the scripts were very short or perhaps tableaux vivantes with speeches. This conclusion is supported by some of the play topics. As at York, there are several plays, here four, dealing with the Creation, Adam and Eve, and the Fall. But one of these is "gravinge & spynnynge." How much action could there be here, given that the preceding pageant depicted the Fall and the following one exhibits Cain? In extant texts this action is just referred to or is a part of the action of the Cain and Abel play. Similarly, the Laborers' pageant is called *The Pinnacle,* not *The Temptation,* and in the Laborers' Ordinance of 1451 the pageant is said to show how the devil took up Jesus and stood him on the pinnacle of the temple. The description and title suggest that the pageant represented only one of the three temptations, and this, in turn, invites us to imagine the Beverley pageants as focusing on one scene, one emblematic tableau, rather than being dramas like those at York, Chester, and Coventry.[34] Finally, since the castles were given prominence in Beverley—and presumably were relatively simple to construct—we ought not to expect that the Corpus Christi pageants were elaborate.

We may conclude, then, that though Beverley had a lot of pageantry, it did not have much of a dramatic tradition. This point is partially supported by the

---

32. Hoskins, *Local History,* estimates that York had a taxpaying population of 7,248 and Beverley 2,663.

33. Clopper, *Chester,* 65 and 49–50, respectively.

34. We might also note that Sir William Pyers, the poet who was paid in 1519–20 for revising *(transposicione)* the Corpus Christi *ludus,* was paid 3s. 4d. for his expenses and labor in coming from Wrassell and for the changing *(alteracione)* of the *ludus.* The governors spent 7s. while with Pyers. By contrast, in 1423–24 Friar Thomas Bynham, a Dominican, was paid twice as much (6s. 8d.) for "making and composing" the banns. In that same year the governors spent 7s. 6d. while managing the pageants going out through the town. Pyers, therefore, appears not to have had to do a lot of labor on the pageants, which suggests that they were rather modest productions to begin with. Suzanne Westfall has identified Pyers or Peres as a member of the earl of Northumberland's chapel who would have been involved with musical entertainments and pageants (*Patrons and Performance,* 18).

rather modest Pater Noster produced in 1441 and 1467. The governors assigned pageants of each of the seven Deadly Sins to collections of guilds (for example, the Shoemakers, Saddlers, Fullers, Tilers, Ropers, and Capmakers were assigned Pride) and an eighth pageant, that of "Vicious," to the gentlemen. According to the 1467 order they were to be played at seven places, the same that were assigned for the Corpus Christi play. Since the players are apparently restricted to the seven sins and Vicious (see the 1467 order), the play would appear to be composed of monologues of the sins, including presumably how they violate clauses of the Pater Noster,[35] but there may also have been some dialogue or action between them and Vicious unless Vicious simply acted as the presenter of each of the sins. What little information we have indicates that the play was more presentational than representational.

Both Newcastle and Beverley are examples of mid-sized towns with substantial freedoms, self-governance by a small oligarchy of prestigious citizens, and relatively favorable economic conditions. But they are limited by size and therefore by economics. Both engaged in dramatic representation, perhaps in imitation of cities like York, but their productions seem rather more modest.

Lincoln provides an example of a city in which a cycle of plays did not develop, perhaps because of the importance of its religious guilds and the prominence of the cathedral. Once thought to have been the home of the N-Town plays, Lincoln seems to have had relatively modest dramatic and ceremonial aspirations; furthermore, the activities that they did engage in seem to have remained fairly segregated along secular and ecclesiastical lines.[36] The two important powers, at least with regard to ceremony, were the cathedral and the Guild of Saint Anne (founded in 1344). There was some dissociation between these two factions even in their observance of Corpus Christi and Saint Anne's Day. From the records available, it appears that the city's *ludi*, called the Corpus Christi or Pater Noster play, usually went one year, and the cathedral's Assumption and Coronation *visus* was displayed in alternate years. The Saint Anne procession was annual in the sixteenth century, but it does not seem to have included performances of plays if, as appears to be the case, the Assump-

---

35. The Pater Noster was traditionally divided into seven petitions, and some texts associated each petition with the request to be protected against one of the sins. See, for example, sermon 9 in Ross, *Middle English Sermons*.

36. The discussion is largely condensed from Kahrl's introduction to the records: *Plays and Players in Lincolnshire*. Stephen Spector summarizes the current thinking on the placement of N-Town in East Anglia rather than at Lincoln ("Provenance of the N-Town Codex"; and see his discussion of dialect in *The N-Town Play*, xxix–xxxviii.

tion and Coronation was a mechanical device rather than a dramatic reenact-ment.[37]

York, which had a strong craft-dominated government from an early period, produced a cycle of biblical plays, but the city also had important religious guilds, two of which were responsible for plays.[38] The two religious guilds represent different corporate bodies from those of the civic government; consequently, their motives for performing the plays and the conditions under which they were performed differ from those of the city's plays. The Corpus Christi guild, made up of laymen, laywomen, and priests, sponsored the *Creed Play*, which was performed fairly regularly at ten-year periods from the late fifteenth century up to the aborted performance in 1568. The Pater Noster guild, which merged with the Guild of Saint Anthony in 1446, was responsible for the production of the Pater Noster play. It too seems to have been performed on a regular (possibly decennial) schedule until 1572.[39] The citizens of York, therefore, would have had occasion to see annual productions of the Corpus Christi plays as well as performances of the Creed and Pater Noster plays at regular intervals. But the auspices of the productions were different. In the guild returns of 1389 the Pater Noster guild claimed that it had no property other than that pertaining to the play and that it existed solely for the purpose of sponsoring the play to the greater glory of God and the reproving of sins and vices. Similarly, the purpose of the Corpus Christi guild had been to hold the properties, books, and other appurtenances of the play and to see that it was performed as the city requested.[40] The city regulated these plays, as it would any activity that fell within its jurisdiction, but I think that, at least initially, the productions of the Pater Noster and Creed plays were acts of personal piety for the good of the commonwealth. After the dissolution, when the mayor and the city were more directly involved in the production of the plays and when the craft guilds financed them, as they did in 1558, they became more like the city's cycle of biblical plays, a production of a corporate body for the good of that corporate body.[41]

The situation at Norwich provides one other configuration.[42] At the end of

---

37. For further comment, see my "Lay and Clerical Impact," 121–22.
38. Johnston, "Plays of the Religious Guilds of York."
39. Johnston and Rogerson, *York*, 352–68.
40. Ibid., 6–7, 87–88.
41. Ibid., 327–28.
42. The discussion is based on JoAnna Dutka, "Mystery Plays at Norwich." I have departed from her analysis of the significance of the 1527 alterations in customs. Also see her "Lost Dramatic Cycle of Norwich."

the fourteenth century the Great Guild, composed of the city notables, was the center of political influence. As a consequence of the civic disturbances of the first half of the fifteenth century, the Great Guild disappeared, in 1452, and the Guild of Saint George took over as the center of influence and wealth. There is no evidence that either the Great Guild or the Guild of Saint George undertook to sponsor plays or other religious ceremonials in the city (except for the Saint George riding). At some point in the fifteenth century, the Guild of Saint Luke, which was made up of Painters, Stainers, and other related crafts prominent at the time, became responsible for the production of "diuers disgisinges and pageauntes as well of the liff and marterdams of diuers and many hooly sayntes as also many other lyght and feyned figures and pictures of other persones and bestes."[43] In 1527 the Guild of Saint Luke petitioned the city to request that other guilds be required to share the costs of the show. JoAnna Dutka has argued that their motive for making this request was not that the guild could not pay for the show but that the city and other crafts profited from the concourse of people brought in by the ceremonies and the Whitsun fair. Most significant, Dutka says, is that the fair, formerly owned by the priory, had been transferred to the city in 1524; consequently, city companies were no longer forced to pay the priory in order to sell in their own city, and, it might have been argued, those fees could be applied toward the costs of the show. In this case the development of the drama seems to have been a consequence of an improvement in the economic situation coincident with an increase in the city's privileges and responsibilities.[44]

Norwich seems never to have produced a cycle of plays as we usually understand the term.[45] The first eight pageants listed in the Old Free Book constitute a typical Old Testament sequence: *Creation, Hellecarte, Paradise, Abell and Cayme, Noah, Abraham and Isaac, Moses and Pharoah,* and *David and Goliath*.[46] There are nativity, shepherd, and magi plays, but the last three plays in the sequence depict only the baptism of Christ, his Resurrection, and the descent of the Holy Ghost. Davis concluded that this was an incomplete list of the cycle because it did not include the Passion or Doomsday. But Davis's logic can be accepted only if one also accepts his assumption that all sequences of bibli-

43. Norman Davis, *Non-Cycle Plays,* xxvii–viii.

44. Hoskins, *Local History,* 127, lists Norwich as paying the highest subsidy in 1523–27. For further analysis of the situation in Norwich, see my "Lay and Clerical Impact," 123–25.

45. David Staines has examined the history of the word *cycle* in the criticism of the medieval drama from the nineteenth century onward; see his "English Mystery Cycles."

46. Norman Davis, *Non-Cycle Plays,* xxix–xxx.

cal plays must be complete cycles.[47] The Norwich plays resemble the ones at Newcastle insofar as they do not achieve the complete cyclic form of those at Chester, York, and Coventry.

I think the evidence of Norwich is important for two reasons. First, if I am correct in believing that Norwich instituted its plays after it took over the fair from the priory, then Norwich provides an instance, as does Chester, of a city establishing a sequence of plays at a point in its history when it gains some kind of new political dominance. Second, I think these events provide additional evidence against the evolutionary model and the assumption that the cycle drama was common. Chambers's and Craig's impression that cycle drama was widespread is a consequence of their assumptions about the evolution of drama from the church into the streets. When they found only partial evidence of a cycle—a list of stories from the Bible, for example—they concluded that the evidence proved the existence of a cycle but that the evidence for the remaining parts of the cycle was no longer extant.[48] Recent study suggests that cycle drama was rare.[49] Most smaller towns did not mount lavish dramatic productions but contented themselves with performances of single biblical episodes or other cooperative projects. Most civic or town drama was not cyclic at all, if by that term we mean a series of plays from Creation to Doomsday. In some cities—Lincoln, for example—such a concept seems never to have developed. In others—Coventry, Chester up to the sixteenth century—the cycle was probably confined to New Testament subjects. In other cases—Norwich, Newcastle, and Beverley—there were incomplete cycles or ones that do not fit modern conceptions of what a cycle is.

This examination of the published documentary evidence from the northern cities allows some tentative conclusions but raises many questions that require further study. The evidence suggests a divorcement between the ecclesiastical and the secular establishments with regard to plays. Religious, especially monks, had their liturgical dramas within their abbey precincts; corporations had their vernacular plays within the city's precincts. Many clergy, no doubt, supported lay vernacular drama, but these were not their plays. This separation is not so rigid in the case of processions, for there is evidence that proces-

---

47. See also Kolve, *Play Called Corpus Christi*, 53–54, who makes a similar assumption.

48. Ibid., chaps. 3–4.

49. Johnston, "What If No Texts Survived?" Johnston's argument that cycle plays were few is confirmed by Reginald Pecock's comment, ca. 1449, that "a quyk man . . . sett in a pley to be hangid nakid on a cros" occurs seldom and in few places (*Repressor*, 1.221).

sions were originally initiated by the clergy and that often they continued to walk in them. Indeed, Corpus Christi processions, as well as those of many religious guilds, required clerks to carry the Sacrament. At Lincoln, the mayor and council ordered that a guild priest was to oversee the arrangements for the Saint Anne's procession,[50] and, of course, processions often ended with a mass either at the church or, in the case of religious guilds, at the church or friary where they maintained their chapel. Yet Lincoln also provides evidence of clerical resistance, for in 1419 Bishop Repington had to exhort the clergy to take a proper place in the citizens' procession on Corpus Christi.[51]

At some point, but possibly from the beginning, civic governments took over the management of processions insofar as they decided who could march and what the order was to be. It is not clear how or why civic government became involved, but it was very probably a consequence of the preponderantly lay participation; many processions were instituted, in fact, in order to encourage lay participation in the religious life. But the ultimate source of the cities' involvement may arise from their jurisdiction over the secular parts of the city. A mayor greets a visiting dignitary not only to show respect but to grant him and his entourage admission to the city. Similarly, within cities where there are competing jurisdictions, one jurisdiction must grant permission, especially if there is a body of people involved, for the other one to move through it. The secular governments may have become overseers of religious processions simply because the procession was going to move through the city's jurisdiction.

Most, if not all, processions remained processions; that is, once they were established, they continued as processions even if plays later came into existence. Furthermore, plays seem to have remained distinct from processions throughout their respective histories. If a play is connected with a procession, it is performed at the end or in the afternoon of the feast day. In cities where the plays themselves were processional—performed in more than one place through the city—the religious procession usually went one day and the play another.

It is not clear why cycles or large sequences of plays occurred in the north or why Old Testament subjects seem to have dominated in places where single plays were performed or even why Old Testament subjects had a preponderance in sequences that were not complete cycles. No single explanation will account for the diversity of the phenomena. Economics, no doubt, placed certain

---

50. Kahrl, *Plays and Players of Lincolnshire*, 45.

51. Ibid., 29; from other records, it would appear that the monks preferred to have a feast for themselves instead.

limits on dramatic extravaganzas. Some cities simply could not afford to mount large numbers of plays; indeed, the large cities that did mount them ultimately were forced to require all the guilds or a large part of the populace to finance the city's dramatic activities. In places where individual plays were performed, there may have been a preference for Old Testament stories because they were of limited scope in the sources, because they were particularly given to moral interpretation, and because there were some who were wary of representations of Christ's Passion. It is difficult to know the extent to which attempts at suppression of *miracula* and the somergame reported in the sermon discussed in chapter 2 may have had a dampening effect on productions involving the Passion.

The most intriguing question is why civic governments put on cycles of religious plays in the streets. They often tell us that they produced them to the honor of God and the profit of the citizenry. Without denying the existence of the profit motive, I think it equally clear that the plays were intended to educate and confirm laymen in their religion. The preacher in the *Hundred Merry Tales* says that if you wish to understand the articles of the creed, then go to Coventry, where you can see them enacted.[52] The Wycliffite preacher points out that you can see the articles of the Pater Noster enacted at York.[53] The curious fact is not that these plays were intended to instruct but that the providers of the instruction were secular guildsmen and secular governments rather than the clergy. If the cycle plays were invented at the end of the fourteenth century or even in the fifteenth century, then they came to life during the period of the rather intense late medieval lay pious movements. I think that civic magistrates, when they gained power, recognized themselves to have a separate responsibility from the clergy for the morals and education of their people. They were expected to entertain the citizens at great personal expense and they were expected to present a moral example to the city that involved public worship. Once the obligation to provide a moral example and to educate is recognized, there is the problem of finding the means of fulfilling it. One method, a very successful one for churches in the Middle Ages, was to provide "pictures," either paintings or statues, for laypeople who were unlettered. However, guilds and city governments did not have places suitable to large concourses of people; they had no churches or cathedrals. Consequently, they placed their "pictures" in the streets.

---

52. Rastell, *Hundred Merry Tales*, 115–16.
53. Wyclif, *English Works of Wyclif Hitherto Unprinted*, 429.

The London Aesthetic

Although provincial cities used spectacle in the reception of noble persons and staged processions that reflected corporate identities, many of these with pageants, public display within London proper was confined to these two kinds of activity; neither the court nor the ruling oligarchy presented fully enacted scripts of biblical or moral dramas, either publicly or in private, until well into the sixteenth century.[54] This sweeping generalization must be modified in some respects—there were dramas being performed in households in the early Tudor period, and some of these presumably were in London—nevertheless, the general principle stands that the London aesthetic was for elaborate display and formal speech rather than narrative representation involving dialogue.[55]

If we think of London not as a city but a complex of parishes, then at that stratum ceremonial life is much like that elsewhere in England.[56] A number of parishes had boy bishops, but there are also Hocktide gatherings, May games, and "plays" in the churchyard.[57] Another fairly common practice was to have Palm Sunday Prophets, usually children in beards, sing or read prophecies from a frame or scaffold over the porch of the church.[58] At Saint Mary Magdalen Milk the prophets then rode in procession. In some parishes, Saint Peter

---

54. I do not discuss London's royal and civic processions in this section, for which see Clopper, "Engaged Spectator."

55. Scholars and antiquarians at least since John Stow's *A Survey of London* (1590) have believed that there was a cycle of biblical plays performed over several days by clerics at Clerkenwell (or at Skinners' Well) in the fourteenth century and the opening decades of the fifteenth and, according to Stow, until his own day (Stow, 1:93; Chambers, *Mediaeval Stage*, 2:379–81; Craig, *English Religious Drama*, 153; and Nelson, *Medieval English Stage*, 170–73). There are a number of problems associated with this tradition, including contamination in the chronicles that report it as well as in the reception of the tradition. I believe that at most there was a biblical spectacle of some kind only in 1390 and 1409. See my essay "Problem of the Clerkenwell Plays."

56. Barron, "Parish Fraternities of Medieval London."

57. All items cited are from transcriptions made by Mary Erler and deposited at the office of Records of Early English Drama. There is a boy bishop as early as 1432 at Saint Mary at Hill and 1431 at Saint Peter Westcheap as well as in other parishes (Saint Nicholas garb is described in the 1469 inventory of Saint Nicholas Shambles); Hocktide appears in the accounts of Allhallows Staining (dating from 1491–92), Allhallows London Wall (dating from 1457–58), and Saint Mary at Hill (dating from 1496–97); May games took place at Saint Botolph's (1535–36) and Saint Nicholas Shambles (as early as 1458); "plays" or "stage plays" occur in the accounts of Saint Botolph Aldersgate (for 1530–32) and Saint Katharine Cree (in 1527 and 1529, by special license), among other places.

58. This occurred at Saint Mary at Hill (dating from 1493–94). See Erler, "Palm Sunday Prophets."

Westcheap, for example, there were readers or singers of the Passion on Palm Sunday.[59] In 1536–37 Saint Mary Magdalen Milk created a more dramatic scene, for they had persons to play God and Longinus and filled bladders with "lyker that Ran owt of the Crosse." The records do not specify what the "plays" in the churchyard might have been, though they could have been any of the above.

But since London is a city, it has a civic organization based, as in most of the other larger towns, in guilds who regulate the economy. Since these guilds wish to establish their own prestige and that of their oligarchic governance, they exhibit the kind of behavior that marks them as an elite: building of guild halls, sumptuous activities within the guild, and public display. London also differs from the other cities in having the monarch as its "first citizen." Since the monarch does not reside in London proper, however, there is both rivalry and imitation, the latter of which is another kind of rivalry.

Lydgate's mummings and disguisings for the court and London illustrate the taste shared by their monastic author, the court, and members of the ruling oligarchy in London in the early fifteenth century.[60] The 1429 mummings written for the Mercers and the Goldsmiths in honor of Mayor Eastfield are alike in being orations delivered by a disguised mummer, a Herald and Fortune, respectively.[61] The sudden appearance of the Herald at the feast recalls the romance conventions of other courtly revels. His speech ends with the (possible) appearance of three ships from which descend Oriental merchants with gifts for the mayor. Whereas most of the Herald's speech is made up of classical allusions and a journey through an allegorical romance landscape, the mumming for the Goldsmiths is centered on Old Testament figures: the conceit is that by means of the twelve tribes of Israel, David sends the Ark of the Lord to the mayor as a material gift—presumably something made by the goldsmiths— but that also contains the gifts of "konnyng, grace and might" so that he might govern with wisdom, peace, and right. Although there is action in the arrival of the merchants and tribes and their presentation of gifts, they do not speak;

---

59. As early as 1448 in this case. The reading also took place at Saint Mary Woolnoth in 1539–40 and the years following.

60. Little has been written on Lydgate's mummings; see Wickham, *Early English Stages,* 1:191–201, and Pearsall, *John Lydgate,* 183–88. P. H. Parry argued that Lydgate established features of the genre that were still evident in the sixteenth century: "On the Continuity of English Civic Pageantry."

61. Lydate, *Minor Poems of John Lydgate,* 2:695–98, 698–701.

rather, the presenter identifies them. The other striking feature of this mumming is its appropriation of royal prerogatives: the mumming is said to be "ordeyned ryallych by þe worthy merciers . . . of London" and the gift is sent by the king of Israel to the "king" of London to exhort him to rule righteously. That there is divine sanction embedded in this gift is signaled by the gifts, "konnyng, grace and might," which are the appropriated attributes of the Son, Holy Spirit, and Father, respectively, and which produce the analogous trinity of righteous governance: wisdom, peace, and right.

Some of Lydgate's court presentations are no more elaborate than these civic ones: for example, the "Soteltes at the Coronation Banquet of Henry VI (1432)" or the "Mumming at Eltham."[62] But even the grander ones are in the same mode. The mumming at London, circa 1427, has a presenter who introduces and "reads" the figure of Fortune, the first to appear: she inhabits an island in temperate bliss until a wave attacks the island; one side of the island is fair, the other hideous; and the "picture" continues with other images of mutability.[63] The presenter says that there are four ladies who can overcome Fortune's power: Prudence, Righteousness, Fortitude, and Temperance. Each of these ladies is "read" as she comes forward. The disguising ends with a song by the four virtues and the banishment of Fortune.

Lydgate's most elaborate, though flagrantly antifeminist, piece is the mumming at Hertford Castle, 1430.[64] Instead of using allegorized virtues or romance figures, Lydgate chose to make this piece "a disguysing of þe rude vpplandisshe people" complaining about their wives with the wives' robust answer. The mumming is organized like a *débat*, with first the husbands' position, then the wives', and then the adjudication of the case by the king. Lydgate imagines the scene to be the prince's court, to which the swains come to complain of mischief and great adversity, a kind of parody of royal supplication. Although apparently six rustics are present (see the marginal note at line 25), they do not speak; instead, the presenter speaks in their voice: here is Hobbe the Reeve, who complains that his wife, Beatrice Bittersweet, spends the day drinking rather than preparing his dinner and then beats him with her distaff when he complains. At the conclusion of this gallery of small town inhabitants, the speaker appeals to the prince once more: These Holy Martyrs, he says, appeal to his majesty to grant them "franchise" and liberty, since they are fettered

---

62. Ibid., 2:623–24, 672–74.
63. Ibid., 2:682–91.
64. Ibid., 2:675–82.

and bound in marriage, and a safe passport out of the country; or the prince could restore Old Testament and natural law, which does not recognize the superiority of women over men. The next speech is rubricated, "Takeþe heed of þaunswer of þe wyves" (line 162), and appears to be spoken by the wives, since they say, "We six wyves beon ful of oon acorde." Their rebuttal is heavily indebted to the thinking and words of the Wife of Bath. The final speech is said to be the judgment of the king, but it reverts to the third person of the opening speech. The king is said to weigh the husbands' tribulations against the wives' claim of custom, nature, and prescription and then—in a parody of Chaucer's Lady Tercelet—decides to delay the decision for a year, leaving the women to reign until the men by some process of law demonstrate that they should have sovereignty. Let men beware, he concludes, before they marry, for a man who marries lives ever in servitude.

The Hertford mumming bears the greatest contrast to others that Lydgate wrote. Rather than being "moral, pleasunt and notable," at he called the one at London, or allegorical and romantic, as most are, this mumming contains only a perverse moral. More important, it is set in the provinces—the participants are "rude vpplandisshe people"—as a consequence of which the "action" can be made farcical and humorous.[65] It is possible that while the presenter reads, the swains and their wives act out the situations being described. If one of the wives delivers their response—for surely all six did not speak simultaneously—there is even greater opportunity for satire in the fleshing out of the Wife of Bath herself. I am not convinced, however, that the wives speak; it is quite possible that the presenter ventriloquizes them. If this is the case, then we have a situation of female impersonation something like that of the Bessy on plough days. Indeed, Lydgate's mumming seems situated in folk game, for the contest between the men and the women probably reflects a Hocktide game like that at Coventry, where the women capture and beat the men.[66] Whatever ludic impulse may lie beneath the mumming, Lydgate created a diversion in the comic mode, as understood in rhetorical texts: the "art of blame" or vituperation. Though satirical, and presumably meant to be funny, Lydgate's mumming ridicules by using rustic types even though the message of the piece presumably is that all married men suffer the like. The use of rustics, however, permits an

---

65. Similarly, Chaucer provincializes the few references he makes to biblical drama, as if to say that he does not regard them as appropriate *spectacula* for his city. Equally significant, he links these activities to persons who are not refined or urbane: the Miller, Absolon, and the Wife of Bath.

66. I do not mean to imply that Lydgate was familiar with Hockday customs in or near Coventry; these festivities appear widely in England.

extravagance in gesture and content that is foreign to Lydgate's other works and, in any event, normally inappropriate for persons of high estate. The debasement of the characters allows the audience to imagine that the situation is not theirs. But this assumption is illusory, as the closing statement suggests, since (all) wives are allowed to continue to reign. There is a subtle critique of the limits of power in the whole set-up of the mumming but particularly in the prince's "resolution." The swains have come asking for justice, but the prince cannot provide it; his court has no jurisdiction in the matter; there is no process at law that can reverse the situation. The year's delay for a decision creates the illusion of power—that the matter can be settled—even while the prince acknowledges that the conflict is beyond redress.

Despite the liveliness of the mumming at Hertford Castle, Lydgate's art is presentational rather than representational. With the possible exception of the wives in this piece, Lydgate's "characters" do not speak in their own voices; they are presented and "read" by a Herald, Fortune, or some unnamed speaker. Although there may be action, there is little or no verbal interaction between participants. The pieces are structured very simply: either there is an oration followed by a bit of action—gift giving, a song—or there are a series of allegorical figures whose portraits and significance are read by the presenter. This predisposition toward "reading" can also be seen in Lydgate's "Bycorne and Chychevache," in which a speaker apparently elucidates the meaning of a series of painted scenes, or in "Procession of Corpus Christi," thought by some to be a description of a London Corpus Christi procession but which seems to me to be a sermon, or "process," centered on imagined *figurae* or pictures of them.[67]

---

67. Lydate, *Minor Poems of John Lydgate*, 1:35–43. The poem opens: on this feast of Corpus Christi, "In youre presence fette out of fygure, / Schal beo declared by many vnkouþe signe / Gracyous maisteryes grounded in scripture" (lines 6–8). Many arcane signs, he says, shall be declared in your presence, which secrets are brought out of *figurae*, the "vnkouþe signe[s]." In the stanzas that follow, Lydgate emphasizes the role of memory in this meditation: "Seoþe and considerþe in youre imaginatyf" how Christ was crucified for Adam's sin (line 10); "Remembreþe eeke in youre Inwarde entente" Melchisedeck's offering of wine and bread "In fygure" of the Sacrament (lines 17–19). Lines from the last stanza suggest that the sermon may have been intended to elucidate a series of pictures (in a window or painting): With these "fygures shewed in youre presence, / By diuers likenesses you to doo pleasaunce, / Resceiueþe hem with devoute reverence, / Þis bred of lyfe yee kepe in Remembraunce" (lines 217–20).

The word "fygures" suggests "images" to the modern reader, but Lydgate has used the term throughout in the technical sense of *figurae*. For the modern reader, "shewed" compounds the sense of "images," but it need mean nothing more than "presented" or "demonstrated." However, when he says he intends to do pleasure by "diuers likenesses," we seem to be dealing with something more

Lydgate is a presenter, not a playwright. The mumming at Hertford is the closest he comes to creating a piece centered on an agonistic struggle or interaction between participants. His rhetorical style, his presentational mode, is representative of an aesthetic desired by the audiences that paid for his services. Lydgate was patronized by the court and merchant oligarchs because he could produce the rhetorically elegant and morally edifying spectacles and conceits they desired. Presumably, it was an aesthetic that Lydgate felt was compatible with his clerical status; his mummings and disguisings are primarily monovocal, allegorical, descriptive, "read" texts.

Although court revels in the Tudor period became much more elaborate—and extraordinarily expensive—they retain the same aesthetic. Sidney Anglo regards some early pageants for Henry VII as an attempt to imitate the splendors of the Burgundian courts, but this form of entertainment reached its apogee in the early years of Henry VIII's reign. We can see how these spectacles are indebted to the Lydgatian model and moved beyond it in the entertainment at Greenwich in 1514 that culminated in a spectacular disguising at the final feast on 7 October.[68] These events were part of the celebration of the Anglo-French marriage negotiations and the Treaty of Universal Peace. After the feast, Henry and the court retired to a large hall on the ground floor for the pageant. It opened with the entry of a group of Turks playing on drums. They were followed by the principal characters: a winged horse, Pegasus, and his rider, Reaport. Pegasus says that he has flown throughout the world to announce the marriage, but, since he cannot sing, he has two children sing the good news. Pegasus introduces the castle pageant-car that Reaport reads for the audience. The car had a castle, a rock, and a gilded cave with silk curtains through which nine damsels with candles could be seen. Hidden within the rock were the musicians, and there were nine youths in livery outside the cave. Above the rock were five trees bearing the arms of the pope, the emperor, the king of France, Henry VIII, and the king of Spain. Reaport reads the significance of the cart. As he concludes, a Turk comes forward to dispute Reaport's claims. Fifteen men take sides against one another and engage in a tourney. The

---

tangible. If the poem functions like the "Bycorne" piece, then it is quite possible that Lydgate is using a series of images to make his sermon vivid. In any event, I think we can dispel the notion that he is describing a London Corpus Christi procession. None of the processions for which we have documentation are patterned on an orderly and chronologically disposed set of Old and New Testament figures (not to mention a series of Fathers and commentators). Nelson, *Medieval English Stages*, 4–5, 173–74, regards the poem as a description of an actual series of plays.

68. Anglo, *Spectacle*, 130–33.

pageant is drawn before the king for a concert of instrumental music, and then the car returns to its former position and the youths and damsels descend to perform a dance. This pageant has the ingredients of most of these elaborated disguisings: one or more pageant cars with allegorical significance and romance settings, an interpreter of the scene, a *débat* of some sort, music, and finally dancing.

Other performances are more reminiscent of Lydgate's mummings. For example, the Dialogue of Love and Riches, given at an Anglo-French diplomatic reception at Greenwich in 1527, opened with the appearance of eight choristers who sang English songs.[69] A youth dressed as Mercury stepped forward to deliver a Latin oration extolling the friendship between England and France. He then announced that Jupiter, who had heard disputes between Love and Riches, had deputed Henry VIII to adjudicate the issues. The eight choristers, divided into two groups, return to present the respective cases of Cupid *(Amor)* and Plutus *(Richezza)*. At the conclusion of the statement of their cases, the matter still being unresolved, three knights appear for each side and fight across a barrier in the hall. After the combat, an old, silver-bearded gentleman enters and pronounces that both love and riches are necessary for princes.

The actions of these presentations are obviously elaborated beyond those of Lydgate; nevertheless, they remain more presentational than representational. The agonistic element, which Lydgate used only in the mumming at Hereford, is more fully present in the form of *débat* or of tourneying. Yet speeches tend to be formal, declarative, and rhetorical. Even though persons represent "characters," they do not reveal meaning by inhabiting their characters and engaging in mimetic action; rather, they state a position or, in the case of Reaport, read the scene for the audience.

Although Medwall, Rastell, and others began to present dramas privately in and around London, the preference in public ceremony remained Lydgatian. The Lord Mayor's Show contained costumed figures, guilds in their livery, and pageants showing biblical and mythological subjects. Royal entries featured elaborate tableaux with speeches, or at times the pageant would be explained by a presenter. Edward VI's coronation entry into London on 19 February 1547 was, in fact, based on the John Lydgate poem describing the 1432 entry of Henry VI.[70]

Henry Medwall's *Fulgens and Lucrece* is often cited as the decisive move to

---

69. Ibid., 220–21; Streitberger, *Court Revels*, 127–29.
70. Streitberger, *Court Revels* 180–81. Lydgate's poem appears in *Minor Poems*, 2:630–48.

secular drama that anticipated the explosion in theatrical activity of the later sixteenth century[71]; however, his *Nature* can stand as an emblem of how Lydgatian mummery can move from the kind of formal aesthetic that I described above to the moral dramas we associate with the provinces. The opening of *Nature* looks much like the Lydgatian mummings except that the personators "read" themselves in their own voices.[72] Throughout the play these formal speeches are in rhyme royal, Lydgate's preferred stanza. The play moves into tail-rhyme (usually) as it descends into the world of Man's fallen state. The play opens with processions of Nature and World, who then station themselves so as to point to their potential opposition. In this lengthy and formal presentation Nature explains that she is God's agent, tells man of his nature, and insists that Reason should rule over Sensuality, to which the latter objects. Reason and Sensuality enter into a kind of body-and-soul debate in which Reason asserts his supremacy and Sensuality resists. Innocence intrudes to say that he will remain with Man as long as he follows Reason, but Man, bewildered by this debate, is finally told by Reason that Man is created as a combination of Reason and Sensuality when he is brought into the world. So they go off to World as Nature demands. The first part of the play is a formal *débat,* which, if this were a court disguising, then might proceed to a ritual battle followed by reconciliation.

Medwall's play moves into the arena of moral drama, however. The opening part, as we learn after the *débat,* is to be read as occurring prior to Man's birth or as the period before he comes to reason. Note, for example, that when he comes to World (lines 430 ff.), World comments on Man's nakedness even though both Man and Innocence believe Man to be sufficiently clothed as Nature brought him forth—that is, in innocent nakedness. World responds that this is not paradise, that Man will get cold, and so World clothes him. World counsels him to get rid of Innocence and hire a larger retinue. When Man

---

71. For example, Wilson, *English Drama,* 7.

72. Medwall, *Plays of Henry Medwall.* Nelson says (2–3) that both plays were composed between 1490 and 1500, during Medwall's employment by the archbishop of Canterbury, John Morton, who was also Lord Chancellor of England and a cardinal (9–13). The plays presumably were performed in the dining hall at Lambeth Palace, London. Nelson also indicates that *Nature* borrows from Lydgate's *Reason and Sensuallyte* (ca. 1430) and that *Fulgens* is indebted to the Latin humanist de Montemagno's treatise *De vera nobilitate;* thus, *Fulgens* is a drama akin to the disguising, *The Dialogue of Love and Riches. Fulgens* also incorporates many of the features we would expect in court maskings: a song, a wrestling match, a comic joust, and elaborate mumming (a dance accompanied by musical instruments). Suzanne Westfall, *Patrons and Performance,* 56–57, thinks these features and the large cast of twenty-two suggests chapel performance at the archbishop's.

agrees to banish Innocence (at line 637), his speech moves from the rhyme royal of the opening portions to rime couée, a verse form associated with northern provincial writing (by Chaucer and in the northern cycles and romances). The plot is a delightful variation on the theme of the Fall and Redemption that we see in the East Anglian *Castle of Perseverance* and *Mankind*. The play does not end with a unifying image of a dance, as in the court mummings, but rather with a communal singing of a religious carol (see lines 1409–12). If Medwall's *Fulgens and Lucrece* is to be taken as the decisive lead into secular drama, then we may construe *Nature* as a moment when the tradition of moral drama was introduced to new aristocratic and clerical audiences.

⁂

This chapter has suggested that drama occurred within certain cities and towns, especially in the north, when there was sufficient population and a lay power base. This is not to say that if these conditions were there, then drama necessarily came forth, London being the prime example. Furthermore, if we take into account the material presented in the preceding chapter, then we see that until the early sixteenth century, drama, that is, use of enacted scripts of biblical and moral content, was the ludic mode of provincial laypeople, whether in the north or the larger East Anglian area, and not of aristocrats or monastics and other religious. Moreover, this mode continued to predominate in the provincial areas, and even after it was introduced into more aristocratic and courtly circles, the presentational mode continued to predominate at court and in London well into Elizabeth's reign.

Texts and Performances

Having described the practices we might expect to find in cities, towns, monasteries, and parishes and among clerics and laypeople, I would like in the next three chapters to turn to the texts that survive in order to consider their traditions of performance and their content. I begin by describing the texts and production techniques that we find in the two primary geographical areas of dramatic presentation, the swath across the top of the Midlands from Chester to York, and the area of Greater East Anglia. Chapters 6 and 7 focus on issues with which the texts present us. With regard to the northern biblical cycles, I wish to explore further how the texts encode the piety of laypeople rather than that of clerics. Although I will argue that biblical drama may have arisen as a solution—religious, political and otherwise—to clerical attempts to suppress and control play and game, I do not take the position that clerics did not support biblical drama, only that they did not participate in or produce it. Rather, they seem to have accepted the new drama as appropriate for laypeople. Nevertheless, we can see that the biblical drama did not support a clerical educational agenda but a spirituality reflective of late medieval lay piety. Chapter 7 turns to selected plays of East Anglia, *Mary Magdalene, Castle of Perseverance,* and *Wisdom,* in order to explore different problems: the mixing of genres, allegorical technique and the representation of character, and the reading of allegorical texts. Although I have treated the East Anglian dramas and the northern biblical cycles separately, I wish to claim finally that the two traditions constitute one broad theatrical tradition of provincial drama.

Most of the *ludi* that I described in the preceding chapters have no extant texts, assuming that there ever were texts rather than orders for processions or just free play and games. This chapter describes the current status of research on extant texts primarily from the north and in East Anglia. Not many years ago scholars thought they knew what the extant Middle English texts represented. Even though there were questions about locations for some of these texts, what the texts stood for, and how they were performed, there was a consensus that the Chester, Wakefield, York and N-Town cycles were the remnants of a widespread phenomenon of late medieval life in which cities and towns throughout England put on extensive sequences of biblical plays. As we now know, these cycles were rarities, but discussion continues about what the extant texts represent: when were they written, who performed them, and how were they performed?

The corpus of works we now associate with East Anglia did not attract the attention that the northern biblical cycles did until rather late in the twentieth century; however, one would have to add that none of the texts as dramas garnered much commentary, especially when compared with the interest shown in their histories. The dominant thinking was that the northern cycles were the typical representatives of the dramatic tradition and the "moralities" and "saint plays" constituted a simpler, less dynamic tradition even though eventually it was through the moralities that one arrived at the golden age of Elizabethan drama.

Much has changed in the past twenty-five to thirty years as new editions of the texts have appeared, as performances of almost all of them have been presented, and as a more systematic search of dramatic and ceremonial records has been undertaken.[1] The republication of the texts has drawn attention to—and raised questions about—the manuscripts in which they appear. There is a much more sophisticated knowledge of manuscript culture and the "stories" manuscripts can tell us now than there was when the texts were first published and the scholars familiar with manuscripts few. Every recent edition of these manuscripts, and the work done on them as a consequence, has challenged what we thought we knew about these play texts, their auspices, and numerous other matters. Modern productions of the plays have convinced viewers of their dramatic vitality and viability, and performers, and audiences, have come to an appreciation of the suppleness and effectiveness as stage speech of the

---

1. I am referring, of course, to the new EETS editions of the plays (though York was published outside this series), to the performances at Toronto, York, Chester, Leeds, Lancaster, and many other places (for many years now calendared and often reviewed in *Research Opportunities in Renaissance Drama*), and to the efforts of the Malone Society and the Records of Early English Drama. Since I have already described much of the records research, I will not be particularly concerned with it in this and the following chapter.

many verse forms in these plays. Performances that have tried to re-create something of the conditions of production by staging plays on moveable carts or stationary pageants have taught us a lot about the capacities of relatively simple stage structures—though some, as in *Castle, Mary Magdalene* or N-Town, are by no means simple.

Before we can assess the contents of the extant plays, we need to know something about what their manuscripts represent. I will talk primarily about the plays that exist only in manuscript, but toward the end of the chapter I move into a discussion of the earliest plays to be printed in order to provide some contrast with those that did not get printed. In addition, I will use the printing history of some of these plays, especially those that were printed sometime after they were originally written and performed, in order to make us more conscious of the fact that the "medieval" plays continued to be "published" in performance long after they were originally written and that they weathered some of the greatest upheavals in English history. Although I refer from time to time to performance conditions, I am not primarily interested in plays in performance; rather, I am concerned, where appropriate, with the circumstances under which they were staged. My purpose in this chapter is to provide information and to raise questions about the texts that survive.

Texts and Performances: The Northern Cycle Plays

There are two performance conventions in English drama: the ambulatory stages of the northern biblical plays and the fixed stages of the biblical and moral dramas chiefly written for production in East Anglia (Norfolk and Suffolk) and southeastern England (Essex and Kent) but common in England wherever there are references to dramas.[2] As we have seen, however, records of dramatic performances—except for folk plays—are rather sparse outside the two principal areas under discussion.[3]

Archival records of York, Coventry, and Chester indicate that the cities' pageants were performed on pageant wagons *seriatim* at various stations

---

2. At one time it had been argued that there was a third performance convention, that of *The Conversion of St. Paul*, in which the audience moved from stage to stage, but I think most commentators now agree that this convention was based in a misperception of what *process* and *processioun* mean in this text and in the region. *Process* means "entertainment" or the "narrative that is being performed," as is apparent from the Digby *Killing of the Children* (lines 49, 484 s.d.) and *The Conversion of St. Paul* (lines 14, 157) (both in Baker, Murphy, and Hall, *Late Medieval Religious Plays*) and John Bale's *The Temptation of Our Lord*, line 21 (in Bale, *Complete Plays*).

3. This conclusion must remain tentative, but the REED project material collected thus far suggests the generalization will hold.

throughout the towns: ten to sixteen places for York; an uncertain number for Coventry; and usually four for Chester.[4] Individual plays are constructed in the same manner in all three cycles. Although they may vary considerably in length and number of episodes, each is a self-contained unit meant to be performed by the guild who sponsored it. As a consequence, large numbers of actors were required, since each pageant that had God or Christ required an actor; each pageant that showed Christ and his apostles presumably had to have thirteen actors. These requirements suggest that only large cities with an elaborate corporate structure could afford to produce and man a long sequence of plays.

There are four extant sets of plays from the north: the York register (circa 1467), the Towneley (Wakefield) manuscript (circa 1500), the two surviving pageants from Coventry (in the past referred to as "True Coventry"; both texts are revisions dated 1534), and the antiquarian manuscripts of Chester (five manuscripts, 1591–1607; there are also some fragments and separate pageant manuscripts). All of these texts are problematical.

The York register came about when the city required all participants to record their texts with the city; however, even as late as the final performances, some of the guilds had not registered their texts and others were performing texts different from those in the register.[5] It is difficult to know, therefore, what the text was at any given performance. A reading through of the Passion sequence, with its repetitions and inconsistencies, suggests that individual guilds did not consult with one another about the matter of their plays. Further, even though the city clerk sat at the first station in order to hear the plays and check them against the register, neither he nor apparently anyone else ever attempted a systematic rewriting of the guild texts into a more continuous and economical narrative.[6] The York register has a certain chaotic quality to it that suggests the individualism of the guilds within this great civic enterprise; the producers were not New Critics.

---

4. Johnston and Rogerson, *York,* 8, 10–12, 119–20, 298, 311, 356, 366, 406. For discussion, one might begin with Twycross, "'Places to Hear the Plays'"; E. White, "Places for Hearing the Corpus Christi Play in York"; and Crouch, "Paying to See the Play." For earlier studies of the feasibility of performing at so many stations, see Nelson, "Principles of Processional Staging"; the essays by Margaret Dorrell and Martin Stevens in *Leeds Studies in English;* and the summary in William Tydeman, *Theatre in the Middle Ages.* Ingram estimates there were three stations at Coventry; see "'To find the players,'" 30. For Chester, see Clopper, "Rogers' Description of the Chester Plays."

5. Beadle, *York Plays,* 10–19; Beadle and Meredith, *York Play: A Facsimile;* and Beadle, "York Cycle."

6. Meredith, "John Clerke's Hand."

Although there are records referring to the Coventry plays as early as the 1420s, we have an incomplete knowledge of the cycle's content.[7] Only two plays survive, both revised by Robert Croo in 1534. Traditionally, the number of pageants has been placed at ten (on rather insecure evidence).[8] The records, by my count, demonstrate the existence of at least eight. The two Croo revisions concern the events of Christ's birth up to his meeting with the Doctors in Jerusalem. There are perhaps four pageants on the Passion, from the betrayal at Gethsemane to Emaus (the latter first noted only in 1552).[9] My list concludes with the Mercers' *Assumption of the Virgin* and the Drapers' *Doomsday*.[10] Conspicuously missing are any references to Old Testament plays. A number of other subjects are also missing: Christ's ministry and early miracles, early stages of the conspiracy against Christ, the Last Supper, appearances to the disciples (except for Emaus), the Ascension, and Pentecost. Since most of the guilds known to be active can be assigned to plays, it seems unlikely that all of the missing actions could have been performed by the remaining guilds. Consequently, the evidence implies that Coventry's play was principally a Passion play with some material from Christ's nativity and childhood and the obligatory Marian play and *Doomsday*.

The Towneley manuscript is the most problematical of all the northern texts.[11] The manuscript, which approaches luxury quality, appears to contain a cycle of plays intended for performance in one town—traditionally Wakefield because of the local allusions in the *Mactacio Abel* and the Wakefield Master's plays—but in recent years there has been growing uneasiness with this

---

7. Ingram, "'To find the players'"; and "'Pleyng geire accustumed belongyng & necessarie.'" Also see Phythian-Adams, "Ceremony and the Citizen."

8. Craig, *Two Coventry Corpus Christi Plays*, xi–xiv.

9. The Smiths' accounts from 1477–91 show that they had scenes of the betrayal, the trial before Pilate, Annas and Caiphas, the trial before Herod, and the dream of Pilate's wife; Judas appears first in 1489, and the late accounts, 1573–78, suggest that the play had the betrayal, cockcrowing, and Judas's suicide (Ingram, *Coventry*, 59, 61, 71, 72–74, 264–65, 269, 285, 289). The Cappers provided the scenes of Crucifixion and the Deposition through the Appearance to Mary Magdalene, as is shown in records that are nearly continuous from 1534 (ibid., 139–40 ff.; Emaus appears in the account on 191).

10. There are no records that specify the Mercers' subject, but their badge was of the Assumption (Ingram, *Coventry*, 125, 564 n). The Drapers have annual accounts for their *Doomsday* from 1561 (ibid., 216–17 ff.), but there are some undated accounts from earlier in the century (ibid., app. 2, 455–81).

11. Stevens, "Missing Parts of the Towneley Cycle"; Cawley and Stevens, *Towneley Cycle*; Stevens, *Four Middle English Mystery Cycles*; and Stevens, "The Towneley Plays Manuscript."

assumption.[12] The manuscript has a number of puzzling features. First, it has been assigned to Wakefield because two of the pageants have that name written at the head of their texts. But if the whole cycle belongs to Wakefield, why are only two pageants rubricated that way? Or, perhaps more to the point, why should there be any rubric at all? Indeed, the first rubric, the scribe's prayer for assistance, is not a guild ascription at all; it may be no more than an indicator of where the scribe was working. There are other anomalies: there are two shepherds' plays but no nativity; several plays are not in their proper order; five of the plays come from the York cycle; and five plays written in an idiosyncratic stanza have been assigned to the Wakefield Master, but there are instances of this stanza at other places in the manuscript. There are five guild ascriptions in a sixteenth-century hand, but it is not known whether there was sufficient guild structure in Wakefield to mount a cycle of plays. Individual plays in the manuscript are constructed as they are at other places where we know the cycle was processional—as opposed to the N-Town Passion plays—but Wakefield appears to be too small and economically underdeveloped in the late medieval period to have mounted a cycle of plays equivalent to those of York, Coventry, and Chester.[13] On the other hand, there is reason to believe that by the mid–sixteenth century there was a Corpus Christi play of some sort in Wakefield.

Several solutions have been offered to resolve these anomalies. In his acting edition of the Wakefield plays, Martial Rose suggested that the cycle was performed at one station; however, his argument was based on internal evidence, which is unreliable.[14] An alternative recently offered is that the manuscript is a compilation of plays from the West Riding or Yorkshire area, the implication being that Wakefield never had a cycle of plays even though some of those in the manuscript may derive from there.[15] This approach suggests that a compiler, probably a drama aficionado, collected plays from the region and put them together in one manuscript in order to imitate the cycles he knew to exist at York and Coventry or in order to create a providential history like the *Cursor Mundi* and other vernacular biblical histories. This "cycle" may have been made up of occasional plays—Shepherds plays from Christmas—and single Old Testament plays such as *Noah* and *Abraham,* and then filled out with

---

12. D. Mills, "'Towneley Plays'"; Palmer, "'Towneley Plays'"; and Epp, "Hazards of Cycling." For the Wakefield allusions, see Stevens and Cawley, *Towneley Plays*, 2:xix–xx.

13. The argument that Wakefield could sustain a cycle because it was similar in population to Beverley would seem not to hold given my analysis of the Beverley records in chapter 4.

14. Rose, *Wakefield Mystery Plays*, 19–48; see also Stevens, "Staging of the Wakefield Plays."

15. Palmer, "'Towneley Plays.'"

texts, such as those from York, for some of the missing parts. This line of reasoning works to a point: one can well imagine the Wakefield Master writing several entertainments for the Christmas season and perhaps the *Coliphizacio* for a midsummer fest; but how likely is it that there would have been separate plays of the Creation and Fall, the killing of Abel, Abraham and Isaac, Jacob, and a procession of prophets in the surrounding region?[16] Further, the manuscript contains plays in which the Wakefield Master's idiosyncratic stanza is used to add to or fill out texts of plays (especially in the Passion sequence, for example, about one-half of the *Flagellation*). Since the Wakefield Master's own work appears in the Old Testament, Nativity, and Passion sections of the volume, and since the idiosyncratic stanza appears piecemeal throughout the Passion sequence and the *Judicium*, the stanza is not localized but exists throughout the manuscript; as a consequence, Martin Stevens has made the argument that the Wakefield Master is the final "auctor" of the Towneley Manuscript.[17]

Even if we were to accept the argument that the existence of the stanza need not indicate that a single poet wrote all of the plays, we would still be bound to observe that this idiosyncratic stanza exists only in this manuscript, a fact that would in turn argue for some relation between the scripts in the manuscript. Further, this stanza is a dramatic verse; it is colloquial and dialogic, a speaking verse form. It seems hardly conceivable that a poet would have gone through a compilation of scripts adding these stanzas to fill out a *reading* text.

On the other hand, as Garrett Epp has argued, if the Wakefield Master is the auctor or compiler, he ought not to be regarded as a "master" since a number of plays are out of order,[18] there are unexpected omissions,[19] and there are repetitions and inconsistencies.[20] Epp raises the legitimate question whether we

---

16. Alexandra Johnston has located single-episode "plays" on Jacob and his twelve sons in Thame, Oxfordshire, in 1481, and on Adam and Eve in 1506–7 and Cain in 1511–12 and 1515–16 in Reading, Berkshire; see "What Revels Are in Hand?" 98. The records, which I have seen at the REED office, do not provide much detail, and one wonders whether these are dramas or pageants or, in the case of Jacob and his sons, a reference to costumed figures in a parish procession. In any event, there are no such records for the area around Wakefield.

17. Stevens, *Four Middle English Mystery Cycles,* 88–180.

18. *Pharaoh* follows *Prophets; Flight into Egypt* precedes *Herodes;* and *Lazarus* appears after *Doomsday.* The *Suspencio Jude,* which comes at the end of the manuscript, is in a later hand.

19. Omitted are plays on the nativity, temptation, Christ's ministry, Pentecost, and a trial before Herod, even though the scene is referred to in *Scourging* (22.53).

20. Christ's robe is diced for three times; Pilate is present for the Crucifixion but seems to know nothing about it in the next play; Mary is presumably nine months pregnant in *Joseph's Doubt* but

want to regard the Wakefield Master as the "author" rather than the auctor of the Towneley Manuscript, whether we want to think of him as the gatherer of texts rather than someone who tried to create a consistent and well-articulated master text, for if the Wakefield Master's intervention into texts in this manuscript was intended to provide a master text, then we must conclude that he failed. On the other hand, repetitions and inconsistencies do not disprove that these plays constitute a cycle, for we see the same pattern in the register at York, where guilds had control of their texts and apparently did not consult with one another. And so we return to the same question: what is the significance of the Wakefield Master's interventions in plays throughout the manuscript?

Many of the interventions are made with little apparent purpose.[21] The remaining interventions, which are substantive, are more easily explained. The Wakefield Master wrote five stanzas of an opening rant for Pilate for the *Conspiracy*, a play borrowed from York.[22] Arnold Williams has argued that the rant helps characterize Pilate as an evil figure rather than the benign one generally found in the other cycles.[23] The *Flagellation* opens with a rant by Pilate followed by stanzas 5–27, about half of the play, in the Wakefield meter. We might conclude in this instance that the Master was working with a defective script or that he chose to replace the text before him (after this intervention the play moves to scenes between John and Mary before the torturers' encounter with Simeon, so the Wakefield Master's portion is an entire piece). The last intervention is in the *Judicium* and scholars have assumed that this is an instance in which the Wakefield Master chose to exercise his remarkable—and colloquial—sense of humor by placing a comic scene between the now-lost traditional opening of the Doomsday pageant and the final Judgment.

If we look at the majority of these interventions as evidence of the Wakefield Master's interests, then we might gain a better understanding of why he

---

Elizabeth is only six months pregnant in the *Salutation* even though she conceived earlier (the problem exists in N-Town as well). In addition, we might note that Christ's miracles are listed a number of times by different characters in the Passion plays.

21. Stanza 57 in *Crucifixion* and stanzas 57–58 in *Ascension* add nothing new. Stanza 4 in *Peregrinus* looks like an editorial intervention to restore symmetry that is observed elsewhere in the pageant.

22. Stanza 6 has the shape of a Wakefield stanza but only twelve lines and thus may be defective. Cawley and Stevens, *Towneley Cycle*, 2.545, argue that lines 624–75 are identical in form, tone, and diction to the opening stanzas. These lines form the conclusion to the scene of Judas's betrayal and are spoken by Malcus, the two soldiers and, at the last, by Pilate.

23. Williams, *Characterization of Pilate*, 28–30, 75, and passim.

worked with these texts. First, he seems fond of opening rants: the Garcio speech in *Mactacio Abel* (if the play is his), and the Pilate speeches for *Conspiracy* and *Talents*. But in the *Coliphizacio* he makes the unprecedented move of starting abruptly with the soldiers herding Christ into the platea. If we were to remove the rant from the *Flagellation,* then that play would begin in the same way. The abruptness of the opening of the *Coliphizacio* and the potential for a similar one in *Flagellation* might argue that the Wakefield Master was trying to construct a fluid drama broken into scenes for some reason. But when we compare the two Pilate rants, we notice a startling number of similarities, sufficient to suggest that one writer is imitating the other. Does the imitation at the beginning of the *Flagellation* indicate a redactor later than the Wakefield Master? Or is the Wakefield Master the imitator? I do not see a way to resolve that question, but the rant at the opening of the *Flagellation,* if it is the imitation, allows that there was a redactor after the Wakefield Master. Perhaps the Wakefield Master was not only a writer but a collector of plays, some of which he revised or tinkered with before seeing them performed. But some of the plays in the manuscript show no sign of his intervention, suggesting that if he was the collector—and producer—he was content to have them played as they were. I think the question whether the Wakefield Master was the auctor of the Towneley Manuscript must remain open—he may have been collected rather than being the collector—but I also think we can conclude that he was not an author of a cycle, as we usually understand that term.

If we think of the Wakefield Master as an author of plays rather than of a cycle, we can see that his work—whether whole scripts or interventions—links him to two powerful ludic sources: folk culture and liturgical parodies and intrusions. He seems to have been intent on appropriating the carnivalesque character of the seasonal year—the Christmas laughter of choirboys, the grotesqueries of *miracula* at midsummer, and the great repasts of festival—in virtually every one of the plays he composed. He is fond of the folkloric rebellious servant: Slowpase in the *Prima Pastorum,* Daw in the *Secunda Pastorum,* and Froward in *Coliphizacio.* If the Wakefield Master wrote the *Mactacio Abel*—and I remain skeptical that he did—he seems to have appropriated elements of the plough play into which he intruded a parody of the mass.[24] The Shepherds plays are less sedate versions of the liturgical *pastores* for Christmas insofar as they engage in the ludic indiscretions of the choirboys' activities on the eves of Saint Nicholas, Holy Innocents, and Saint Stephen. The most sug-

---

24. For the latter, see Stevens and Cawley, *Townely Plays,* 2.447, the note to line 468.

gestive elements in them are the grotesque feast and the parody of the *Gloria* (only in Wakefield and Chester, though there might be a little in N-Town). Banquets in carnivalesque, according to Bakhtin, are banquets for the world, yet the grotesque feast in the plays at first is a negative reference to this carnivalesque one because the master shepherds wish to keep the food to themselves and try to deny any to the apprentice; it is anticarnival, private, deprivatory. But in the quantity and variety of the food eventually produced we see the grotesque realism of carnival, and the wrestling match among the shepherds in Chester provides a good example of topsy-turveydom since the apprentice overturns his superiors.[25] The banquet is finally shared with the servant, and at Chester it becomes a true carnival banquet when the shepherds distribute their excess to the audience.[26] The Wakefield Master transposes the liturgical *representatio Herod*—a licit *representatio*—but in adapting it for the vernacular stage, instead of the Rachel *figura,* he intrudes the "grotesque realism" of the slaughter scene (from the choirboys' less decorous action on Holy Innocents?). Is the Herod of the *Magnus Herodes* constructed as a Christmas Lord?[27] At the beginning of the play Nuntius has a rather long rant preceding Herod's own, whereas the common practice in other cycles is to start with Herod's rant. Nuntius' speech is comparable to Garcio's in the *Mactacio Abel* and a fairly clear borrowing from folk drama. If the *Mactacio Abel* is a Christianization of a plough play, is the Herod a textualizing of liturgical parody or of Herod's antics at the Feast of Holy Innocents? In keeping with carnival there is death, tragedy, sorrow, and comic reversal in the women's beating of the soldiers, which also has a regenerative effect on the audience as well as a tie to the thematic idea of resurrection from death. The torturers in the *Coliphizacio* say they will teach Christ a "new play of Yoyll" (= Hot Cockles, EETS 21.498); they call him King Copin (line 241), a name for a Christmas King of Fools, according to Cawley and Stevens;[28] and in the *Conspiracy,* they say they will lead

---

25. Wrestling has a link to festive activity; it was one of the sports against which bishops and others complained because it took place in churchyards on saints' days and Sundays.

26. The sharing is suggested by the fact that the Chester Painters purchased multiple items of the foods named in the shepherds' list of foods and by the directive in the Chester Late Banns that the Bakers "caste go*des* loues abroade with accustomed cherefull harte" (Clopper, *Chester,* 245). The latter hint at the use of bread as a token presented to the onlookers much as favors are thrown to the crowds at Mardi Gras. Scholars in the past have thought that the shepherds' food was imaginary; see Cawley, "Grotesque Feast."

27. Stevens, "Herod as Carnival King"; and Weimann, *Shakespeare and the Popular Tradition in the Theater,* 64–72.

28. Cawley and Stevens, *Towneley Cycle,* 2:558.

him in a "dawnce" to Pilate's hall (22.92)—an echo of events in a somergame? All of this festive laughter coalesces in Titivillus the Great, who is identified by the other devils as a boy when they say that he will be a great shrew "when he comes of age" (30.337–38). Later he is called a chorister ("querestur" at line 306), and the play is associated even further with the parodies of the schools when the Second Demon compliments him on his knowledge of grammar, actually the bad Latin of line 364. Then Titivillus takes off on a long litany of the seven deadly sins, which may have been patterned on clerical rants at Christmas, a kind of anti-sermon. Given that the torturers in the *Coliphizacio* characterize their torments as a Christmas game, we well might ask whether the Wakefield Master's plays were not occasional pieces for that season. Or, if we take the tormentors' remarks simply as allusive, we may ask whether the plays may have been designed to be played alone at appropriate seasons of the year. Since so many of these plays could have been performed as single pieces, and since a number of them seem to be associated with Christmas, perhaps the Wakefield Master is to be identified as the *ludimagister* of a school in or near Wakefield.[29]

In all of these examples the Wakefield Master intrudes laughter into "serious" matter. Why does he do this? Does he celebrate festive culture by bringing it into the plays? Does he write these as lay *ludi* to match clerical *representationes*? Or does he write them in order to co-opt and suppress lay festive culture, to substitute appropriate game for *ludi inhonesti*? Perhaps he had more than one motive; in any event, rather than thinking of these instances as "secularization" with its connotation of debasement, as less artful examples have been labeled in the past, we should think of them as deliberate appropriations of folk play and liturgical parody.

We have little additional evidence to suggest what the tradition may have been at Wakefield, if indeed that is where some or all of these texts are to be located. As A. C. Cawley, Jean Forrester, and John Goodchild have demonstrated, many of the items that J. W. Walker published as entries in the Wakefield Burgess Rolls are actually records from other towns.[30] Nevertheless, the rolls for 1556 and 1559 do contain three references to a Corpus Christi play: one is an order that every guild is to bring forth "theire pagyauntes of Corpus

---

29. Alternatively, Westfall, *Patrons and Performance*, 49, notes that the *Second Shepherds Play* has a number of features, especially sophisticated music, that suggest that it may have been a chapel play of a noble household.

30. Cawley, Forrester, and Goodchild, "References to the Corpus Christi Play." See also Cawley, *Wakefield Pageants*, 124–26.

Chr*isti* daye," as accustomed; another calls for Giles Dolleffe to bring in the "regenall" of the play; and a third requires the masters of the play to come make their accounts before the gentlemen and burgesses of the town. The first two are reminiscent of records in other towns, and the second suggests that there was either a text or a document that described the order of pageants. But the third is unusual because if the pageants belong to the guilds, the accounting, as at Chester and elsewhere, would have been internal. Why do the guilds make their accounts to the civic officials? Is the play, like a parish ale, some kind of centralized commercial endeavor?

Although we have no assurance of the content of the Wakefield Corpus Christi play, the assumption has been that it was the cycle of plays contained in the Towneley Manuscript, and this assumption was believed to have been partly substantiated by a 1576 directive sent from York by the Ecclesiastical Commission to the bailiff and burgesses of Wakefield saying that "no Pageant [is to] be vsed or set furthe wherin the Maiestye of god the father god the sonne or god the holie ghoste or the administration of either the sacramentes of Baptisme or of the lordes Supper be counterfeyted or represented."[31] Since the message was addressed to the overseers of Wakefield, our presumption has been that the Ecclesiastical Commission knew the contents of the Wakefield play; however, it may be that the commission only knew that there was a Corpus Christi play and assumed, given their knowledge of the York Corpus Christi play, that it might contain the subjects listed. I no longer remain certain that the York officials had specific knowledge of the Wakefield play.

The other evidence we have, some sixteenth-century notations in the Towneley Manuscript that assign some plays to guilds, does not help clarify the situation. The marginal notes give the *Creation* to the Barkers, the *Mactacio Abel* to the Glovers, the *Pharaoh* and the *Suspencio Jude* to the Listers, and the *Peregrinus* to the Fishers. Although these guilds are not specifically linked to Wakefield by the notator, it has been assumed, since these names occur in various parts of the manuscript, that in the sixteenth century, the town of Wakefield produced a cycle of plays comparable to those at York and Chester and that these were some of the guilds who performed them. But, if this was the case, why do only some of the plays have guild ascriptions? There are other ways to read this evidence. If we take Norwich rather than York as a model, then the guild ascriptions might suggest that Wakefield—or whatever town these guilds were a part of—mounted a selection of plays rather than a cycle

---

31. Cawley, *Wakefield Pageants*, 125.

(though, admittedly, the *Suspencio Jude* seems an odd choice). Perhaps they performed them together or perhaps as self-contained dramas over a number of years. Perhaps the Towneley Manuscript is, after all, a compilation from which dramas could be chosen for performance in any given year.

It may be that the Towneley texts were never performed in their entirety in Wakefield or elsewhere; the manuscript could be a compilation of texts from Wakefield or somewhere nearby to which texts from other places such as York were added to create a "cycle" that would imitate those at York and Coventry. Perhaps the Wakefield Master or a disciple prepared a Passion sequence and the *Judicium* as Wakefield's Corpus Christi play and his Shepherds and Noah plays for other occasions; or perhaps there was a collection of Old and New Testament plays performed at Wakefield but not the entire sequence in the manuscript. However we ultimately interpret the often baffling evidence, it seems clear that a substantial number of these texts are somehow associated with one another.

The Chester plays are unique in that they exist in five manuscript copies and some parcels of individual plays.[32] The five manuscripts were copied by antiquarian scribes from the city "Regenall" (apparently something like the York register); they were probably collected together after the cycle's expansion into the three-day Whitsun play sometime in the decade 1521–31.[33] The puzzling feature about the five manuscript copies is that there is disagreement about the content of the cycle and the division of some of the plays; even more puzzling is that one scribe, George Bellin, made two copies that do not entirely agree with one another. This state of affairs has led to the conclusion that the "Regenall" was not only a master text but that it was a body of texts from which a cycle could be constructed—the implication being, as at York, that the script for the cycle might change from year to year. If this reconstruction is accurate, then we may conclude that the antiquarian manuscripts record a "text" from an unknown recension probably conglomerating pieces of text that were never performed at the same time. Perhaps the most obvious example is the Shepherds play, which contains two humorous analyses of the angels' song in two different meters. I suspect the two were never performed in any given year, but that they constitute alternates. An acting text would choose one or the other version.

Despite these cautionary words about the status of the extant manuscript

---

32. Lumiansky and Mills, *Chester Mystery Cycle,* and *Essays and Documents,* 3–86.
33. Clopper, "History and Development," 220–23.

versions, I want to emphasize that the Chester manuscripts read as more thoroughly integrated scripts than York's or Towneley's. Despite variation in meter, the Chester plays more consistently use one rhyme scheme, in this case, an eight-line rime couée, than do any of the other cycles (the revised Coventry texts excepted); indeed, York and Towneley are notable for their variety of stanzaic forms. More important, at Chester there seems to have been one playwright rather late in the day who went through the entire cycle adding his own distinctive meter with the result that the cycle has a more pointed thesis and set of interests (for example, the details of the old law in the Old Testament plays) than do other cycles.[34] It would appear that this kind of tailoring of the "text" could come about because there was a master text that someone decided to work through—as no one at York did. Although the guilds had copies of their plays, they registered them with the city, consulted the city register, and in one case in 1575 brought two versions of a play before the mayor for him to choose the better.[35]

Despite the fact that the Regenall had to be copied anew in 1568, many of the texts or parts of them are undoubtedly pre-Reformation.[36] This argument is largely suppositious, but there is some evidence to suggest the conclusion is probable. First, the Antichrist play in the antiquarian copies is very close to that in the Peniarth Manuscript, dated rather insecurely as circa 1500, as is the Manchester fragment of the opening of the *Resurrection*, dated late fifteenth or early sixteenth century.[37] These two external witnesses to the earliness of their respective plays does not demonstrate that all of the plays in the antiquarian copies are pre-Reformation; nevertheless, they do suggest the continuity of at least some parts of the text from the period of their composition until the last years of the cycle. Some texts are clearly Catholic, which suggests that they are pre-Reformation, although there is no way for us to distinguish pre-Reformation from Marian texts. Chester's *Last Judgment*, for example, includes a saved pope (24.41–80), numerous references to purgatory (lines 69–70, 89–90, 165–66, and 437ff.), and an allusion to the intervention of Mary and the saints (lines 613–16). It is difficult to see how this text could have been seen as an acceptable one in the

---

34. Travis, *Dramatic Design;* and Clopper, "Principle of Selection."

35. Clopper, "History and Development," 241–42. There is also evidence in the Banns and the "Lists of Companies and Their Pageants" that the cycle was continually in revision.

36. Randall Trever was called before the mayor to answer charges that he had taken but not returned the "originall book of the whydson plaies" (Clopper, *Chester,* 80; Salter, *Mediaeval Drama in Chester,* 50–51). There are subsequent expenditures in the guild accounts for recopying the Regenall (Clopper, *Chester,* 85, 82, 91).

37. Lumiansky and Mills, *Chester Mystery Cycle,* ix–xii.

reigns of Edward or Elizabeth, for the play would have had to have been edited in order to conform it to Anglican practice. There are occasional references in other plays that imply Catholic auspices; for example, in the *Creed Play*, Peter is referred to as the heir of Christ and the deviser of the first article of the creed (21.307–8); in the *Shepherds Play* two of the shepherds take on the vocations of hermit and anchorite (7.666–80); and in the *Resurrection* (18.167–85) and the *Creed Play* (21.343–46) there are problematical allusions to the Eucharist that might express belief in transubstantiation.

On the other hand, there are many plays that would have posed no significant problems for Anglican authorities. For example, the *Purification* dramatizes Mary's presentation of Christ to Simeon, the origin of Candlemas, a event celebrated by both Catholics and Anglicans. Similarly, the *Magnificat,* which was sung and then translated in the *Nativity,* is one of the few Marian pieces that continued under Anglican practice. With the occasional exception, it is difficult to see how these texts could not have functioned under Anglican auspices because they do not exhibit a specifically Catholic doctrine or point of view as far as the texts are concerned. Of course, we must allow that Catholic sympathizers could have imported a Catholic spirit into the plays through gesture, costume, singing, and other effects, but the texts themselves are not irretrievably Catholic.[38]

Indeed, there is little evidence that the cycle was materially altered during Henry's reign.[39] The Early Banns in their present state were copied into the White Book of the Pentice and into a parallel record during Henry Gee's second term of office, 1539–40, and remained unchanged until perhaps 1548, when several erasures were made in order to make the Banns conform to the suppression of the Corpus Christi feast. The Newhall Proclamation, which precedes the Early Banns, was originally written in 1531–32 in order to make the division of plays conform to the three-day performance schedule and to incorporate numerous changes in individual plays and responsibilities. The Proclamation was amended in 1539–40 to eliminate all references to Catholic sponsorship—the monkish authorship, the granting of pardon, and the like. But the content of the plays, according to the Lists of Companies and Their Pageants, did not materially change until the reign of Edward.[40] The wives

---

38. See Sally-Beth MacLean's discussion below of the Chester *Purification,* which she believes to retain its Catholic representation ("Marian Devotion").

39. Clopper, "History and Development," 225–33; Lumiansky and Mills, *Chester Mystery Cycle: Essays and Documents,* 176–92.

40. This finding is generally in accordance with Harold Gardiner's conclusions in *Mysteries'*

continued to produce the *Assumption* and the clergy their Corpus Christi play at least until 1539–40, when the Banns were copied into the Pentice book. Randle Holmes, the antiquarian scribe who copied this material, notes that the section that describes the play at Corpus Christi was erased, but this probably did not occur until Corpus Christi celebrations were suppressed in 1548; it certainly seems unlikely that the Pentice book scribe would have copied the section if it had already been erased before 1539–40.

The meager evidence for the period 1548–61 suggests that (1) the cycle remained more or less unchanged throughout the early Reformation period, but (2) in 1548 the clergy's Corpus Christi play was put down and (3) the Bakers' play was suspended, if not in that year, certainly by 1550. It is also possible that the wives' *Assumption* was suppressed; however, there is no concrete evidence to substantiate this supposition. There may have been other alterations in the texts; unfortunately, we do not have any records of expenditure on the plays, except for the Shoemakers' account, that are earlier than 1561, and, thus, we cannot be certain that there was any systematic rewriting or revision of the entire cycle during this period.

Thus far I have stressed that these pre-Reformation plays apparently were not perceived as antagonistic to Anglicanism, but there is one play, the *Abraham*, that strikes me as having been written in order to incorporate Anglican doctrine. The Melchisedech episode is not mentioned in any document until the Late Banns; therefore, it seems possible that it was written either in the 1560s or the 1570s. The play has three episodes: the meeting between Abraham and Melchisedech; God's covenant with Abraham with regard to circumcision; and the sacrifice of Isaac. Each episode concludes with a speech in which the Expositor explains the significance of the event with regard to future promises. In the first episode Abraham returns from defeating his enemies, as a consequence of which he vows to begin the practice of tithing. He intends to make his tithe to Melchisedech, king and God's priest. Melchisedech comes out of the city and offers Abraham wine in a standing cup and white, pure bread.[41] The Expositor explains that Christ's death is remembered with the bread and wine that Christ gave his disciples at the Last Supper. The incident is, of course, based on biblical story, but the decision to dramatize this presentation of bread

---

End, 61–62. During Edward's reign there is evidence of one major alteration in the cycle when the Bakers' *Last Supper* dropped out; however, the Shoemakers apparently expanded their play to include the Supper in a new version that, according to records in 1550, went from the *Entry into Jerusalem*, their usual play, to the *Captivity* (Clopper, "History and Development," 232–33).

41. Lumiansky and Mills, *Chester Mystery Cycle*, 4:57–88.

and wine to a layman in effect distinguishes Anglican from Catholic practice. Moreover, the fact that Melchisedech is priest and king would inevitably conjure up the figure of Henry, specifically, but in any event the English monarch, who is both head of the Anglican church and ruler. After the second episode the Expositor says that circumcision was a sacrament in the Old Law that, when Christ died, was replaced by baptism (lines 192–200). The play, therefore, enacts the precursors of the only two sacraments that the Anglican Church accepted: communion and baptism. These concerns place the Abraham and Isaac episode in a context unlike that of the other cycles. Moreover, although the play has three scenes, it has one programmatic theology.

Looking back over all the evidence, we could read Chester's continued performance of these plays, many of them pre-Reformation, as a sign of a determined Catholic opposition to Anglicanism. Or we could read it as evidence that the local people—or at least some of them—did not see the relevance of the religious debate to their plays, which had been performed "time out of memory," as many documents claim. One playwright may have taken the opportunity to rewrite the Abraham play to incorporate an Anglican point of view, but I suspect that the majority of texts that we possess are pre-Reformation. We have seen that until Edward's reign, the old practices continued; these were restored in Mary's reign, but the local populace seems to have thought that the old practices were not inconsistent with the Protestantism of Elizabeth and so the plays continued.

Texts and Performances: Greater East Anglian Drama and *Ludi*

The plays from Greater East Anglia—Norfolk, Suffolk, Cambridgeshire east of the Ouse River, and Essex north of the Blackwater—constitute the largest bulk of extant texts other than that of the northern cycles and exhibit the greater diversity of form.[42] Most of the plays are contained in three manuscripts. Bodleian MS Digby 133 (the Digby plays) preserves the *Mary Magdalen* (end of the fifteenth century), a combination of morality, biblical history, and saint legend; *The Killing of the Children* (circa 1512), a farcical *Slaughter of the Innocents*; *The Conversion of St. Paul* (1500–1525), a saint play; and a fragment of *Wisdom* (circa 1470–75), an allegorical drama about the seduction and eventual restoration of the three faculties of the soul, Mind, Understanding, and Will.[43] Folger MS. V. a. 354 (the Macro plays) has *The Castle of*

---

42. John Coldewey provides a convenient summary in "Non-cycle Plays."
43. Baker, Murphy, and Hall, *Late Medieval Religious Plays*.

Perseverance (1400–1425), an elaborate *Psychomachia; Mankind* (1474–79), a morality with burlesque features; and a complete text of *Wisdom.*[44] Cotton Vespasian D.8 contains the N-Town collection (the *Mary Play* is dated 1468 but the manuscript was probably assembled toward the end of the century).[45] A number of other texts survive in miscellaneous manuscripts: the Norwich *Grocers' Play* (in two versions dated 1533 and 1565); the Brome *Abraham and Isaac* (late fifteenth century); the Croxton *Play of the Sacrament* (circa 1461), a legend of the torture of a Eucharistic wafer by Jews; *Dux Moraud* (circa 1425–50), a player's part for a moral play that centers on incest; and some other fragments.[46]

The East Anglian texts in some respects are less problematical than those of the northern biblical cycles. They are self-contained, smaller-scale productions for the most part, although it still remains unclear who their producers were and why the majority of them should end up in three manuscripts. Are we to understand these collections to be performance texts for itinerant groups of actors? Or are they collections made by someone interested in the drama after their performance life had ended? The latter seems to have been the case for the Digby manuscript, for we know that in the mid–sixteenth century it was owned by Myles Blomefeld, an avid collector of books.[47] The Macro manuscript was owned at some point by a monk named Hyngham of Bury St. Edmunds, but though this provenance might tempt us to speculate that Hyngham or the monks were producers of these vernaculars plays, we should keep in mind the distance canon law attempted to maintain between the clergy and the *spectacula* of the laity, and we should also recall, with the Terence manuscripts in mind, that collections of play scripts were a monastic reading genre in the Middle Ages.[48] We might also remember that John Lydgate, that rather worldly monk of Bury, wrote disguisings, mummings, and scripts for royal entries and civic entertainments but never play texts. Possession of a text does not signify the acting of it.

The N-Town plays have usually been grouped with the northern cycles because the manuscript in which they appear presents them as if they were a cycle from Creation to Doomsday; however, it is obvious that the manuscript is a

---

44. Eccles, *Macro Plays. Macro* refers to a former owner of the manuscript, Rev. Cox Macro.
45. Spector, *N-Town Play.*
46. Norman Davis, *Non-cycle Plays.*
47. Baker, Murphy, and Hall, *Late Medieval Religious Plays,* xii–xiii.
48. Eccles, *Macro Plays,* xxvii–viii; the case for monastic performance has been made by G. Gibson, *Theater of Devotion,* 107–35. We will return to this matter below.

compilation of plays originally of separate and earlier origin that were brought together by the scribe-compiler no earlier than the last decade of the fifteenth century.[49] The manuscript opens with a proclamation that has been interpreted as banns to be read wherever the text was to be performed. The reference to "N-Town" near the end of the proclamation is taken as a sign that the banns-reciter is to introduce the name of the town where the sequence is to be played. The descriptions of the pageants in the Proclamation often deviate from the texts in the manuscript, however, in addition to which it is apparent that whole sequences—the *Mary Play, Passion Play I*, and part of *Passion Play II*—had independent existences. From other indications in the manuscript, it seems clear that the main scribe tried to integrate disparate material on an ad hoc basis without complete success.

It is unclear what the manuscript was intended to be. It is not a register like that at York—indeed, there are no guild ascriptions for individual pageants— and its location—the scribe's dialect is East Anglian, more particularly, Norfolk—suggests that it belongs to a different dramatic tradition than that of the northern civic cyles.[50] In any event, East Anglia has no large cities—outside perhaps Norwich—capable of producing a cycle of plays of this magnitude, and surviving texts and records from Norwich indicate that the plays of N-Town do not belong to that city. The evidence suggests that the manuscript was not put together with an eye to performing the entire sequence of plays; nor is it a record of a cycle of plays that was once performed at some now-lost location. On the other hand, it does preserve in recoverable form the kinds of plays that we can associate with East Anglia and the southeast—plays intended for production in single locations, often with elaborate staging that included multiple loci and complicated stage machinery.

Despite the large quantity of external records collected from East Anglia and the southeast, scholars have yet to discover an entry that indicates a performance of any of our extant texts (the Norwich plays excluded).[51] Nevertheless, the method of production suggested by the extant texts and those in the

---

49. Spector, *N-Town Play*, xiii–xxix; and Meredith, "Manuscript, Scribe and Performance." There is a facsimile edited by Peter Meredith and Stanley J. Kahrl, *N-Town Plays: A Facsimile*. For an overview of the discussion, see Fletcher, "N-Town Plays." The manuscript has also been referred to as *Ludus Coventriae*, because of a flyleaf note giving that title, and as the Hegge manuscript, from the name of a family that once owned it.

50. Eccles, "*Ludus Coventriae*: Lincoln or Norfolk?"

51. John Coldewey has argued that the Digby plays were revived in Chelmsford, Essex, but the details of character and costume do not suggest these plays to me; see his "Digby Plays and the Chelmsford Records."

documentary records indicate that the most common method of performance was stationary, either indoors or out. Some of these plays—*Mankind,* for example—could have been played in an innyard or a manor hall and required few actors, props, or costumes. Other plays are more elaborate; indeed, there is a lengthy history of large-scale production spanning 150 years that includes the *Castle of Perseverance* (1400–1425), the N-Town *Passion Play I and II* (1450–75), *Mary Magdalen* (end of the fifteenth century), and the New Romney *Passion* (1555, 1560). These four dramas are akin in that they require numbers of scaffolds or stages constructed specifically for their performances. The text of the *Castle of Perseverance* is followed by a stage plan, the significance of whose details is disputed; nevertheless, the plan suggests that there was a castle in the central playing space, perhaps with a moat, around which scaffolds were raised for God, Covetise, and the World, the Flesh and the Devil and the Sins associated with them, for a total of six stages.[52] The castle structure had to be large enough to hold the Mankind figure, Humanus genus, and the Seven Virtues when they are besieged by the Sins. The stages for the evil characters must also be large enough to hold the Sins and whatever other retinue there might be. There is considerable spectacle: a crucial scene shows the Virtues to be initially successful in battle—their weapons are roses—until Humanus Genus succumbs to Covetise.

The N-Town *Passion Play I* calls for a stage each for Annas and Caiaphas, an oratory in the middle of the place, and a garden to represent Mount Olivet. The requirements for the second part are more elaborate: there are stages for Herod, one for Annas and Caiaphas together, Pilate, hell, a council house separate from Pilate's stage (see 1.319, 323), the sepulchre, and possibly a temple (1.335).[53] Both plays make extensive use of the place as an acting area; for example, Christ is surrounded and captured in the place, and he and the two thieves are crucified there.

The *Mary Magdalen* is the most elaborate of all; it has not only separate stages for the emperor, Herod, Pilate, the World, the Flesh, and the Devil (all

---

52. Southern, *Medieval Theatre in the Round;* Schmitt, "Was There a Medieval Theater in the Round?" and Pederson, *Tournament Tradition.* See also the stage plans for the Cornish plays in Joyce and Newlyn, *Dorset / Cornwall,* 551–56.

53. It is difficult to know where *Passion Play II* ends because there are no markers such as there are at the end of *Play I* and the beginning of *Play II*. I have assumed that it ends with play 36, dealing with the Marys at the Tomb and their report of the Resurrection, because play 37, the *Hortulanus,* repeats part of the preceding play and has an opening rubric that suggests it is a self-contained play. It also does not have the kinds of stage directions that appear in the Passion plays.

with military retinues or sins) but a castle, a tavern for Mary's seduction, a garden for her meeting with Christ after his resurrection, and also Marseilles, the Near East, a rock in the middle of the Mediterranean, and a boat to traverse the latter. When the Devil enters, he comes in a movable stage with hell underneath, and when Mary eventually retreats to the desert, she encounters two angels suspended in a cloud; two more angels raise her up to it to feast on the Sacrament she is offered, all presumably part of the heaven scaffold.

The New Romney Passion, for which we only have accounts of expenses, suggests that *Castle* and the N-Town *Passion* were typical of these larger productions: there are expenditures for stages for Pilate and the Princes, Annas and the Tormentors, the Pharisees, Herod, heaven, hell, the sepulchre (called the cave), and the city of Samaria, for a total of eight.[54] The Crucifixion apparently was staged in the place, for there is also expenditure on the mortices for the three crosses. The records tell us that wealthier patrons lent money for the building of the stages, while many other townspeople offered a certain number of days of labor. Money was also obtained from nearby towns. The sponsors were reimbursed from the profits of the play, which, in this case was held over a period of four days. Unfortunately, the records do not give us the arrangement of the stages, but the accounts do indicate that they were raised platforms. There is no expenditure for digging earthworks at New Romney or elsewhere, as far as I have determined, so there is no evidence for stage construction like that which Southern proposed for *Castle*.

The second distinguishing feature of East Anglian dramas and other *ludi*, as I have just suggested, is that they were often produced for profit by local parishes, towns, or other cooperative groups. Of course there were communal processions that were not for profit, such as the one at Ipswich or that at Norwich, in which during Pentecost week there were "diuers disgisinges and pageauntes as well of the liff and marterdams of diuers and many hooly sayntes as also many other lyght and feyned figures and pictures of other persones and bestes" or the more modest one in which Margery Kempe participated at King's Lynn.[55] But dramas, parish ales, and other *ludi* could be profitable. Since towns and parishes within the region were too small to produce dramas of the size of the great northern cycles or even the more modest collection of

54. For details, see J. Gibson, "'*Interludum Passionis Domini.*'" The recognances for these performances were edited by Dawson, *Plays and Players in Kent,* 202–11. Gibson has found additional records.

55. Wasson, "Corpus Christi Plays"; Norman Davis, *Non-cycle Plays,* xxvii; and Kempe, *Book of Margery Kempe,* 184–87.

Old and New Testament plays found in Norwich after 1527, they produced only the occasional single play, especially Old Testament ones that could be moralized, or they divided larger projects into smaller units. The N-Town *Passion,* for example, has two Passion sequences to be played in alternating years, and the prologue to the Digby *Killing of the Children* refers to the fact that in the preceding year they played the *Shepherds* and the *Magi* and that in the present year they intend to perform the *Purification* and the *Slaughter* and, in the year to follow, *Christ and the Doctors.*[56] But perhaps the most common practice in the region was to contribute toward a cooperative *ludus* or to advertise one's *ludus* throughout the surrounding area.[57] There are numerous records of messengers being sent to nearby towns to proclaim the banns of the initiating town's *ludus;* there are other records of corporate contributions to the *ludus* of one town by other towns and religious institutions; and there is evidence that boy bishops, for example, went from town to town to make their collections. I should emphasize that we do not know whether many of these activities were anything more than boy bishop ceremonies and church ales or other kinds of display. It would certainly be rash to conclude that every time we see *ludus* or "pley" the record refers to a drama.

By the 1530s printed texts "offered for acting" began to appear; they were modest plays especially designed for small troupes or household performance.[58] They required few stage props and costumes, and, most important, were written so that one actor could play more than one part. It is believed that this practice began sometime during the fifteenth century, when troupes of minstrels and musicians added stage plays to their repertoire.[59] Of the East Anglia dramas, *Castle* and N-Town, but especially *Mankind,* have been seen as precursors of this form of popular drama. Like N-Town, *Castle* has a set of banns that leaves a space to name the town in which they are to be played; however, it has been estimated that *Castle* would require a minimum of twenty-two actors, not to mention the elaborate stage set that would have had to be constructed.[60] Since earlier scholars tended to think of N-Town as a "cycle," perhaps located at Lincoln, they paid little regard to the space in the banns for the presumed insertion of a town's name. Although Peter Meredith believes the manuscript to

---

56. N-Town *Passion Play II,* 295, lines 5–6; *Killing,* lines 25–28, 561–62.

57. Coldewey, "Non-cycle Plays," and "Last Rise and Final Demise," and see my discussion in chapter 3.

58. Bevington, *From "Mankind" to Marlowe.*

59. But now see Meredith, "Professional Travelling Players."

60. Bevington, *From "Mankind" to Marlowe,* 49, 72.

be a compilation of originally separate texts, he also thinks it would have been exceedingly difficult for a troupe to use the manuscript as a collection of texts from which a piece could be extracted for performance.[61] I agree that the manuscript is a compilation, yet I do not understand why Meredith thinks it would be difficult to extract smaller plays from it for performance. Many are self-contained. In addition, the proclamation could function as a source for short proclamations introducing smaller units from the manuscript. The banns reader could begin with the opening general section and then move to the part of the banns announcing the play to be performed and then to the concluding lines of the banns.

The problem of the *Castle*-text seems more easily resolved than those of the perplexing N-Town collection. Rather than thinking of *Castle* as a text for a traveling troupe, perhaps we should think of it as a text "offered for acting"; perhaps it was the text that moved rather than the performers. A town or parish wishing to raise some money could opt to perform *Castle*, a spectacular play but not one beyond the talents of local groups (as modern performances have demonstrated).[62]

Mankind, on the other hand, would seem to be the quintessential—and earliest—popular drama for a traveling troupe.[63] A number of features suggest that it is a modest professional drama performed in an inn: the seven parts could be played by six actors; props and costumes are minimal; and the play is stopped before the entry of the devil Titivillus, so that the actors can collect money. The inn location is suggested because one of the vices, New Guise, calls for the hostler, the keeper of horses at an inn (line 732), but the performance is inside the inn rather than the innyard, as earlier scholars thought, because Mankind says, "I wyll into þi ȝerde" (line 561). The audience is socially mixed, since it is addressed as "ȝe souerans þat sytt and ȝe brothern þat stonde ryght wppe" (line 29), but its popular orientation is indicated when the yeomanry are invited to join in the singing of the lewd Christmas round (line 333). Because there is a series of personal names at one point in the text (lines 504–15), the performance has been localized in the Cambridgeshire-Norfolk region, and

---

61. Meredith, "Manuscript, Scribe and Performance."

62. Bruce Moore has made a similar suggestion in "Banns in Medieval English Drama." Peter Meredith has also suggested that N-Town is a touring manuscript, not a touring play; see "Scribes, Texts, and Performance," 19–20.

63. Bevington, *From "Mankind" to Marlowe,* 15–18. The text is edited by Mark Eccles in *Macro Plays,* 153–84.

a reference to February (line 691) perhaps indicates that it was performed at Shrovetide (but then why is there the Christmas song?).

Although this interpretation of the text is admirable—and one would have to admit that *Mankind* would make a great traveling play no matter what it original auspices—one has to wonder whether it is entirely accurate.[64] Ought we to read lines in the play as literally as we have? Does the reference to a hostler indicate that the performance is in an inn, or does it suggest that the performers imagine themselves to be in an inn? Or that the place of the performance is being reconstructed as an inn? The personal and place names have been used to localize the play, but might not these be names of some of the persons at the production? Let us imagine *Mankind* to be a Christmas or Shrovetide amusement at some manor house.[65] The host or his clever author decides to get a laugh by writing some of the names of the guests into the script. During such a celebration there certainly would be "souerans" who are sitting and "brothern" who are standing, the latter either servants or others invited to the entertainment but not the banquet. When the "yemandry" are invited to join in the lewd carol, are only the "yemandry" expected to sing or is this a sly joke that constructs all who sing as yeomen? The play is very clever; there is a lot of witty Latin play. The trial scene parodies formulae that suggest proceedings at a manor court. But whoever wrote this drama evoked the festive spirit of the end of the year—in the vices Nought, New Guise, and Nowadays; the allusion to the mock beheading in mummers' plays; the topsy-turveydom; and, of course, Titivillus the Great—and of Lent in the figure of Mercy, who at the beginning attempts to save Mankind, the audience, from the frivolity of the season and who ultimately is able to return them to the sobriety of the upcoming Lenten period.[66] The drama is reminiscent of the elaborate mummings in which a group of masked persons arrive at a hall and perform an action that engages some members of the audience. One mark of such mummings and other folk *ludi* is the *quête*, the collection of money or other goods by the participants as the price of their entertainment. Seen in this light, *Mankind* looks much more like an interlude such as *Fulgens and Lucrece* than it does other popular fare.

---

64. I proposed a slightly different argument years ago in "*Mankind* and Its Audience."

65. Suzanne Westfall, *Patrons and Performance*, 54–55, suggests that *Mankind* may have originated in chapel performance before being taken over by traveling players. John Marshall has recently suggested that it might belong to a religious guild; see "'O 3E SOUERENS.'"

66. Gash, "Carnival Against Lent."

Plays in Print to 1540

None of the texts I have discussed thus far was printed in the early modern period; indeed, the printing of dramatic texts begins rather late and excludes the public drama of the north, greater East Anglia, the southeast, and elsewhere.[67] There are undoubtedly many reasons for this neglect. The printing industry was centered in London, whereas dramatic activity took place away from the city. Perhaps printers did not have access to these play texts. But given the fame of the Coventry plays, why was no printer tempted to produce an edition? Here we should keep in mind that guilds, corporate bodies, and other groups owned their texts. What would be the incentive for such a body to give up its text to be printed? They would gain no financial advantage from such a commission; indeed, they might lessen their attendance figures.

Printers may also have felt that there was little audience for plays. After all, a play is not so much a text as a spectacle. Medieval and early modern audiences were used to seeing, not reading, contemporary plays. That they were classed as ephemera is suggested by the failure initially to print descriptions with texts of royal entries and other public displays, activities that had enormous expenses but that apparently were thought to have accomplished their purpose once they were seen.[68]

Most of the plays to be printed in or before 1540 were connected to educational interests or to the Rastell family or both. The earliest dramatic text was Pynson's edition of Terence in 1495–97, reissued by Wynkyn de Worde in 1504 and circa 1510.[69] Pynson's publication roughly coincides with the introduction of Terence into the English school and university curricula. Around 1520 there was an edition of Terence in English, printed in Paris but distributed in England.[70] Of the remaining nineteen plays from this period, twelve were printed by John and William Rastell: Medwall's *Fulgens and Lucrece* (1512–6); Rastell's *Nature of the Four Elements* (1520?); Skelton's *Magnificence* (1519–20); Heywood's *Gentleness and Nobility* (1519–28); *Calisto and Melebea* (circa 1525); *The Prodigal Son* (1530?); Medwall's *Nature* (1530–

---

67. An exception, though rather late, is "Play of Robin Hood for May-Games" (ca. 1560; in Greg, "Play of Robin Hood"; see also Wiles, *Early Plays of Robin Hood*, 72–79).

68. For an excellent discussion of these issues, see Walker, *Politics of Performance*, 6–50.

69. The Terence is in Lancashire, *Dramatic Texts*, item 79. The list that follows is compiled from Greg, *Bibliography*; Berger and Bradford, *Index of Characters*; and Lancashire, *Dramatic Texts*. I have excluded a broadside, ca. 1500, with texts assigned to allegorical figures, since it may not represent a playing script (Lancashire, *Dramatic Texts*, 72).

70. Lancashire, *Dramatic Texts*, item 101.

34); Heywood's *Pardoner and the Friar, The Play of the Weather,* and *Johan Johan* (all in 1533); *Old Christmas* (1533); and Heywood's *Play of Love* (1534). The Rastells' interest in the use of drama for educational purposes is apparent in this list, as is their promotion of works written by members of the Rastell-Heywood circle. Of the remaining early prints, two are in Latin or are Latin-derived: *Palamedes,* a Latin comedy (1512–13), and Palsgrave's translation of *Acolastus* (1540), the original of which was used to teach Latin grammar. Thus there are only five English play texts in this period that were not printed by the Rastells: *Everyman* (1510?), *Hickscorner* (1515–16), *Mundus et Infans* (1522), *Temperance and Humility* (circa 1528), and *Interlude of Youth* (1532–33).

Everyman is the anomaly in this collection. Not only is it very early—indeed, the first printed play text in English—but it is not a native play. Furthermore, it is not presented to the reader as a text to be acted but one to be read: it is called a *Treatise . . . in Maner of a Morall Playe.*[71] I am not trying to suggest that *Everyman* is not a drama, for the text betrays its stage origins throughout; rather, it would appear that the printer thought the text could be better promoted by calling it a *Treatise,* a reading rather than a playing text.

When we look at extant texts not printed in the period to 1540 and, for a larger backdrop, the records of London, we find a much broader range of events but most of them ephemeral and thus unlikely to be put into print: pageants, disguisings, tournaments, parish Palm Sunday prophets, Midsummer shows, and smaller household moralities. Royal entries, Lord Mayor's shows, and other pageants in London and elsewhere are often noted in varying detail in chronicles, but full "texts" are not usually provided even if some of the speeches are occasionally remembranced or, less frequently, printed (Latin verses from Charles V's entry in 1522 translated into English and printed by Pynson in 1522).[72] The extensive documents and script for the reception of Katharine of Aragon are preserved in manuscript but were not printed in their entirety until 1990.[73] Also unprinted were fragments of several moralities— *Albion Knight* plus two sets possibly by John Redford—and two Heywood pieces, *4PP* and *Witty and Witless,* the first of which was published in 1545(?). Not only did *The Conversion of St. Paul, Mary Magdalene,* and the Digby *Killing of the Children* go unpublished, but so did the *Interlude of John the*

---

71. Bevington, *Medieval Drama,* 940.
72. Lancashire, *Dramatic Texts,* item 105.
73. Kipling, *Receyt of the Ladie Kateryne.*

Evangelist (written before 1520 and published circa 1550) and the Protestant *Resurrection of Our Lord* (1530–60). Bale's plays, written about 1538, were not published until 1547–48. *Thersites,* written 1537, was not published until 1562(?), and *Godly Queen Hester,* written circa 1529, was not published until 1561.[74] There are also a few references to no-longer-extant polemical dramas from the period: among others, one in 1533 that occasioned a papal complaint that Henry allowed persons dressed as cardinals to play in ignominious farces and another that elicited a report from 1535 that Henry saw a triumph on a chapter of Apocalypse in which heads of ecclesiasts were chopped off.[75] Printers were not timid about printing polemical tracts, but perhaps the texts of these two plays, assuming they had fixed texts, were too radical and satirical to risk printing—or the texts may not have been available. Bale's texts may not have appeared because they were written under patronage and he was performing them with his troupe.[76] When he was forced into exile, they would not have been good candidates for a print shop, but once he returned, under Edward, they could again be put to use and were printed on the Continent at the beginning of Edward's reign (1547–48).[77]

Most of the early printed plays were published one to two decades or even longer after they were written and first performed. This lag implies that printers were uncertain of a market, but it may also indicate that the texts were not available property. The printing of plays became increasingly tricky as statutes prohibiting plays that dealt with scriptural texts or matters of state became more common. We have some interesting case studies in the plays of Bale and two other texts written before 1540 but published afterwards.

The *Interlude of St. John the Evangelist,* written before 1520 and not published until circa 1550, provides an example of what an interlude centered on a saint might have been in the early sixteenth century.[78] John opens the play with a speech in which he says that the sweetest life is to have meditation of Christ; therefore, he goes continually to church to rest, reverence, and worship. Eugenio and Irisdision enter and become involved in an anticlerical squabble. Eugenio apparently is a cleric who knows little except some Latin. Irisdision, using allegorical names for geographical locations and buildings, describes for Euge-

---

74. Lancashire, *Dramatic Texts,* item 128, dates *Godly Queen Hester* to ca. 1541–42 and says that Aman is Thomas Cromwell, but most scholars prefer the earlier dating (see below).

75. Ibid., items 1018, 1021.

76. P. White, *Theatre and Reformation,* 15–27.

77. Bale, *Complete Plays,* 1:5–6.

78. Farmer, *Interlude.* 349–68; also in Greg, *Interlude.*

nio the simple way to heaven of which Eugenio is ignorant. Perhaps because Irisdision uses such simple language and teaching, Eugenio accuses him of being a "lowler," with the result that Irisdision describes the way to hell and leaves.[79] Eugenio confesses his lechery, meditates on women and marriage, and leaves. John reenters to preach a sermon to the audience and leaves. Eugenio reenters meditating on whether he should follow Irisdision's advice and give away all his goods and follow willful poverty only to meet Actio, an idler and a lecher, who leads Eugenio off to Evil Counsel. Evil Counsel takes the stage with Idleness, and they enter into a witty dialogue about bedding other men's wives and related matters. They leave and Eugenio and Actio, who have been wenching, reappear and listen to John deliver a sermon on the parable of a Pharisee and a Publican. Eugenio and Actio are drawn to penance and John ends the play with an address to the audience.

Interlude is not a saint play, as we have understood that genre, but an appropriation of a biblical text for moral purposes. It imagines what the tasks of early Christian preachers might have been. Although it predates the Reformation, it offers a simple understanding of the faith in English, an agenda promoted by the friars, which may account for Irisdision's advice that Eugenio give away all his goods and follow "willful poverty."[80] The *Interlude* could have had continued success in the early years of the Reformation because of the characterization of the Latin-speaking cleric, Eugenio, as a Pharisee and hypocrite, but the text might have drawn unwanted attention in the later years of Henry's reign as he moved back toward a more traditional Catholic position; consequently, it is not surprising that it is published in Edward's rather than Henry's reign. Under Edward the play could be read as approving a simple understanding of matters of faith. Its hero is a preacher who has textual authority and who draws an errant Catholic priest from his lechery through biblical parable.

Even though there seems to have been a concerted effort to use drama to attack Catholic institutions and practices, Bale's plays were not printed at the time they were being performed.[81] By the time Bale might have been willing to have them published, the religious tide had turned and Henry was moving back toward traditional usages; consequently, some of Bale's polemic came to sound too radical, and eventually his work was condemned by royal proclamation on

---

79. Farmer, *Interlude*, 354.
80. "Willful poverty" is the term used by critics of the friars to describe the voluntary *(spontanée)* poverty they claimed to pursue; see Clopper "'Songes of Rechelesnesse,'" 58–60, 317–28.
81. P. White, *Theatre and Reformation*, 12–41.

8 July 1546.[82] The *Temptation of Our Lord,* "compyled" by John Bale in 1538, according to the title page, and published in 1547(?), provides a good example of a text of the moment caught by change.[83] At first glance the play might not seem to be so beyond the pale that it could not survive the final Henrician years, but the profundity of its objections to observance—and presumably Bale's other writings—would make it suspect. Baleus Prolocutor opens the play with an implicit denial of baptism as a sacrament; baptism, he says, signifies instead that men are the sons of God and Christ is to be their only teacher. In anticipation of rejecting monastic withdrawal in imitation of Christ, Baleus says that Christ has gone into the desert with the Holy Ghost to begin his office; he will be tempted but will withstand the Devil in order to betoken men's resurrection ("rayse") and Satan's inevitable fall. The story foretells persecution; if you follow Christ, you must expect to be assaulted as he was.

In Bale's version Satan recognizes that successfully to tempt Christ he must disguise himself and use subtlety, so he assumes the garb and demeanor of a religious (lines 74 ff.). He praises Christ for his virtuous life, his wandering in contemplation, and his living alone in the desert (a description of the monastic ideal). He moves naturally from Christ's fasting to his physical condition and the challenge that, if he is God's son, he can turn the stones to bread to provide the food necessary to sustain him and to allow him to execute his vocation (preaching, for example). Christ turns aside these temptations: God will provide, he says, instancing Moses and the Israelites in the desert. Satan tempts Christ twice more, but each time Christ rejects his advances by reasons that echo or cite biblical texts. The action ends with the descent of two angels who give spiritual solace and food. Jesus eats the food in their presence, at which point the angels praise Christ for taking on man's humanity and frailty. The angels present Christ to the audience emblematically: he fulfilled the law and resisted Satan; therefore, follow his teachings. Baleus returns to urge the people not to be aggrieved that they are tempted; Christ was as well in order to give example of how to resist. Faith, he says, will protect you. Then in the last stanza he says,

> Let non report us that here we condempne fastynge,
> For it is not true—we are of no soch mynde.
> But thys we covete: that ye do take the thynge
> For a frute of fayth as it is done in kynde,

---

82. Bale, *Complete Plays,* 1:10.
83. Ibid., 2:51–63.

And onlye Gods worde to subdue the cruell fynde.
Folowe Christ alone, for he is the true sheparde;
The voyce of straungers do never more regarde.

A number of polemical points are made, most of which might fit the agenda of any Protestant. There is the attack on religious institutions (Satan as the desert hermit) at a time when the monasteries are being disendowed. Bale makes it quite clear that Christ's sojourn in the desert was not to give example for withdrawal into the desert or institutions modeled on them; rather, it was to give example of how one was to resist temptation. Later in the text Satan comes to represent the Catholic hierarchy—priests, bishops, and the pope—and their hypocritical predecessors, the Pharisees and the Scribes.

The second polemical point centers on the matter of fasting. Christ says he did not fast in order to establish this as a tradition; rather, he used it as a way of provoking the devil's temptation so that he might teach men how to resist. Satan has no agency in this action; instead, he is Christ's dupe, a means of giving an example of the way to salvation. Resistance is the teaching Christ offers. Thus, an outward ritual is demonstrated not to be effective in itself; rather, the inward resistance to the Devil and the world is the effective cure. Hence, at the end Bale is able to claim that he does not dismiss fasting per se (because it is a kind of purifying tribulation) even while noting that Christ's teachings are superior in effectiveness to ritual practice.

The final scene with the angels is innovative in going beyond its counterparts in biblical drama. The angels' descent is an elaboration of the biblical comment that angels came to comfort him after the temptation. The angels do not appear at all in Chester; that play concludes with a Doctor who explains the commonplace that Christ overcame the three temptations that Adam failed, those of gluttony, avarice, and vainglory (12.169–216). The York angels (22.181–210) engage in a dialogue with Christ to allow him to assert the meaning that Bale attaches to the play: Christ gives an example of steadfastness. In N-Town 23.196 we are told that the angels come ministering to him, singing "Gloria tibi Dominie," but it is Christ who urges the audience to take his action as example.[84] Bale seems uninterested in the three sins of Adam; his focus is on fasting, but more important, on food. Neither York nor N-Town suggests that the angels bring food as solace, and Gertrud Schiller gives no

---

84. N-Town incorporates the exposition that the Chester Doctor makes into Christ's responses to the Devil.

iconographical example in which the angels give more than spiritual support.[85] Food is important in Bale's representation because it affirms Christ's
humanity, and it makes him mankind's perfect example because he rejected Satan's temptation to miraculously create (transsubstantiate?) food in order to
suffer the tribulations of the flesh. But the food is also implicitly antisacramen-
tal: the angels give Christ real food, real bread. The subtext is unmistakable:
the food that Christ gives in the Eucharist is real food—that is, bread—which
is symbolic of the spiritual food that he is—his example.

A play that might have seemed safe and useful in 1538 would not have been
so in June 1539, when Henry issued the Act of Six Articles. Two of the articles
maintained the doctrine of transsubstantiation and upheld monastic vows.
Bale's *Temptation* was not in conformance with the Six Articles, and after
Cromwell's fall in 1540, he fled to Germany. Bale chose to have Dirik van der
Straten, who maintained a Protestant press at Wesel, to print his plays as he
prepared to return to England as Henry's death neared.[86] Bale's plays, if they
ever circulated widely, would have served Edward's agenda well. The king
eventually named him bishop of Ossory. As part of his missionary work he
caused to be performed three of his plays as part of the celebrations welcoming
Queen Mary to Kilkenny on 20 August 1553.[87] The performance caused an
uproar and Bale left Ireland in haste for Basel.

There is a certain logic to the publication of the two examples I have cited.
The *Interlude of St. John the Evangelist* and Bale's plays found an appropriate
second audience because of the political and religious climate. It is difficult to
imagine, on the other hand, why the publishers of *Godly Queen Hester*
thought they could pull off their brazen attempt to re-present a play in Elizabeth's reign that had been written in resistance to what became part of the Reformation agenda.[88] In *Hester*, written following the fall of Wolsey in 1529,
the playwright made no attempt to disguise the fact that he was borrowing an
Old Testament story in order to write a political allegory.[89] There are numer-

---

85. Schiller, *Iconography of Christian Art*, 1:143–45.
86. Bale, *Complete Plays*, 1:9–10.
87. Ibid., 1.6–7.
88. Greg, *New Enterlude,*
89. Greg Walker dates the play more narrowly (1529) than does Bevington, who places it in
1527–29. See Walker, *Plays of Persuasion*, 102–23; Bevington, *Tudor Drama and Politics*, 86–94;
and Greg, *Newe Enterlude*, vii–x. All three identify Aman as Wolsey. Walker, 105 n. 5 and the surrounding text, explains why he thinks the play is concerned with Wolsey's rather than with
Cromwell's fall (1540). Although for my purposes the exact political context is unimportant, I
think Walker's analysis bears out the traditional identification of Aman as Wolsey.

ous references to English custom and law, but most important, the Jews whom (H)Aman proposes to execute are represented as English monks. King Ahasuerus is, then, a figure of Henry and, if the dating is correct, Esther is Jane Seymour, who is depicted as an intercessor for the old religion. The play is framed within the discussion of the kind of person(s) the king should appoint to high honors in governing his kingdom. His counselors insist that justice is the highest principal, not riches, power, wisdom, or gentle blood. Greg Walker believes that the counselors argue that the king errs when he thinks that if he chooses a just lieutenant, then he will himself rule justly whereas the counselors seem to argue that he must rule in his own person. In any event, the king chooses Aman as his lieutenant and must come to a realization of the error of his choice. In the meantime, the king is without a consort and eventually chooses Hester, who also instructs him in good governance, her principal warning being that he should beware of accumulation of great wealth among a few. He should see that wealth is distributed to those in need.

Although *Hester* has the trappings of historical drama, it is a political morality. After Hester gives her advice, there is a comic scene in which Pride, Adulation, and Ambition come together in order to lament that Aman has denuded them of all power and effect. The hypocritical Aman enters to complain to the king of attacks on himself and his good intentions. He warns him of the Jews within the kingdom who think to convert the populace to their religion. The king is persuaded by Aman's oration and gives him ring and seal to execute the orders against the foe. Fearful that the Jews will be destroyed, Hester prepares a banquet for Aman and the king in order to expose Aman. She reveals that Aman wants the Jews' goods so that he will become wealthier and more powerful than the king. When the king says that he thought the dispossession was authorized by the Jews' failure to aid the poor (the monastic obligation) and their voluptuous living (the old charges against religious), Hester disabuses him and seeks his intervention to protect the Jews (and English monastic houses). At the conclusion the king draws the moral: by this action one can see that the multitude is hurt by the head's negligence. Hester adds that though people like Aman may reign for a while, they inevitably fall.

William Pickerynge and Thomas Hacket printed the play in 1561, only a few years after Elizabeth's accession to the throne. Although there is no indication that Elizabeth ever saw or read the play, one might wonder why the printers thought it an appropriate text for distribution. How would one read the play in the political situation at the time of its printing? Since Elizabeth often referred to herself in the masculine, as "the prince," one might be inclined to read the king as Elizabeth and the text as a *furstenspiegel*. But then how would one read Hester? I suppose that Hester could be construed as the embodiment of the wise governance of Elizabeth, but this association would run into difficulty once Hester begins to plead for the preservation of the Jews. There undoubtedly would be many candidates for Aman, but the identification of the Jews with monks would be even more uncomfortable in 1561 than under the play's original auspices since Henry undertook to accomplish what Wolsey was unable to carry out and since Elizabeth, Henry's daughter, would not seem interested in reinstituting monasticism or other Catholic practices. Indeed, one wonders how to read a play in which the villain is hanged for doing the work of later Protestant rulers.

The printers used two ploys on the title page to try to direct the readers' attention away from the inappropriate matter. First, they claim that it was newly made and that it was biblical history: "A NEWE ENTERLUDE drawen oute of the holy scripture of godly queene Hester, verye necessary newly made and imprinted, this present yere. M.D.LXI." One wonders why this interlude was "verye necessary newly made." The repetition about the play's "newness" betrays an awareness of the dangers of its political content. The claim that it is drawn out of Holy Scripture is a patent attempt to make this political drama a history play, and a sacred one at that.

The printers also claim that this history play has a moral content:

> Com nere vertuous matrons and wome*n* kind
> Here may ye learne of Hesters duty,
> In all comlines of vertue you shal finde
> How to behave your selues in humilitie.

Esther is represented as a heroine in the Old Testament, as she has remained in the Judeo-Christian tradition, but can we say that Esther is the epitome of "duty" and "humilitie," whether we are speaking of the Old Testament Esther or the Hester of this text? To read the text as the printers suggest requires that we be oblivious to what the text says. Finally, the publication of this play—it was entered in the Stationers' Register—would suggest that the oversight of plays was rather lackadaisical.[90]

---

90. Arber, *Transcript of the Registers*, 1:154. There is another possible scenario behind the publication—though I think it unlikely. Perhaps the printers hoped *Hester* could function as a covert Catholic drama in which the king and Hester represent Philip and Mary in order to encourage hopes of a second restoration of Catholicism. The emphasis on the text's "newness" and "historicity" would be their protection against charges of production of a seditious pamphlet, but at the

Although most scholars no longer subscribe to the evolutionary thesis—that the medieval drama moved from the liturgy to the biblical cycles to moral drama and saint play before growing from early Tudor into the Elizabethan drama—the notion lurks in our histories, in our curricula and textbooks, and in the variety of other ways we talk about and organize what we have to say about the early drama. This way of thinking not only remains evolutionary but favors print culture in writing the story of the drama.[91] I would like to conclude this chapter on texts and performances with a few remarks about what my foregoing discussion implies.

First, there is little evidence in the documents of an extensive performance record of either moral dramas or saint plays. Not only do we not have any documentation of the performances of the *Castle, Mankind, Wisdom, Mary Magdalene, The Conversion of St. Paul* and other texts that survive in fragments, but there is little evidence for the production of such plays in the areas from which these texts survive. That is not to say that these plays did not have a performance life; certainly they did, or we would not have the texts or, more important, the detailed stage directions for their production. Nevertheless, there is an enormous hole in the records that suggests they were occasional, rare, and without extensive runs. The gap is even more apparent when we consider other kinds of festive activity: ales, processions, boy bishops, hockings, king games, Robin Hood games, and the other activities that are recorded on annual or regular bases all over England.

The record of printed dramas, like that for moral plays, is equally sparse. We can document that Terence and Plautus and plays modeled on them were performed in certain venues, chiefly schools, universities, and related institutions, and we can determine that these authors and texts had some influence on plays that were later printed or performed in new venues. But we cannot demonstrate that most printed plays in this tradition were produced after their initial performances. We have few repertories of the kind preserved by *The Book of Sir Thomas More*, a play written circa 1590, that suggests its audience would be familiar with some earlier plays: the *Cradle of Security, Hit the Nail*

---

same time they could provide their Catholic readers with a hagiographic account of the reign of the late queen.

91. John Wasson has challenged these commonplaces, suggesting that the moral play is not the predecessor of later Elizabethan dramas and that our attention to early printed books has obscured the importance of the folk traditions and saint play; see "Morality Play."

o' the Head, Impatient Poverty, Heywood's *4PP, Dives and Lazarus, Lusty Juventus,* and the *Marriage of Wit and Wisdom.*[92] There are other exceptions. Bale was able to see that his plays were performed over a number of years while he had his company and when he was working in the interests of the government, but they were not produced in England during his exile, and the only later performance of which we know, that in Kilkenny, was apparently the last, since Bale went into exile after it was mounted. The Rastells clearly intended to save the works presumably first performed under their auspices, but we can at best describe a publication, not a performance history, for most of John Heywood's work, for example.[93] Printing turns plays into texts; actors are no longer necessary and the drama, in some respects, makes its way back into being the reading genre that it was for most medieval readers of Terence and Plautus and other texts in which the author does not speak in his own voice but in that of others.

Printing created an archive of early dramatic texts, fortunately for us. Nevertheless, the scripts that had the longest performance histories in the sixteenth century were those that were never printed: the Creed and Paster Noster plays of York and the biblical cycles of York, Chester, and Coventry.

---

92. Bevington, *From "Mankind" to Marlowe,* 18–19. Two of the plays, *Hit the Nail* and *Dives,* are no longer extant. Heywood's *4PP* was written ca. 1520–22 but not published until 1545(?). *Cradle,* also not extant, is ca. 1565–75; *Impatient Poverty,* 1553–58; *Lusty Juventus,* 1550–53; and *Marriage of Wit and Wisdom,* 1570 or 1579 (ibid., 22). With the exception of the Heywood, none of the plays are from More's lifetime.

93. An inventory (1547–51) of John Dudley, Lord Lisle, lists Heywood's *Play of the Weather, 4PP,* and *Play of Love* among the five plays in his possession (Greg, *Bibliography,* 4:1651).

⚡ S I X ⚡

The Matter of These Plays

Earlier I surveyed the kinds of *ludi* represented in the cities and towns of England in order to argue that the productions of dramas were announcements of political dominance by their lay producers. By contrast, the East Anglian and southeastern dramas seem to have been more driven by motives of profit even if they were also expressions of corporate identity and local piety. In this chapter I wish to argue corollary theses: that we can read the development of religious and moral drama by and for the laity as a contestation for space within the religious arena even though the laity seem to recognize clerical authority in some areas, and that the ecclesiastical hierarchy acknowledged the power of lay corporations to authorize these dramas, a recognition that helps account for the lateness of the demise of biblical drama. The arena in which dramas were performed, not surprisingly, is a negotiated space.

Perhaps the Franciscan William Melton's attempt in 1426 to influence the York production is typical of the clergy's response to vernacular drama. His defense of the York plays is very much like that provided by Pauper in *Dives and Pauper* even though he was not entirely happy with the event.[1] Melton appealed to the city of York to move its play to the day after Corpus Christi. He was sympathetic toward the play and commended it because it instructed the common people in the elements of the faith and because the viewing of it could accrue to the merit of the participants. But he also noted that its performance on Corpus Christi day sometimes led to distractions such as drinking and feasting with the result that the inhabitants of York did not attend masses and other services for which they would receive Pope Urban IV's pardons. The Melton af-

---

1. Johnston and Rogerson, *York*, 43–44; Johnston, "Procession and Play of Corpus Christi."

fair indicates that the friars recognized the value of civic and lay worship in the form of plays and supported those efforts as long as they did not interfere with more traditional forms of worship. The city's decision to ignore Melton's advice suggests perhaps that it felt the play was an appropriate kind of "secular" celebration on the feast day—so it moved the procession rather than the play.

Melton understood the plays to be primarily for the benefit of the laity. Similarly, David Rogers, in an echo of the Late Banns, justifies the Chester plays on the grounds that they provided a "bible" for the laity: "The matter of these plays weare the historie of the bible, composed by the said author [the Benedictine monk Ranulph Higden] in a holy deuotion, that the simple mighte vnderstand the scripture, which in those times was hid from them."[2] Described in the Late Banns as "not Monckelyke" (line 10), Higden is constructed as a proto-Protestant in order to retain the tradition that the plays had been authored by Chester's famous inhabitant, the writer of the *Polychronicon,* the most important chronicle of the late Middle Ages. But these statements also tell us that these plays were written for laypeople because they could not read the Latin of the Bible. These are not clerical plays.

Most scholars accept, I think, that the vernacular drama of the later Middle Ages reflects lay spiritual interests rather than a strictly clerical agenda. The thesis seems self-evident, but some clarification is necessary. The historical record provides little evidence that clerics were the sponsors, promoters, or writers of vernacular religious dramas. Whether or not clerics were involved, when lay governors or other groups produced biblical and moral dramas, they put themselves into positions of authority, ones normally occupied by the clergy. Even if lay groups hired clerics to write their dramas, lay sponsorship inevitably reconfigured the relationship between the laity and the clergy. How far did producers of these dramas observe the distinction between the two spheres? What was an appropriate role in religious instruction for groups who had no formal position among the ordained? What did clerics think lay people ought to know about their religion and what was the response on the lay side?

Technically, lay producers of religious dramas could argue that they were only exercising every Christian's right to exhort his or her neighbor to penance and belief; their dramas did not preach doctrine.[3] The distinction is significant because preaching—that is, instruction in Christian doctrine—resides in the

---

2. Rogers's *Breviarye,* in Clopper, *Chester,* 324–25. The claim of authorship is erroneous; see Salter, *Mediaeval Drama in Chester,* 33–45; and Clopper, "Arnewaye, Higden and the Origin of the Chester Plays."

3. Gregory the Great, *Moralia in Job,* PL 76: 186, para. 79.

office of the bishop. The bishop is obliged to preach; no one else may unless he be authorized by the bishop by license (as in the case of many friars) or by ordination (as in the case of parish priests). The priest is to preach and edify; the deacon may only read the gospels and give moral instruction; but any person may exhort to the good life. What may a lay corporation do? To contextualize the question further: given that English translations of the Bible were forbidden by the Arundel Constitutions at the beginning of the fifteenth century, how far could lay people go in representing biblical narrative without crossing forbidden boundaries?[4] How "safe" are biblical dramas? One's first response might be that biblical dramas are not threatening; indeed, like texts such as the *Northern Passion*, the *Cursor Mundi*, and *Meditations on the Life and Passion of Christ*, dramas can be seen as obviating the necessity of biblical translation. Nevertheless, the purveyance of this material by secular authorities poses a challenge to the clergy; further, an investigation of the texts should tell us something about how far the laity were willing to extend their authority. In the short term, I think it can be argued that lay producers observed the distinction between clerical control of doctrine and lay exercise of neighborly exhortation. But there is unease and anxiety along the line of separation, a situation that not only lays the groundwork for greater lay participation in religious life and controversy but also results in troubling representations of central events in providential history. We can read our dramatic texts as indicators of lay piety as well as illustrations of the anxiety of belief.

Drama and the Clerical Agenda

Early scholars of the drama believed that the cycle plays originated in the choirs and naves of churches; however, there is no direct evidence of a performance of a *cycle* in Latin or the vernacular in any English church or within any ecclesiastical precinct (the steps, close, cemetery, or the like); there is no evidence of *vernacular* plays within any church before the sixteenth century; and there is little evidence of ecclesiastical sponsorship of cycle plays at any time during their documented histories.[5] Indeed, it is at the time of the cycles'

---

4. Wilkins, *Concilia Magnae*, 3.314–19; and Hudson, "Lollardy: The English Heresy?," 146–49.

5. The *Ordo repraesentationis adae* or *Jeu d'Adam* is the one exception to the first clause, and there may have been plays in churches in the sixteenth century. See Kahrl, "Medieval Drama in Louth"; Nicholas Davis, "Allusions . . . (4): Interludes," 77, 87–90; P. White, *Theatre and Reformation*, 130–62. Some of these latter records may be to plays in church halls rather than churches, however, as is the case in a reference from Tewkesbury, 1600–1601, to performances in the abbey,

demise that we find ecclesiastical intervention in the production and regulation of civic religious drama.[6]

At the present state of our studies, we lack the substantive and documentary evidence that would establish much of a clerical presence in civic biblical drama.[7] And we cannot, I think, attribute the absence of references to the clergy in the dramatic records solely to the loss of documents because, in cities where records are extant, the clergy still do not seem to play a very significant role. Although it is difficult to generalize from so many different situations, the rule seems to be that the clergy were involved in initiating, and often participated in, Corpus Christi and other feast day processions in which craft guilds and other groups marched. But even in these the city usually regulated the procession, the participants, and the ordering of those groups. The clergy were also involved through religious guilds in processions, and, in some cases, in the performance of plays like the Creed and Pater Noster plays. But the cycles of Old and New Testament plays seem remarkably free of ecclesiastical control and participation, as do the moral plays from other parts of the country. The cycles are the products of the citizenry, and their composition and development often reflect the power structure of the corporation. The same argument can be

---

formerly site of the parish church but by then the church hall (Douglas and Greenfield, *Gloucestershire,* 339–42, 429 n). For the liturgical drama, see K. Young, *Drama of the Medieval Church;* Hardison, *Christian Rite;* and Flanigan, "Roman Rite," "Liturgical Drama and Its Tradition," and "Medieval Latin Music-drama."

6. Attempts by the government and cities to regulate dramas will be discussed in the next chapter.

7. I have given the data for this claim in "Lay and Clerical Impact," 112–18. At the time I wrote the essay, I did not consider the possible role of schoolmasters, some of whom may have been clerics. We know that Geoffrey of Saint Albans and Gerhoh of Reichersberg, both in the twelfth century, were *ludimagistri* who engaged in *ludi theatrales,* and we have several records from England in the sixteenth century of schoolmasters who wrote plays, but little in between these two periods. In the later medieval and early modern periods, however, when the vernacular plays were written, schoolmasters, as Nicholas Orme has shown, did not have to be celibate clerics or even university graduates. The largest group of schools—fee-paying town institutions—allowed masters to be priests, clerks, or married laymen. Monasteries also appointed masters from each status. Only small endowed schools were restricted to priests. See his "Schoolmasters," in *Education and Society,* 52–53. It was not until the early stages of the Reformation that we get the names of clerics who had taken to playwrighting. John Bale had been a Carmelite friar, Lewis Wager, the author of the Protestant *Life and Repentaunce of Marie Magdalene,* had been a Franciscan friar, and Thomas Wylley, who appealed to Cromwell for patronage in 1536, was Vicar of Yoxford, Suffolk (see P. White, *Theatre and Reformation,* 15–16, 80, 69, respectively). Wylley was engaged in writing polemical and pietistic dramas but claims that he was disdained by the greater number of priests in Suffolk since he made a play against "the popys Conselerrs, Error, Colle Clogger of Conscyens, and Incredulyte."

made for the dramatic productions of East Anglia and southeastern England. Where we have evidence at all, dramas are produced and controlled by lay officials.[8] We might recall that when the citizens of New Romney and Lydd in the period 1526–33 wished to write or revise their plays of the Passion and of Saint George, respectively, they took their texts not to a cleric but to Richard Gibson, who provided the spectacle for court occasions.[9]

Further, it should be noted that by the late fourteenth century the materials were available that would enable laymen who were unlearned in Latin to write plays for laymen. The *Stanzaic Life of Christ,* the *Northern Passion,* the *Cursor Mundi,* the *Gospel of Nicodemus,* and the Franciscan *Meditations on the Life and Passion of Christ* were available in English and alone could supply all of the materials that playwrights would need to construct a cycle or part of a cycle of plays. These vernacular works were part of the phenomenon of northern and late medieval lay spirituality. In some cases, for example, *Cursor Mundi,* they were presented as counters to inappropriate texts (gestes and romances); they are what lay people might wish to know about scriptural events (though presumably the lesser clergy might find them useful as well). If their existence made it possible for laymen ignorant of Latin to write biblical dramas—and source studies suggest that these vernacular pieces were often the immediate precursors of the extant dramatic texts—then the distance between the civic biblical plays and the liturgy may be greater than has been assumed in the past.

My position is that though we have no evidence that clerics wrote vernacular plays in the medieval period, the clerical voice is apparent to varying degrees in the extant texts; however, it is not the voice for a clerical agenda, as we can see by comparing the Pecham and Thoresby constitutions to the content of the dramas.[10] Whoever wrote these dramas noted the need for moral instruction and religious affirmation; what they brought into the plays and what they left out define for us the lay religious life. Although writers of religious drama were not obligated to incorporate the educational agendas of Lateran IV (1215), Archbishop Pecham's *Ignorantia sacerdotum* (1281), and Archbishop Thoresby's Constitutions (1357, elaborated in the vernacular as the *Lay Folk's Catechism*), there was certainly the opportunity to do so. And, if the drama

---

8. The extensive records of the New Romney *Passion* do not contain the names of any obvious clerical supporters or participants. For the demographics, see J. Gibson and Harvey, "Sociological Study of the New Romney Passion Play."

9. Dawson, *Plays and Players in Kent,* 132–33, 199–200.

10. Also, see my forthcoming essay, "Framing Medieval Drama: The Franciscans and English Drama."

were being driven by the clerical orders, then one might wonder why the opportunity was not seized, since it would have aided the directive that the laity were to be taught the elements of the faith in the vernacular in Sunday sermons. Looking at the ways that the drama got the Christian message across will show us something of the relation these texts have to clerical agendas.

The laity had long been urged to learn their Pater Noster, Creed, and Ave, but the reform programs of the later Middle Ages instructed the clergy to teach the laity the Fourteen Articles of the Faith, the Ten Commandments, the Two Evangelical Precepts, the Seven Works of Mercy, the Seven Capital Sins and their progeny, the Seven Principal Virtues, and the Seven Sacraments.[11] These directives resulted in the production of a massive literature in both Latin and the vernacular. The larger efforts, such as *Ayenbite of Inwyt* or the *Lay Folk's Catechism*, attempted to present the agenda systematically; moreover, the *Catechism* became a magnet for once separate texts, on the Commandments, for example, so that it moved from a relatively simple listing to a lengthy disquisition on the elements within each category.

When we analyze the dramatizations of biblical texts, we find that much of this clerical agenda is absent, which is perhaps not so surprising since the dramas are narratives, not treatises.[12] Only the Chester *Pentecost* repeats the creed in its entirety. None of the northern cycles refers to the Seven Principal Virtues. None lists the Seven Sacraments even though there is the occasional reference to the fact that there are seven: in the Towneley *Baptism,* for example, where the passage is subsequently censored and "not playd," and in the N-Town *Shepherds,* where the angel says there will be seven sacraments without naming them. The sacraments of baptism and the Eucharist are represented, and there are calls to repentance by John the Baptist and Jesus, but there is little attention paid to them as sacraments.[13] None of the cycles refers to the sacraments of confirmation, extreme unction, or ordination, but we could say that these are inappropriate to the biblical narratives since these sacraments were instituted by the church, not in Christ's ministry.[14] But we

---

11. For a succinct overview, see Boyle, "Fourth Lateran Council and Manuals of Popular Theology."

12. N-Town does not conform to many of the generalizations in the next several paragraphs.

13. Again, N-Town is the exception. In the Gethsemane scene the Father sends the chalice and host for the new sacrament (28.1117), and in the *Baptism* Christ is said to come to be baptized and to confirm the sacrament (22.64). The sacrament of penance *as* sacrament gets much more attention in the nonbiblical plays.

14. The N-Town *Shepherds* (16.5), though, says that Christ will institute seven sacraments.

might also wonder why the sacrament of matrimony is omitted. There are at least two opportunities to dwell on the sanctity of marriage—in the garden before the Fall and in the union of Mary and Joseph—but the playwrights show little interest in the subject in the first case, and in the second, they take the opportunity to show the woes that originate in matrimony, not only in the cases of Adam and Joseph but in Noah's as well.[15] The Seven Sins are referred to in the biblical drama only in passing and are rarely listed in their entirely except for N-Town, which has each of the damned sinners in the *Judgment* represent one of the sins. Obviously some of the characters can be seen to personify specific sins: Pilate as Pride, Herod as Anger, Caiaphas and Anna as Envy and Anger, and perhaps Judas as Covetise. The Acts of Mercy appear in all the Last Judgment plays, yet only N-Town lists all seven, York, Towneley, and Chester omitting the burial of the dead.

From this preliminary survey we can say that in general the extant biblical drama responds to but does not systematically promote the clerical agenda. Old Testament selections, though they tend to focus on origins and on certain apocalyptic themes (as in the *Noah*), dwell primarily on the virtues of obedience and faith. Where there is explicit interpretation, it tends to be moral rather than doctrinal—thus preserving the distinction between the duties of the bishop and his designates and the moral exhortation allowed the laity. The dramas tend toward the eschatological and apocalyptic but primarily are penitential. Again I think this observes the distinction between the clerical obligation to preach doctrine and teach the elements of the faith and the right of any layperson to draw someone to penance. Indeed, the Christianity of these dramas is that of urban and town populaces that seem largely content with the ecclesiastical structure and teaching of its day (at least until the Reformation). They are historical plays with tropological interests; they are not particularly given to typology beyond the simplest sort (for example, Isaac who is Christ) or to anagogy, the latter two of which might be characterized as the higher (particularly clerical) senses of scriptural texts.[16]

To illustrate how the plays sometimes fail in transmitting elements of the clerical agenda, let us look at how the texts handle what should be a relatively

---

15. The N-Town *Marriage of Mary and Joseph* is an exception.

16. I think clerics make this distinction when they put tropology before typology, the implication being that obedience to the text (and in one's life) is necessary before one can achieve any higher revelation. See de Lubac, *Exégèse médiévale*, I.i.119–69, 410–15. For an overview of the question of typology and its effectiveness in the Middle English drama, see Meyers, "Typology and the Audience." Arnold Williams was the most prominent critic of typological readings; see "Typology and the Cycle Plays."

straightforward scene: the presentation of the Ten Commandments. The commandments are given at two places in the biblical plays: in the *Procession of Prophets* or *Moses* (Chester [play 5], Towneley [7], and N-Town [6]) or in *Christ and the Doctors* (York [20], Towneley [18], Coventry Weavers' Play, and Chester [11]). The latter four plays are related even though they also have significant differences.[17] Arthur C. Cawley observed that the placement of these scenes calls forth two sets of commandments: when they are produced by Moses, they are based on the Old Testament versions in Exodus and Deuteronomy; when they are expressed by Christ, what Cawley calls the New Testament version, the first two commandments are rephrased as the Two Precepts, to love God and one's neighbor.[18] In the two cycles where both versions are present, Cawley adds, they form a typological pair. Chester 5 gives a fairly simple rendering of the Old Testament version, as does Towneley 7, except that Towneley elaborates the texts a bit. The N-Town *Moses* puts them within an ancient tradition, from Augustine, that divides them into two sets: the first three, inscribed on the left tablet, pertain to God (on strange gods and image worship, on taking God's name in vain, and on honoring the Sabbath), and the remaining group of seven relate to man and his salvation. The division is a commonplace in manuals of instruction and sermons.

The Christ and the Doctors plays fuse two elements of the clerical agenda: the Two Precepts and the Ten Commandments. This novelty seems to have occasioned less comment—partly because it can be found elsewhere—than the fact that the four versions of this play are textually related. Rosemary Woolf, in fact, found it "curious" and "unclear" why "this dull and infelicitous version should have had such a diffusion."[19] Greg's interest in the *Christ and the Doctors* was focused on the kind of testimony the four closely related texts might give to the larger question of influence and borrowing among the cycles. Cawley narrowed the issue to why York and Towneley, which are very much alike elsewhere, should diverge at the point when the playwrights introduced the last eight commandments. Greg attributed this divergence to a lacuna in the York urtext that Towneley and the others had to supply when it reached their hands; Cawley countered that Towneley borrowed its version from the *Speculum christiani*, which uses a quatrain stanza preferred by some of the Towneley

---

17. Greg, "Bibliographical and Textual Problems."
18. Cawley, "Middle English Metrical Versions."
19. Woolf, *English Mystery Plays*, 212. An antidote to Woolf's position is Kline's "Structure, Characterization, and the New Community."

playwrights, because the *Speculum* gives a fuller accounting of the commandments.

I would like to reshape the discussion. If, as Cawley suggests, the Chester and Towneley playwrights wished to give the commandments twice in order to establish a typological relationship, would this not have been better accomplished in the *Doctors* by Jesus' assertion of the Two Precepts, which, after all, contain the whole of the law? We would have had a simple restatement of the Old Law in the Two Precepts. Further, Cawley's model does not exist in the other cycles. In York we have only one version of the commandments, and it is not that of the Pecham-Thoresby Constitutions but a compilation of the precepts and the last eight commandments. How do we account for this "transformation" of the commandments? Let us presume, for the moment, that the playwright initially decided to use the Two Precepts in the *Doctors* because it would graphically symbolize the institution of the New Law without the abrogation of the Old. Then, since this is his only opportunity in York for a statement of the commandments, he—or perhaps some later writer—anxiously fills in the remaining eight commandments despite the fact that this does serious damage to the integrity of the Decalogue. It would not have been difficult for him to have incorporated the Two Precepts into a rendering of the commandments; all he would have had to do was to take the traditional division of three and seven and place the first three under the first and the last seven under the second precept, as the *Lay Folks' Catechism* does when it follows the Decalogue with the Two Precepts.[20] This may have been what the Chester playwright was attempting to do when he began with the first precept and then the second and third commandments; however, he does not follow through with the second precept and completely botches the order of the remaining commandments, giving the seventh ("Thou shalt not steal") twice. The Coventry Weavers' play attempts to resolve the disruptive effect of this fusion by replacing the ninth commandment (against coveting one's neighbor's wife) with an injunction against swearing oaths, usually a part of the second commandment, which in most other versions has been replaced by the second precept. Effective as the various versions of *Christ and the Doctors* are as dramas—and I do think they look deceptively simple on the page—they are not the best instructors of the Decalogue. My purpose here is not to attack the playwrights as dramatists but simply to point out that they do not handle the instructional agenda as succinctly and clearly as do the clerical manuals. If there was a cleri-

---

20. Simmons and Nolloth, *Lay Folks' Catechism*, 60–61.

cal author involved, he certainly lost control of his script; if there was a clerical overseer of the extant texts, he seems not to have been paying attention.

The Problems of Literalism

The central purpose of the northern cycles and the N-Town collection is to enact the second seven Articles of the Faith, those concerning Christ's manhood: conception by the Holy Spirit (not always clearly stated), birth to the Virgin, Crucifixion, Harrowing of Hell, Resurrection, Ascension, and return at Judgment. Old Testament plays serve to fill out the larger history of the Fall, which necessitated a redemptive plan. That plan is anticipated by covenants with Noah, Abraham, and Moses and prophecies of Jesus' institution of a New Law. Thus, these collections of dramas succeed in fulfilling Thoresby's requirement that laypeople be taught the precepts of both the Old and the New Testaments. Thoresby means, literally, that laypeople be taught the Ten Commandments and the Two Precepts, as Pecham has it, and, as we have seen, the biblical dramas do this, though not always with the precision our archbishops might have desired. The other Old Testament actions can be said to fill in the story and to justify, to make righteous Jesus' suffering—according to reason, as God expresses it in his opening speech in the Towneley *Annunciation:* a man for a man, a woman for a woman, a tree for a tree (10.31–34). Indeed, I would say that the larger project of the Old Testament plays is not to provide a series of typological relationships with New Testament subjects but to outline the logic of redemption. Although God cannot be obligated to do anything other than that which he chooses, these Old Testament plays portray the deity, who, being "riʒt," is also one who establishes a covenantal relationship with man that fulfills a reason (a logic) for the redemption.

Insofar as biblical plays aim at describing the logic of history, their mode is narrational, anecdotal, and assertive. The plays shy away from subtle or technical matters of doctrine, but in pursuing the historical, they often open rifts in what we like to portray as the seamless garment of the church's teachings. These rifts concretize urgent and problematical questions of belief, what Langland regards as impertinent inquiries into the "whyes" that can only lead laymen astray. In rereading these texts I have been struck by the way that they set out to affirm Christian truth at the same time that they inevitably make difficult that truth for their audiences by remaining at the literal level of biblical events. This, of course, was one of the reasons that church authorities did not wish the Bible to be translated into the vernacular, where narratives bare of their exegetical commentary could lead one to misinterpretation or doubt.

My analysis, as with all discussions of biblically derived narrative, is going to be a bit tricky because if, as I have been intimating, the playwrights aimed at a literal narration of biblical texts, then can we attribute to their efforts the problems I will try to outline, or should these be assigned to their ultimate sources? Certainly, we can trace some of the anxieties in the biblical drama to those in the Bible, but medieval poets are not obliged to bring these problems to the surface of their texts. Moreover, we can at times see how playwrights attempted to meet difficulties in their narrative sources and also how, having confronted the problems, they resorted to the "logic of iteration," especially in the reassertion of the providential plan. My purpose in the discussion that follows is to characterize the limits of these dramatic projects and then to highlight some of the rifts that might show us something of the reception of Christian orthodoxy and its concomitant questioning.

Most scriptural dramas shy away from the tougher matters of doctrine. For example, the first seven Articles of the Faith, those that address the nature of the deity in his Godhead, are rarely expressed in the technical vocabulary of clerics, with the result that sometimes the doctrine of the Trinity is not fully nuanced.[21] Such is the case in the York cycle despite the fact that God in the first pageant uses a vocabulary that alludes to trinitarian distinctions:

> *Ego sum Alpha et O: vita, via, veritas, primus et nouissimus.*
> I am gracyus and grete, God withoutyn begynnyng,
> I am maker vnmade, all mighte es in me;
> I am lyfe and way vnto welth-wynnyng.
> I am formaste and fyrste, als I byd sall it be.
> My blyssyng o ble sall be blendyng,
> And heldand, fro harme to be hydande,
> My body in blys ay abydande,
> Vnendande, withoutyn any endyng.
> Sen I am maker vnmade and most es of mighte,
> And ay sall be endeles and noghte es but I,
> Vnto my dygnyté dere sall diewly be dyghte
> A place full of plenté to my plesyng at ply:
> *(York, 1.1–12)*

In comparison with the opening of the Towneley *Creation,* York provides a fairly full analysis of God's Being, but to see what the playwright does and does

---

21. The division of the fourteen Articles of Faith into two sets of seven dealing with the Godhead and Christ's Manhood is commonplace; Pecham's *Ignorancia sacerdotum* provides only one instance.

not do, we need a brief overview of trinitarian doctrine. The paradox that must be explained in any discussion of the Trinity is that God is three Persons but one God, three subsistences (Greek *hypostases;* Latin *personae*) and one essence (Greek *ousia;* Latin *essentia*).[22] But the Persons have proper or personal names, as well: Father, Son, and Holy Spirit. These names express relations that are real and existent rather than nominal or notional.[23] The commentator must avoid suggesting that the persons are three gods (tritheism) or emanations (Manichaeism and related Neoplatonisms); in addition, he must avoid suggesting that the Persons are only nominal distinctions (Sabellianism). There are two kinds of relations in the Trinity. The first is that which obtains between the Father and the Son, paternal and filial, and the second that which obtains between the Father and the Son together and the Holy spirit. The latter relation is more difficult to describe because there is not a word like *paternal* of *filial* to attach to it. The first set of relations can be better expressed in the second: the Father is ingenerate, the Son is generated from the Father alone (generation, filiation), and the Holy Spirit proceeds from both the Father and the Son (procession, spiration). The relation between the Holy Spirit and the other two Persons of the Trinity is unlike that of the Son to the Father insofar as the Holy Spirit proceeds from both the other Persons whereas the Son is generated only from the Father. These two distinctions are real; they state that the Father is not the Son nor the Holy Spirit and that the Father and the Son are not the Holy Spirit. Nevertheless, the Persons are not distinct from the Essence: they are neither species of the genus Essence, nor does the Essence in any way form a quaternity.

In addition to these two relations, many fathers of the patristic period as well as later medieval theologians associated particular attributes with each of the Persons, the most common being those of power *(potestas)* with the Father, wisdom *(sapientia* but also *scientia)* with the Son, and goodness *(benignitas, caritas)* with the Holy Spirit.[24] These "appropriated attributes," as they are

---

22. The points of orthodoxy discussed below can be found in Lombard's *Sententiae in IV libris distinctae,* e.g., I, dist. 2, caps. 1–2; dist. 5; dist. 9, cap. 3; dist. 11, cap. 1, and passim) For commentary, see Fortman, *Triune God;* and Pelikan, *Christian Tradition,* 1:219–20, 3:277–84.

23. A *relation* is "the ordination of one thing to another; it expresses the connection between two things united by a special bond (i.e., the transcendental relations revealed by the paternity of the father, the filiation of the son, the procession of the Son from the Father, and the spiration of the Holy Spirit from both the Father and the Son). Relations in God are not accidentals but absolutely identified with the divine essence itself; apart from these 'relations' everything else is identical in God" (*New Catholic Enclopedia,* 12:216–17).

24. Lombard, *Sententiae* 2, dist. 22, cap. 4 in fine; Aquinas summarizes the patristic and medieval tradition to his day in *Summa theologica* I, q. 39, art. 7–8.

called, denote logical or mental, not real, distinctions, for, if they were real, they would seem to deny the power of the Father to the Son and the Holy Spirit and so forth. Commentators excused the usage on the grounds that these were the names by which men might better know the Persons of the Trinity; consequently, it is common to find an association of each of these appropriated attributes with one of the Persons. But since the association could also suggest an unorthodox third set of relations, the careful commentator might note that the distinction was mental and that power was not only in the Father but also in the Son and the Holy Spirit.[25]

Now let us return to the York passage. God expresses the eternality of his Being—*Ego sum Alpha et O*—in a variety of ways—"wythoutyn begynnyng," "maker vnmade," and so forth—but some of these formulations may have been intended to have more specific trinitarian meanings. God is "withoutyn begynnyng" insofar as he is ingenerate; his ingeneracy makes him "formaste and fyrste" not in the sense of superior to or temporally before the other two Persons but in relation to them. The Person represented is not the Divine Being but God the Father; he is "maker"—all "mighte," the appropriated attribute, is in him. This constitutes a rather literalist reading of the Genesis narrative; there is little evidence in the speech of the fifth Article of Faith: that the Trinity *and* the One God created heaven and earth. The Son, who is the *scientia* through which the Father creates (contrast *Piers Plowman* B, 17.140–86) is absent from the passage, though there is an allusion to the Holy Spirit a few lines down (see lines 17–18). In the absence of a fully articulated doctrine of the Trinity, one wonders what the effect might have been of God saying that he is "formaste and fyrste." Listeners who are weak in theology might well conclude that the Father is both prior and superior to the other two Persons of the Trinity.

Towneley, by contrast, makes a simple assertion that gets around the technical vocabulary:

> Ego sum alpha et o,
> I am the first, the last also,
> Oone God in magesté;
> Meruelus, of myght most,
> Fader, and son, and holy goost,
> On God in Trinyté.
>
> (lines 1–6)

---

25. Augustine, *De trinitate libri XV*, 6.1.2–2.3, 7.1.2–2.3; Bonaventure, *Breviloquium* 1.6.1.

The playwright appeals to common epithets for the Father, "magesté" and "myght," and adds the alliterative "Meruelus," before asserting that the Deity is a Trinity. This assertion is rather frequent in Towneley, but it is also the case that Towneley rarely goes beyond this kind of simple statement of the faith.

The N-Town collection is more sophisticated in its language of trinitarian relations. Although God's opening speech focuses on God as Father and Creator, it does assert that he is a Trinity "Knyt in oo substawns" (1.13); he is the Father of "Myth" whose Son "kepyth ryth" and whose Ghost has light and grace (lines 22–26). More interesting, and unique to N-Town, is the discourse in the *Doctors* in which Christ provides a common trinitarian analogy— splendor, heat, and light—and explains the appropriated attributes of the three Persons—might, wisdom, and goodness (21.65–104). He continues with an assertion of the Immaculate Conception as well as explanations of why the Son was incarnated and of the significance of his double lineage. Although the N-Town collection, and even more so *Wisdom,* which uses Augustine's primary analogy of mind, will, and understanding, shows some sophistication in the handling of trinitarian doctrine, they largely avoid trying to express real relations within the Godhead, opting instead for the more easily understood trinitarian analogies and explanations that draw on the appropriated attributes.[26]

If we look at the opening of John Bale's *Three Laws,* we see the difference between the popular trinitarian expression of the biblical cycles and the precision of clerical teaching:

> I am Deus Pater, a substaunce invysyble,
> All one with the Sonne and Holy Ghost in essence.
> To Angell and Man I am incomprehensyble,
> A strength infynyte, a ryghteousnesse, a prudence,
> A mercy, a goodnesse, a truth, a lyfe, a sapyence.
> In heaven and in earth we made all to our glory
> Man ever havynge in a specyall memory.
>
> (lines 36–42)[27]

---

26. The exception to this generalization is God's opening speech, partly macaronic, in the Chester *Fall of Lucifer.* The lines in question are in a unique stanza form, however, which suggests that they are later additions to a play that probably did not enter the cycle until the 1520s; thus, they may have been intended to clarify a doctrine that, as we have seen, is represented rather casually and incompletely elsewhere in the vernacular drama.

27. Bale, *Complete Plays,* 2:1–34. Compare *God's Promises,* lines 36–49, which is even more carefully articulated.

The speech—and its continuation—expresses the same sentiments as those of God the Father in the Creation plays: man is God's special creature, made in his own "symylytude" (line 56). Bale, however, invokes a technical vocabulary to make clear that God is an invisible "substance" and one in "essence" with the Son and the Holy Ghost. The phrase "I am incomprehensyble" insists on the single essence, but the attributes that follow are names by which the Persons might be known; they suggest abundance and plenitude. The stanza concludes with "we," a pronoun that can be read both as a royal prerogative meaning "one" or as an assertion that the three Persons made heaven, earth, and man together. Bale often takes care to make these relations apparent; for example, in *Johan Baptystes Preachynge* he has Christ say when he enters that he is the son of the living God (which is not surprising), but also that he is the "ymage of hys substaunce," "ymage" being a common analogical term for the Son's relation to the Father (line 339).[28] Later, Christ says he is God and is "coequal" with his Father (line 367) in order to insist that they are of the same substance.

Perhaps the most surprising omission in many cases is any nuanced discussion of the relation of the Holy Spirit to the Father and the Son. None of the Creation plays realizes the Holy Spirit's participation in the making of the world and man, a belief that arises from Genesis 1:2: "and the Spirit of God was moving over the face of the waters." In the Annunciation scenes, when Mary asks how the Incarnation will take place, Gabriel usually says that the Holy Ghost will alight in her and protect her (Chester 6.27–29; Towneley more pointedly says it is to protect her maidenhead [10.69–74]). The preacher at the beginning of the York *Annunciation,* recalling an exegetical commonplace, compares the Holy Ghost to the morning dew of prophecy. The remarkable variant is the N-Town *Parliament in Heaven,* where the three Persons jointly instruct Gabriel in what he is to say, the Holy Spirit adding that if Mary should ask how the Incarnation might take place, Gabriel is to say that the Holy Ghost shall effect it so that she will be saved through "oure Vnyté" (11.205–7). The miraculous event is strikingly visualized; according to the stage direction: "Here þe Holy Gost discendit with iij bemys to oure Lady, the Sone of þe Godhed nest with iij bemys to þe Holy Gost, the Fadyr godly with iij bemys to þe Sone. And so entre all thre to here bosom" (11.292, s.d.). Remarkable spectacle though this is, one might question its theological soundness. Obviously the three beams in the hands of each of the Persons are intended to represent the Trinity and thus to suggest that the Incarnation is the united act of the three

---

28. Ibid., 2:35–50.

Persons (and even that all three Persons are in each of the Persons), but is the effect not undermined by the sequential descent of each of the persons and even more so by the specification that the Son descends to the Holy Ghost and the Father to the Son? I do not wish to dwell on the heterodox reading one could give to the scene, but I think the action illustrates the potential difficulties that arise from the necessary literalization of texts and their theology in theatrical production.

Other problems with regard to doctrine are apparent in these plays. If one reads through the Towneley Passion narrative—which, of course, is possibly not the way it was presented—one is struck by the frequency with which Christ insists that he and the Father are one. It could be argued that the playwrights are simply quoting scripture or are attempting to assert a point of orthodoxy. From another point of view, we could read the insistence on the point as a sign of anxiety.

Perhaps the scene that poses the greatest potential risk is the Agony in the Garden of Gethsemane. The scriptural narrative is quite bare: Christ goes with his disciples to the garden to pray. Three times he says a variant of the prayer: "My Father, if it be possible, let this cup pass from me; nevertheless, not as I will, but as thou wilt" (Matt. 26:39; Luke 22:40–44).[29] The scene has tremendous emotional potential (Luke adds that Christ's agony was so great that his sweat became like great drops of blood [22:44]). However, the scene could also raise questions: If Christ is God, then why does he not know what is about to occur? Why does he not know the providential scheme?

If we look at how writers of nondramatic biblical narratives treated the scene, we can see that they—and the biblical commentators on whom they sometimes based their work—recognized the potential for misreading the episode.

The Pseudo-Bonaventuran *Meditations on the Life of Christ* creates an elaborate scenario in order to focus the meditator's attention on an appropriate understanding of the event. As is his wont, the speaker seeks to evoke vivid scenes in Christ's life at the same time that he controls their significance.[30] He

---

29. In the Lucan version Christ only prays once, after which an angel appears to comfort him. In some of the Middle English harmonized narratives the angel appears at the end of the first prayer, in others at the conclusion of the three-part ordeal.

30. Ragusa and Green, *Meditations on the Life of Christ*. Similarly, the narrator of *Cursor Mundi* (ca.1300–1350) emphasizes the moral instruction of Christ's action *before* the narrative gets under way. By making his moral point first and then intervening as the story continues (e.g., lines 15611–622), the narrator deflects the potential question of why the action occurs at all. His commentary is that Christ teaches through his example. See the edition of Richard Morris, 3.15578–706.

points to Christ's humanity, his human will(s), as an explanation for his suffering and fears; as the narrative progresses, the narrator shifts to Christ's divine will and his volition in choosing his Passion. The speaker tells the reader to have compassion for Christ and marvel at his profound humility: "Although He is God and equal to His Father and co-eternal, He appears to have forgotten that He is God and prays like a man."[31] He is like "any other little man of the people." The strategy is to remind the meditator that Christ and the Father are one but then to imply that Christ sets aside his Godhead to participate in the condition of man. The narrator elaborates the biblical prayer: in his version Christ remarks on his willingness to be incarnated and to do the Father's will before he says, "if it be possible, remove this great bitterness." The other two prayers are alluded to but not recounted. The archangel Michael is sent to him to say that he took the blood that Christ had sweated before the whole supernal court and that they prayed that the chalice be removed from him, but the Father said, "My most beloved Son knows that the redemption of mankind, which we so desire, cannot be accomplished properly without the shedding of His blood; consequently, if He wishes the salvation of souls, He must die for them."[32] Then Christ tells Michael that he chooses to die for the salvation of souls. The narrator is very careful to distinguish the human from the divine Christ. Christ indicates his willingness in the incarnation and his preparation to be obedient before asking that the chalice be removed from him. When he gives Michael's report, he has the Father state that Christ knows what is needed. And after Michael's report, Christ chooses to proceed with the Passion.

The *Northern Passion* and the *Southern Passion,* both from around the beginning of the fourteenth century, tend to keep to a simplified narration of biblical events.[33] The *Northern Passion* echoes the Matthew-Luke harmonized text closely and provides no commentary though the emphasis is on Christ's obedience. The *Southern Passion* also follows the biblical narrative closely. The narrator emphasizes Christ's agony, even unto the third prayer, during which, he suggests, Christ's dread was greatest. However, he uses Christ's suffering to segue to the reader's sense of sin, thus deflecting the questions the event might occasion. Another strategy is to suppress or otherwise elide the episode. The *Pepysian Gospel Harmony* (late fourteenth or early fifteenth century) suppresses the problematical parts of the biblical scene. The narrator says, "And Je-

---

31. Ragusa and Green, *Meditations on the Life of Christ,* 320–21.
32. Ibid., 321, 323.
33. Foster and Heuser, *The Northern Passion;* Brown, *The Southern Passion.*

*s*us went hym hastilich *fra*m hem a stones cast, and fel on knees to þe erþe, and bisouȝth to his fader ȝif þat it were his wille, þat he schulde hym bynyme þat passioun."[34] He places Christ's willing obedience in the forefront whereas in the scriptural texts it comes after he has asked that the cup be allowed to pass from him. Robert Mannyng's *Meditations on the Life and Passion of Christ* suppresses the incident even more.[35] Rather than recounting the incident, he focuses on the detail of Christ's blood-sweat in order to change it into a highly emotive image: in the well of blood that sprang out of Christ's flesh, he says, a fresh flower is dyed. The sharp sword of Christ's earthly love has made his body all bloody. The ardor of his love has made his body a red rose bush. His body is decorated with the drops of blood as the stars adorn the firmament. The narrator appeals to Christ to aid him and to remind the reader that by this example Christ taught men to pray for aid and that by the angel he would provide comfort. Mannyng turns the scene into an icon of Christ's Passion; for the viewer gazing on the rose, Christ's praying is an exemplum for all Christians.

Mannyng's strategy perhaps gives us a clue as to what could happen in a production. Even though a text might raise questions, the play's producers could divert the audience's attention to the emotive image of the bleeding Christ.

These various tellings of the Agony indicate that writers were aware that the event might occasion unwanted readings. Some chose to suppress or elide the event. Others interceded to guide understanding. All would like to place the emphasis on Christ's human suffering, the approach that affective piety took in the later Middle Ages. Playwrights who come to this moment in the Passion have narrower choices. They could suppress the event or they could introduce an Expositor figure to function much as the narrators or commentators in the poems described above. None chose either alternative; instead, each tried to find other ways to control the viewers' understanding.

Both Chester and N-Town replicate the biblical action but embellish the prayers to direct interpretation of the action. Just before Christ goes to Gethsamane he insists to his disciples that he and the Father are one; what they ask of the Father, they ask of him (Chester 15.221–40). In the garden, he does not repeat the scriptural prayer; rather, he prays that the Father glorify the Son so that he may glorify the Father. On earth he has been given "postie" and he has done the work intended of him with "harte free." He has made the Father's name known and taught that he was sent from the Father. He prays that the Fa-

---

34. Goates, *Pepysian Gospel Harmony,* 90–91.
35. Mannyng, *Meditations on the Life and Passion of Christ,* 366–88.

ther save his disciples (lines 265–80). It is not until the second—and in this version the last—prayer that Jesus confesses his fears, but his dread is carefully hedged: "My hart is in great mislikinge / for death that is to me commynge. / Father, if I dare aske this thinge, / put this aweye froe mee" (lines 289–92). He makes this conditional request in the knowledge that the Father can do anything (line 293) and then immediately accedes to the Father's will, which is his own will. In Chester the Son's relation to the Father is not allowed to occasion questions about that very relation but is used to solve that potential query. The first prayer to the Father is an act of intervention on behalf of mankind (in the guise of his disciples); the second prayer expresses his humanity, his fear, without compromising his will. There is no reference to Christ's blood nor any intimation that he demonstrates physical agony. The scene seems to be handled very coolly, the emphasis being on the assertion of the unity of will of the Father and the Son.

The N-town playwright faces the crux in order to convey the agony of the human Jesus at the same time that he has Christ's words provide a kind of explication of the event. The scene is presented as a figure of the Crucifixion. The first quatrain gives us a version of the biblical text with a twist: "O fadyr, fadyr! For my sake / Þis gret Passyon þu take fro me, / Wech arn ordeyned þat I xal take / Ʒyf mannys sowle savyd may be" (28.25–28). The "ordeyned" of the second half of the prayer indicates that Jesus' knowledge is in conflict with his human feelings. In the next two prayers, the playwright focuses on the intensity of Christ's suffering, made more heinous by the fact that it is undeserved: "And lete me fro þis deth fle, / As I dede nevyr no trespace. / The watyr and blood owth of my face / Dystyllyth for peynes þat I xal take. / My flesche qwakyth in ferful case / As þow þe joyntys asondre xuld schake" (lines 39–44). The third line from the end anticipates what shall take place, but the last two lines make of Christ's physical torment a present crucifixion. The angel who comes to comfort Jesus and who says that the Parlement of Heaven has determined that men's souls shall now be saved brings a chalice and the host with him as if to signal that Jesus' present and future suffering will be transformed into the Sacrament: "Þis chalys ys þi blood, þis bred is þi body, / For mannys synne evyr offeryd xal be. / To þe Fadyr of Heffne þat is almythty / Þi dyscipulis and all presthood xal offere fore the" (lines 61–64).[36] The scene ends with Christ's quiet assertion that he will fulfill the prophecy.

---

36. Spector, *N-Town*, 2.502, note to 28.52 s.d., on Rosemary Woolf's authority (*English Mystery Plays*, 236, 397 n. 62), notes that the angel's appearing with a chalice and the host accords with late iconographic representations of the scene.

York 28 illustrates how another playwright evoked Christ's emotional agony to great effect while avoiding fairly well the question of Christ's relation to the Father along with the attendant question of why he does not know the providential plan. When Christ returns to the disciples, he says that the evil spirit is near (lines 79–80), a remark that indicates that Christ knows what is coming. When he returns to pray, he makes it clear that it is his flesh, his "man-hode," that makes him fear, but that he will be "buxum" to the Father's bidding. An angel appears to give Christ comfort and to assert the need for his death, to which Christ quietly submits. Although the angel's speech allows the question to arise of why Christ does not know why he is to suffer, the playwright is fairly effective in orienting the scene to Christ's fears for his flesh, a point with which the audience can empathize, and to the purpose of his suffering, the angel's speech, which also functions as instruction for the audience.

The Towneley version of the scene (*Conspiracy*, 20.456–583) seems to me to exhibit greater anxiety with the result that it goes to greater efforts, not entirely successfully, to try to quash potential questions. Christ's speech that he will return to the disciples after he goes to the Father is a pastiche of scriptural verses—"I am the way"; "I am in the Father," "He is in me" (lines 456–511)—and other sentiments: since I owe love to the Father, I must do as he commands. Christ's agony is confined to three prayers based closely on that quoted above from Matthew; the emphasis, therefore, is on Christ's willing obedience should his Passion not be allowed to pass from him. The Towneley playwright elected at this point to have Christ comforted by Trinitas (how was this represented?), who repeats the pattern of providential history, the implication being that Christ's death, since he is a man, is necessary, but that, insofar as he is God's son, he ought not be condemned to hell. Trinitas says that when one (that is, Christ) is "borrowed," all will be. In some respects we might say that this strategy is the same as the York playwright's: the speech of comfort is used to educate the audience in the logic of providential history. Trinitas's speech more obviously raises the question of why Christ does not know this plan, however, and if we reflect on Christ's earlier insistence that he and the Father are one, then we begin to wonder whether these scenes—indeed, the appearance of Trinity—are not also registering anxiety about the relation of Christ to the Father.

The playwrights recognize the need to address the issue of this relation and find a variety of ways of asserting that Christ is one with the Father; nevertheless, they at the same time reveal that this urgent issue is not easily understood and so they simply repeat the doctrinal points. I suspect that Towneley's iteration of the divine plan in the *Conspiracy* and elsewhere is intended to move the discourse from these lurking questions to the assertion that there is a divine plan. Ultimately, this strategy implies that there is no logical "logic" to God's plan; one can describe the providential plan and assert that it has a logic, but why it is so is a matter of faith.

Representations of the Sacraments

The anxiety I have just described is expressed as reformist policy in a directive from York to Wakefield in 1576: The burgesses are told "that in the said [Corpus Christi] playe no Pageant be vsed or set furthe wherein the Maiestye of god the father god the sonne or god the holie ghoste or the administration of either the Sacramentes of Baptisme or of the lordes Supper be counterfeyted or represented."[37] Although this document has been read as an attempt to suppress the play at Wakefield, in fact it prohibits the representation of any of the three Persons in their Godhead, not Christ in his humanity.[38] The reviser of the Late Banns at Chester expresses similar reservations and directs that since the Godhead cannot be proportioned to the shape of man, and since face gilt disfigures the performer, those who play God should come down in a cloudy covering allowing only the voice to be heard.[39]

As we also see in the directive to the Wakefield burgesses, there was opposition to the counterfeiting of ritual, another area of discomfort in our extant texts. The baptism can rather easily be represented as a historical event focused on the institution of the sacrament; the representation of the Last Supper is more problematical, especially given the eucharistic controversies of the late medieval period and the increased scrutiny they endured during the Reformation. There seems not to have been a *Last Supper* at Norwich, and there is no reference to one at Coventry. Towneley simply elides the matter; there is a stage direction that reads "*Tunc comedent*" (18.351), and the scene moves on to the discussion of the betrayal and the washing of the disciples' feet.[40] Chester

---

37. Cawley, *Wakefield Pageants*, 125.

38. Gardiner, *Mysteries' End*, 78–79, and Wickham, *Early English Stages*, 1:115, read the document as an attempt at suppression.

39. Clopper, *Chester*, 247, lines 14–20. These anxieties point to another problem of literalism: anthropomorphism. How do you make God "disappear" so that Lucifer can seize the throne? I think some of the revisions in the Chester *Fall* constitute attempts to get around the problem.

40. Lauren Lepow has shown that, even though the scene of the Last Supper is briefly represented, eucharistic references occur elsewhere. For example, the *Baptism* is not only about the sacrament of baptism but is linked to the Eucharist through the giving of the lamb to John (Christ, echoing the Mass, says the "lamb is me"). John's initial reference to Christ as "that frely foode"

opens with Christ's directive that they eat the paschal lamb as the law commands, but when the group actually arrives at the chamber, Christ says that the time has come to reject all signs, shadows, and figures, so that he may begin a new law to help man out of his sin (15.65–88). At this point, the text reverts to two stanzas that echo the scriptural version of the dispensing of the bread and wine. This literalizing of the scriptural text has the effect of historicizing the moment; Christ establishes the Sacrament, the players do not counterfeit it.[41] The most elaborate presentation of the Last Supper, however, is in N-town, where the Jewish ritual is duplicated in detail, with an exposition, before Christ says that this figure shall cease. Then he takes the sacramental wafer into his hand, prays to the Father, and explains that the wafer is transsubstantiated into his own flesh. When he gives the disciples the wafer, he adds that it is his flesh *and* blood (27.449). After the interlude with Judas, we return to the supper, where Christ offers the chalice of his blood and commands the disciples to offer the Sacrament to his sheep. This is our only extant text of the Last Supper that explicitly insists on the doctrine of transsubstantiation; moreover, it asserts that the wafer contains the body and blood of Christ, a significant point because the laity receives both in the wafer alone. When we return to the sacrament and Christ offers the blood to his disciples with the directive that they offer the Sacrament—not the blood in itself—he, in effect, sets the disciples aside as a priesthood that is to take the Sacrament in both forms. Although this rendition makes the action seem quite close to duplication of a ritual, it can be argued that it historicizes and explicates the moment; moreover, it exhibits anxiety about correctly teaching the doctrine of transsubstantiation, a move into dangerous territory but one that could be justified by contemporary eucharistic controversies. By contrast, Chester evades the issue of transsubstantiation, relying instead only on the words of the Gospel. If, as has been suggested, our texts for Chester derive from the decades when England moves

---

(young man; 19:39) is recalled in the eucharistic reference a few lines later (line 56) and in a possible pun when the angel later calls Christ that "frely foode" once again (line 164). It is in the *Peregrinus* that the Mass, granted in the *Resurrection*, is first celebrated: Cleophas says that he first recognized Christ when "he brake this brede in thre" (27.335). See Lepow, *Enacting the Sacrament.*

41. The Late Banns writer was sensitive to the issue; he tells the Bakers to "see yat with the same wordes you vtter / As Criste himselfe spake them to be a memorall" (Clopper, *Chester,* 245, lines 3–4). It would appear that the banns-writer understood the scene to be a "memorall"—rather than a counterfeiting of the Sacrament—as long as the key words that the player uttered had scriptural authority. This, at least, is what is going on at the level of text. We must keep in mind that performers through gesture and stage props could have expressed a Catholic ritual while using a text that would have been inoffensive to the censors.

toward Anglicanism or are even later Protestant revisions, then Chester stands in marked contrast to N-Town, which overtly expresses Catholic orthodoxy, or, even more dramatically, to the Croxton *Play of the Sacrament,* which shows the stolen eucharistic wafer being cast into an oven, whereupon the oven splits and blood begins to flow through the cracks and a life-size image of Christ emerges to speak to the perpetrators.[42]

The Last Supper was a volatile site in the years of uncertainty, the 1530s to the 1570s, and we have seen evidence of suppressions, wariness, and other signs of anxiety about this action. The Baptism plays seem safer even though some might say they too enact a ritual. John Bale's *Enterlude of Johan Baptytes Preachynge in the Wyldernesse* provides a test case of sorts; it allows us to see how a Protestant polemicist handled these biblical materials at the same time, I argue, that it indicates that pre-Reformation texts could safely navigate the turmoil of the Reformation. I juxtapose Bale's *Enterlude* with the three Middle English Baptism plays in order to illustrate that there is a commonality among them. Of course, Bale's polemical interests lead to a far more discursive play—though one that is surprisingly close to the reformist outlook of N-Town. If we were look at these plays chronologically—York and N-Town, circa 1460s, Towneley, circa 1500, and the *Enterlude,* circa 1530s—then it would be easy to conclude that Bale's play is a more highly developed piece standing between the medieval drama and the Renaissance to come.[43] However, that would be to ignore the fact that it is quite possible that all four plays were performed in the same year. If we were to look at them synchronically, we could read Bale's *Enterlude* not just as an exploitation of an older dramatic form but also as a response to the dramas being performed in the same arena: the streets and greens of England.

Although the York and Towneley versions of the *Baptism* employ different meters, they are very close in structure; indeed, there are sufficient echoes of York lines in Towneley to suggest that the latter may be a rewriting of the former. York opens with John's prayer, in which he distinguishes his baptism by water from that of the Lord who will come to baptize in "fire and gaste"

---

42. Much has been said about dramatic representations of the Sacrament and the way that the "acting" of the ritual might challenge the notion of transsubstantiation and drain the ritual of mystery (e.g., Beckwith), yet we do not find opposition to the representation of the sacraments until late in the history of the drama. When it comes, it comes from Protestants. It would appear that it is not the duplication of the ritual that they fear so much as the performance of one that would recall Catholic ritual. See Beckwith, "Ritual, Church and Theatre."

43. Bale as a transitional playwright was at one time a commonplace; see Harris, *John Bale.*

(21.14). After explaining the moral content of his penitential preaching, John is visited by two angels who tell him that he is to baptize Jesus. John initially resists (21.59–61), appears to submit, but then questions why Christ requires baptism since it is intended to wash away sins, which Jesus does not have. Christ gives him two reasons: baptism is necessary to salvation and since he has become incarnate, he must be baptized for mankind's sake; and so that Christ's virtues will dwell in the water of baptism. John hesitates once more, trembles, and asks Christ's aid in baptizing him, and Christ tells him to proceed that righteousness be fulfilled. After—or perhaps during—the baptism, the angels sing "Veni creator spiritus," and Christ affirms that he takes baptism to destroy the dragon's power and to save mankind.

The central action of the Towneley *Baptism* is much the same: John distinguishes the two baptisms; an angel appears to tell him that he should baptize Christ; Christ appears and John asks to be excused because of his unworthiness; Christ explains that he must be baptized to fulfill the law; the angels urge on John, who, trembling, completes the ritual. The playwright, however, both complicates the action and elaborates the significance of the event. It is much more self-exegetical than York. It is also more sacramentally centered in that it uses the baptismal formula and comments that this is but one of the seven sacraments.[44] Towneley also makes more explicit Christ's intent to fulfill the old law in order that a new sacrament may be instituted, an action that is played out in the second baptism by oil and cream.

The N-Town *Baptism* differs from York and Towneley in reading the event almost exclusively as a figure not of baptism but of penance. Despite the fact that John distinguishes the two baptisms and that Christ says he has come to take baptism in order to confirm the sacrament, the emphasis throughout is on humility, both John's and Christ's, and the need for penance. John reads Christ's withdrawal into the wilderness as a sign that men should do penance. His sermon is on the three elements of the sacrament of penance—contrition, shrift of mouth, and penance—but shrift of mouth is the insistent note (see lines 155 and 167 and the repetition of the three parts of the sacrament at lines 175–79). He warns that those who do not do penance will be cut down like a tree that bears no fruit.

---

44. The reference to the seven sacraments in lines 193–200 is crossed out with the marginal comment, "corected & not playd." The erasure suggests that the play was being performed in the post-Reformation era, but it also suggests that the performers found nothing else in the play inconsistent with Reformation sentiment.

Of these three versions, the York *Baptism* seems most content with representing the historical event and with providing a rationale for why Christ should have sought John out for baptism; although it is not a simple translation of the gospel text, it remains closest to that narrative. The N-Town version goes further than York's or Towneley's in stating an agenda. Not only is the play interested in the event of baptism, but it does not distract with questions of why Christ should have been baptized. It is not as insistent as the other plays on the fact that Christ's baptism instituted one of the seven sacraments; instead, its message is that there is great need for penance. But it stresses even more urgently the threefold sacrament of penance. This displacement from the sacrament of baptism to that of penance is revealing in its insistence on the virtue of shrift of mouth. The N-Town plays have long been recognized as a voice in opposition to Lollard sentiments; its emphasis on shrift of mouth certainly seems to place it in that camp. But it also illustrates that long before John Bale, writers of biblical plays could see the polemical value of the medium.[45]

John Bale's *Enterlude* retains many of the common features in the biblical plays we have just examined—John's hesitation, the distinction between the two baptisms—but fleshes out the story considerably.[46] Since it is a self-contained piece, Bale offers himself at beginning and end as presenter and explicator. Baleus Prolocutor situates himself in the present by his direct address to the audience, but he is also in the time between the Old and New Testament laws; the events to be represented are not designated as occurring in the past but are to come. By declaring that the Law and the Prophets, the shadows and figures of Christ's coming, are now drawing fast to an end, Bale brings into alignment Christ's new law and the Protestant re-formation of that law. Like the N-Town playwright, Bale interprets Christ's submission of himself humbly and in poorness of spirit as the model for the Christian life. John the Baptist enters to preach to the audience the imminent coming of Christ. He is overheard by Turba Vulgaris, Publicanus, and Miles Armatus, each of whom responds joyfully to the good news. John catechizes each of them in order to get them to repeat what he said. He explicates his teachings and exhorts them to repent, but also warns them to flee man's traditions, the shadows observed by the Pharisees, and to justify themselves by works. John asks who each of the three lis-

---

45. *The Play of the Sacrament* is another obvious example of polemical drama.

46. Bale, *Complete Plays*, 1:12–13, believes that Bale's play is indebted to the biblical drama. If Bale returned to the Carmelite house in Norwich where he resided as a child, he could very well have seen the city's baptism play.

teners is, leads them through confession, and baptizes them. He transforms the mode of sacrifice from the offering of beasts to acts of charity. When the Publican asks for precepts to follow, John says he will not tell him to dispense with all of his possessions; rather, in future he should tax justly and mercifully. The reformed Publican says he will no longer tax the poor through bribes. Neither the Publican nor the Soldier is told to reject his profession, only to practice it justly. Bale seems to be striking at two targets simultaneously: first, he counsels the Publican that he need not give up his possessions, which both legitimizes possessions and ridicules monastic withdrawal from the world (man's traditions); and second, he recognizes the legitimate need for soldiers while suggesting that they often misuse their power.

While John is explaining the two baptisms, the Pharisee and Sadducee enter and, like the Jews in the Passion, decide to act against John lest his "new learning" destroy their law and their livings. But, knowing that they must be crafty to be successful, they present themselves as seekers after truth. John knows, however, that their words and wills differ: "ye playe most wycked partes," he says (line 218). They leave intending to take measures to ensure that John no longer is allowed to preach. The Sadducee fears that John will cause an insurrection because an infinite company of worldly rascals (the audience) comes to hear his new learning. After they leave, John identifies the Pharisee and Sadducee as blasphemers. Christ, he says, will come to cleanse and to restore the perfect Israelites. The targets of the polemic are obvious, but here and elsewhere Bale uses theatrical invective to denigrate the evildoers.[47] Just as denizens of the *theatrum* were characterized as hypocrites for feigning emotions they did not feel, so the Pharisee and the Sadducee are represented as "actors" who hypocritically take on roles that they do not indeed enact.[48] Their transparent craft is obvious to John and the audience alike. No doubt costume and gesture heightened the theatrical effect. The true "actor," like John, is distinguished from them because of his deeds, in this case, preaching and baptizing; he feigns nothing because this historical moment is placed in the "now" and John—and the Prolocutor—lead the audience into the new age.

Christ enters, and like a preacher, explicates the significance of his incarnation: He is the son of the living God, coequal with the father, the image of God's substance, who, born of a virgin, was sent to suffer death. Insofar as he is man, he is subject to the law and therefore must submit to baptism. When John hes-

---

47. P. White, *Theatre and Reformation*, 34–41.
48. Bale, of course, is not an actor but himself, the expositor.

itates to baptize Christ, the Lord explains again that he came to fulfill the law, that he must follow the same way as sinners. To John's objection that sinners are far from his perfection, Christ responds that the circumstance makes it all the more necessary to have a guide to the way; baptism, he says, is the "lyverye token" of Christ's brotherhood with man (line 413).

As the dove descends, the voice of the Father says that Christ has procured grace in the Father's sight as a consequence of which he is pacified and content to make peace with mankind. The Father commends Christ's teachings and warns the listeners not to affiance themselves to men's traditions; they are to listen only to Christ. John admonishes them to praise the three Persons as one God.

Baleus Prolocutor returns to draw the moral and theological points. God considers an individual's humility, not his highness nor his learning. John, who was a preacher, did not preach man's traditions or his own holy life but only the gospel and that only to sinful people, not the "paynted" Pharisee. John did not teach the wearing of harsh clothing, long prayers, wandering in the desert, or eating wild locusts; rather, he taught that faith would purify the heart. John taught penance, saying that one should forsake the old life. Bale says to give ear to Christ, not to Francis, Benedict, Bruno, Albert, or Dominic, for they invent new rules. Men should believe neither pope nor priests but follow only Christ's gospel.

Bale's attack on the monastic orders at the end might be expected from a person who left one himself, but the theoretical foundation for this assault is laid much earlier in the text. Bale rewrites biblical narrative and its interpretation when he has John insist that his example of retreat into the wilderness should not be followed (and see the point iterated at 472–74). Thus John repudiates the traditions that were appealed to as founding principles of religious orders.[49] The confrontation with the Pharisee and the Sadducee provides a similar critique of the priestly orders. So what is left? Baptism of the spirit, inward reformation reflected in outward acts, faith in the teaching of the gospel. The rite of baptism is sanctioned by Christ through his insistence that John perform it, but John makes it clear that the ritual in itself is insufficient; it only calls people to repentance or reminds people of the terms of justice. Only Christ can effect salvation. The ritual, then, is an aid, not a cleansing in itself; inward reformation completes the outward ritual and opens the sinner to Christ. Bale never refers to baptism as a sacrament.

---

49. In his *Temptation* Bale says that Christ did not fast in order to establish a ritual but to lure the devil into tempting him (Bale, *Complete Plays*, 2:51–63).

The playwrights and producers could have made the argument that as long as they reported the words of the gospel, they were not counterfeiting the rituals of the sacraments. None of the texts literally enacts the sacraments as the viewers would have experienced them in their churches; each focuses on the institution of the sacrament. These texts could be placed before a censor and very likely pass the test. However, the performers could act a text in such a way that it evoked ritual. Only a censor on the spot would know whether a written text "deviated" in performance.

The Reception of Biblical Dramas

In the discussion above I have treated the biblical scripts as if they were unchanging, that is, not only that the words did not change but that the play's meaning did not, either. Now I would like to consider ways in which the representation of texts can preserve meaning that is no longer in the text or in which the text remains constant but its reception alters its meaning.

Sally-Beth MacLean's analysis of the Chester Smiths' *Purification*, which is based on the research for her 1983 production, argues that the 1572 performance continued a largely Catholic interpretation of the event (Luke 2:22–39).[50] The play is called the *Purification* in the lists of plays attached to the Early and Late Banns and in the play heading in the manuscripts of the play.[51] In the Early Banns it is called "Candilmas dey."[52] The Late Banns only refer to the Smiths' *Christ and the Doctors;* however, the Smiths' accounts for 1572 and 1575 indicate that the *Purification* was performed in addition to the *Doctors.*[53] Although the Candlemas procession with lighted candles was suppressed under Edward and again under Elizabeth (and perhaps accounts for the deletion in the late banns), the celebration of the Purification continued in the Anglican Church.

MacLean presents a persuasive case that the extant text and accounts of expenditures indicate numerous Catholic associations. The play begins with a legend in which Simeon attempts to correct what he believes to be an erroneous reading in Isaiah—"virgin" for "good woman"—only to have an angel appear to reinsert "virgin" where Simeon has scraped it away.[54] This apocryphal story anticipates the insistence on the purity of the Virgin.

---

50. MacLean, "Marian Devotion."
51. Clopper, *Chester,* 32, 250.
52. Ibid., 36.
53. Ibid., 91, 105–6.
54. The miracle appears in English only here and in the *Stanzaic Life of Christ;* the legend

Clues from the Smiths' accounts suggest some production elements. The indications for music in the play signal conservative liturgical practice. For example, the *Nunc dimittis* was apparently sung in Latin, if, as Richard Rastall has suggested, the English translation that follows is not a metrical version associated with a musical setting.[55] The Smiths' accounts record payments to singers that suggests a group acquainted with Latin polyphony.[56] They also indicate that Simeon wore liturgical garb and may have received Christ at an altar in accordance with the prevailing pre-Reformation iconography of the scene. Expenditures on the child indicate that his face was gilded up to and including the 1572 performance, a practice that the Late Banns writer would seem to reject.[57] Finally, there is a payment for the repair of the Virgin's crown, an emblem that many reformers tried to eradicate from windows and other representations of the Virgin.

MacLean's analysis, if correct, suggests that the Smiths continued to perform a (probably) pre-Reformation text through 1572.[58] On one hand, the production indicates that some Cestrians resisted the imposition of the Act of Uniformity of 1559 and like government measures for reformation in matters of religion. On the other, it tells us that a performance can say more than a text does. It would have been relatively easy to edit out the references to Mary's purity and to substitute the spoken English translation of the *Nunc dimittis* for the sung Latin anthem. Yet a cleansed text would not necessarily result in an unobjectionable performance because Simeon could express through gesture and costume what is not stated in the text; moreover, the stage properties, an altar within a Gothic arch, could arouse associations with older practice through traditional iconography. If the Smiths presented the Purification text that the Chester scribes transmitted, then it seems expressly Catholic. But, if we

---

draws on material in the *Legenda aurea* and Ranulph Higden's *Polychronicon*. The dialect of the *Stanzaic Life* is Cheshire, so it, like the play, is probably a local product (Severs et al., *Manual of the Writings in Middle English*, 2:392–93).

55. "Music in the Cycle," in Lumiansky and Mills, *Chester Mystery Cycle: Essays and Documents*, 129.

56. MacLean, "Marian Devotion," 241–42.

57. The Late Banns underwent revision—we do not know how many times—but the objection to gilding may indicate that the lines in which the reference appears were added for the final performance.

58. Clopper, *Chester*, 105. They apparently became sensitive to the problems of their text because in 1575 they performed two plays "before the Aldermen to take the best," probably an indication that they had made some changes and were submitting the work to the civic authorities as called for in the minutes for the final performance (ibid., 104).

consider the pre-Reformation texts from elsewhere in which some of these emphases are not stated, then we can see that an inoffensive text could become an embodiment of the old values in post-Reformation performance.

Similarly, a play may have a relatively stable text and be received differently at various times in its performance history. Richard Emmerson has provided three interpretative moments of the Chester *Antichrist* over a seventy-five-year period, a period that encompasses the shift from Catholicism to Anglicanism.[59] The Peniarth copy of the *Antichrist* has been dated circa 1500. This text is very close to the texts that were copied twenty to thirty years after the last performance of the play; consequently, we may assume that the text remained fairly stable through the last seventy-five years of its performance history. Emmerson uses the Peniarth version to establish a traditional, medieval reading of the legend: the Antichrist is a figure who will come at the end of time to persecute believers and to seduce those not firm in faith.[60] The Chester *Antichrist* follows the sequence of events described in Adso's *Libellus,* the originary version of the story. Emmerson then imagines a performance during the latter years of Henry VIII's reign when Henry wavered between Protestant and Catholic positions. Through this period "Antichrist" was an epithet used to designate various persons and institutions. For many Protestants the Antichrist was the papacy and its institutions, but Henry at times was called the Antichrist.[61] Emmerson concludes that since "the interpretation of the sign 'Antichrist' was vehemently contested,"[62] the reception of the text would have been diverse and the Henrician performance a more complex theatrical experience than that in 1500. Emmerson then turns to a production in the Elizabethan period, by which time pressure against the plays had begun to mount. Chester seems to have been resistant to the imposition of religious conformity, and it is probable that the plays went only in those years in which the mayor and his ruling party were traditional in their religious practice. The plays in 1572 were opposed by the archbishop of York and the earl of Huntingdom, who was the lord president of the Council of the North. The inhibition against the plays

---

59. Emmerson, "Contextualizing Performance."
60. Emmerson is aware of the various Joachist traditions that identify the Antichrist with specific popes and the like but does not think these had much circulation in England, whereas the legend was widely known ("Contextualizing Performance," 116 n. 46). Lollards also identified the Antichrist with the pope, but Chester does not seem to have been much influenced by Lollardy (100).
61. Ibid., 104–6.
62. Ibid., 105.

purportedly arrived too late to stop them;[63] nevertheless, sometime in the Elizabethan period lines were added to the Late Banns that indicate there was concern that the "Antichrist" be read aright:

> And then yow Diers & hewsters. Antechrist bringe out
> ffirste with his Doctor that godlye maye expownde
> Whoe be Antechristes the worlde rownde aboute
> And Enocke. and. Helye persones walkinge on grownde
> In partes well sett yow out the wicked to confownde
> which beinge vnderstanded Christes worde for to be
> Confowndethe all Antechristes and. sectes of yat degree
> (lines 20–26)

The description indicates that late in the cycle's history additions were made to the text to give it a polemical edge. Emmerson believes that the significant changes are that the play opens with Antichrist and his Doctor, the latter of whom functions as an Expositor to identify Antichrist and his cohorts (note the plural in line 22).[64] The play now identifies Antichrist with the papacy and the "Antechristes" and the "sectes of yat degree" with Catholic adherents, whereas the medieval tradition points to him as a figure to come. The identification of Enoch and Elijah suggests a Protestant interpretation of the Two Witnesses as preachers of Scripture against Catholicism during the Reformation. Given this Protestantizing of the text, some, perhaps many members of the audience are constructed as Antichrists. Emmerson concludes that in some ways this new text is a paradigm of the emerging popular religion: here we have an old text that preserves Catholic eschatology surrounded by a Protestant commentary, but one that does not succeed in resolving the tensions between the two texts and their traditions.

If Emmerson's and MacLean's readings of the late performances of *Antichrist* and *The Purification* are correct, then the Chester cycle would seem not to have promoted a single political or religious agenda. And we should not expect that they would, since individual plays remained the responsibility of independent craft guilds. Although the mayor and the city council theoretically could control the texts, and perhaps did to some extent, they could not entirely control the representation of those texts.

---

63. Clopper, *Chester*, 96–97.
64. Emmerson, "Contextualizing Performance," 109–11.

✠ S E V E N ✠

Variety in the Dramas of East Anglia

As we have seen, East Anglia and the southeast have a greater variety of drama than the midlands or the north. Not only are there biblical dramas in the region, but also the Digby and Macro plays and other isolated fragments and single pieces. These plays—moralities, saint plays, and *The Play of the Sacrament*—received less attention from early scholars than the biblical plays for several reasons. According to the evolutionary thesis, the biblical cycles were crucial because they made the link between liturgical origins and popular drama. The other medieval dramas, often presented in poor editions, were thought to be uninteresting because they were allegorical or vulgar *(Mankind)* or even more crudely secularized than the biblical plays. Histories of medieval drama generally segregated these other plays into a single chapter where their shortcomings were lamented.[1]

Typically, scholars distinguished between the biblical—and therefore historical—dramas and this second tradition, moral dramas, largely because the moralities were seen to be the heirs of the biblical plays and the immediate predecessors of the Elizabethan theater. But this categorization did not quite cover everything; two plays, *Mary Magdalene* and the *Conversion of St. Paul,* were set apart as the only surviving examples of an extensive inventory of dramatizations of saints' lives, and the *Play of the Sacrament* was acknowledged to be anomalous (and troubling), though sometimes classed as the only surviving example of a play about a miracle.

These generic distinctions have proved awkward in part because they at-

---

1. For example, Craig, *English Religious Drama*, 320–53. By contrast, Pamela King gives a probing rethinking of the "genre" in her "Morality Plays."

tempt to shoehorn plays of considerable variety into categories that impede recognition of their differences. Five texts in this tradition—*King of Life, Castle, Wisdom, Mankind,* and *Everyman* (which is not East Anglian)—have been grouped as moralities because they are medieval in origin, share an interest in the sacrament of penance, and use personifications.[2] Despite their similarities, none of these plays can be called typical because they differ so much in length, production, auspices, and action; indeed, in some respects their similarities are smaller than their differences. Moreover, the *Mary Magdalene,* despite its mix of allegory, history, and romance, is a penitential drama if there ever was one. It is the closest of the extant texts to *Castle* in terms of production needs and is as unlike the *Conversion of St. Paul* as it is like nonhistorical morality plays.

Rather than talking about how we might put these plays together into a tradition different from that of the biblical plays, I would like to focus on their variety and the issues that they raise in our apprehension of them. Indeed, I would like to suggest that, different as they are, biblical, morality, and related plays share a number of assumptions about character, representation, and theatricality. Caesar, Herod and Pilate in *Mary Magdalene* speak in the same voices as their counterparts in the biblical plays. The high priests in the *Conversion of St. Paul* present the same motivation for their antagonism toward the Christians as did Annas and Caiaphas in theirs against Christ. The shipmaster's boy and the pagan priest's servant in *Mary Magdalene* speak in the same scurrilous and disruptive voices as do Garcio, Slowpase, Trowle, and others. Is Pilate so different from World? I am not trying to suggest that moralities and saint plays are the stepdaughters of biblical dramas and simply borrow characterizations from the biblical drama; rather, I would argue that playwrights have stereotypes of how tyrants and apprentices act. These are familiar figures to them and to their audiences. The similarities that cut across genres might indicate to us that there is a shared theatrical tradition that can call on the stereotypes of the playwrights' trade and, in some cases, call up figures that we see in folk *ludi* and games of various sorts. I wish to suggest that one reason these plays are viable and theatrically effective is that they appeal to their audiences' sense of reality.

I will focus on three plays, *Mary Magdalene, Castle of Perseverance,* and *Wisdom,* the first and last of which have received little attention until fairly re-

---

2. Robert Potter would add *Mundus et Infans, Hickscorner,* and *Youth* to this group since they share the penitential pattern but come before Skelton's *Magnificence,* which is commonly thought to have transformed the mode into political drama (*English Morality Play,* 30–31).

cently. I have selected these three because they bring before us issues of genre (saint play), mode (allegory), and auspices (monastic production), respectively. My analysis is twofold: by approaching these plays from assumptions about genre, mode and auspices, we have created impediments to reading what the playwrights were attempting to do and we have failed to see how these plays, no matter how we classify them, form part of a larger dramatic tradition that includes biblical plays, romance narratives, and other forms of pageantry.

Mary Magdalene

The Digby *Mary Magdalene* was once thought to be an incompetent piece that haphazardly strung together its narrative in three different modes—history, allegory, and romance—a play that only medievals could approve. Despite the poor transmission of the text, which, its recent editors assert, made the text as we have it unplayable, *Mary Magdalene* can be recouped as the theatrical masterpiece that it was.[3] Since we have had some excellent analyses of how the play is held together thematically and visually, I would like to focus on the matter of the three modes of its representation in order to argue that, unlike some modern commentators, the playwright did not think it inappropriate to mix genres and that he selected genres appropriate to the different sections of his narrative. Second, the playwright did not just create his narrative by largely bringing together material from his two principal sources, the Bible and the *Legenda aurea;* rather, he radically reworked his materials in order to create his own idiosyncratic version of Mary's narrative, which he articulated by drawing on the various dramatic traditions of his day.[4]

Although we might try to keep history, allegory, and romance separate,

---

3. The play's reputation improved considerably with the early appreciative analysis of David Jeffrey and the commentaries of John Velz and Theresa Coletti. See Jeffrey, "English Saints' Plays," 75–82; Velz, "Sovereignty in the Digby *Mary Magdalene*"; and Coletti, "Design of the Digby Play of *Mary Magdalene.*" A recent production has drawn attention to its playability; see the reviews of Meg Twycross, "*Mary Magdelene* at Duraham," Peter Meredith, "*Mary Magdalen* at Durham," and John McKinnell (the director), "Staging the Digby *Mary Magdalen.*"

4. On the sources, see Baker, Murphy, and Hall, *Late Medieval Religious Plays,* xl–xlii. Darryll Grantley believes that there are sufficient correspondences between the version in the *South English Legendary* and the play to suggest that *Legenda aurea* is not the direct source, but that the play depends on some version closer to *SEL* ("Source of the Digby *Mary Magdalen,*" 457–59). I wish to emphasize here, however, that the play deviates significantly from all sources suggested and from all other Middle English versions of the narrative: Horstmann, *Early South-English Legendary,* 462–80; Horstmann, the expanded *Northern Homily Cycle,* 81–92; the Auchinleck version, in Horstmann, *Sammlung Altenglischer Legenden,* 163–70; Mirk, *Mirk's Festial,* 203–8; Bokenham, *Legendys of Hooly Wummen,* 136–72; and Weatherly, *Speculum Sacerdotale,* 170–74.

most medievalists would probably concede that the distinction between history and romance was slippery for medievals. When one begins *Mary Magdalene* with the rants of Caesar, Herod, and Pilate and then moves on to Simon's house, one is in the familiar territory of the historical biblical plays. The opening scenes, though rhetorically embellished, tell the story recounted in the Gospels. The first part of Mary's story seems historical as well, insofar as the Cyrus narrative is parallel to and similar in appearance to the Caesar, Herod, and Pilate scenes that surround it. Within this historical frame, we have the allegorical action in which the World, the Flesh, and the Devil arrange to draw Mary into sin, followed by her life in sin and her eventual repentance, which leads to the scene at Simon's house. The compartmentalization of these modes, it might be argued, keeps them in their own registers while allowing the audience to see how the allegorical generalizes the historical or the individual condition. The play does not continue this neat kind of restricting of modes, however, for Mary returns to her castle and the historical biblical narrative (the death and resurrection of Lazarus) before the action turns to the romance of the king and queen of Marseilles. The king's opening rant reminds us of those at the beginning of the play, and we would seem to be starting anew, yet the text does not segregate history and romance as it did history and allegory. After the Marseilles scene at the opening, the play returns to the biblical narrative, with the visit of the Marys to the tomb and the *Hortulanus*, then returns to the pagan temple scene and back to the Pilate scene, reminiscent of that in the cycle plays after Christ's Resurrection, and finally to an invented historical scene with Mary and Christ before moving on to the romance legend. These scenes are thoroughly mixed together; the beginning of the romance legend is enmeshed in the biblical scenes, whereas in the sources the biblical events are demarcated from the romance narrative.

Although I raised the possibility that the playwright kept the allegorical and the historical in different registers, I do not think this to be entirely the case; these modes, as we will see, are connected in much the same way the romance and historical strands are. Nevertheless, one wonders why the playwright decided to use allegory at all in the first part of the play. Why not continue Mary's life in sin as history since the events are biblically documented?[5] I see the move to allegory as a strategy to contain our negative evaluations of Mary as a sinner before she becomes a saint.

---

5. I am, of course, referring to the way three separate individuals in the Bible were read as the single Mary. See Haskins, *Mary Magdalen*, 3–32.

The playwright's treatment of Mary's life in sin might seem counterproductive if his purpose is to isolate the saint as the heroine amid the forces of good and evil. Although the legendary accounts must mention Mary's life in sin, they do so rather succinctly and move rapidly to the conversion narrative; it is the latter that is the informing action of Mary's life and the pattern for those who read her legend. The playwright elaborates Mary's life in sin, but he offsets overly negative perceptions of Mary by choosing personification allegory as his medium. Rather than making these scenes historical, as the other opening scenes are, the playwright elected allegory because the genre emphasizes the typical. He readily mixes the historical personage, Mary, with the deadly sin Lechery, Mary's alter ego before she is seduced by the "gallaunt," Curiosity (later revealed to be Pride at line 550). The scene is an amalgam of popular themes and social satire. The besiegement of the Castle Magdalene by the Seven Deadly Sins recalls the siege of *Humanum Genus* in *Castle*. Not only does Lechery's messenger speech parallel those of the tyrants at the opening part of the play, but its aureate diction reminds us of hymns written in praise of the Virgin:

> Heyl, lady most lavdabyll of alyauvns!
> Heyl, oryent as þe sonne in hys reflexite!
> Myche pepul be comfortyd be your benyng afyavuns.
> Bryter þan þe bornyd is your bemys of bewte,
> Most debonarius wyth your aungelly delycyte!
> (lines 440–444)

This diction is intended to seduce Mary, to suggest to her that she is something that she is not; nevertheless, it anticipates a second scene—an annunciation this time—that is modeled on Gabriel's appearance to the Virgin. Just prior to Mary's mission to Marseilles, the heavens open to reveal Christ enthroned (line 1348). He utters a speech in praise of his mother before sending an angel to Mary to announce that she should go to Marseilles to convert the king and queen and "byn amyttyd as an holy apostylesse" (line 1380).[6]

If the seduction scene sets up a perverse annunciation, the tavern scene is constructed as a parody of courtly love in conjunction with the humor of those lyrics that show a silly young man or cleric attempting to seduce a young girl. The scene opens with a mock rant in which the Taverner extols the virtues of his wines. This is not an alehouse but a better sort of place—hence the wine.

---

6. The scene is invented by the playwright. The annunciation motif is continued when the angel is sent to Mary in the desert (lines 2011–15) and when the priest first greets her (lines 2045–52).

Lechery is dressed as a gentlewoman (line 513). Curiosity is one of those ridiculous figures who counterfeits the manner of the court:

> Hof, hof, hof! A frysch new galavnt!
>   Ware of thryst, ley þat adoune!
> What? Wene ȝe, syrrys, þat I were a marchant,
>   Becavse þat I am new com to town?
>   Wyth sum praty tasppysstere wold I fayne rownd!
> I haue a shert of reynnys wyth slevys peneawnt,
> A lase of sylke for my lady constant!
> A, how she is bewtefull and ressplendant!
>   (lines 491–98)

When he is away from his mistress, he is full of sighs; he disdains everyone and everything but her. His opening speech to Mary is a riot of affectation:

> A, dere dewchesse, my daysyys iee!
>   Splendavnt of colour, most of femynyte,
>   Your sofreyn colourrys set wyth synseryte!
> Consedere my loue into yower alye,
>   Or ellys I am smet wyth peynnys of perplexite!
>   (lines 515–19)

The gallant's precipitous falling in love is matched by Mary's quick decision to follow him in a (no doubt) sensuous dance and a quicker exit.

The scene skillfully demonstrates how easily people are fooled by appearances and language, how the flesh so willingly follows the world. On one hand, the scene functions as an exhibition of how everyone, not just the historical Mary, falls into sin. The genre helps deflect attention from Mary's fault; she becomes exemplary of all humankind's faults. The genre also allows Mary to move easily toward redemption and the historical plot, perhaps indicating the playwright's sensitivity to the problem in the legend of Mary's sudden conversion. The *Legenda aurea*, for example, says that Mary's sins became so manifold that she lost her identity as Mary of Magdalene and simply became known as the "sinful one." Why would such a person have a conversion experience? The *Legenda* skips quickly from Mary's fall into sin to her appearance at Simon's house. The playwright, by contrast, constructs a bower scene where Mary awaits her lovers.[7] Mary dreams not of her dream man, but of her good

---

7. One wonders whether the bower scene is patterned on popular spring festivals in which a girl is chosen as a queen to sit in her bower where she is to be honored by the young men of the parish or village.

angel, who gets her to convert and to follow the Prophet, as Christ is called throughout these sections. The scene, still operating within the conventions of allegory, makes the point that Christ acts as an intercessor for any sinner; it is as easy to convert to the good life as it is to accede to the evil one. Mary, once again, is presented as the example for all Christian people. When the playwright moves her from the bower to Simon's house, however, he shows us the extraordinary actions of a singular, historical person. The move from allegory is significant since it is one from the universal to the singular, from Humankind to Mary Magdalene. It is because Mary acts in such an untypical way that she is honored above Simon and all the others and becomes worthy to be one of Christ's apostles.

We see in the Marseilles portion of the story that the playwright has made even more extensive changes in the legend. These changes cannot be tied to limitations of sets or other production values because the playwright had all that he needed in order to render his text as it exists in his sources; therefore, we may conclude that his changes are strategic and theatrical ones.

Briefly, the sources say that fourteen years after Christ's Passion the disciples were dispersed, the reason given being that the Jews wished to exterminate the Christians. Mary, who was entrusted to Maximin, was placed with him, Martha, Lazarus, and others in a rudderless boat in order that they perish at sea. They providentially arrive in Marseilles and take refuge in a portico of a local shrine, where Mary calls the local pagans away from idolatry. The legend says that all "who heard her were in admiration at her beauty, her eloquence, and the sweetness of her message."[8] The governor and his wife are also eventually converted. During the conversion process Mary appears twice to the wife in dreams to ask angrily why she and her husband, who live in great luxury, allow the saints of Christ to live in such poverty and distress. The wife is afraid to report these dreams to her husband, but on the third night Mary appears to both, and, out of fear, they agree to offer them shelter.

The governor seems resistant to Mary's teachings and asks if she can "defend" her faith, by which he apparently means to see whether she can corroborate it. Mary says she can because she is strengthened by the daily miracles and preaching of Peter in Rome. The governor and his wife move closer to affirmation of their faith when they ask to be granted a child. After the birth of the child, the governor decides to go to Rome to find out from Peter whether what Mary has taught is the truth. During the sea voyage there is a great storm, the

---

8. Jacobus de Voragine, *Golden Legend*, 376–77.

wife dies, and the child's life is threatened by the lack of his mother's milk. The governor decides to place his wife's body on a rock and leaves the son with her. He reproaches Mary for his losses.

When he meets Peter, Peter comforts him, tells him not to despair, and shows him the sights of Jerusalem and instructs him for two years in the faith. On his return voyage to Marseilles the governor stops at the rock and discovers his son alive (the child had continued to nurse at the breast of his mother). The "dead" wife returns to life and says that she has accompanied the governor in all his journey and instruction except Mary was her guide.

When they return, they find Mary preaching. They take baptism from Maximin and make Lazarus the bishop of Marseilles and Maximin bishop of Aix. They destroy the temples and build churches.

Abruptly Mary decides to withdraw to the wilderness, where she remains for thirty years in contemplation, sustained by angels who come each day to raise her up to heaven for spiritual sustenance. She needs no material nourishment, the text insists. A priest who had also retired to the desert goes to seek Mary out when he sees signs of the daily miracle; however, he is physically unable to come into her immediate presence. Mary reveals herself to the priest and sends him to Maximin to tell the bishop that in a year she will appear to him in the church accompanied by angels. She appears, with a choir of angels, floating two cubits off the floor. She calms the fears of Maximin and tells him she is about to die and ascend to heaven, whereupon he calls the clergy to perform a mass and to give her the sacrament. She lies before the altar until she dies. The legend concludes with a history of the translation of her relics from Aix to Vezelay and a few posthumous miracles.

The modern reader is struck by the ways in which Mary is made subordinate to male figures in her own legend despite Jacobus's assertion that Jesus conferred such great graces and showed so many marks of love.[9] Mary is "entrusted" to Maximin; although she preaches, she subordinates herself and her words to Saint Peter, who "proves" them; Mary preaches and converts, but Maximin and Lazarus are made bishops; we hear her angry words in the visions but not those of her message to the governor and others. Mary's subordination to the males in her narrative may seem odd but is not surprising. Jacobus de Voragine is a Preaching Friar and, though he cannot obliterate Mary's preaching, he can play it down and suggest ways in which it was authorized by males. There is still risk in presenting a female preacher, but some of

---

9. Ibid., 376.

the risk is taken away by statements such as his claim that Christ so loved her that he "had her do the housekeeping on his travels."[10]

The *Magdalene* playwright has radically rewritten the narrative. If one knew the legend, then one might think that the opening scene, in which Caesar instructs Herod and Pilate to kill those disobedient to his gods, but especially the preachers of Christ's incarnation, is intended to initiate the action that leads to Mary Magdalene's banishment from the Holy Land along with her sister and brother, Maximin, and other Christians. The playwright does not follow this scenario; instead, he uses the Caesarean plot to demonstrate the folly and futility of a worldly power that ends in defeat at the empty tomb. When he follows Mary to Marseilles, he shows that the journey is not a consequence of banishment but a directive from Christ that Mary convert the heathen of southern France. She goes alone, a trimming of the legend that makes Mary here and elsewhere even more obviously the center of the narrative. Mary's role in Christ's life is very carefully managed from the moment of her appearance at Simon's house and her elevation by Jesus, to her attendance on Lazarus, and, most important, in the scene in which she is the first to encounter Christ after his resurrection. Although Mary Magdalene and one of the other Marys say that they will report their findings to the disciples, we do not actually have the scene of the report, as we do in N-Town, for example.[11] The omission is significant since it is Mary's report to the disciples that earns her the title of *apostola apostolorum*.[12] The playwright also leaves out other key scenes—Mary's presence at the Crucifixion and the Deposition—scenes of great emotional force in the popular iconography of the late Middle Ages. The decision to suppress these scenes would not seem to be the result of the playwright's inability to include them in his monumental drama—he has an elaborate stage to work with—rather, it would appear that he wished to keep the play focused on Mary. The absent Passion narrative is a backdrop to be imagined, one that centers her in that larger drama.

The *Magdalene* playwright not only brings Mary to the forefront of her narrative but insists on her as the "apostylesse" to the apostles, one who received the gift of tongues, as the apostles did (lines 1343–44) and who preached, as did they. When Mary arrives in Marseilles and asks the king for a mansion, the king angrily demands to know who this Christ is in whose name she claims

---

10. Ibid., 176.

11. *Mary Magdalene*, lines 1104–09, 1121–24, 1131–32; cf. N-Town, 35.95–102, 37.58–93.

12. Haskins, *Mary Magdalen*, 58–97.

protection. Mary delivers a sermon on the Savior who is the second person of the Trinity but also from the beginning; he is the Creator who in the course of six days made all things that are (lines 1471–1525). The king threatens Mary but determines to make a test of his god against hers at the temple. He demands that the priest cause the idol to speak. When it does not, the priest desperately claims that the idol will not speak in the presence of a Christian. Mary calls on God—in Latin—and the idol trembles. Mary prays that the temple be destroyed, whereupon a cloud appears and sets the temple on fire while the priest and his clerk sink into the ground (1561 s.d.).

The king promises to convert if Mary can help him and his wife produce a child. Mary and two angels appear to them, in a single dream, and not to rebuke them for letting Christ's saints suffer, but to urge them to repentance and a renunciation of their goods. The king offers aid to Mary, asks about heavenly bliss, and reveals the queen's pregnancy. Mary turns away the king's thanks and tells him to thank Peter, who will baptize him. The king seizes her in all his possessions while he is gone. The events of the journey and the abandonment of the queen are much as they are in the legendary accounts except that the king does not rebuke Mary when he believes himself to have lost his wife and child. When the king and queen arrive home, Mary returns all the king's goods to him and then preaches a sermon about how Christ bought them and reminds them that even if they were in poverty, they should thank God, for poverty is the gift of God. She then provides a condensed version of the Sermon on the Mount.

Mary decides to turn from worldly governance of the king's estate to purchase ghostly strength (line 1960). After her departure the king and queen lament the loss of their guide, and the king vows to establish churches and to punish those who resist the faith; thus he reverses the action initiated by Tiberius Caesar.

The playwright changes a number of details in the scenes of Mary in the wilderness. Since he eliminated Maximin and others from his text, he cannot conclude with Mary's appearance at Maximin's church; instead, he has the priest in the wilderness fulfill the bishop's function. The priest—as well as the audience—sees Mary elevated by angels to the heavens, where she is given an oble, the Sacrament, for food (line 2018 s.d.). The Sacrament and the doctrine of transsubstantiation are important in this final scene. The priest says he is attended by angels at the mass: "I sakor þe body of ower Lord Jhesu Cryst / And be þat holy manna I leve in sowthfastnesse" (lines 2067–68). When Jesus appears to announce that Mary shall have possession by right of an eternal crown, he tells the angels to go to the priest's cell to bring Mary "My body in forme of bred" to housel her (lines 2079). These additions to the source indicate not only that the playwright wanted to take the opportunity to remind his audience of the orthodox position on the Sacrament but also to imply, through the priest's words, that when the watchers hear the mass, they are joined by saints such as Mary. The text suggests that just as Christ sustained Mary with his body, so the priest, with the aid of the saints, sustains those repentant Marys at the mass.

The playwright does keep the sacraments of baptism and the Eucharist in the hands of men, but Mary is not otherwise subordinated to males in this narrative. Although Peter baptizes the king and instructs him in the faith, Peter does not act as the proof of what Mary has taught. The whole question of whether Mary is telling the truth is elided. Furthermore, the king's conversion is brought about as a result of Mary's confrontation with the idol after she has preached a sermon. She is the active agent. When he returns from the Holy Land, she preaches another sermon. Given the fact that women were not to preach, and given the suspicion that there were Lollard women preachers, it is daring to have Mary speak a sermon in the play.[13]

Clearly, the playwright wishes to present Mary as an apostle in her own right. Mary is often referred to as the apostle to the apostles since she was the first to witness the Resurrection and to report it to the other apostles.[14] This title appears as early as the third century, and though it is retained in later vitae, Mary is subsequently and usually presented as the quintessential figure of penance. Jacobus inserts the title "apostle to the apostles" at the end of his account of her actions in the Gospels, just before he turns to the story of Marseilles. The *Mary Magdalene* playwright, by contrast, has an angel tell Mary that she "only" is to be the "apostylesse" to the kingdom of Mercille (lines 1380–83). Her title is linked not to her witnessing of the Resurrection but to her new office as missionary. When the playwright took Maximin, Lazarus, Martha, and the others out of his narrative, he isolated Mary as an apostle. She performs miracles, as the other apostles did, but more important, she received the gift of tongues at Pentecost, as they did. She is shown preaching, and she instructs in matters of doctrine—on Jesus and the Trinity, a matter of doctrine reserved to bishops or their delegates—as well as relating Christian history, the Creation, and the Sermon on the Mount.

---

13. Aston, "Lollard Women Priests?"; and for the broader view, see Blamires, "Women and Preaching."

14. Haskins, *Mary Magdalen*, 67, 87–88.

The playwright makes an even more extraordinary move at the end of his play when he imagines Mary's reception into heaven as a kind of second Coronation of the Virgin. The angels who are sent to Mary with the manna say that she will be elevated above virgins (line 2022), reversing the traditional hierarchy. Christ says, "Now xall Mary have possessyon, / Be ryth enirytawns [inheritance] a crown to bere" (lines 2073–74), and the angels welcome her in the final echo of an annunciation scene (lines 2093–96). Mary's soul is received into heaven with angelic singing and, one supposes, her coronation.

This carefully designed presentation of Mary Magdalene is motivated by more than a pious interest in telling the legend of this saint's life. The sponsors of the text must have had a deep commitment to the Magdalene cult, or perhaps the playwright himself did. Without documentation, it is difficult to say more about the location and auspices of the texts, but the play's odd emphases on property and poverty are suggestive. When Mary appears in the vision, she tells the king to renounce his possessions, yet the text seems to accommodate his possessions later when she makes the odd remark that should he be poor, he should thank God because poverty is the gift of God. Equally curious is why Mary should be seized in the king's property and take over governance of his realm if it is desirable that he renounce possessions.[15]

The renunciation of possessions probably derives from Mary's demand, in the sources, that the king provide for Christ's saints, but in the play the renunciation intended seems more absolute. The apostles in Acts called for followers to renounce all property in order to put it in the apostles' governance for the use of the community. Mary is an "apostylesse"; the renunciation she seeks from the king is the commitment of his resources to the building of a Christian community, something that is accomplished when he returns from the Holy Land. The seemingly odd "seizing" of Mary with his property during his travels is a representation of the ideal that a ruler submit his office and his possessions to the control of his bishop. The economics of these scenes, then, suggests the workings of an ideal apostolic church. When she says that if the king were poor, he should praise God, she does not require that he be literally poor; rather, she asserts that poverty is superior to properly used riches. It is significant, therefore, that we are told that Mary decides to turn from worldly governance of the king's estate to purchase ghostly strength: she chooses to leave the apostolic life for one of contemplation in which she has no material possessions, not even earthly food and drink and possibly not even shelter since the

---

15. Theresa Coletti discusses these and other issues in her essay "'*Paupertas est donum dei.*'"

text does not refer to a dwelling but only to the wilderness. The playwright does not present her withdrawal from the world for the purpose of contemplation as the election of a monastic vocation; rather, it is more like the life of pre-monastic ascetics, the Desert Saints and the like, who figure in the originary myths of the Augustinian Friars and the Carmelites. On the other hand, the creation of Mary as an apostle, a sort of itinerant preacher, might also suggest the ideals of the Franciscans and the Domincans, who characterized their members as apostolic men. I am not trying to suggest that mendicant friars performed this play, only that the text may speak for some of their interests in moments that do not seem strictly necessary to the relating of the legend.

The puzzle, for me, is why this playwright elected to make Mary a missionary-apostle. It might be argued that the play speaks for a Lollard agenda in which laypeople, whether male or female, have the right to evangelize. However, this would seem to be inconsistent with the playwright's intrusion of orthodox statements about transsubstantiation. Were the play not so obviously a public production in the tradition of *Castle* and the N-Town Passion, it might be thought that it was a private production for women. Mary Magdalene was especially appealing to women in the late Middle Ages; indeed, the mendicants in particular seem to have promoted worship of her in their ministrations to women.[16] But Mary the Apostle does not fit entirely comfortably within mendicant presentations of the saint, either. Aquinas, a Dominican, insisted that Mary's title, *apostola apostolorum*, referred to her *private* announcement of the Resurrection to the disciples; it did not authorize her *public* testimony.[17] Mary's announcement could not be used to argue for the ordination of women or for their right to preach. Perhaps the playwright thought that by reserving the sacraments of baptism and the Eucharist to men, he could suggest that Mary was not preaching but only testifying, but if this were his desire, then he should not have called her an "apostylesse" or given her doctrinal matter to preach. My only conclusions, if they can be called that, are that the text exhibits some mendicant ideas and is representative of the affective piety promoted by the mendicants, especially among women, and that it would seem to have been written for a community with a significant investment in and devotion to the cult of the Magdalene. Perhaps the play was written for a church dedicated to the saint or for a guild of some prominence in an East Anglian town.

---

16. On the Digby *Mary Magdalene*, the mendicants, and female devotion, see Dixon, "'Thys Body of Mary'"; Coletti, "Design of the Digby Play"; and Milner, "Flesh and Food." See also Coakley, "Gender and the Authority of Friars."

17. Haskins, *Mary Magdalen*, 178.

The Castle of Perseverance

As a consequence of its hybridity, the *Mary Magdalene* presents another question for scholars that might prove enlightening to our understanding of allegorical drama, that is, of a play in which allegory is the mode throughout: How do personification and history get into the same arena? How do Pride and Christ exist in the same play? To enlarge the question: How does World, a king in *Castle,* differ from a king in a history play? Do they not wear the same clothes? How does Philologus in *Conflict of Conscience* differ from Doctor Faustus? Not in dress, perhaps, but in speech, one might say. But is not the "realism," the individuality of Doctor Faustus in part a consequence of modern productions of Marlowe's play? Would we perform *Conflict of Conscience* and *Doctor Faustus* with the same intonations, the same gestures? Or would we mark *Conflict* as a morality play in some way and *Doctor Faustus* as a "modern" play by dressing the doctor in basic black and setting the action in some indeterminable but "modern" existential space and time? There is no disputing the power of Marlowe's verse, but would *Conflict* and *Faustus* have looked so different from one another in the late sixteenth century?

In the critical tradition concerning medieval drama, the moralities took second place to the biblical plays because they were thought to be lifeless and insubstantial: they were allegorical texts.[18] This stance is indebted to the romantics' characterizations of allegory, which continued to hold sway through much of the twentieth century. There were those who spoke on behalf of allegorical texts, but their advocacy seems to have had little effect on appreciations of the moralities (*Everyman* being an early exception).[19] It was undoubtedly the production of moralities such as *Castle* that occasioned a rethinking of the effectiveness of allegorical dramas as theater. Nevertheless, in the commentary on the moralities there remains a romantic understanding of the nature of allegory—that it is lifeless—that must be combated in order to save the phenomenon—that allegories are theatrically effective.

The question of how allegorical drama can be theatrically effective is premised in the assumption that personification is by nature abstract and unrelated to the real world except through conceptualizations that have been drained of all life. Moralities are dramas of ideas, not persons, and therefore cannot be

---

18. At the same time we might recall that the biblical dramas were thought to be unliterary, with the result that scholarly interest was focused on their history rather than their words as effective dramatic instruments. See G. R. Coffman's early and largely unheeded "Plea for the Study of the Corpus Christi Plays as Drama."

19. For example, Tuve, *Allegorical Imagery.*

said to be mimetic; rather, they are presentational.[20] Characters are uninteresting because they are not persons but representations of ideas; since they are personifications, they must consistently represent what they are and thus are incapable of change and development, a criterion expected of mimetic action.

When moralities were presented in modern productions, however, the abstractions were seen to be more palpable than the name on the page suggested they were. The reader is continuously reminded of the abstract quality of the character because of speech tags, whereas the viewer sees an actual person fulfilling a part. To account for the theatricality of morality drama a theory was developed that has a contradiction or paradox within it: the character functions on the level of abstraction but the actor infuses the character and the action with a certain element of reality.[21] The character remains an abstraction with all the limitations that personification figures have. The theory accounts well enough for what happens, but one wonders whether it describes the phenomenon historically. Moreover, our descriptions of the genre ignore some important facts: Satan and God, both of whom appear in *Castle,* are not abstractions, at least to their medieval audiences. God mingles with his Daughters as easily as Satan does with *Mundus* and *Caro.* Further, the central figure, the Mankind personification, necessarily changes; otherwise there would be no drama. I would like to suggest that our perceptions of allegory are sufficiently distorted that we no longer respond to personifications in the ways medieval writers and viewers may have responded.

Modern commentators on allegory acknowledge the difficulty of characterizing the genre because the language of allegory seems to do things that language normally does not do: a literal text, which is of course a personified narrative, is said to give rise to a meaning other than that of its literal level.[22] How does such a narrative signify? What is the relationship between signifier and signified? I do not propose to offer a new theory of personification; rather, I wish to point to what I believe to be a fundamental misconception about medieval allegorizing: that personification takes a quantity of actual individuals sharing a quality and turns them into a mental construct that has no real substance but is an idea only. This theory of cognition, grounded in scientific methodology, reverses the relationship between sign and thing in Augustinian-derived cognitive systems.

---

20. Potter, *English Morality Play,* 3–4.

21. Ibid., 32–34; and Kelley, *Flamboyant Drama,* 22–24.

22. Carolyn van Dyck is particularly good at characterizing the issues and the attempts to resolve them in the opening pages of her book *Fiction of Truth,* 15–46.

When we look at discussions of allegory, we find the basic assumption to be that the allegorist abstracts—makes immaterial and unreal—the reality, the materiality of the world he wishes to examine. The real is signified by and subsumed into the abstract—most often as a personification. As Coleridge, following the lead of the German romantics, put it: "Now an allegory is but a translation of abstract notions into a picture language, which is itself nothing but an abstraction from objects of the senses; the principal being more worthless even than its phantom proxy, both alike unsubstantial, and the former shapeless to boot."[23] The abstraction or the conception does not have the vivacity of the real; consequently, the intrusion of anything that we would call real into an allegorical frame would seem to conflict with the allegorical impulse.

Coleridge's definition of the operations of allegory is not disinterested. His statement denigrates work of prior periods in order to advance a new poetry. Coleridge had no obligation to history, yet his description of allegory would lead us to suppose that for a thousand or more years writers wrote texts that listeners dutifully consumed while being bored stiff.

Did medieval writers and listeners understand allegory to operate as Coleridge says it does? At first an authority such as Isidore of Seville might sound as if he does: "Allegory is a kind of other speaking *(alieniloquium)*, since one thing is said and another thing is signified."[24] Rabanus Maurus (early ninth century) concurs: "Allegory is, properly speaking, a technique of grammar. . . . It alleges one thing in words, and signifies another thing in meaning."[25]

Although Coleridge and Isidore and Maurus might seem to be speaking of the same operation, I think they are not. Coleridge speaks of abstraction; the medieval authorities do not mention abstraction. Instead they speak of a distinction between words and meanings. Arguably in distinguishing words from meaning, they are suggesting a process like abstraction, but that is not what they say. They say there are words and there is meaning. Jon Whitman suggests that whether we are talking about allegory within the rhetorical tradition or as a method of reading, the basis for the word *allegory*, its theory, is *obliquity*—a term that is better for our purposes than *abstraction* or *conceptualization*. Perhaps we should think of the medieval notion of the operation of allegory as

---

23. Coleridge, *Statesman's Manual*, in *Critical Theory Since Plato*, 476.

24. Isidore of Seville, *Etymologiarum* 1.xxxvii.22: Allegoria est alieniloquium, aliud sonat, aliud intelligitur. The definition derives from Cicero via Quintillian. For a succinct history of the term, see Whitman, *Allegory*, 263–68.

25. Whitman, *Allegory*, 266.

a lateral move rather than a tiering of the literal and of meaning on different levels.

Let us consider a theory of allegory based on medieval philosophical realism.[26] In such a theory a universal—what we would consider a concept or abstract—is a substance, the real. A universal is not words, not a construct that we have put together. It is real and existent; indeed, it preexists our cognition of it. Mundane manifestations of the universal—things that we can feel and sense—are individuals. Another way of thinking about this is to distinguish substance from accidence. A substance—chairness—is something that all things called chairs share even though individual chairs may be differentiated by shape, weight, color, density, and so forth, all of which qualities are accidents.

When we read an allegory and come across a term such as *Anger, Charity,* or *Will,* we might understand the name to designate a substance. This substance is manifested, or made known to us, can be recognized by us, through its accidents. This leads to the crux of the problem of cognition in realist systems: what is it that allows us to know that a set of accidentals points to a substance that we recognize? For example, why do brownness, woodenness, and four-leggedness possibly lead to "chair" when some chairs are white, three-legged, and upholstered? or when there are other things that are brown, wooden, and four-legged like desks and so are recognized not to be chairs?

However the realist thinker works out this problem, his emphasis is not on the sight end of the cognitive relationship but on the knowledge end. That is, "chairness," which exists in the mind of God like a Platonic idea, is placed in the mind so that the mind, as it processes sensory data, can recognize that a particular set of sense data represents "chair" and not "desk."

The important point that I wish to make is that in cognitive theory the individual—what we moderns might call the concrete, or real—is not in opposition to substance—or what we might call the abstract, or the conceptual. Rather, the real exists invisibly but makes itself known to us through its accidents. If a realist were to write allegory, then he would name that which is real—Anger, Charity, Will—and make it known to us through its accidents, that is, its manifestation in individuals.

It is not insignificant that the Mankind figure in *Castle* is called *Humanum Genus* because he constitutes—he is—that substance, *humanitas,* that makes him and every member of the audience what they are: the genus of humankind,

---

26. Woozley, "Universals." For a modern approach that comes to conclusions similar to mine, see Emmerson, "Morality Character as Sign."

or humankind as a universal. When in *Wisdom* Anima is revealed to be the trinitarian image of the Creator, we know that Mind-Will-and-Understanding is the substance that is the soul. They cannot be thought to be abstractions; they are real faculties that constitute and animate the human being. They are the image of the divine and are immortal. Accidents are ephemeral.

When a character appears in *Castle*, his genus is revealed by the accidents of his representation. Caro, not unsurprisingly, is substantial, but he is also luxuriant:

> I byde as a brod brustun-gutte abouyn on þese tourys.
>> Euerybody is þe betyr þat to myn byddynge is bent.
> I am Mankyndys fayre Flesch, florchyd in flowrys;
>> My lyfe is wyth lustys and lykynge ilent.
> Wyth tapytys of tafata I tymbyr my towrys.
>> In myrthe and in melodye my mende is iment.
> Þou I be clay and clad, clappyd vndir clowrys,
>> 3yt wolde I þat my wyll in þe werld went
>>> Ful trew I 3ou behyth.
>> I loue wel myn ese,
>> In lustys me to plese;
>> Þou synne my sowle sese
>>> I 3eve not a myth.
>
> (lines 235–47)[27]

Caro is further characterized by the knights who are his servants, Gluttony, Sloth, and Lechery. They are the actions that express Caro's substance as well as being substances in their own right, but each with a set of accidents that distinguishes him from the others.

In this opening speech Caro not only defines himself and reads his character but also provides clues to his physical representation on the stage; these are the accidents of his substance, the things that make him more than just a blob of flesh or the idea of one. He is immensely large, but his largeness occupies a tower, a representation of the status accorded to him by those who share his substance. He claims that everyone fares better who obeys him, thereby suggesting the sensual pleasure that all people take in their bodies. When he says he is adorned with flowers, he describes the luxuriant costume he wears, a costume that in its way personifies *Caro*, a luxuriance that fades like a flower.[28]

---

27. Eccles, *Macro Plays*.

28. The costume may be traditional; see *Mary Magdalene*, where upon his entrance Flesh says that he is "florychyd in my flowers" (line 334).

When he says that he decorates his tower with taffetas, he not only expresses his desire for sensual and rich things but describes for us the construction of his stage with its painted cloths. These are the outward signs of his being; indeed, it is the very signedness of the *painted* cloths that signify his insubstantiality. He acknowledges his real substance (clay) and its inevitable disposition, to be rejoined to the sod, yet he willfully seeks out pleasures; he chooses to value his flesh above his soul. It might be said that Caro is necessarily limited to that which he personifies and thus is uninteresting as a character, but this brief introduction suggests a whole range of activities that he might engage in and still express fleshliness. Moreover, he is not simply imagined to be trapped by his flesh because he wills to pursue his lusts. Caro is active; he is present; he is not just an idea.

Thus far, I have tried to suggest ways that characters in moralities are more than mental concepts. There are other ways in which moralities are joined to the realities of the world of their audience. It is a commonplace that moralities are set in no time or outside of time, that they describe eternal verities and archetypal patterns and thus are uncluttered by the accidents of individual histories or even the unique history of Providence. There can be no doubt that the plays describe universal actions—the pilgrimage of life, the fall from innocence into knowledge and sin and the return to innocence through penance. But it is also true that at its inception an allegorical text cannot escape its historical moment. A play like *The Castle of Perseverance* (circa 1400–1425) imagines its allegory in terms of the very real concerns and experiences of its projected audience.

Castle appears to have been written for a popular audience. But we can be more specific than this. The dialect indicates that the playwright was from Norfolk. Later records from greater East Anglia indicate that towns, even small ones, mounted dramas or organized other kinds of entertainments and festivals in order to raise money. A project as large as *Castle* would have required substantial support from relatively wealthy sponsors, so let us assume that *Castle* was mounted by a town—not a city—in East Anglia. The major supporters, for there would have to be some willing to underwrite the costs of building the stages, would be the counterparts of the urban bourgeois guildsmen who produced the biblical cycles.[29] Presumably they would be freemen interested in advertising their status and accumulating money for a civic or religious project.

---

29. See the discussion of the New Romney *Passion* above, for which townsmen lent money for the construction of scaffolds.

Since the town where the play was to be held would have been too small to make it profitable within its own environs, however, the play would have had to be advertised in other nearby towns; hence the need for the *vexillatores* to cry the banns that precede the text. When the criers come to the end of their speeches, they first fill in the name of the town where the *Castle* is to be performed (line 134) and then the names of the towns where the banns are cried (lines 145, 148). We might expect the play, then, to be cast in images that its sponsors would find meaningful.

It is difficult to imagine, let alone reconstruct, a historical moment in the past for a text such as *Castle;* nevertheless, the Revolt of 1381 and the issues associated with it were probably still in the minds of local inhabitants since the struggle over feudal obligations continued.[30] The revolt, which was occasioned by a poll tax and the means its collectors used to extort the tax, drew together persons of various classes and ranks: members of the lower clergy and peasants as well as lay authorities of small towns. Among the rebels' desiderata was the elimination of all vestiges of feudal obligations, which were particularly irksome to persons who otherwise held free status and position within the community. To such people feudal duties were stains on their honor, a reminder of a time when they were unfree or only partially free servants.

The *Castle*-playwright uses feudal imagery to characterize life in sin.[31] When *Humanum Genus* is presented to World, he is promised the status of kaiser, king, or knight as well as power and great wealth; however, at the same time, World and others call him "servant," so the promised overlordship is, in fact, a servitude. As the drama continues, *Humanum Genus* is enfiefed by the Sins, who are the knights in the retinues of the World, the Flesh, and the Devil; consequently, his status is lowered even further insofar as he is subinfeudated. Given the fact that civic freedom is a consequence of an abdication of rights by a secular or ecclesiastical lord, to be fiefed is to be returned to a nonfree status. These early scenes in *Castle,* then, suggest that allying oneself with the World and the Sins is like losing the free status that townspeople gained when they receive freedoms or charters of incorporation.

Depending on their costumes and actions, the retinues of World, Flesh, and the Devil may also have suggested to the audience the gangs of liveried men who attempted to coerce others, to manipulate justice, by threats of force. If

---

30. Dobson, *Peasants' Revolt of 1381;* Hilton, *Bond Men Made Free;* and Justice, *Writing and Rebellion..*

31. Riggio, "Allegory of Feudal Acquisition," 187–208. I have extended Riggio's discussion.

the retinues were liveried or bore banners suggesting their association, they would have been seen as powerful reminders of the threats that some lords posed to local freemen.[32]

Later in the play the feudal imagery nearly disappears and *Humanum Genus*'s sins become those of a mercantile class: not the desire for power so much as the desire for goods. The greatest sins are sins of acquisition, like that of the steward who buries his talents in the field; the failure to perform charitable acts, specifically the seven acts of mercy, which are always the deciding factors at the final judgment, leads to damnation. *Castle* captures the two sides of the town and urban oligarchic mind, which is also present in the northern cycles: a recognition that overlords are the primary enemy and that superfluity is the principal danger.

Wisdom

Wisdom strikes me as one of the most sophisticated and complexly structured of the Middle English moral plays. It exists in all-time, yet at certain points it exists in historical times: the time of the Fall, the times of each person's fall, and the 1460s–1470s.[33] *Wisdom* looks like a court disguising in the Lydgatian manner into which a political satire has been introduced.[34] This structure is not all that dissimilar from *Mankind*'s, in which there is an outer frame, the sermons of Mercy, and an inner plot focused on social satire. *Widsom* differs in having elements of court disguisings in the center of the play: dances that are deployed as what we might call anti-masques. It also differs from Lydgate's model in having Wisdom, once he has "read" himself, engage in a lengthy dialogue with Anima before the scene returns to the disguising mode with Mind's, Understanding's, and Will's readings of themselves. The opening is grand but also mysterious; we understand what is said but not the conditions under which these statements are made. It is the uncertainty about where we are that has occasioned much of the modern commentary on the play's auspices and thus its political interests.

---

32. See McFarlane, *Nobility of Later Medieval England*, 102–21, and "'Bastard Feudalism.'"

33. Scholars have traditionally dated the play thus; however, Milla Riggio has recently suggested it should be dated to the 1480s or at the earliest the late 1470s (*Play of Wisdom*). She bases her argument on a revisionary thesis regarding the relationship of the Macro and Digby versions of the text (6–18), which require consideration, and on the rising concern about maintenance in Richard III's and Henry VII's reigns. The latter part of the argument is not persuasive given the concern about maintenance in Richard II's reign and in the early decades of the fifteenth century and the renewed concern in the 1450s. See the references to McFarlane in the preceding note.

34. Riggio, *Play of Wisdom*, 69–75, and see Westfall below.

A visually spectacular drama, as the stage directions indicate, *Wisdom* uses a largely static structure to frame a lively seduction plot. In the first scene Wisdom, who is the second Person of the Trinity, enters in rich purple cloth of gold; he is a regal and celestial monarch. Anima, a maiden clad in white cloth of gold covered by a black mantle, kneels before Wisdom to ask to have him as her spouse and lover. Wisdom offers himself to her and all those who would have "sekyrnes of joy perpetuall" (line 60).[35] When Anima asks what she may offer Wisdom, he tells her to give her heart; when she asks to be taught the "scolys of yowr dyvynyte," he says she should not desire to savor in too excellent cunning (line 87) but fear him and conform her will to his. When she asks how she might have knowing of his Godhead incomprehensible, he says that by knowing herself she may have a "felynge" of it (line 95). The catechism continues: What is a soul? It is the image of God. Since humankind did not participate in Adam's sin, why do people suffer the consequences? Because all creatures come from Adam, they take on the filth of original sin. When first born, souls are disfigured and cannot be worthy of heaven (lines 115–18). The soul is restored by the seven sacraments—though at this point Wisdom only specifies that of baptism.

The conversation turns to how the soul has knowledge. Wisdom tells her that the soul has knowledge from sensuality (the five sensible wits) and reason (the image of God properly). By the "neyther parte of reson" the soul knows discreetly how all earthly things are to be used (lines 145–46). The soul is bipartite: sensual and rational. Sensuality, "flechly felynge," is served by the five outward wits (line 136); when they are not properly ruled, sensuality is then made the image of sin. The point is that the five senses are not sinful per se but can turn to evil if not regulated. The other part of the soul is reason, appropriately called the image of God, for by the reason, the soul has cognition of God, which should cause the soul to serve and reverence God. By the "neyther parte of reson," the soul knows "dyscretly" how all earthly things are to be used and what is not to be refused (lines 145–48). The first part of the statement says that the soul has an innate knowledge of God and, as a consequence, how it is to act; the second part says that within the reason there is an innate or practical knowledge of how to use the world, that is, what is necessary to preserve the human condition. Wisdom concludes by saying that the soul is both "fowlle and fayer," foul as a beast "be felynge of synne" and fair as an angel by reason's knowledge of God (lines 157–60). The statement that the soul is "fowlle" is puzzling because in the narrative neither Anima nor her Mights have been

---

35. I cite the Eccles edition, *Macro Plays*.

tempted; therefore, Wisdom is either talking about the sin of Adam that each soul has or he is trying to emphasize Anima's vulnerability to sin through the senses.

Anima is then divided into her component parts. The Five Wits, who are described as virgins, enter singing the antiphon, "Nigra sum sed formosa, filia Jerusalem" (line 164 s.d.; based on Canticles 1:4). Anima, who is identified with the Shulamite here, says that her Five Wits, whom she identifies as the daughters of Jerusalem, do not interpret her outer blackness, the mantle or the darkness of the Shulamite, as a reproach because they know she is as white within as the beautiful skin of Solomon (lines 165–70). Wisdom says that the soul has three Mights, which are "applyede" (line 178) to the Trinity.[36] Each of the Mights explains who he is and what he does: Mind signifies Faith, Will, Hope, and Understanding, Charity; Wisdom links them with the Father, the Son, and the Holy Ghost, respectively.[37] Wisdom elaborates the trinitarian analogy while insisting that the three Persons of the Trinity are one and thus so are the three Mights one in Anima; consequently, we must keep in mind as the play progresses that though the Mights speak in three voices, they are one soul. Opposed to these Mights are the three enemies: the World, the Flesh, and the Devil. The Mights are warned to beware of sensuality, the inclination of the sensible part of the soul toward the material and sensuous.

Scene 2 opens with a replaying of the Fall (line 325): Lucifer enters in his demonic garb, though instead of returning as a serpent, he comes back as a gallant, a more appropriate guise to tempt the three Mights of the audience's time. Lucifer lures them away from what is characterized as their "contemplatyff lyff" (see lines 417, 421, 431). Lucifer intends to seduce them to Pride, which will lead to Covetise and Lechery (lines 529–34), the sins to which Mind, Understanding, and Will later confess.

---

36. "Applyede" probably plays on the technical sense of "appropriated" in trinitarian theology. "Wisdom" is an appropriated attribute of the second Person, that is, a name that is proper without being exclusive to him (which would suggest difference in the single essence). See lines 9–10, where Wisdom says that "wysdom ys propyrly / Applyede to þe Sune by resune." The three Mights are "applyede" to the Trinity but are not "propyrly" so; they do not have the same existential status as the Persons but are only images of them.

37. There is a change in the ordering of the Mights at this point. Augustine's order, on which *Wisdom* is largely based, is *memoria, intelligentia,* and *voluntas (amor),* and these are usually linked with the Father, the Son, and the Holy Ghost, but here the playwright puts Understanding last in his initial introduction and then reverses the order of the last two in Wisdom's exposition. Will is associated with Charity a number of times in the play. Placing Will before Understanding may be a simple mistake, for elsewhere, the writer follows Augustine's ordering.

In Scene 3 the Mights joyously describe the forms of their sins before the playwright fixes the particular manifestations of their life in sin on maintenance, legal corruption, and lechery. Each of these phases is personified in a dance of liveried companies: Mind describes the allegorical figures in his retinue, those who constitute the features of maintenance, as do Understanding and Will theirs. Wisdom reenters to recall each to his former self. Mind is somewhat moved, but the others say they will repent later. Mind's inclination is significant because he is also *memoria,* the remembrance of his Creator; the memory of divine origin precipitates the sequence of action that results in the soul's willing to return to God. It is not until Wisdom shows Mind the disfigured Anima that Mind remembers his sins and shows them to Understanding, who recommends the return to God. Will concurs. This inward reformation is followed by a sacramental one as Anima goes through penance: Mind must have contrition, Understanding must make confession, and Will must make satisfaction, after which Wisdom offers absolution through Holy Church (this takes place offstage). While Anima and the Mights are absent, Wisdom preaches a sermon on the nine points *(Novem virtutes)* that please God (lines 997–1064). The gist of the sermonette is that people should perform acts of mercy or think on Christ because these actions are more pleasing to God than outward penances and extravagant acts of atonement and penance. In other words, the sermon justifies the active life as long as the person so engaged performs spiritual, especially charitable, acts.

Anima, the Mights, and the Five Wits reenter in the clothes they wore in the opening scene. Anima offers herself to Wisdom and asks forgiveness. Wisdom says that she has wounded his heart and relates his present agony to the pangs of his crucifixion, which were payment for Anima's sin. Since Anima was first reformed by baptism and is now brought back by the sacrament of penance, Wisdom admonishes her not to revert to evil. The Mights recommit themselves; the play ends with Anima's submission to Wisdom, Sapientia Patris.

Although the sponsorship of *Wisdom* has been attributed to almost every venue imaginable—monastic, household, Inns of Court, school or university, town or religious guild, touring troupe—the strongest arguments have been that the play was staged by monastics for a monastic audience (or one that combined monks and aristocrats) or by the chapel players of a noble household.[38] Since the Macro manuscript, in which one copy of the play resides, was

---

38. Baker, Murphy, and Hall, *Late Medieval Religious Plays,* lxx–xxii, surveys the earlier literature, to which should be added Baker, "Is *Wisdom* a 'Professional Play?'" and J. Marshall, "'Her

owned and possibly transcribed by a monk of Bury Saint Edmunds, it has been argued that the location of the performance was Bury.[39] The attribution to a monastic setting is based on the presence of the manuscript at Bury, on a reading of the scenes in which the Devil appears to be seducing the principals, Mind, Will and Understanding, from monastic contemplation to a debased *vita mixta* in the world, and on the sources, which are said to be monastic. However, since the social and political satire in the middle portion of the play is centered on maintenance, corruption of the legal system, and lechery and some other issues of particular concern to the laity, and since the sermon on the nine virtues seems pitched to a lay audience and discourages outward penances and extravagant acts of atonement and penance, some scholars have argued that the play had a mixed audience in the monastic venue. Suzanne Westfall's recent analysis of the production requirements—the number of speaking parts, the use of dancers and music, and other features—suggests that the play belongs to a noble household and is perhaps a chapel play. She does not speak to the issues that led others to associate the play with a monastic setting, but her argument that chapel players had the kind of talent that a play like *Wisdom* requires strikes me as persuasive.

In reading the case for the monastic thesis, it seemed to me that location within a monastic setting creates serious impediments to a simple understanding of the text. My initial skepticism arose from a lack of evidence in monastic records that these institutions initiated dramatic productions.[40] But more, what motive might we impute to an abbot for putting on before a partially lay audience a play that criticizes monks for leaving their cloisters in order to engage in worldly affairs? One of the common injunctions to medieval preachers was that they were not to rehearse the sins of the clergy before the laity; clerical misdemeanors were only to be broached in sermons to clerics.[41] It would be

---

virgynes, as many as a man wylle'" (town or religious guild production). The monastic argument was first advanced by Walter K. Smart, *Some English and Latin Sources,* and later taken up by Milton McC. Gatch, "Mysticism and Satire in the Morality of *Wisdom*" (at the Bishop of Ely's palace, London); G. Gibson, "Play of *Wisdom* and the Abbey of St. Edmund"; and Milla Riggio, in a series of essays leading up to her edition, in which the argument is restated (also see her notes). Suzanne Westfall has argued for performance in a noble household; see *Patrons and Performance,* 52–54.

39. There are notations after each of the three originally separate plays that it is owned by "monk Hyngham," who is identified as Thomas Hingham, a monk of Bury, whom Richard Beadle has argued is the scribe of the manuscript ("Monk Thomas Hyngham's Hand"). Beadle notes earlier discussions, including his own, on Hyngham and the manuscript.

40. See chapter 3 and Alexandra Johnston, "*Wisdom* and the Records: Is There a Moral?"

41. Spencer, *English Preaching in the Late Middle Ages,* 66.

extraordinary for an abbot to confess to lay lords, who, after all, are his competitors, the venality of his monks.

I wish to begin by trying to clarify some of the issues. In the temptation scene Lucifer appears to the three Mights, who are united in prayer and devotion, to raise the question whether a lay person with wife and children should leave his worldly labors to enter the contemplative life (lines 400–412). When he asserts that Martha pleased God, Mind says that Mary, identified with the contemplative life, pleased him more. Lucifer eventually lists the difficulties of the contemplative life, describing how it leads to despair, sickness, and other ills, and calls the Mights away from that life to live in the world and to use necessary things. The seduction has been understood as an inducement for monastics to leave their monasteries to engage in secular activities and to take worldly office. The question Lucifer poses, however, is whether a layperson should leave the world for the contemplative life, not the other way around.

Scholars who support the monastic thesis, and who suggest that the monastery was Benedictine (as Bury was), give as support for their position the monastic sources that have been identified for the play: Henry Suso's *Orlogium sapientiae,* Walter Hilton's *Scale of Perfection,* the *Meditationes piissimae de cognitione humanae conditionis,* Bonaventure's *Soliloquium,* and the anonymous *Novem virtutes,* once attributed to Richard Rolle.[42] First, one is struck by the fact that none of these texts is associated with Benedictine monasticism; rather, they derive from orders most immediately involved with ministration to the laity: Suso is a Dominican, Bonaventure is a Franciscan, as is the author of the *Meditationes,* and Walter Hilton is a Augustinian Canon. None of the groups to which these persons belonged was committed to the enclosed contemplative life of the Benedictines; all practiced some form of the mixed life.[43] Further, the texts that have most influence on *Wisdom,* Suso's and Hilton's and the *Novem virtutes,* exist in Middle English rather than in the Latin of the monasteries, and the playwright used the Middle English versions.[44] Scholars

---

42. Smart, *Some English and Latin Sources,* is the principal work on sources; his findings appear in the introductions and notes to recent editions.

43. There is an excellent chapter, "The Social and Domestic Content of the Religious Literature of the Diocese," on the mixed life and Hilton, among others, in Hughes, *Pastors and Visionaries,* 251–97. The *Meditationes piissimae* frequently goes under the name of Bernard of Clairvaux but is Franciscan; see Wittig, "'Piers Plowman' B."

44. For the Middle English versions of *Novem virtutes,* see Jolliffe, *A Check-List of Middle English Prose Writings,* items I.12(a)–(*l*), 106–8.

who have promoted the monastic thesis have mischaracterized these texts as monastic; nevertheless, they do understand them to be part of the late medieval flowering of religious culture in which texts that originated in clerical circles were transmitted to laypeople in the vernacular, a fact that I do not dispute. But my point about the promoters of these texts makes it difficult to sustain the argument that the play is a monastic production and that it understands "contemplative life" in the sense of monastic withdrawal for the purposes of continual prayer, study, and meditation. Why and how, then, is the contemplative life used in this text?

The opening chapters of Walter Hilton's "Epistle on the Mixed Life" provide the subtext for the temptation scene and ultimately the logic of *Wisdom*.[45] The letter is written to a layperson who has expressed a desire to withdraw to the contemplative life: "I knowe wel þe desyre of þin herte, þat þou coueytest gretli for to serue vr lord by gostli ocupacion al hol[i] wiþ-oute lettyng or troublyng of worldli bisynes. . . . Neuerþeles hit is to refreyne and to rule hit be discrecion as aʒeynes outwarde doyng, aftur þe state þat þou art in, ffor charite vnruled turneþ sumtyme to vice."[46] The text returns to the matter of charity frequently with the argument that it would be uncharitable to God to cast off the office to which one was called for another one. Hilton describes the lives of Martha and Mary in order to set up the threefold distinction that is his subject: the active, the contemplative, and the mixed ("medled") lives. There are three manner of lives, he says: the active, which belongs to worldly men and women who are "lewed, fleschly, & boistous" in their knowledge of spiritual occupations, for they feel no fervor or devotion; the contemplative life "alone" (that is, without any form of active life), which belongs to those who forsake the world to occupy themselves inwardly with spiritual matters; and the "medled life," which pertains to prelates and other curates who use the active life to aid others but at other times busy themselves with prayers, meditations, readings of Holy Writ, and other ghostly occupations. There are lay counterparts to these secular clerics: "Also hit longeþ generali to sum temporal men þe wʒuche han souereynte wiþ muche hauyng of worldli godes, and also han as hit were a lordschipe ouer oþur men to gouerne & susteyne hem, as a fader haþ ouer his children, a Maister ouer his seruauntes, and a lord ouer his tenauntes; þe wʒuche men also han receyued of þe ʒift of vr lord grace of deuocion, and in

---

45. Horstmann, *Yorkshire Writers*, 1:264–92.
46. Ibid., 1:267.

parti sauo*ur* of gostli ocupacion. To þise also lo*n*geþ þis medled lyf." If such men were to leave the active for the contemplative life, "þei do not wel, for þei kepe not þe ordre of charite."[47]

Let us imagine a performance of *Wisdom*'s temptation scene before a noble patron who knows Hilton's "Epistle." After Lucifer reappears as a gallant, we see the Mights in prayer and devotion, for which Lucifer sarcastically taunts them by calling them "fonnyde fathers, founders of foly" (line 393).[48] Lucifer suggests that their activities are idleness (line 394), that their devotions will lead them to perish. When Mind insists that he "ys not ydyll þat wyth Gode ys," Lucifer says that he can prove otherwise:

> Thys ys my suggestyun.
> All thynge hat dew tymes
> Prayer, fastynge, labour, all thes.
> Wan tyme ys not kept, þat dede ys amys,
>   Þe more pleynerly to yowr informacyon.
>
> Here ys a man þat lywyt worldly,
> Hathe wyffe, chylderne, and serwantys besy,
> And other chargys þat I not specyfye.
>   Ys yt leeffull to þis man
> To lewe hys labour wsyde truly,
> Hys chargys perysche þat Gode gaff duly,
> Ande yewe hym to preyer and es of body?
>   Woso do thus wyth God ys not than.
>   (lines 400–412)

The question that Lucifer poses is a challenge, though it echoes Hilton's open-ing remarks, which are pastoral. The Devil's question is whether it is appropri-ate (whether it is something that falls into "dew tymes") for laypeople to engage in prayer and fasting when they have other obligations—to labor, wife, children, servants, and other charges. His "suggestion" constructs the Mights as laypeople; the trick in the question is the implication that labor is an entirely separate activity from prayer and fasting. Either one is active or one is contem-plative.

---

47. Ibid., 1:268–69.

48. Riggio, *Play of Wisdom*, 230, says that this identifies the Mights as contemplatives, whereas I argue that Lucifer characterizes them as clerics in order to ridicule their devotions and set up the question that follows.

When Lucifer premises his argument on Martha, Mind responds with what he has been taught: that Christ praised Mary much more. The response does not indicate that Mind is a contemplative, only that he recognizes two degrees of perfection (line 417). Lucifer counters with the argument that Christ did not exemplify the contemplative life and that it cannot, therefore, be the better life (lines 418–29).[49] By Christ's example Mind should pursue the *vita mixta* (line 428). Lucifer's point is not that Mind should leave the contemplative life; rather, he is trying to persuade Mind that an active life is not only physically more comfortable than the contemplative life (lines 431–39) but that a worldly life is more pleasing to God (lines 440–44). We must keep in mind that this is the reasoning of the Devil. It is a false reasoning insofar as it persuades Mind that not only is the *vita mixta* the better life but that it is a life of sensuality, one in which the Mights' concern for their spiritual welfare is put off to the distant future. The Devil may be quoting, but surely is not promoting, Walter Hilton; he is trying to persuade the Mights that their prayers and devotion are so excessive that they constitute a "contemplative life." Lucifer seduces them to the sinful life by misrepresenting the *vita mixta*.

If the temptation is not a seduction of contemplatives into the world, then how are we to read the opening scene, which has been understood as taking place within a monastery? First, we must recognize that the opening scene is not conceived of as occurring within a cloister, unless it is in some metaphorical sense. It is the court of heaven where Wisdom sits in his throne; it is not the world. Although the spectators may be at first confused about where the action is placed, they come to know in the temptation scene, if not before, that the opening scene has taken place prior to the Fall/fall. In other words, the opening action shows the education of the soul before it is born into the body.[50]

If we accept that the play is given in a noble court or some related lay venue, then some of the puzzling features of the opening scene can be better explained. Although presumably the figure of Anima is a representation of all souls, within this text she is characterized in ways that might suggest all souls or souls

---

49. Lucifer's ploy is interesting; in the Devil's mouth it can be read as a jab at what we call Lollard thinking, with its emphasis on scriptural authority: the gospels do not authorize a monastic life. But the contents of his "suggestion" are based on Hilton's chapter 5: "Hou vre lord Ihesu Crist & holi men in hei3 degre schewed ensaumple of medled lyf in lyuyng" (269).

50. The idea may seem far-fetched, but Guillaume de Deguileville begins his *Pèlerinage de la vie humaine* with his dreamer's vision of the New Jerusalem before he is born into the world in which he goes on pilgrimage. Similarly, Medwall's *Nature* opens with a scene that occurs before Man descends to the world.

who are intended for the *vita mixta*. Anima's initial appearance is not wholly comprehensible; the audience is presented with a puzzle when she appears in white cloth of gold with a black mantle. As the scene continues the black mantle is read in a variety of ways. Anima's first action, kneeling at the feet of Christ, might suggest Mary, the personification of contemplation. But the language of the text, drawn from Song of Songs and reflecting the commentary on that book, suggests that Anima is the Shulamite lover of the shepherd-king. As we have seen, this identification is made explicit later in the text in the encounter between Anima and her Five Wits (at line 165). The opening dialogue not only suggests that worship of Wisdom is appropriate but that it is natural, that the soul's love for God is innate, a kind of predisposition. Toward the end of the passage, which derives from Suso's mystical theology, Anima turns to the issue of how she will know the Godhead. She asks, "Teche me þe scolys of yowr dyvynyte" (line 86), a course of study that Wisdom rejects in favor of fear of the Godhead.[51] When Anima asks how she will have knowing of the incomprehensible Godhead, Wisdom offers the Augustinian path: "By knowynge of yowrsylff 3e may haue felynge / Wat Gode ys in yowr sowle sensyble" (lines 95–96).[52] Although some form of this advice might be offered to any soul, it implicitly tells this Anima that she should eschew intellectual pursuit and mortifying discipline because any person has the potential for an inward prompting that orients the soul to God. I think this exchange prepares the way for the discussion of the *vita mixta* evoked later in the play and the rejection of contemplative exercises and discipline at the end of Wisdom's sermon on the nine virtues.

Given the traditional Christian symbolism of black and white, the audience might at first think that Anima is an already fallen soul even though this would wreak havoc with the narrative line. Anima is said to be a "mayde" in the stage direction at her entry; she is crowned as a queen and is the image of Wisdom in her costume; and she is explicitly identified as the Shulamite at the end of her dialogue with Wisdom (lines 165 ff.). As the beloved of the Bridegroom and a virgin, she cannot be conceived of as an active sinner, a point that Wisdom makes clear in his analysis of the properties of the soul. But his description is

---

51. I think Wisdom distinguishes here between the way of the clergy, "þe scolys," and that of the laity, "fear."

52. Hilton remarks: "This I can tell you, that [the fire of love] is neither physical nor physically felt. A soul which is in the body may feel it in prayer or devotion, but he feels no bodily sense. . . . But the fire of love is not physical, for it is only in the spiritual desire of the soul" (*Scale of Perfection*; cited by Hughes, *Pastors and Visionaries*, 272).

also a history: he says that the soul is the image of God but also his "lyknes" (similitude). The soul was the fairest of all created things until Adam's offense. The black mantle, therefore, is also the sign of Adam's original sin. This sin can be removed by the sacrament of baptism, but Wisdom warns that the soul can give in to actual sin if the senses are unregulated by the reason. In terms of the plot Anima has not yet committed actual sins.

The soul always maintains the image of the Trinity, because it is created in that image, but depending on how it acts it may retain or deform its similitude to God.[53] That the soul—not the body—is the image of the Trinity shows Anima that God loves her, in making her in his image, but also that the body, the senses, and sensuality are farthest from God and have the potential for transforming the soul's likeness. The allegory of the opening scene demonstrates that the soul has knowledge of first principles: that the soul is an image of the Trinity, that God loves the soul and that therefore the soul should love God in return. The scene also suggests that the soul has innate knowledge of how to redeem itself through the sacraments. The knowledge the soul has, however, is darkened by the occasion of sin, specifically Adam's, with the result that the nether part of the soul can be easily led into sensual errancy. But the soul always retains memory (Mind) of its divine origin and can turn itself back to God if it wills to remember.

Wisdom's discourse on the nature of the soul and my suggestion that the scene takes place before Anima is born into the world can help clarify who the Five Wits are and why they are virgins. There has been some dispute about the Five Wits because they would at first seem to be the five senses, but if so, why are they said to be virgins? Some scholars think they represent the five inner wits, but Anima identifies them in the contrition scene as her "five wits bodily" (line 1076) and Wisdom contrasts Anima's offending Five Wits with the recompense he made through each of his senses during his Passion (lines 1093– 1101).[54] If the scene portrays Anima before she is born into the world, then her Five Wits are virginal because they have not consented to the seductions of taste, smell, hearing, feeling, or seeing. But they are also virginal because the senses in themselves are not sinful; sensibility is what enables the soul to know how to use the world properly (lines 135–60). But, as Wisdom later warns the

---

53. Hill, "Trinitarian Allegory."

54. Riggio, *Play of Wisdom*, 204, says they are the inner or spiritual wits, citing the *Lay Folks' Catechism*, which defines the five as Will, Reason, Mind, Imagination, and Thought. Since some of these faculties are separate characters in the play, however, they could not also be the five wits. See also Clifford Davidson, who identifies them as the inward wits: *Visualizing the Moral Life*, 96.

three Mights, the senses are susceptible to suggestion and to delectation, neither of which is sinful unless the will consents to the urging of the senses and allows the will to be overruled (lines 288–305).

This prologue tells us that the soul was created pure and enters the world that way except for the consequences of Adam's original sin, a sin that can be remedied by baptism. We can imagine that Mind, Understanding, and Will are in a baptized state of grace and have not yet committed actual sin. Since one cannot assent to sin until one has reached the age of discretion, perhaps we may visualize Mind, Understanding, and Will as the young boys the actors perhaps were. If we see the temptation scene as the occasion of their first sin, then we can read their initial confessions and delight in sin, which are generalized ones, as those one experiences in youth (lines 552–620). After their jolly song, however, they enter into the sins of their adulthood: maintenance, perjury, and lechery (lines 621 ff.). At some indeterminate point in their life, but presumably before their old age (see line 890), Wisdom recalls Mind to the knowledge of his sins and the redemptive process begins that ends in the purification of Anima, her Five Wits, and her three Mights.

※?⁂

In 1556 New Romney produced a *Passion* in which the tormentors were named Mischaunce, False-at-need, Untrust, Fainthart, Unhap, and Evil Grace. One wonders how these "personifications" were represented. Were their names embedded in their speeches or were the torturers somehow to signify by action the temperaments they personified? However they did it, we may assume that they acted like the tormentors in other biblical plays: amid their noisy and crude humor, concerned perhaps with the quality of their workmanship, they stretch and nail Christ on the cross. They are neither "real" nor "merely ideas": they are grotesques who represent the evil of which humans are capable.

These characters or ones like them could move as easily into the worlds of *Castle* and *Mary Magdalene,* where they could play villains, as they could those of *Wisdom* and other plays like it, where they could play the lapsed Mind, Will, and Understanding or be their companions. My point is that a stage representation is as palpable in a historical, biblical drama as it is in a morality or personification allegory. Denizens of the stage are masks; they are *hypocritae,* something other than what they represent themselves to be. Though they may convey ideas by their name, their speech, or the action of the plot, they remain persons who are recognizable to us.

266

By focusing on three East Anglian texts I have tried to convey not only the variety of medieval and early modern drama but the commonality of its traditions. When we compartmentalize the texts, we diminish them. When we do not sufficiently historicize them, we can easily misread them. If we look at the arc of dramas across the midlands and down the eastern counties from Norfolk to Kent, we see an extraordinary, popular, and provincial theatrical tradition, but it is in East Anglia and the southeast that we are made most aware of the intermingling of history, allegory, and romance within that larger tradition.

The Persistence of "Medieval Drama" in the Tudor and Elizabethan Periods

Drama appeared in England in the late medieval and early modern period in part because there was no antitheatrical tradition in the Middle Ages. Indeed, the antiludic tradition that I have tried to describe, in conjunction with late medieval lay pious interests, seems to have created a desire for the representation of biblical stories and moral plays by laypeople for laypeople. The antitheatrical traditions of late antiquity and the antiludic ones of the late medieval reformist period were centered on indecorous behavior, especially in sacred places or by clerical persons. As I argued earlier, the medieval antitheatrical tradition used theatrical language in order to demonize clerical excess. As the reformers enlarged their efforts, they attempted to control a wide variety of ludic activities—somergames, scotales, wrestling in churchyards, and the like—but we have no evidence that clerics or the church attempted to regulate or curtail vernacular religious or moral drama until well into the sixteenth century, and even then, they did not attempt to regulate the northern biblical cycles until approximately fifteen years into Elizabeth's reign.[1]

The instruments for controlling ludi were episcopal letters, church synods, canon law, and the like. English-language dramas were not affected by these measures because they were not perceived to come within their purview. Con-

---

1. Glynne Wickham argued that the church sponsored and therefore controlled the religious drama until the Reformation, when the state undertook to suppress it beginning in the 1530s. Most scholars who work on medieval and early Tudor drama would not support this view of the church's relationship to these plays, but I mention it here because it has been restated recently in Richard Dutton's essay "Censorship," 290–91.

trol of these dramas was maintained by their producers: the trade guilds, civic and town governments, and in a few cases, religious guilds. Indeed, it was in part because these lay groups authorized vernacular religious and moral drama that it took the state and the church so long to make the move to suppress them. But it was also because there was no antitheatrical tradition—opposition to dramatic representation—that medieval plays persisted in the early modern period.

My last formulation presents a problem, however, in the way we articulate the periodization of early English drama, for how can a text written or performed in the Tudor or Elizabethan era be medieval? Is it not willy-nilly Renaissance or early modern—if those terms have any credibility? I would like to pursue this conundrum as a way of concluding this study. If we approach the texts of "medieval drama" as we have in the past—that is, chronologically—then we are struck by the persistence of these medieval texts far into the Elizabethan period, at which time they begin to falter. But we also need to look at them synchronically so that we can recognize the "medieval" character of these plays in the early modern period and the early modern indebtedness to and sharing with the persistent "medieval" traditions. I do not wish to deny newness in the sixteenth century—I will point to some—but I do wish to emphasize that a history of the drama that encourages in any way an evolutionary model—medieval to early Tudor to Renaissance or Elizabethan drama—or that ignores the persistence of medieval drama in the sixteenth century is an intellectual scam to maintain a distinction between us, we moderns, and them, those medieval people.[2]

My approach is to offer two itineraries, the first in the pre-Reformation 1520s and the second in the 1560s, in order to represent the diversity of drama and ludic activity across England. Between these two itineraries, I will reconsider the argument that the Protestant church and state began systematically to destroy the traditional drama represented by the northern biblical cycles. There is, indeed, a new antitheatrical movement in the sixteenth century, but its initial stages are intended to control some of the very forces the church and state unleashed when they began to use polemical drama against Catholic practice and belief. There is no evidence that the state or the church took action against the biblical cycles before the 1560s; nor is there any evidence that producers of biblical plays, whether in the north, East Anglia or the southeast, imagined that proclamations and other instruments of control were directed

---

2. For a discussion of these matters, see Richard K. Emmerson, "Eliding the 'Medieval.'"

against their plays. The last section of the chapter reviews the events of the 1560s and 1570s that resulted in the cessation of large-scale biblical drama in England.

This chapter is designed to conclude this study by pursuing the logic of my thesis that the absence of an antitheatrical tradition in the west enabled the development of dramatic representation and also accounted for the continuance of biblical drama during the explosive historical changes of the Reformation.

Itinerary: The 1520s

For our first itinerary I have chosen the 1520s because there are by this time sufficient data to suggest the range of ludic activities in England.[3] Perhaps more important, it is a period far enough in advance of the Reformation to suggest traditional practice. And finally, it appears to be a time in which new dramatic initiatives can be documented.

In the north, the great cycles that had begun up to 150 years earlier continued to be mounted. The Coventry and the York plays were performed through the decade. In other cities processions were at the center of spectacle: at Lincoln on Saint Anne's day, with the *visus* of the Annunciation; at Beverley on Rogation Monday, when castles were built along the route through which the relics of Saint John were carried from the Minster to Saint Mary's.

There are also signs of changes in practice. At Chester there was a major reorganization of its play: in the years 1521–1531 the play moved from Corpus Christi to Whitsuntide and was performed over three days rather than in one. Chester also performed Robert of Sicily at the High Cross in 1529.[4] There is a reference to "new plays" at Coventry in 1518–19, and we know that Robert Croo revised at least some of the Corpus Christi texts in 1534; the Louth plays seem to have begun about 1515; and at Beverley in 1519 William Pyers, a poet, was hired to make a "transposing" *(transposicione)* of the Corpus Christi pageants, but they seem to have ceased the next year. At Norwich, in 1527, the Painters' Guild of Saint Luke, which alone had sponsored a procession with three-dimensional figures, pictures, and other works, petitioned the city to be relieved of the expense and to have it shared by other guilds. In 1529 the first biblical plays were introduced. Richard Gibson worked on the New Romney

---

3. The survey cannot be all-inclusive but aims to be representative.

4. Clopper, *Chester,* 26. Glynne Wickham cites a letter (now lost) discovered by J. P. Collier concerning this performance (*Early English Stages*, vol. 2, pt. 1, 56 [hereafter, e.g., 2.1.56]). The letter is directed to a noble at court asking whether the matter is suitable (since Robert is reformed through his stay at the papal court).

Passion and the Lydd *Saint George* in the middle years of the decade, though the *Passion* apparently was not allowed in 1528–29. In 1527–28 one Mr. Parnell of Dunmow, Essex, is said to have made Corpus Christi pageants and plays with other games.[5] There are notices of a Pater Noster play at Lincoln and one of the Twelve Articles of the Creed at Coventry.[6]

Evidence of dramatic activity in East Anglia and the southeast counties is rather sparse, largely because of gaps in the records. Besides the Norwich and New Romney plays, the *Conversion of Saint Paul* may come from this period, though we do not know where it may have been performed. There are a number of references to the *ludi* of saints—Saint Christina at Bethersden, Saint Swithin and Saint Andrew at Braintree, Saint Thomas Becket at Canterbury, Saint Martin at Colchester, "Holy John of Bowre" at Grimsby, Saint George at Lydd—but all but the last of these were probably not *vitae* of saints but parish games and ales on the saint's feast day or processions with the image of the saint. There was also a Saint Catherine *ludus* of some kind at Shrewsbury in 1525–26.

If we were to join the retinue of Cardinal Wolsey we would witness some of the most fantastical shows of the period. William Streitberger has argued that the revels and spectacles of the 1520s rivaled any produced earlier, and he attributes much of their grandeur to Wolsey's recognition of the importance of spectacle to statesmanship.[7] From the Field of the Cloth of Gold in 1520, where he showed himself as comparable to the king, to his fall in 1529 Wolsey contrived spectacles to direct the king and others and to compliment himself. Streitberger says that Wolsey's court was "as likely a place as Henry's to find revels associated with negotiations of diplomatic moment . . . and his court rivalled the king's in the prestige and power such magnificence implied." Although not all of the events I mention here were engineered by Wolsey, they reflect his use of spectacle and his encouragement of disguisings, maskings, and other court rituals. Streitberger summarizes the arc of Wolsey's involvement in spectacle:

> In January 1520, the king and nineteen of his companions costumed in masking apparel, were entertained with a banquet and revels at Wolsey's, and in January 1521 another revel was held there. A year later, the cardinal

---

5. Coldewey, "Early Essex Drama," 235–36.
6. Kahrl, *Plays and Players in Lincolnshire*, 27–50; Rastell, *Hundred Merry Tales*, 115–16.
7. Streitberger, *Court Revels*, 121; the descriptions that follow are based on Streitberger's account, 121–36.

hosted some of the main revels in connection with the Anglo-Imperial treaty negotiations. On 3 May 1522 the king and the imperial ambassadors attended a banquet, a play performed by the Cardinal's Gentlemen, and a mask at Wolsey's court, and on the following evening another banquet and pageant-disguising—*Schatew Vert [Chateau Vert]*—was produced there by [Richard] Gibson under Sir Henry Guildford's supervision at the king's charge. Cornish's political allegory in June of that year celebrated the importance of the Anglo-Imperial treaty in checking the power of France. The height of Wolsey's power in international negotiations came in connection with the negotiations for the second Anglo-French treaty in early 1527 and early 1528.[8]

This last series of events marks the high point of Wolsey's spectacles. The treaty concluded on 30 April 1527 was celebrated by a tournament on 6 May and other entertainments staged in a banqueting house built, like that at the Field of the Cloth of Gold, for the occasion. The revels began with a Latin oration in praise of Francis I, Henry, and Wolsey and were followed by an elaborate pageant, *Love and Riches,* involving a dialogue about whether one was better than the other. The unresolved dialogue was succeeded by knights who defended their parties at the bar, and the entertainment was concluded by the appearance of an old man who announced that both were necessary. This pageant was followed by another in which Princess Mary and other ladies arrived in a cart in the form of a cave, followed by dances. The revels in November were even more elaborate but of the same kind. After the courtly masks, there was an interlude in Latin in the "manner of a tragedy" in which Saint Peter appears to Wolsey to urge him to negotiate the pope's rescue and that of the king of France's sons. Although the plot sounds simple, there are payments to thirty-eight characters including Luther and his wife. The play was written by John Rightwise, then High Master of the Children of Saint Paul's.

Wolsey also encouraged classical comedy. At the revels at Hampton court on 3 January 1527 for the papal legate, the Venetian and French ambassadors, and some of the leading English nobles, Wolsey had arranged a performance in Latin of Plautus's *Menaechmi* by the Cardinal's Gentlemen. This refined entertainment had been preceded by the impromptu(?) arrival of Henry and other maskers dressed as shepherds with beards of gold and silver wire. They played at dice with the cardinal and some of the ladies before discovering themselves

---

8. Ibid., 122.

and joining the festivities. In the following year Wolsey had the boys of Saint Paul perform Terence's *Phormio* at his palace as part of the revels celebrating the pope's escape from the emperor.[9] Streitberger notes that one of the things that distinguished Wolsey's revels from Henry's is that Henry's were inspired by medieval romance and the courtly ethic, whereas Wolsey's imitated those of Italian courts, with their emphasis on the classics and mythology.

Perhaps because Wolsey was so adept at using spectacle for political and religious purposes, he was also suspicious of others who did the same. Edward Hall reports that Wolsey was outraged by a play written by John Roo for performance at Gray's Inn at Christmas 1526–27 because he took as a picture of himself the lord governor of the play, who was "ruled by dissipacion and negligence, by whose misgouernance and euill order, lady Publike weele was put from gouernance."[10] He had Roo arrested despite the playwright's claim that the play had been written twenty years earlier and so could not refer to Wolsey. The playwright and one of his actors were eventually freed by intervention of the archbishop of Canterbury. Whether or not Roo's play was intended as a veiled attack on the Cardinal, *Godly Queen Hester* (1529) celebrated the fall of Henry's evil, voracious minister.

Clearly, there is a lot of dramatic activity or change in the early decades of the sixteenth century, and it is occasioned by a diversity of situations. Some towns attempted public dramas and succeeded; others failed. Those with long histories of dramatic production continued even when the plays had become economic burdens. As we travel from play site to play site through towns, villages, and parishes we come across parish ales and other activities in which there were collections of money—Mayings, Hocktides, Robin Hood plays, saints' feasts—or other kinds of celebration—Palm Sunday prophets, readings of the Passion narrative, Easter sepulchres, and processions of all sorts. We might encounter traveling companies of musicians or, perhaps, troupes of men who performed dramas. In London and at court we could see lord mayor shows or midsummer processions, disguisings, mummings, and pageants.[11]

---

9. Lancashire, *Dramatic Texts*, item 1006. The *Phormio* was followed by a politico-religious play on the pope's escape and Wolsey's role in resolving the international crisis (Streitberger, *Court Revels*, 135).

10. Hall, *Union of the Two Noble*, 719 (quoted by Streitberger, *Court Revels*, 135–36).

11. I have omitted reference to the universities and the Inns of Court because there are few records of drama from this period. See Elliott, "Drama at the Oxford Colleges"; Nelson, "Drama in the 1520s: Cambridge University," 64–68; and the other works by these authors cited above. For early printed texts from this period, see chapter 5.

Control 1530–1560: Prelude to the New Antitheatricalism

Harold C. Gardiner made the case that the northern cycles came to their end as the result of a concerted effort by Protestant authorities.[12] Gardiner described the decline of the religious drama from Henry VIII's reign until it received the coup de grâce in Elizabeth's. Part of his argument was that the plays grew increasingly debilitated until they collapsed under the state's orchestrated assault. To my knowledge, Bing D. Bills was the first to challenge the monolithic thesis proposed by Gardiner.[13] Bills says that the acceptance of this theory relies on two interrelated beliefs: that the plays were perceived by both ecclesiastical and state authorities as popish and therefore dangerous to the realm, and that such perceptions led the authorities to destroy the plays. He questions whether the authorities before the 1560s and 1570s perceived the plays to be a threat and asks, if they were so perceived, why they were not swept away early in the Reformation as were many other practices (such as boy bishops) that the local populaces supported. The injunctions, proclamations, and statutes that attempt to regulate or control stage plays do not mention civic religious productions; indeed, as we will see, their focus is on quite another kind of dramatic representation. Bills notes that the plays were not characterized as "popish" until the latter years of their existence or after their demise, that is, not until the beginning of the Puritan antagonism toward theater and other practices. And finally, he points to what now has become obvious: that Protestants were not opposed to drama per se, that drama was used by Protestants in the early Reformation to spread their views, and that drama continued to be used by both religious parties throughout the campaigns, which began in the 1530s, to regulate certain kinds of playing, speech and printing.[14]

Glynne Wickham argues that prior to the 1530s there was no serious desire on the part of the government to interfere with authors or their liberties; there was no precedent for censorship in England with regard to drama prior to this

---

12. Gardiner, *Mysteries' End*. His evidence must be read carefully, especially in light of subsequent research. For example, in n. 10, p. 49, to bolster the claim that Henry became suspicious of dramas as occasions of dissension that required suppression, he instances the Corpus Christi plays at Ipswich, which were taken away forever in 1531 (there were no plays; there was a procession of pageants); the halt of the New Romney *Passion* in 1517–18 (and 1528–29), though he notes they continued to be performed later; and the fact that the Beverley plays are not mentioned after 1520 (which is before any attempts were made to contain seditious plays).

13. Bills, "'Suppression Theory' and the English Corpus Christi Plays."

14. Paul White provides an excellent reappraisal of the Protestant use and regulation of drama during the period in *Theatre and Reformation*.

time.[15] Most of the documents from the 1530s to Elizabeth's reign have been used to argue that the state, with the aid of the church, set out to suppress traditional drama; however, the documents cited were not always aimed at that target but rather at the polemical drama the state and church had promoted and subsequently sought to control. To be sure, there were times when producers of the traditional drama made changes and even suppressed parts of their texts, but these alterations occurred as a result of the change in religion, not because the state was trying to suppress biblical drama. Someone altered the Newhall Proclamation of 1531 at Chester to remove references to the pope and to indulgences for attending the plays peaceably after Henry assumed headship of the English church in 1531. The Marian plays dropped out of the cycles probably during Edward's reign not because Edward sought to suppress biblical drama but because he wanted to rid the church of Marian worship. Other practices were inhibited because of changes in religious practice. Henry prohibited the dressing of children as priests, bishops, and women on the feasts of Saint Nicholas, Saint Catherine, Saint Clement, and Holy Innocents because these were the bad days of the ludic season when choirboys and others dressed as the boy bishops, Saint Nicholas, or Saint Thomas, whose cults had been put down.[16]

What appears to Gardiner and Wickham as evidence of a sustained assault on the biblical drama sometimes looks different when placed in context. Both scholars cite Bishop Bonner's injunction against "common plays, games, and interludes" in chapels and churches as part of the antitheatrical campaign, by which they mean a campaign against religious dramas.[17] If we look at the whole document, however, we see that Bonner's injunctions are a continuation, and sometimes a translation, of decrees from earlier episcopal legislation.[18] Amid the directives for proper services, matters to be taught, and priestly decorum, Bonner instructs the priests to tell alehouse and tavern keepers not to allow young people on Sundays and holy days, in time of divine service, to congregate in their establishments because they exercise unlawful games with great swearing and other enormities. In another paragraph he translates *Mimis:* "Item, that no priest from henceforth do use any unlawful games, or frequently use any alehouses, taverns, or any suspect place at any unlawful

---

15. Wickham, *Early English Stages* 2.1.54–97. Although I agree in general with Wickham's description of the gradual development of a state apparatus to control texts, I interpret some of the documents differently than he.

16. Hughes and Larkin, *Tudor Royal Proclamations,* 1:301–2.

17. Gardiner, *Mysteries' End,* 54 n. 32; Wickham, *Early English Stages,* 2.1.63.

18. Wilkins, *Concilia Magnae Britanniae,* 3:865–66.

times, or any light company, but only for their necessaries." In yet another paragraph, parsons, vicars, and curates are told that they are not to "permit or suffer any manner of common plays, games, or interludes to be played, set forth, or declared within their churches or chapels." These injunctions are not attacks on the stage but inhibitions of the *ludi inhonesti* and other activities that clerics from the time of Lateran IV and earlier claimed desecrated sacred times and places.

There are concerns that public disorder may arise from attendance at *ludi*, but in many instances the fear does not center on performance of dramas but on attacks on the Crown's religious policies. For example, we have a letter from Henry VIII to a justice of the peace complaining that he has heard of a seditious uprising in York at the acting of an interlude of Saint Thomas the Apostle by a group of papists.[19] He asks the justice to do his utmost to prevent and hinder such commotion in the future and to imprison any papists "who shall, in performing interludes which are founded on any portions of the Old or New Testament, say or make use of any language which may tend to excite those who are beholding the same to any breach of the peace." The sedition consists in using biblical texts to incite the crowd against actions taken by Henry in the early years of the Reformation. We can see this same concern in many later documents. For example, a royal proclamation of 1543 (*Statutes of the Realm*, 34–35 Henry VIII, c. 1), states that action is necessary on account of the "diversitie of opinions, sayinges, varyannces, argumentes, tumultes, and scisms (which) have been sprong and arysen amonges his sayd subiectes, within this his realme." It goes on to provide that "it shall be lawfull to all and every persone and personnes, to sette forth songes playes and enterludes, to be used and exercised within this realme, & other the Kynges dominions, for the rebukyng and reproching of vices and the setting foorth of vertue: *So alwayes the saide songes and playes or enterludes medle not with interpretacions of scripture, contrary to the doctryne set forth or to be set forth by the kynges maiestie*, oure saide soueraygne lorde that now is."[20] Although Edward revoked some of Henry's proclamations, he continued the practice of control in order to protect his own Protestant initiatives. His first Act of Uniformity (1549) proscribed

---

19. The original is said to be in Latin, ca. 1535–40. Halliwell-Phillips, *Letters of the Kings of England*, 1:354. See also Johnston and Rogerson, *York*, pp. 649–50, where the editors express some doubt about the authenticity of the document.

20. Emphasis added. Quoted from Wickham, *Early English Stages*, 2.1.352 n. 13, and Nicholas Davis, "Allusions . . . (4): Interludes," 78.

"enterludes playes songes rymes (which) declare or speake anye thinge in the derogac[i]on or dyspisynge of . . . The Book of Common Prayer."[21] Mary reversed directions once more: the royal proclamation of 18 August 1553 bans "playinge of Interludes and pryntyng false bookes, ballettes, rymes, and other lewde tretises in the englysche tonge, concernynge doctryne in matters now in question and controuersye, touchinge the hyghe poyntes and misteries of cristen religion."[22] Finally, in the Act of Uniformity, 8 May 1559, Elizabeth took measures to control those who "shall in any interludes, plays, songs rhymes, or by other open words, declare or speak anything in the derogation, depraving or despising" of the Book of Common Prayer.[23]

It is clear that the Crown increasingly sought to tighten control over speech and printed texts that might contain attacks on or ridicule of its own policies and initiatives, but the apparatus is incredibly cumbersome. If we consider the number of books printed in the early modern period and the number of people who were supposed to read and authorize them, we must wonder how these censors accomplished any of the tasks of their offices, let alone actually read all the books submitted to them. The printing of *Godly Queen Hester* in 1561 suggests that an inappropriate text could slip by.

The fear of seditious speech was not the only reason for attempting to suppress or control ludic activities. In 1545 London issued a proclamation for the abolishment of interludes that complains that "manyfold and sundrye Enterludes and co[mm]en Playes" are more commonly and busily set forth than heretofore "in dyvers & many suspycyous darke & inconvenyent plac[e]s" when the king and the city have ordered that they not be played.[24] The proclamation thus far would seem to be a blanket one, except that it goes on to say: "And namely & cheiffelye upon the Sondaye & other hallydayes in the tyme of Evensonge & other devyne s[er]vice." The objection is the common clerical one about competition during services, but to this the city fathers add the moral argument that these plays encourage idleness and the "wasting of their masters' goods and disobedience to their masters." These last clauses indicate the real concerns of the authors of the proclamation: to Bishop Bonner's com-

---

21. Nicholas Davis, "Allusions . . . (4): Interludes," 79, 80.

22. Hughes and Larkin, *Tudor Royal Proclamations*, 2:5–8; Nicholas Davis, "Allusions . . . (4): Interludes," 83.

23. Chambers, *Elizabethan Stage*, 4:263; Nicholas Davis, "Allusions . . . (4): Interludes," 85.

24. Hughes and Larkin, *Tudor Royal Proclamations*, 1:341–42; Nicholas Davis, "Allusions . . . (4): Interludes," 78–79.

plaints about idleness, sin and sacrilege, the merchant oligarchs add the waste of their goods by their apprentices and laborers.

Those who sought to control *ludi* on Sundays and holidays during the hours of service also attempted to restrict activities in the spring and summer as well. On 6 August 1549 Edward issued a proclamation that since within the realm as well as the city of London, there were interludes containing "matter tending to sedition, and contemning of sundry good orders and laws" which lead to "disquiet, division, tumults and uproars in this realm," he orders that no one is to "openly or secretly play in the English tongue any kind of interlude, play, dialogue, or other matter set forth in form of play, in any place, public or private, within this realm" on pain of imprisonment and further punishment.[25] He demands that the authorities throughout the realm be especially vigilant. This proclamation has been read as evidence of the royal initiative to suppress the religious drama.[26] However, there is a clause that calls that interpretation into question, for the prohibition is to last only from 9 August until the feast of All Saints (1 November). If this proclamation is aimed at religious dramas, why does it only forbid them during three months of the year (and not when the biblical dramas are performed)? Is one allowed to stage seditious plays the other nine months of the year? This curious restriction is repeated in numerous other documents. In the royal proclamation of 16 May 1559 Elizabeth ordered that since "the tyme wherein common Interludes in the Englishe tongue are wont vsually to be played, is now past vntyll All Halloutyde, and that also some that haue ben of late vsed, are not conuenient in any good ordered Christian Common weale to be suffred," all manner of interludes to be played either openly or privately are forbidden unless there is notice given beforehand and a license issued.[27] Historians of the Revels' Office and other forms of control focus on the license clauses but neglect the restriction about the time of the year. We might also note that by this time, the period that is permitted has become customary: the time in which plays "in the Englishe tongue are wont vsually to be played" is past. This is certainly not a new initiative, for we can find earlier in the century licenses in the city of London for stage plays in the normally restricted period: in 1528 the city gave a license to the parish of All Hallows in the Wall for

---

25. Hughes and Larkin, *Tudor Royal Proclamations*, 1:478–79; Nicholas Davis, "Allusions . . . (4): Interludes," 80.

26. Gardiner, *Mysteries' End*, 60–61.

27. Hughes and Larkin, *Tudor Royal Proclamations*, 2: 115; Nicholas Davis, "Allusions . . . (4): Interludes," 85.

a stage play from Easter (12 April) to Michaelmas (29 September); and in 1529 another was given stating that only the parish of Christ Church, Saint Katherine's, could set up a stage play from 20 April to 29 September.[28]

Even though some of these proclamations suggest that the prohibitions are concerned to deter sedition, it might be thought that restrictions on this time period really arise from fear of the spread of pestilence in the densely populated areas. Indeed, London's mayor on 30 September 1563 prohibited all interludes and plays during the infection, and this rationale becomes fairly common thereafter: on 12 May 1569 there is a precept that no plays are to be played from the last day of May until the end of September.[29] The city government expresses the concern that closely packed rooms, the summer season, and so forth, contribute to the spread of infection. They order, in the queen's name, that no innkeepers, taverners, hall-keepers, or brewers set forth stage plays or interludes or allow such in their houses or environs within London or the liberties or suburbs of the city. A precept of 1572 asserts that the persons who attend these plays are of the "meanest sorte."[30] The city fathers have shifted their concern from the idleness of apprentices—which they addressed in other ways—to what would seem to be the more urgent fear of contagion. But the time restriction—from sometime in May to November 1—and expressed concerns about sedition and the stipulation that these "interludes" are in English obscure fears about another kind of contagion—immoderate speech.[31]

Why is it that Elizabeth in the Act of Uniformity says she will fine anyone one hundred marks who after the feast of the Nativity of Saint John the Baptist speaks in derogation of the Book of Common Prayer in interludes, plays, songs, rhymes, or open words?[32] The matter is elaborated in her proclamation of 16 May 1559, noted above: Elizabeth says that the "wonted time" for interludes in English is now past and orders them not to be played between now and

---

28. Mill and Chambers, "Dramatic Records of the City of London," 287–88.

29. Chambers, *Elizabethan Stage*, 4:267.

30. Ibid., 4:269.

31. Edmund Grindal, bishop of London, reveals the connection between two kinds of infection in his letter to Sir W. Cecil, 23 February 1564, five months after London's mayor forbade plays because of the plague. Grindal recommends the inhibition of plays within the city and a three-mile compass for a year because the plague is renewed by the practice of the "idle sorte off people" who attend on "Histriones, common playours; who now daylye, butt speciallye on holydayes, sett vp bylles, wherevnto the youthe resorteth excessively, & ther taketh infection." Then, moving to another discourse, he goes on: "besydes that goddes worde by theyr impure mowthes is prophaned, and turned into scoffes" (Chambers, *Elizabethan Stage*, 4:266–67).

32. Chambers, *Elizabethan Stage*, 4:263.

November 1. She specifies that the officials are to permit no plays wherein either matters of religion or of the governance of the estate of the commonwealth shall be treated (unless by men of authority, learning, and wisdom or before an audience of grave and discrete persons).[33]

We learn from these documents that there is a period in which certain ludic activities are allowed (roughly 1 November into early spring) and that there is a period in which they are feared (late spring until 1 November). In addition, we learn that these interludes are in English and in public and—given the special licenses ordered in the 1520s—sometimes take place in churchyards. They are the *ludi* and stage plays that occur during the summer months, when lay people had their church ales, Robin Hood gatherings, Hocktides, and the like. Interestingly, the proclamations do not focus on these activities by name (even though there is ample evidence elsewhere of attempts to control or put them down); rather, the controls aim to suppress immoderate speech and attacks on state religion and the monarchs—all of which would constitute sedition. The rulings mark off an approved ludic season at the same time as they attempt to suppress one associated with the commons.

It would appear that the Crown and other officials are not trying to control drama so much as activities that are satiric, parodic, and polemical. The season they would shut down is the time of disorder. I would like to suggest that these documents can tell us something about the traditions associated with spring and summer rituals, something about the popular voice on a scaffold high.

As we have seen, the summer months provided occasions for *miracula*, somergames, lords of misrule, king games, Hocktides, Robin Hood, the transgressive Maid Marian, plough plays with their *quêtes*, and many other disruptive folk customs. Bishop John de Grandisson objected to Exeter's Abbot of Brothelyngham (1348) because the mad abbot encouraged attacks on the townspeople.[34] In 1352 he attempted to suppress an objectionable diversion that used derision, invective, and reproach against the Shoemakers and their craft.[35] Plays were a means to ridicule, as More's description of a stage play indicates:

> And in a stage play all the people know right wel, that he that playeth the sowdayne is percase a sowter. Yet if one should can so lyttle good, to shewe

---

33. Hughes and Larkin, *Tudor Royal Proclamations*, 2:115–16; Chambers, *Elizabethan Stage*, 4:263–64.

34. Wasson, *Devon*, 9–10.

35. Ibid., 11–12.

out of seasonne what acquaintance he hath with him, and call him by his owne name whyle he standeth in his magestie, one of his tormentors might hap to breake his head, and worthy for marring of the play. And so they said that these matters bee Kynges games, as it were stage playes, and for the more part plaied vpon scafoldes. In which pore men be but the lokers on. And thei that wise be, wil medle no farther. For they that sometyme step vp and playe with them, when they cannot play their parts, they disorder the play & do themself no good.[36]

More's description suggests that they were disreputable activities of the commoners, ludicrously pretentious (the reference to the sowter, who is a Soldan), and slanderous or libelous.[37] Sandra Billington has described king games, which occur from midsummer until the end of August, as games in which the victor scorns the losers and others (among other examples she cites the wrestling match in the Chester *Shepherds Play*).[38] King games are also linked with the image of Fortune, the death of the summer lord, and king-of-the-mountain games.

Elsewhere More attacks Robert Barnes, a Reformation opponent, who, he says, rails against the laws: "No Sowdan in a stage play may make mo braggyng bostys, nor ronnes out in mo frantike ragys, then may frere frantyke Barns."[39] The words "frere frantyke" may be illuminated by More's description of Tyndale and Luther as "sorte[s] of freres folowynge an abbote of mysrule in a Christmas game that were prykked in blankettes, and then sholde stande vp and preche vppon a stole and make a mowynge sermon."[40] He describes the sermons of Friar Frappe as "lewd," though not so ribald as those of Tyndale: "The tother [= Friar Frappe] where he precheth that men may lawfully go to lechery / he maketh commenly some fonde textes of his own hed / and dare not in such matters medle wyth ye very scrypture ytself," as Tyndale does when he defends clerical marriage. In both instances More focuses on a game in which a figure, a sultan or a friar, one on a stage the other on a stool, in order to mock, amuses with "lewd" remarks probably both salacious and irreverent. The proclamations that forbid "playing" from late spring to 1 No-

---

36. More, *History of Richard III*, 80–81, 258–59.

37. The presence of the tormentors suggests that the play may be some farcical piece in which the audience is to be delighted with the torture of the alien sultan. See also the story of John Adroyns, who played the Devil in a stage play (Rastell, *Hundred Merry Tales*, 67–69).

38. Billington, *Mock Kings*, 63–65.

39. More, *Confutation of Tyndale's Answer*, 919.

40. "Mowynge" probably means "jesting" or "grimacing"; see *OED*, "Mow," v[3].

vember are intended to control the dangerous period of folk custom when "playing" can become polemical, political, and otherwise disruptive.

None of the acts, proclamations, or other attempts at control that I have mentioned thus far are directed at biblical dramas like those produced in the north, at Norwich, or in the N-Town manuscript. Indeed, the only such action of which I am aware before Elizabeth's reign had to do with the New Romney *Passion*. On 26 May 1517 the Warden of the Cinque Ports instructed the Jurats of New Romney that they should not proceed with their play without a license from the king. There is also a note from 1528 or 1529 that there was again a commission concerning no play in New Romney. Both notices are strange because in 1517 there was no apparatus for the licensing of plays as far as we know. The stoppage in 1528–29 might be more understandable given the direction Henry's government had taken; perhaps someone had objected to something in the play and the times were uneasy enough that the warden decided the play should not go forward. It may also be noteworthy that New Romney began negotiations with Richard Gibson with regard to their play a few years before the second prohibition and that Gibson apparently finished whatever work he did four years or so after that action. There are no indications of interference with the play after that. Beyond these mystifying actions at New Romney, we have no evidence of royal or ecclesiastical intervention in the performance of the traditional biblical and moral plays before the 1560s.

Itinerary: The 1560s

The scene in the 1560s had undoubtedly changed since the 1520s, yet there was also a remarkable persistence of the "medieval" drama. Although there are signs of opposition to the northern biblical cycles in the 1560s, Coventry continued to perform its Corpus Christi play annually and Chester its Whitsun Play on an irregular schedule: 1561, 1567, and 1568.[41] There were only to be two further performances: in 1572 and 1575.[42] York might be used as an example of a cycle that began to falter in the 1560s. It is difficult to be certain exactly how many performances there were, but certainly four over the course of the decade. However, evidence of a lack of assurance comes early. In 1561 it is agreed to have the plays—but not the Assumption and Coronation of the Vir-

---

41. Ingram, *Coventry*, 213–51; Clopper, *Chester*, 64–68, 75–86; and Clopper, "Chester Plays."

42. Clopper, *Chester*, 90–97, 101–10.

gin.[43] In 1562 there is an order for either the Corpus Christi plays—which were to be played on Saint Barnaby's day (11 June)—or the Creed play.[44] They chose the Corpus Christi plays but decided they would be played on Corpus Christi as usual. There is an order in 1565 for the plays but the accounts note no income from the playing places; presumably, the plays did not go forward.[45] In 1567 along with the order for the plays is another requiring four guilds to register their plays as the others had done.[46] There is also an order that the Cappers have their text examined against the register and reformed. In 1568 the *Creed* play is ordered, but the text is taken to the dean of the cathedral, who says that it should not be played because "they be Disagreinge from the senceritie of the gospell . . . ffor even thoghe it was plausible 40 yeares agoe, & wold now also of the ignorant sort be well liked: yet now in this happie time of the gospell, I knowe the learned will mislike it and how the state will beare with it I knowe not."[47] When the commons petition that the Corpus Christi play be played instead, the city council decides that it should not until the text can be read and amended.

Now let us look at the new dramas of the 1560s. We will follow an itinerary that begins in the northwest at Shrewsbury and moves through Chester, Coventry, Wakefield, and York on our way to Norwich. Then we will move south through East Anglia into the southeastern counties, ending finally outside the gates of London.

We are told that in 1560–61 Mr. Ashton, the local schoolmaster at Shrewsbury, produced his first play: the *Passion of Christ*.[48] In subsequent years he was paid substantial amounts of money—£25—to write and mount other plays, including in 1556 *St. Julian the Apostate* and in 1569 his second "greate playe" of the *Passion*.[49]

Skipping the cycles of the great midland cities just mentioned, we arrive at Lincoln, where in 1564, 1566, and 1567 there was a great standing play of *To-*

---

43. Johnston and Rogerson, *York*, 331–32.

44. Ibid., 340–41.

45. Ibid., 346.

46. Ibid., 351.

47. Ibid., 353–54.

48. Somerset, *Shropshire*, 207. Although it might seem unlikely that a Protestant would write and produce a Passion play, we have evidence from elsewhere that Protestants did (see below).

49. Ibid., 205, 211–14.

bit over two days in the summer.[50] Lincoln does not have a history of biblical drama; rather, the guilds had participated in the Saint Anne's procession, in which the principal sight was the cathedral's mechanical device depicting the Assumption and Coronation of the Virgin, which was presumably put down with the suppression of the monastery, an action that opened the way for other ludic activities.

In 1565 the Norwich Grocers' "Temptation" was "newely renvid and accordyng unto the Skripture."[51]

As we move south we stop at Chelmsford, Essex, where in 1562 there were four *ludi* beginning at midsummer and continuing into August.[52] These were fund-raisers and may have been performances of a single play rather than performances of four plays. We do not know the content, but there are allusions to costumes for prophets, vices, devils, Aaron, and Christ and payments for a heaven with clouds.

We go on in 1560 to New Romney, in Kent, where we see the "newe playe" performed over a series of days.[53] Although this is said to be a "newe playe," there are records for a similar play in 1554–55, perhaps a Marian revival, and an older text called the *Resurrection* from as early as the mid–fifteenth century.

Probably from somewhere in eastern England comes the *Resurrection of Our Lord,* a text written between 1530 and 1570 for performance over two days. It is clear from the contents that this new play is a Protestant effort.[54]

We end our itinerary in the 1560s outside London at Shoreditch, Smithfield, and the playing fields near Saint Bartholomew's. What kind of drama do we find? None. Although there is evidence for the performance of biblical plays at Clerkenwell in 1390 and 1409, there is no tradition for dramatic performance. Instead, the playing place in Smithfield was the site of wrestling matches from as early as 1300 until they were put down in 1549.

Nevertheless, there are plays that we can associate with London even if only through their being printed there.[55] Prints from this period indicate a contin-

---

50. Kahrl, *Plays and Players in Lincolnshire,* 67–68.

51. Norman Davis, *Non-Cycle Plays,* 11.

52. Coldewey, "Digby Plays."

53. J. Gibson, "'Interludum Passionis Domini.'"

54. Wilson and Dobell, *Resurrection of Our Lord;* see lines 311–20, 548–89, 810–34, and passim.

55. The list given here cannot be exhaustive because there is some disagreement among scholars about the dates of some of these plays; however, I think the list provides a representative sampling of plays printed in the 1560s. We should recall that plays were often printed some time after they were written, so the list represents what is available in the 1560s, not the date of original pro-

ued interest in moral allegories: *Albion Knight* (1537–65); Thomas Lupton's *All for Money* (1559–77); Thomas Preston's *Cambises* (1558–69); Lewis or William Wager's *Cruel Debtor* (circa 1565); *Jack Juggler* (1562–63); *Liberality and Prodigality* (1567–68); Ulpian Fulwell's *Like Will to Like* (1562–68); Lewis Wager's *The Life and Repentaunce of Marie Magdalene* (1566); William Wager's *The Longer Thou Livest* (1560–68); *Marriage of Wit and Science* (1568–70); *New Custom* (1559–73); and *Trial of Treasure* (1567). Other plays based on classical or biblical scripts often include morality figures: R. B.'s *Appius and Virginia* (1559–67); John Pikering's *Horestes* (1567); *King Darius* (1559–65); and Thomas Garter's *The Most Vertuous and Godly Susanna* (circa 1569). Many of these do not follow such moralities as *Mankind* and *Castle of Perseverance* so much as Bale's *King Johan,* in which morality figures are mixed in with characters who have personal names or are historical persons. There are, of course, other ways to categorize the plays. Several concern themselves with proper governance (for example, *Cambises, King Darius,* and *Horestes*). Most in one way or another address religious issues, the growing concern with the effects of a cash economy, political affairs, and related matters. Some clearly are courtly boys' plays for example, *Appius and Virginia* and *Tom Tyler and His Wife* (1550–80).[56] David Bevington lists a number as "plays offered for acting": those requiring four men (*The Longer Thou Livest* and *New Custom*), five men (*Like Will to Like* and *Trial of Treasure*), six men (*Horestes* and *King Darius*), and eight men (*Cambises* and *Susanna*).[57] Although these acting scripts would be suitable for traveling players, they would also work for households with an interest in playing. But those markets would seem too small to encourage publications of plays, so we must assume that printers believed that there was a reading public for play texts.[58]

---

duction. The list is compiled from Greg, *Bibliography of English Printed Drama;* Cawley, *Revels History,* vol. 2; Spivack, *Shakespeare and the Allegory of Evil;* and Bevington, *From "Mankind" to Marlowe* and *Tudor Drama and Politics.*

56. Bevington, *From "Mankind" to Marlowe,* 31–32.

57. Ibid., 265–73. Bevington also lists *Misogonus* for ten men. The text, translated from the Italian, remains only in manuscript.

58. I have omitted reference to dramas at the universities and other elite venues in order to focus on the public and popular traditions. The educational reforms of the early sixteenth century in conjunction with the universities' attempts to control the students' raucous behavior in the Christmas season resulted in numerous productions of plays by Terence, Plautus, and Seneca, as well as some plays in English: Nicholas Udall's *Ezechias,* Richard Edwardes's *Palamon and Arcite* and *Damon and Pythias,* and the anonymous *Wylie Beguylie.* See Boas, *University Drama in the Tudor Age,* app. 4, 387–88; and Nelson, *Cambridge,* app. 8, 968–71.

Persistence, Renewal, and Demise

It has become a commonplace that the northern cycles came to their end at the hands of Protestant bishops because the plays could not be cleansed of their Catholic content. Although it is true that Archbishop Grindal was in office at the moment of the death of the York plays, it is also true that he and others did not act until twenty years into Elizabeth's reign and apparently never moved systematically to put down biblical dramas. Given the archbishop's belated action, we need to examine the situation more broadly because there were, I suspect, a number of factors that led to the cessation these plays.

First, the assumption has been that the biblical drama is irreducibly Catholic, but it is demonstrable that a Protestant biblical drama is possible. This category would include the *Resurrection of Our Lord,* noted above, the New Romney *Passion,* the altered texts of Coventry (circa 1534 and later) and of Chester (some perhaps as late as the 1560s). Indeed, Martin Bucer advocated the writing of comedies and tragedies based on biblical texts, from Adam to the apostles, in the vernacular, Latin, or Greek.[59] Polemical dramatists also used biblical narrative, so we should not assume that biblical drama was perceived to be necessarily Catholic.

I suspect that the northern cycles lasted so long because there was a desire to preserve them; they were, as the records frequently say, a custom from "tyme out of mind," and there is inertia to overcome if one wishes to suppress such a custom. On the other hand, these productions were extremely costly, and I think the economics of the venture helped create the conditions for the intervention of ecclesiastical and royal authorities.[60] Toward the end of the fifteenth century and in the early decades of the sixteenth, the oligarchies in cities such as Beverley, Coventry, Lincoln, and Norwich demanded that nonparticipating guilds and citizens contribute to the costs of plays and processions. In some cases these new contributors were expected to be just that: underwriters, not participants. Such taxation undoubtedly antagonized those impressed into support, but the imposition of the tax suggests that the ruling guilds had come to feel these presentations to have become a burden on them.

---

59. Chambers, *Elizabethan Stage,* 4:188–90; Wyckham provides a translation in *Early English Stages,* 2.1.329–31.

60. Mayor Coton of Coventry wrote to Cromwell in 1539 for redress of the city's economic difficulties, noting, among others things, the great costs to the commoners for the plays and pageants at Corpus Christi (Ingram, *Coventry,* 148–49).

We have much more information about the sequence of events that led to the cessation of the Chester cycle than we do about others; consequently, I will focus on it in order to illuminate the rather complicated set of circumstances that resulted in the cycle's demise.

It has been traditional for us to accept the late Renaissance dictum that the Chester plays were suppressed because of the superstition in them; that is, they were the victims of Protestantism. To be sure, this is to some extent true. For example, one of the chroniclers of the period said of the 1575 performance that some of the plays were left unplayed because of the superstition in them.[61] We have little concrete information about such objections; however, David Mills has recently discovered in a letterbook of Christopher Goodman that Goodman was offended by some of the plays—specifically the midwives' scene in the Nativity and parts of the Last Supper—and attempted to encourage intervention before the performance of 1572.[62] Mills characterizes Goodman as a "convinced Protestant of extreme views" who was associated in Geneva with John Knox during the Marian years. Goodman, who had been appointed to the living of Aldford and made archdeacon of Richmond in 1570, preached against the plays even though he had been deprived of his living in 1571 because of his extreme views. On 10 May 1572 Goodman wrote to the lord president of the Council of the North, the earl of Huntingdon, to tell him that the plays were to be played that year. In one of the "Mayors Lists" for the year 1575 we are told that the plays went forward in that year against the wishes of the archbishop of York and the earl of Huntingdon.[63] In the same note we are told that not only Sir John Savage, the mayor in 1575, but also John Hankey, the mayor in 1572, were summoned to the Privy Council to answer charges that they had caused the "popish plaies" to be performed in those years despite the inhibitions. Goodman confirms that the inhibitions were sent in 1572. His opposition to the plays—and he claims other preachers were opposed as well—was based on the fact that they had been written two hundred years earlier by a monk "in the depth of ignorance" and that Mayor Hankey imposed the plays on the city without the texts' being officially read and the performance sanctioned. Goodman preserved the letter sent on 15 May 1572 by Archbishop Grindal in which he says that he has been informed that within the

---

61. Clopper, *Chester*, 110, line 15.
62. D. Mills, *Recycling the Cycle*, 146–51, 179–80.
63. Clopper, *Chester*, 109–10.

plays are "sundry absurd & gross errours & heresies joyned with profanation & great abuse of god's holy word."[64] He requires Hankey by virtue of her majesty's Commission for Ecclesiastical Causes in the diocese of York to cease preparation for setting forth the plays and to forbear to play them in future "till your said plays shall be perused corrected & reformed by such learned men" as shall be appointed by the archbishop and "till signification of our such allowance be given to you in writing under the hands of us or other our Associates the Queen's Majesty's said commissioners."[65] Hankey later claimed that the injunction arrived too late to be implemented (and one "Mayors List" records this as well), but Goodman claims that he delivered the letters from Grindal and the earl of Huntingdon to the mayor and the bishop of Chester. Goodman's claim may be cast into doubt by the fact that for the 1572 performance the dean and chapter of the cathedral supplied beer to the players, as was their wont.[66] After the performance Goodman wrote to the archbishop once more expressing doubts that the plays had been corrected and asserting that those who objected to the plays were forced to help pay for them with the threat of imprisonment.[67] Grindal seems to have taken no further action at that time.

Goodman apparently attempted to muster support for suppressing the 1575 performance but did not record his efforts in the detail that he did with regard to 1572. In his letter to the archbishop on 11 June 1575 he acknowledges that there was an attempt at correction of the text but implies that it was a superficial one: "For albeit divers have gone about the correction of the same at sundry times & mended divers things, yet hath it not been done by such as are by authority allowed, nor the same their corrections viewed & approved according to order, not yet so played for the most part as they have been corrected."[68] Goodman makes two complaints here: that the corrections were made by the wrong persons (in this case it would seem to have been the civic rather than the ecclesiastical officials) and that the corrections were ignored by

---

64. D. Mills, *Recycling the Cycle*, 147.

65. Note that Grindal did not summarily suppress the plays but allowed the possibility that they were correctable.

66. Clopper, *Chester*, 96. By contrast, there is no record that they did in 1575.

67. Indeed, some apparently refused payment. Andrew Tailer, a dyer, refused to pay his 3s. 8d., as a consequence of which Mayor Savage had him jailed. After Henry Hardware, who objected to many city customs, became mayor, he was approached by John Bannister and Edmund Gamull, who acted on Tailer's behalf by paying the assessment, and Tailer was freed (ibid., 111–12).

68. D. Mills, *Recycling the Cycle*, 179–80.

the performers. Mills cites lines that Goodman quotes from the *Last Supper* that have clear Catholic overtones but that do not correspond to the texts that we have. There is also a quotation from the midwives scene that differs from the extant text. Do these "quotations" indicate revision or the unreliability of Goodman's citations? Is he citing the performed text or some version of the written Reginall?

We might say, then, that some people were offended by some of the matter, but when we read the extant texts of the Chester plays, it is difficult to find much that might be classified as superstition. Although there are some apocryphal elements, there are no wild-eyed stories of saints or martyrs to which most Protestants would have objected.

Perhaps we have been too concerned with the opposition between Catholics and Protestants and not enough with that between groups of Protestants.[69] For example, it is puzzling that the city council thought it would be able to go ahead with a performance of the plays in 1575 when the archbishop of York had inhibited them (or tried to do so) in 1572.[70] There was opposition to the plays even within the council when the council voted on the question of whether it would be "meet" to perform them. It was agreed that it was meet but it was also noted that they should be "reformed," that is, edited, by the mayor and his advisors—but not by the clergy—if they felt it meet and convenient. Whatever editing was done must have been relatively minor, for the plays began less than four weeks after it had been agreed that they should be performed, and the cycle that year seems not to have been shortened since it took three and one-half rather than three days to perform it.[71]

It is possible that the "superstition" thought to exist in these "popish plays" had much to do with their mode of presentation, for there is some evidence that there were objections to the representation of God the Father as a person and of the sacraments "in game." In addition, it is possible that some of the Protestants objected to the representation of material they regarded as fables or in-

69. On the mix in Chester, see Emmerson, "Contextualizing Performance," 89–92.
70. Clopper, *Chester*, 103–05, 112–17; 96–97.
71. Ibid., 116, lines 15–18. The additional half-day for the performance does not necessarily indicate that the plays were expanded. In that year they began in the afternoon rather than the morning and ran for three more days. The stanza added at 5.448 suggests that only five plays were performed on the first day. I would like to take this opportunity to correct a typo in my introduction to *Chester*, lv, where the text says the last performance took place on "one day." It should have read "three and one-half days," as it does in my "History and Development," 244, and as is clear in the certificate issued on behalf of Mayor John Savage, 116.

ventions unauthorized by Scripture, whereas other Protestants within the city felt that such representation was meet. Even though some of the opposition must have been directed at the plays because they were thought to be popish or because they were associated with persons known to be Catholic survivalists, it is a simplification to see it just as a Protestant attack on popish superstition.

We may take the reviser of the Late Banns as a contemporary witness of the concerns about the plays and as a defender of them. In the prologue the reviser gives a history of the cycle and defends Randoll, the monk of Chester Abbey who was believed to have written the plays, on the grounds that he was not "monckelyke" because it had been his desire to reveal to the common man the sacred knowledge of the Scriptures in the English tongue.[72] He also apologizes for the inclusion of "Some thinges not warranted by anye writte" (line 15). He apologizes for the Tanners' *Fall of Lucifer* but adds that some writers warrant the matter and therefore it has been allowed to stand. He points out that the Scriptures do not warrant the midwives' episode in the *Nativity* and that there are few words in the *Shepherds Play* that are true because all the author had to work with was the *Gloria in excelsis*. The Shoemakers' *Entry into Jerusalem* is commended because it is a true story; the Bakers are admonished in their presentation of the *Last Supper* to utter the same words that Christ himself spoke.[73] He acknowledges that it is a matter of faith that Christ descended to hell, but reminds the audience that it is not known what occurred there; the author, he says, wrote the play "after his opynion" and the audience should credit the best learned on the subject.[74] The Banns reviser does not simply assert that the plays do not contain superstition; rather, he at times distinguishes the plays that have scriptural authority from those that do not. But he also defends others by saying that some authorities warrant them. He seems to think that certain apocryphal or invented stories can instruct even if they are not historically true.

If this revision of the Banns was made during Elizabeth's reign—and the ev-

---

72. Ibid., 240–41; Clopper, "Arnewaye, Higden." The statement is not entirely logical. Higden is being reconstructed here as a proto-Protestant.

73. Clopper, *Chester*, 240, line 15; 242, lines 9–15; 243, lines 11–12; 244, lines 21–24; 245, lines 1–5.

74. Ibid, 245, lines 19–25. The Harrowing of Hell seems to have caused difficulties for Protestants because it was a part of the Creed but not scriptural. Bills, "'Suppression Theory,'" 162–63, reports that when John Bale was accused of unorthodox preaching, he responded that he never "denied that 'descendit ad inferna' was an article of the Creed . . . [but] . . . Told them not to believe it 'as they see it set forth in the country there in a certain play.' They must not suppose that Christ fought violently with the devils for the souls of the faithful."

idence suggests that it was—then it might be understood not so much as a defense against the charge that the plays are Catholic doctrinally as a defense against the charge that the plays are nonscriptural and thus untrue. There is some confirmation for this interpretation in the comment made at the end of the play entry in the first edition of the Rogers *Breviary:* "And we haue all cause to power out oure prayers before god that neither wee nor oure posterities after us. maye neuar see the like Abomination of Desolation, with suche a Clowde of Ignorance to defile with so highe a hand. the moste sacred scriptures of god."[75]

If there was a concern about the accurate representation of the scriptural texts, there was also one about the propriety of representing rituals and the deity. At the end of some copies of the Late Banns is an objection both to the former mode of presentation and to the unfortunate quality of the one that the audience is soon to see:

> Of one thinge warne you now I shall
> That not possible it is these matters to be contryued
> In such sorte and cunninge & by suche players of price
> As at this daye good players & fine wittes. coulde deuise
> ffor then shoulde all those persones that as godes doe playe
> In Clowdes come downe *with* voyce and not be seene
> ffor noe man can *pro*portion that godhead I saye
> To the shape of man face. nose and eyne
> But sethence the face gilte doth disfigure the man *y*at deme
> A Clowdye coueringe of the man. A Voyce onlye to heare
> And not god in shape or person to appeare.[76]

The objection to the representation of the Godhead is confirmed in the directive to the burgesses of Wakefield in 1576 that they set forth no pageant or play "wherein the Maiestye of god the father god the sonne or god the holie ghoste . . . be counterfeyted or represented."[77] This directive does not forbid the appearance of Christ *in his manhood.*

Even though large-scale productions in the north were economic burdens, they continued to be produced because some members of the lay oligarchy authorized them; furthermore, it was that authorization, I believe, that deterred ecclesiastical and royal authorities from mounting a systematic campaign against them. Edward VI's actions with regard to appropriate ritual and prac-

---

75. Clopper, *Chester,* 252, lines 4–8.
76. Ibid., 247, lines 8–20.
77. Cawley, *Wakefield Pageants,* 125.

tice seem to have had a far more chilling effect on biblical drama and other customs than did anything in the first two decades of Elizabeth's reign. Part of the reason is that power recognizes power. Earlier in this book, I suggested that the production of biblical plays was a contention for space to develop a lay spirituality but that the form it took implicitly acknowledged the difference between the authority of the clergy in matters of doctrine and the legitimacy of the layman's exhortation of his fellow citizens to a moral life and firm faith. On the other side of this coin is the necessity for the ecclesiastical authorities to acknowledge the legitimate arenas of lay authority. Biblical dramas and processions, the latter of which are particularly encouraged by the clergy, are regulated by the lay participants whenever they occur within the secular sphere. It is not until those participants invite clerical intervention that the clergy has an opening to sequester lay activity. York provides the best illustrations of this principle: in 1568 the dean of the cathedral church was asked to read the Creed play to see if it might be played and he said that some sections deviated "from the senceritie of the gospell" and counseled against it. Archbishop Grindal, by contrast, did not act against civic plays until 1572, after a disturbance at the Pater Noster play, as a consequence of which the mayor and council asked that the book be brought to the *mayor* in order that it be "pervsed amended and corrected"; only after the crisis deepened did Grindal ask to see the book (which he apparently kept). That there was no systematic ecclesiastical campaign to sequester biblical drama is also indicated by the directive to the Wakefield burgesses cited above—it forbids certain kinds of things but not biblical drama per se—and by the fact that the archbishop of Canterbury apparently never took any action against the famous Coventry plays and Grindal made only half-hearted attempts to put down those of Chester. At the same time, one must concede that the pressures—ecclesiastical and royal—were becoming too great. Although neither authority seems to have been willing to crush the phenomenon, they were willing to intimidate and intrude. Given the economic burden of these productions and the growing puritanical reaction against games and *ludi* of all kinds, the urban ruling parties seem to have chosen to cease to authorize large-scale public performances, and, as Puritanism became more entrenched, cities and towns turned away traveling performers and suppressed or altered other customs.[78]

---

78. Peter Womack provides a related analysis of what he calls an "ambiguous program" to suppress the plays. He argues that a broader reason for the suppression was to respond to the rising in the north in 1569–70 that had revealed a regional culture of Roman Catholicism and dynastic loy-

The larger point I have been trying to make about the persistence of the "medieval" tradition can be reduced to a few observations. The final performance of the Chester plays took place one year before James Burbage built the Theatre outside London. Coventry continued annual performances until 1579, three years after the building of the Theatre, and mounted a new play in 1584 written by John Smith of Saint John's College, Oxford, *The Destruction of Jerusalem*, and ordered in 1591, the same year their maypoles were suppressed, that either *The Destruction of Jerusalem*, *The Conquest of the Danes*, or the *History of Edward IV* be performed according to the decision of the commons.[79] These latter Coventry plays are obviously not medieval in composition, but they are products of the same civic mechanisms that oversaw the Corpus Christi cycle for nearly two hundred years. Coventry had a stronger, older, and longer dramatic tradition than did Chester. Although Chester is thought to have been conservative in religion and resistant to Protestantism, it also had a large number of persons with a puritanical bent. Mayor Henry Hardware was one, and in his several terms in office, not only did he not authorize the Whitsun plays but he also "reformed" other civic practices including the midsummer show.[80] Although Hardware opposed the Whitsun plays, he was the mayor the year after Mayor Savage was cited to the Privy Council for having had them performed. Ironically, Hardware had to produce the certificate that exonerated Savage. I think the certificate is revealing because Hardware—like Grindal and other opponents—understood that duly authorized power had to be acknowledged. He certainly objected to the plays, and one assumes he did not attend them, but he knew the importance of defending Savage's and the city council's power to authorize them.

---

alty threatening to the Crown. Grindal and the earl of Huntingdon were instituted to represent the Crown's interests. See "Imagining Communities."

79. Ingram, *Coventry*, 290–93, 332–35; Pendleton, "Mystery's Addenda"; and Ingram, "1579 and the Decline of Civic Religious Drama."

80. Tittler, "Henry Hardware's Moment."

References to *Miracula,* Miracles, and Steracles in Medieval and Early Modern England

I include steracles because a few documents equate steracles and miracles. If the entry appears in Ian Lancashire's *Dramatic Texts and Records of Britain* (1984), I give the entry number rather than a full bibliographical citation. Most items are discussed in my essay *"Miracula* and *The Tretise of Miraclis Pleyinge."*

    1. 1100–1119 (ca. 1250), Dunstable: "quemdam ludum de Sancta Katerina— quem 'Miracula' vulgariter appellamus" made by a certain Geoffrey (Lancashire 616). Rather than dating the Dunstable reference to 1100–1119, the presumed time of the event's occurrence, we ought to date it ca. 1250 because it was then that Matthew Paris wrote the *Gesta abbatum,* and, since he said it was what "we" call *miracula,* it was then, apparently, that the term was commonly used to refer to the *ludi* of the *clerici.* For the date, see Gransden, *Historical Writing in England,* 374–75.

    2. 1188–98, Lichfield, Cathedral Statutes: Provision for *repraesentationes* at Christmas, Easter, and Whitsuntide and for *miraculorum in nocte Pasche et die lune in Pascha.* The latter reference occurs among the duties of the subchanter who was in charge of the choirboys (Lancashire 843). Young, *Drama of the Medieval Church,* 2:522, printed the items without the rubrics and obscured the fact that they come from different sections of the statutes.

    3. Circa 1244: Letter from Grosseteste, bishop of Exeter, to his archdeacons: "Faciunt etiam ut audivimus clerici ludos quos vocant miracula, et alios ludos quos vocant inductionem Maii sive Autumpni et laici scotales" (Lancashire 872).

    4. 1260–72: *Manual des Péchiez* (Lancashire 213; Young, *Drama of the Medieval Church,* 2:417–18). There is a ME prose translation, ca. 1350, in Saint John's College, Cambridge, MS G 30 (located by Nicholas Davis; cited by Twycross and Carpenter, "Masks," 70).

    5. After 1266: Sloane MS 2478 (thirteenth c.) in Wright, *Selection of Latin Stories,* 99–100: a seeress in a *spectaculum* that the Franciscan reporters say "we call *miracula."*

6. 1283, Gloucester: "Item clericis ludentibus miracula sancti Nicholai & eorum Episcopo de elemosina Regis" (Lancashire 684). A boy bishop ceremony.

7. 1301: Clerkenwell prioress's complaint that the people of London "par lur miracles et lutes ke il funt sovent" destroy her crops and meadows (Lancashire 543).

8. 1303: *Handlyng Synne*: Robert Mannyng's version of item 4 (Lancashire 213; Sullens ed., lines 4641–64).

9. 1307, Lanercost Priory: "Regi Capiny Johanni de Cressy et aliis menestrallis ludentibus miracula et facientibus menestracias suas coram Regina de dono Regis per manus Guilloti de Psalterio xl. s" (Lancashire 823). Cited by Richard Rastall in "Minstrels and Minstrelsy," 7. Richard Axton incorrectly cites this as having taken place at Christ Church, Canterbury; see "Popular Modes in the Earliest Plays," 27.

10. 1325–50: John Bromyard, *Summa predicantium,* articles on "Audire (Verbum Dei)," "Bellum," "Chorea," "Contritio," and "Ludus" (Lancashire 216).

11. 1345, Carlisle: The servant of the bishop intervened "Cum Clerici fecerunt quendam ludum in foro dicte ciuitatis karioli . . . sicut clerici inceperunt ludere quoddam miraculum in foro karlioli" (Lancashire 515).

12. 1377, Colchester: A suit in the Hundred court in which Wm. Baroun charged that John Kentyssh had borrowed and not returned a mask, a tunic with tails, and other apparatus for playing "miracles" ("unam laruam vnam tunicum cum tibiis caudis et alio apparatu ad miraculam"). Epitome provided by Jeayes, *Court Rolls of the Borough of Colchester,* 3:140. I wish to thank John Coldewey for providing a photocopy from which I made the transcription.

13. 1390: *Pierce the Ploughmans Crede,* lines 106–7. Some friars say: "At marketts & myracles we medleth vs nevere" (Skeat ed.).

14. 1405–10: *Dives and Pauper.* Pauper defends "Steraclis [Miraclis MSS BY], pleyys & dauncis þat arn don principaly for deuocioun & honest merthe & for no rybaudye ne medelyd with no rybaudye" (Lancashire 241; Barnum ed.).

15. 1408 (Oct.)–1409 (Jan.): Bursar's Acct., Boxley Abbey, Kent. "Item dat' vj hominibus ludentibus unum miraculum de sancta maria in crastino Sancti Thome episcopi & a [*sic*] martirae—ijs." Public Records Office SC 61256/13. Courtesy of Sheila Lindenbaum. Probably a *miracula* on the day after or the morrow of Saint Thomas and his martyrdom; possibly a boy bishop ceremony.

16. 1410–11: Durham Priory, Hostillar's Accounts for 1410–11. "Item Soluti Johanni Horsele Armigero referenti Miraculum Sancti Cuthberti vjs viijd" (courtesy of John McKinnell, editor of the Durham records for Records of Early English Drama; printed in Fowler, *Extracts,* 1:138).

17. Early fifteenth century: *Tretise of Miraclis Pleyinge* (Lancashire 227; Davidson ed.).

18. 1410–20: William Boter deposed as follows: he "saugh diu*er*se times & ofte*n* pleyes pleyed vpon þe fornseyd lyng*is* [the place where the activities occurred] made

be þo me*n* of lucham þ*at* is to seyne steraclis Schetyng*is* wrestelyng*is* ren*n*ing for þo spere renny*n*g at þo fotbal for kak*is*" (Rutledge, "Steracles in Norfolk," 15).

19. Circa 1400: A sermon that refers to holy day abuses: "Make no iangelynge, rownyng, ne cry, ne deene in cherche, ne in cherche yerd . . . ne stryvyng, ne fyghtyng, ne marchandyse, ne markettys, ne ferys . . . ne dauncys, ne werdly songys, no inter-lodyes, ne castynges of the stonne, steraclys, ne pleying at the balle, ne other ydell iapys and pleyis" (Davis, "Allusions . . . [4]: Interludes," 65).

20. 1400–1425: *Jacob's Well*, 105. To be idle is to go "to wakys & to wrestlyng*es*, to dau*n*synges & to steraclys, to tauernys, to reuell, to ryott, to shetinges, to feyrys, to markettys on þe holy-dayes, & to chaffarynge, & levyst þi parysch-cherche & þi seruyse." (Brandeis ed.).

21. Fifteenth century: Pseudo-Mapes, "The Payne and Sorowe of Evyll Mary-age." Women rejoice to see and to be seen, to go on pilgrimage, to walk on the plain at great gatherings, "And at staracles to sitte on high stages, / If they be faire to shewe ther visages" (Mapes, *Latin Poems*, 297). There is no equivalent for "staracles" in the Latin text.

22. After 1468: N-Town *Temptation*. The Devil says, "Whan зu art sett upon þe pynnacle, / Þu xalt þer pleyn a qweynt steracle, / Or ellys shewe a grett meracle" (Spector, *N-Town Play*, 23.114–16).

23. 1540: "Why whippest thou it about, or playest thou thy steracles[?]" (Pals-grave, *Comedy of Acolastus*, 139.20).

24. 1539, 1547–60: Bale's *Kyng Johan*: Dissimulation, a priest, says that Usurped Power (= the pope) will put all men under his obedience, create religious orders, and build them places to corrupt cities and towns: "With ymages and rellyckes he shall wurke steracles" (*Complete Plays I*, line 996).

25. 1563?: Thomas Becon, *Acts of Christ*: "But to pray at places where the devil worketh steracles, I would say, miracles, thus passeth al" (*Worckes*, 3:416b).

Uncertain Entries

26. Circa 1283: Alexander de Alverton is said to have founded the collegiate church of Lanchester, Durham, in 1283, for which he furnished statutes and ordi-nances. Robert Surtees, who makes this report, says that the statutes were in Latin that in an "Old English" translation reads as follows: "None of the said Vicars shal without sufficient cause go into any common taverne nor tarye in the same; neither exercise wrestling, dauncinge, or any other hurtfull gaymes, nor [frequent] such spectacles or syghtes, which ar comonly called *myracles*" (*History and Antiquities*, 2:309). Surtees notes that *miracula* are "tricks of jongleurs and tregeteurs." The first part of the quotation sounds like a translation of *Mimis*. Surtees's note suggests that *miracula* are illusions, and since the "Old English" is modern, it may derive from sixteenth-century texts like those cited above. Surtees (3:462–63) gives Dugdale's *Monasticon* and Prynne's *Antiquae Constitutiones* as his sources, but the Lanchester

documents in these sources do not give the statutes; rather, they concern the conveyance of the church and its properties and rights. The original document has not been located, but the version cited does not sound fabricated.

27. 1602, Cornwall: Richard Carew, in his *Survey of Cornwall*, says: "The Guary miracle, in English, a miracle-play, is a kinde of Enterlude, compiled in Cornish out of some scripture history, with that grossenes, which accompanied the Romanes vetus Comedia" (Joyce and Newlin, *Cornwall*, 537). He says that the producers raise an earthen amphitheater, that the country people flock to them because they have therein "deuils and deuices, to delight as well the eye as the eare," and finally that the actors do not memorize their lines but are prompted by the "Ordinary." Much of the description seems dependent on Isidore or some Isidorean treatment of the ancient theater: the plays are gross like Old Roman comedy; they are played in an amphitheater; and the "poet" reads the lines while the performers act them out. The statement is also a muddle: why would plays taken from Scripture be said to have the grossness of Roman comedy? I think Carew has confused *miracula*—note the "deuils and deuices"—with what he knew about the Cornish religious drama (or some other biblical drama). Similarly, William Borlase in his *Observations on the Antiquities, Historical and Monumental, of the County of Cornwall* (1754) seems as much influenced by the ancient tradition (he quotes Ovid on seating arrangements) as anything else (Joyce and Newlin, *Cornwall*, 403). His description of the amphitheaters makes them, as they are in Isidore, places not only for dramas but for athletic competitions and war games. I suspect that both antiquarians, under the influence of their classical educations, have fused several native and ancient traditions.

Entries Rejected Because the Generic Terms Is Not *Miracula*

28. 1170–82: William Fitz Stephen's *Vita S. Thomae* (Lancashire 878). "Londonia pro spectaculis theatralibus, pro ludis scenicis, ludos habet sanctiores, repraesentationes miraculorum quae sancti confessores operati sunt, seu repraesentationes passionum quibus claruit constantia martyrum" (Young, *Drama of the Medieval Church*, 2:542). The *miraculorum* refers to content, not genre *(repraesentationes)*. See appendix 2, item 30.

29. Circa 1390: *Wife of Bath's Prologue*, D.555–58. "Therefore I made my visitaciouns / To vigilies and to processiouns, / To prechynge eek, and to thise pilgrimages, / To pleyes of myracles, and to mariages" (Benson). The line could mean that she went to clerkes pleis of *miracula*.

Communitas: The Play of Saints in Late Medieval and Tudor England

This appendix attempts to list all citations in the critical literature and documentary records of *ludi* that have been called "saint plays," that is, plays that enact the vita of a saint or some crucial moment in the saint's life.[1] I exclude Marian plays that occur within the cycle drama as well as ones that may have recounted a miracle of the Virgin. As far as I know, however, there are few references to miracles of the Virgin in the English dramatic tradition except for the York *Fergus* (pageant 44A) and possibly the *Durham Prologue* (the Theophilus legend) and *Dux Moraud.*[2] I am also not concerned to focus on miracles performed by the saints or others, but again there are few references in England to such texts. I also exclude folk plays, conversion stories—like that of Robert of Sicily, which may have been performed in Lincoln in 1452–53 and Chester in 1529–30—and Tudor polemical dramas traveling under the names of saints.[3] Since there are instances of revivals or new saint plays in Mary's reign, I have surveyed the English records through 1558. At the end of the appendix I give an index to the saints by name with the item number in which they appear in parentheses.

If the entry appears in Ian Lancashire's *Dramatic Texts and Records of Britain* (1984), I give the item number rather than a full bibliographical citation.

An asterisk (*) indicates that the entry is discussed in my essay "*Communitas.*" Double asterisks (**) indicate that the item is also discussed above. There are some entries below that are not in my earlier list.

𝖆𝖘𝖅𝖆𝖘

Saint plays for which we have texts include the following:

---

1. See chapter 3, note 77, above for the sources I have consulted.
2. Davis, *Non-Cycle Plays,* 106–13; Hieatt, "A Case for *Duk Moraud.*"
3. Kahrl, *Lincolnshire,* 31; Clopper, *Chester,* 29; Happé, "Protestant Adaptation of the Saint Play."

1. Digby *Conversion of St. Paul* (Lancashire 74): Not a vita but a series of episodes on the major event in Paul's life. Called a "process" at l.13, the explicit reads *Finis conuercionis Sancti Pauli.*

**2. Digby *Mary Magdalene* (Lancashire 75): No title; ends *Explycit oreginale de Sancta Maria Magdalena.*

3. *The Life of Saint Meriasek* (Lancashire 430). Cornish.

4. The Ashmole Fragment (Lancashire 70) may be from a Saint Lawrence play (see Wright, "Ashmole Fragment"; earlier scholars [e.g., Robbins, "Dramatic Fragment," and Davis, *Non-Cycle Plays,* cxix] thought the fragment was from a lost Nativity play.)

Saint plays for which we have sufficient evidence to suggest that they were enacted vitae of the saints or significant events in their lives include the following:

*5. Lydd, Kent (Lancashire 1162, 1164): Saint George: Perhaps as early as 1456; new playbooks and other accounts from 1526–34.

*6. York: Saint George, 1554 (Lancashire 1580).

Saint *ludi, miracula,* and other games arranged geographically in alphabetical order. An index to saints appears at the end of the list.

All of these are either doubtful, for lack of evidence, or erroneous, when the extant evidence argues against their being saint plays. I do not attempt to list all appearances of saints in processions and royal entries; however, I have listed those that mistakenly have been or might be taken to be saint plays.

7. Ashburton, Devon: Saint Rosemont, 1555–56 (Lancashire 352): The churchwardens' accounts for this *ludus* on Corpus Christi day include Robin Hood (1526–27, 1541–42), Herod (1537–38), and Christ (1558–59; Wasson, *Devon,* 21, 25, 24, and 29, respectively). The most frequent payments are for "players' garments" and the "players ale" and tabernacles (which I assume contained an image of a saint). References to devils' heads and "rattylbagys"(mummers' properties) in some years suggest that there was a folk revel, perhaps in conjunction with a Robin Hood play and processions with images of the saints (Ibid., 20, 26, 29). There is insufficient evidence that there was a play about Saint Rosemont. Nor do I know who the saint is. Neither the *Acta sanctorum* nor the other standard references cite this saint. I suspect Rosemont is some local popular figure, not a real saint, who was the center of a parish game. Perhaps he was king of a bower known as "Rose Mont."

**8. Bassingbourne, Cambridgeshire: Saint George, 1511 (Lancashire 365): An effigy carried in procession on Saint Margaret's day. Anne Brannen, "Parish Play Accounts," believes this to be a play about Saint George.

*9. Bethersden: Saint Christina, 1519–21 (Lancashire 374): This may have been a three-day *spectaculum* of some sort.

10. Braintree, Essex: "Plays" of Saints Swithin, 1523; Andrew, 1525; and "Placy Dacy als St Ewe Stacy," 1534 (Lancashire 394–96; John Coldewey provided me with his transcriptions). The plays of Saint Swithin and Saint Andrew are said to have occurred in the church, which should make us suspicious. Noting the parallel phrasing of "Placy Dacy" and *Roister Doister,* Coldewey has suggested to me that the Eustace might be a school drama, perhaps written by Nicholas Udall, who was the schoolmaster at Braintree at the time. Clifford Davidson ("Saint Play and Pageants," Web site), however, says that Udall was not appointed vicar until 1537 and should not be identified as the possible author.

**11. Bristol: Saint George, 1461 (Lancashire 405; and see Pilkington, "Pageants in Bristol"): A mock battle during a procession at the reception of Edward IV.

*12. Bungay, Suffolk: Saint Thomas Becket, 1539 (Lancashire 1804): Erroneous citation; see Lancashire.

13. Bury: Saint Edmund, 1509. The refectory of the abbey was used for the performance of "Saint Edmund's play" (Bury Saint Edmund's West Suffolk Record Office, IC 500/2/4; cited by Beadle, "Monk Thomas Hyngham's Hand," 56). Gibson, *Theatre of Devotion,* 115, gives this as a bequest from Thomas Pykrell of "all my pleying garements to Seynt Edmunds pley in the Frayt[er]" (Register Pye, fol. 209). She also notes that in 1494 John Benale left a long black gown and a short gown of damask "to the gylde of Seynt John Baptyst in Bury and also for the revell on Seynt Edmund's nyght" (Register Pye, fol. 25). She concludes that the guild participated in a revel in the monastery's refectory on the eve of the feast that commemorated the translation of Edmund's relics to Bury. It is uncertain what the "revels" may have been.

**14. Canterbury: Saint Thomas Becket, 1501–38 (Lancashire 501): A pageant transported by four knights (his assassins?) with an effigy of the saint and a mechanical angel.

**15. Canterbury: Saint Thomas Becket, 1505–43 (Lancashire 501): A "pley" with "tormentors." Possibly some kind of parish game.

16. Chelmsford, Essex: Saint Nicholas (see Lancashire 521): John Coldewey's transcriptions of the Chelmsford accounts for "play days" list a vestment of Saint Nicholas but also two vices' coats, five prophets' caps, three "flappes" for devils, four sheephooks, beards, and so forth. In 1562–63 they paid for a frame for heaven and cord for clouds. The mixture is bizarre; in any event, the records do not suggest any of the Saint Nicholas legends.

*17. Chester: Saint George, 1431 (Lancashire 525). Uncertain. Entry appears in a *List of Mayors.*

18. Colchester, Essex: Saint Martin, 1527 (Lancashire 553): May be a parish ale. The item is a fine for gathering corn (for the ale?) for Saint Martin's "pley."

19. Coventry: Saint Catherine, 1490–91 (Lancashire 563) and Saint Christian, 1505 (Lancashire 567). Uncertain. Entries are casual references in chronicles and a

writ about *ludi* in Little Park. However, in a proof of majority taken in 1528 the latter play is called "Magnum ludum vocatum seynt christeans play" (Ingram, *Coventry*, 128).

**20. Dunstable, Bedfordshire: Saint Catherine, ca. 1100–19 (Lancashire 616): A *miracula* (see Clopper, "*Miracula* and the *Tretise of Miraclis Pleyinge*," 879, 885, 886).

**21. Durham: Saint Cuthbert, 1410–11: A *miracula* (see *Extracts*, 1.138; and Clopper, "*Miracula* and *The Tretise of Miraclis Pleyinge*," 905).

**22. Gloucester: Saint Nicholas, 1283 (Lancashire 684): A *miracula* with a boy bishop (see Douglas and Greenfield, *Gloucestershire*, 290, 421–22; and Clopper, "*Miracula* and *The Tretise of Miraclis Pleyinge*," 880, 885).

23. Grimsby, Lincolnshire: The "play of holy John of bowre," 1527 (Lancashire 738): Uncertain. "Holy John" has been identified as John the Baptist, but it is unclear why he is "of bowre," and there are no additional records to establish what the "play" was. He could be a local "saint," a May king who is enthroned in a bower.

*24. Ham, Kent: Saint Thomas Becket, 1453–54: Erroneous reading.

25. Hereford: Saint Catherine with Three Tormentors, 1503 (Lancashire 768): A tableau in the Corpus Christi procession, which also included biblical scenes (Klausner, *Herefordshire/ Worcestershire*, 114, 116).

**26. King's Lynn, Norfolk: *Interludium* of Saint Thomas the Martyr, 1385 (Lancashire 806): Uncertain; the term is used to refer to a variety of activities.

**27. Lincoln, Saint Thomas Didymus, 1321–69 (Lancashire 851): The *ludus* is a liturgical *representatio*, some form of the *Peregrinus*, performed at Easter.

*28. Lincoln: Assumption of the Blessed Virgin Mary, 1393–1561 (Lancashire 856): A mechanical device called a *visus* or *orlogium*.

29. Lincoln: *Ludi* of Saints Lawrence, 1441–42; Susanna, 1447–48; James, 1454–55; and Clare, 1455–56 (respectively, Lancashire 859–60, 861–62): Uncertain. These appear as notations in a list of majors, sheriffs, and so on.

**30. London: Saint Thomas Becket, 1170–82 (Lancashire 878): William Fitz Stephen says that there were "repraesentationes miraculorum quae sancti confessores operati sunt, seu repraesentationes passionum quibus claruit constantia martyrum." Fitz Stephen is contrasting the rites of the *theatrum* of ancient Rome with those of the Christian church. *Representationes* suggests that they are liturgies of the saints rather than vernacular saint plays.

31. London: Saint Catherine, 1393 (Lancashire 908): Uncertain. Entry in the *London Chronicle*.

**32. London: Saints Blythe (1512), Thomas Becket (1519), Blessed Virgin Mary and Elizabeth (1519), John the Evangelist (1521, 1529, 1525, 1535), Elizabeth (1536), Margaret (1541), and others (Lancashire 969): These are figures or pageants in the midsummer watch and lord mayor's show.

33. Maldon, Essex: Saint John the Baptist, 1539–40 (Lancashire 1168): Although there are payments in 1539–40 for calves' skins for the man who "played" John the Baptist and for Christ's coat, the entry also contains expenditures for dancers' bells and gunpowder, which suggests it was not the saint's vita (courtesy of John Coldewey). Davidson ("Saint Plays and Pageants," Web site) thinks that the bells may signify the presence of Salome, but I suspect they are bells for Morris dancers (note the plural).

**34. Mildenhall, Suffolk: Saint Thomas (Becket?), 1505 (Lancashire 1183): Uncertain but glossed in the manuscript as a "chyrchall."

35. Morebath, Devon: Saint George, 1531–47 (Lancashire 1189): A parish ale? The earlier records suggest that the George was an effigy, but John Wasson thinks there may have been a play in 1540 (see "St. George and Robin Hood Plays," 66).

36. New Romney, Kent: Blessed Virgin Mary, 1512–13 (integrated with references to a Passion play in Lancashire 1207): Uncertain. Payment for "lusorum beate mariae" of 8d. seems insufficient for play production. There's a note in the records deposited at the Records of Early English Drama that they are the players of Saint Mary in the Marsh and thus probably musicians.

*37. New Romney, Kent: Saint George, 1489–90 (Lancashire 1163): Erroneous citation.

38. Norwich, Norfolk: Saint George, 1471 (Lancashire 1223): Mock battle at the end of a procession. The procession later included Saint Margaret (see McRee, "Unity or Division?")

*39. Oxford, Magdalen College: Mary Magdalen, 1506–7 (Lancashire 1261): "pro scriptura lusi b[ea]te marie magdalene xd" and "Solutum kendall pro diligentia sua in luso Sancte marie Magdalene . . . xijd." And in 1518–19: "Solutum domino porett pro tinctura et factura tunice eius qui ageret partem Christi et pro crinibus mulieribus ijs vjd." Uncertain. Perhaps a liturgical piece, the *Hortulanus* or the Marys at the tomb.

*40. Shrewsbury, Shropshire: Saint Catherine, 1525–26 (Lancashire 1391): Probably a *miracula* or some kind of *spectaculum;* there are payments to a Lord of Misrule and for a fool's head but none to the saint.

*41. Shrewsbury, Shropshire: Saints Filiciana and Sabina, 1516–17 (Lancashire 1388; Somerset, "Local Drama," 2): The entry reads: "In vino, pomis, waffers, et aliis novellis datis et expenditis super abbatem Salop et famulos suos ad ludem et demonstrationem martiriorum Felicianae et Sabinae in quarera post muros" ("In wine, fruit, cakes, and other novelties given to and expended upon the abbot of Shrewsbury and his servants at the play and *demonstrationem* of the martyrs Feliciana and Sabina in the quarry outside the walls"). First, one wonders why these two saints are placed together. Sabina's feast day is 29 August, and Feliciana, who is paired with Primus, has a feast day on 9 June. Second, the word *demonstratio* is unusual. The only other usages I have come across are from the same period and refer to games and pageants rather than plays. On Bishop Longland's visitation of Newark College on 27–28 November 1525 the bishop questioned the canons, vicars, and other ministers of the church whether Lady Hungerford and her husband, Sir Richard Sacheverall, had held bear baitings and other May games and common spectacles at the college, ones prohibited to the clergy within the college (transcriptions by Alice B. Hamilton at the office of the Records of Early English Drama for Leicestershire). One of the deacons confessed that there were bear baitings (which some of the deponents call *demonstraciones*), and added that "Maygames and Robyn hode & sanct George . . . vseth . . . to comme into the colledge" whether Lady Hungerford was there or not. Dominus John Butchard, vicar, affirmed the article that *demonstraciones,* i.e., Saint George, the "months [of the year]," and public processions took place there. William Harvey, vicar, says he saw two or three bear baits and other "ostensions" such as ridings of Saint George, the Riding of the Months, and Robin Hood, all of which used to be done yearly for the wealth of the churches. The *ludus* or *demonstratio* of Saints Filiciana and Sabina, therefore, may have been a pageant rather than a saint play.

42. Shrewsbury, Shropshire: Saint Julian the Apostate, 1556–57 (Somerset, *Shropshire,* 205). Why is Julian called a saint? Surely this is not a saint play! James Gibson has transcribed an attack on superstition (Canterbury, 1561), to wit, a "contemptuouse mockerye" on midsummer eve, otherwise called the vigil of Saint John Baptist's nativity, in which bonfires were made in the streets "for vpholdynge the olde frantyck supersticyons of papistrye. The next daye, preached one maistre Clarke, a man sober, godly and learned: and amonge other talke he towched the orignyall of superstityouse bonefyers, and declared that they first came from Iulianus apostata, whych tyrannously brent the bones of *Saint* Iohan Baptyst" (transcription in the office of the Records of Early English Drama). If the play was connected with a bonfire on the eve of Saint John Baptist, it would still not explain why Julian is called a saint unless it is meant ironically.

43. Southwark, Surrey: Saint Lucy and Saint Margaret, 1444–59 (Lancashire 1405): Uncertain.

44. Taunton, Somerset: Mary Magdalen, 1504 (Lancashire 1435): Bequest "vnto the said Sepulcre service there [the church of Saint Mary Magdalene] my rede damaske mantell & my mantell lyned with silke that I was professid yn to thentent of Mary Magdalen play" (Stokes, *Somerset,* 1.227). Uncertain, but would appear to be a liturgical *representatio* at Easter.

45. Thame, Oxfordshire: Saints Fabine and Sabine, 1488–89 (Lancashire 1444): Erroneously cited by Ellis, an earlier transcriber, as "Fabianus and Sebastianus." Davidson ("Saint Plays and Pageants," Web site) has: Expenses "when ye box of ye play of Fabine & Sabine was sett open on the morowe of the Apostles Peter & Paul" were 1d. It is not clear what such expenses might be, but the box might be for keeping the money raised from a *ludus* or ale. Uncertain.

46. Thame, Oxfordshire: Saint George, 1482–83 (Lancashire 1443): A figure in a procession (see Briscoe, "Deserts of Desire," 268).

**47. Thetford Priory, Norfolk: Saint Trinity, 1520–21 (Lancashire 1449): Not a saint play but the *ludus* of Saint Trinity's.

48. Winchester, Hampshire: Saint Agnes, 1409: A court case involving a *ludus* of Saint Agnes in which four men agreed with Richard Syngere that, if he provided the costumes and props, they would play the parts of the steward, the tormentor, and the soldiers. When Singer did not comply, the four broke into his house two days before the *ludus* and carried off "*unum originale Sancte Agnetis et unum pannum vocatum pleyngcloth*" (see Keene, *Survey of Medieval Winchester*, 393). The cast does not fit the legend as we have it. Although there is an executioner or torturer in the legend, there are no references to soldiers. Agnes herself (unless the "*originale Sancte Agnetis*" is an image) is not present in the account, nor are the spurned lover and the debauchees of the brothel on whom the legend is centered. The reference may be to some kind of game centered on the image of Saint Agnes. On the other hand, at the 1999 Leeds Medieval Conference Jane Cowling argued that "*origenale*," elsewhere attested as a script or document, in conjunction with the reference to the "pleyngcloth," demonstrates this to be a record of a saint play despite the absence in the record of the expected cast (paper forthcoming).

**49. York: Saint George, ca. 1502–58 (Lancashire 1580): Except for 1554, a riding (from ca. 1502–58). White, "'Bryngyng Forth of Saynt George.'"

**50. York: Saint Dionysius, 1456 (Lancashire 1570): Uncertain.

**51. York: Saint James the Apostle, 1446 (Lancashire 1566): Uncertain.

52. York: Saint Thomas the Apostle, temp. Henry VIII (Lancashire 1574): Alleged performance that resulted in a riot owing to the "seditious conduct of certain papists." May have been a polemical drama, but the document may also be spurious (Johnston and Rogerson, *York* 2:649–50).

Unlocalized *ludi* include the following:

53. Saint Catherine: The Anglo-Norman vita of Saint Catherine, preserved in John Rylands Library MS French 6 (ca. 1250), has some speech tags but is a narrated text, not a play (text and discussion in Fawtier-Jones, "Les Vies de Sainte Catherine d'Alexandrie").

54. Saint Francis: Craddock read the lyric, "On the Minorites," as a description of plays on the life of Saint Francis, but I agree with R. H. Robbins that the poem refers to a pictorial cycle (see Craddock, "Franciscan Influences"; and Robbins, *Historical Poems*, 335).

55. Saint John the Baptist: John Bale's *Vitam Dixi Ioanis Baptisti* in fourteen books (Lancashire 282/1; ca. 1534–36). I doubt this is a saint play. With the excep-

tion of *Kyng Johan,* in two books, Bale's other extant plays are fairly brief. The presumption that the *Vitam* is a drama arises from the rubric for the section titled "In idiotame materno, comoedias sub vario metrorum genere," which suggests that all the items are comedies. However, *comedy* can refer to narratives with a happy ending or to versified tales (for the latter, see Raby, *History of Secular Latin Poetry,* 2:54); further, the list also includes "Pammachij tragoedias transtuli," which indicates that Bale's rubric did not specify the content of all items in the list. Finally, most of the items are said to be in *libri,* whereas items 2–8 are designated "Com.1" or "Com.2," another indication that some of the texts are comedies and others are something else (for the lists, see Bale, *Complete Plays,* 1:6–11).

56. Saint Mary Magdalene: Lewis Wager's *Life and Repentaunce of Marie Magdalene,* ca. 1547–66 (Lancashire 143): Although the play depicts Christ's casting out of the seven devils and Mary's anointing of Christ's feet, the play is mostly an allegorical morality play.

57. Saint Nicholas, ca. 1250 (Lancashire 207): A sermon prologue to a play? The sermon is so turgid that it is difficult to know what might be going on.

Index of Saints

Agnes (item 48), **Andrew** (10), **the Blessed Virgin Mary** (28, 32, 36), **Blythe** (32), **Catherine** (19, 20, 25, 31, 40, 53), **Christian** (19), **Christina** (9), **Clare** (29), **Cuthbert** (21), **Dionysius** (50), **Edmund** (13), **Elizabeth** (32 [2]), **Eustace** (10), **Fabianus** (45), **Feliciana** (41), **Francis** (54), **George** (5, 6, 8, 11, 17, 35, 37, 38, 46, 49), **Holy John of Bowre** (23), **James the Apostle** (29, 51), **John the Baptist** ([23], 33, 55), **John the Evangelist** (32 [4]), **Julian the Apostate** (42), **Lawrence** (4, 29), **Lucy** (43), **Margaret** (32, 43), **Martin** (18), **Mary Magdalene** (2, 39, 44, 56), **Meriasek** (3), **Nicholas** (16, 22, 57), **Paul** (1), **Rosemont** (7), **Sabina** (41, 45), **Sebastianus** (45), **Susanna** (29), **Swithin** (10), **Thomas Becket** (12, 14, 15, 24, 26, 30, 32, 34[?]), **Thomas the Apostle** (27, 34[?], 52), and **Trinity** (47).

⚒WORKS CITED⚒

Primary Sources

Adam of Orleton. *Registrum Ade de Orleton, episcopi Herefordensia* A.D. MCCCXVII–MCCCXXVI. Edited by A. T. Bannister. London: Canterbury and York Society, 1908.

Aelred of Rievaulx. *The Mirror of Charity.* Translated by Elizabeth Connor. Kalamazoo: Cistercian Publications, 1990.

———. *Speculum charitatis.* In PL 195:501–658.

Alton, R. E., ed. "The Academic Drama in Oxford: Extracts from the Records of Four Colleges." In *Collections 5.* Oxford: Malone Society, 1960. Pp. 29–95.

Anderson, J. J., ed. *Newcastle Upon Tyne.* Records of Early English Drama. Toronto: University of Toronto Press, 1982.

Andrew, Malcolm, and Ronald Waldron, eds. *Sir Gawain and the Green Knight.* In *Poems of the Pearl Manuscript.* Berkeley: University of California Press, 1979.

Arber, Edward, ed. *A Transcript of the Registers of the Company of Stationers of London: 1554–1640 A.D.* 5 vols. London, 1875–94.

Augustine. *The City of God.* Translated by Marcus Dods. New York: Modern Library, 1950.

———. *Confessions.* Edited by James J. O'Donnell. 3 vols. Oxford: Clarendon Press, 1992.

———. *De trinitate libri XV.* Edited by W. J. Mountain. 2 vols. Turnholt: Brepols, 1968.

Baker, Donald C., John L. Murphy, and Louis B. Hall Jr., eds. *The Late Medieval Religious Plays of Bodleian MSS Digby 133 and E Museo 160.* Early English Text Society, vol. 283. Oxford: EETS, 1982.

Bale, John. *The Complete Plays of John Bale.* Edited by Peter Happé. 2 vols. Cambridge, U.K.: D. S. Brewer, 1985–86.

Barnum, Priscilla Heath, ed. *Dives and Pauper.* 1 vol. in 2 pts. Early English Text Society, vols. 275, 280. Oxford: EETS, 1976, 1980.

Basing, Patricia, ed. *Fraternity of the Holy Trinity and SS. Fabian and Sebastian in the*

Parish of St. Botolph Without Aldersgate. London Record Society, vol. 18. Kendal: London Record Society, 1982.

Beadle, Richard, ed. *The York Plays.* London: Edward Arnold, 1982.

Beadle, Richard, and Peter Meredith, eds. *The York Play: A Facsimile of British Library MS Additional 35290.* Leeds: University of Leeds, 1983.

Becon, Thomas. *The Worckes of Thomas Becon* . . . 3 vols. London: I. Day, 1564. (STC 1710.)

Bede. *Commentary on the Acts of the Apostles.* Translated by Lawrence T. Martin. Kalamazoo: Cistercian Publications, 1989.

————. *Expositio actuum apostolorum et retractatio.* Edited by M. L. W. Laistner. Cambridge, Mass.: Medieval Academy of America, 1939.

————. *A History of the English Church and People.* Translated by Leo Sherley-Price. Baltimore: Penguin Books, 1955.

Bernard of Clairvaux. *Lettere.* Edited by Ferruccio Gastaldelli. 2 vols. within *Opere di San Bernardo,* vol. 6. Milan, 1986.

————. *The Letters of Bernard of Clairvaux.* Translated by Bruno Scott James. London: Burns Oates, 1953.

Bevington, David, ed. *Medieval Drama.* Boston: Houghton Mifflin, 1975.

Bokenham, Osbern. *Legendys of Hooly Wummen.* Edited by Mary S. Serjeantson. Early English Text Society, o.s., vol. 206. Oxford: EETS, 1938.

Bonaventure. *Breviloquium.* Vol. 5 of *Opera omnia.* 10 vols. Edited by the College of St. Bonaventure. Quaracchi, 1882–1902.

Brandeis, Arthur, ed. *Jacob's Well.,* pt. 1. Early English Text Society, o.s., vol. 115. London: EETS, 1900.

Bright, John, trans. *Jeremiah.* Vol. 21 of *The Anchor Bible.* New York: Doubleday, 1965.

Bromyard, John. *Summa predicantium.* Venice: D. Nicolinus, 1586.

Brown, Beatrice Daw, ed. *The Southern Passion.* Early English Text Society, o.s., vol. 169. London: EETS, 1927.

Bullinger, Henry. *The Decades of Henry Bullinger, Minister of the Church of Zurich, trans. by H.I.* 4 vols. Edited by Thomas Harding. Cambridge, U.K.: Parker Society, 1849–52.

Capgrave, John. *The Life of St. Katharine of Alexandria.* Edited by Carl Horstmann. Early English Text Society, o.s., vol. 100. London: EETS, 1893.

————. *Ye Solace of Pilgrimes: A Description of Rome, circa A. D. 1450, by John Capgrave, An Austin Friar of King's Lynn.* Edited by C. A. Mills. London: H. Frowde, 1911.

Cawley, A. C., ed. *The Wakefield Pageants in the Towneley Cycle.* Manchester: Manchester University Press, 1958.

Cawley, A. C., and Martin Stevens, eds. *The Towneley Cycle: A Facsimile of Huntington MS HM 1.* Leeds Texts and Monographs. Leeds: University of Leeds, 1976.

Chaucer, Geoffrey. *The Riverside Chaucer.* 3d ed. Edited by Larry D. Benson. Boston: Houghton Mifflin, 1987.

Christine de Pisan. *The Middle English Translation of Christine de Pisan's Livre du corps de policie.* Edited by Diane Bornstein. Heidelberg: Carl Winter, 1977.

Clopper, Lawrence M., ed. *Chester.* Records of Early English Drama. Toronto: University of Toronto Press, 1979.

Coleridge, Samuel Taylor. *The Statesman's Manual.* In *Critical Theory Since Plato.* Edited by Hazard Adams. Rev. ed. Fort Worth: Harcourt, Brace, Jovanovich, 1992.

Craig, Hardin, ed. *Two Coventry Corpus Christi Plays.* 2nd ed. Early English Text Society, e.s., vol. 87. Oxford: EETS, 1957.

Davidson, Clifford, ed. *Tretise of Miraclis Pleyinge.* Washington, D.C.: University Press of America, 1981.

———. *Tretise of Miraclis Pleyinge.* Rev. ed. Early Drama, Art, and Music Monograph Series, vol. 19. Kalamazoo: Medieval Institute Publications, 1993.

Davis, Norman, ed. *Non-cycle Plays and Fragments.* Early English Text Society, s.s., vol. 1. Oxford: EETS, 1970.

Dawson, Giles E., ed. *Records of Plays and Players in Kent 1450–1642.* In *Collections 7.* Oxford: Malone Society, 1965.

Decretalium copiosum . . . Paris: Uldaricus Gering and Bertholdus Rembolt, 1504.

Decretum Gratiani seu verius decretorum canonicorum collectanea . . . commentarijs Hugonis ac Joanis Teuthonici . . . Paris: Jolanda Bonhomme, 1550.

Douglas, Audrey, and Peter Greenfield, eds. *Cumberland / Westmoreland / Gloucestershire.* Records of Early English Drama. Toronto: University of Toronto Press, 1986.

Dugdale, Sir William. *Monasticon.* Rev. ed. Edited and translated by John Caley, Henry Ellis, and Bulkeley Bandinel. 6 vols. London: James Bohn, 1846.

Eccles, Mark, ed. *The Macro Plays.* Early English Text Society, vol. 262. Oxford: EETS, 1969.

Fabyan, Robert. *Fabian's Chronicle.* London: Richard Pynson, 1516.

———. *The New Chronicle of England and France, in Two Parts; by Robert Fabyan.* Edited by Henry Ellis. London: F. C. and J. Revington, 1811.

Farmer, John S., ed. *Interlude of St. John the Evangelist.* In *Recently Recovered "Lost" Tudor Plays.* London: Early English Drama Society, 1907; rprt. 1966. Pp. 349–68.

Fitz Stephen, William. *Vita S. Thomae.* In *Memorials for the History of Thomas Becket.* Vol. 3. Edited by James Craigie Robertson. Rolls Series, no. 67. London, 1875–85. Pp. 1–54.

Foster, Frances A., and Wilhem Heuser, eds. *The Northern Passion.* Early English Text Society, o.s., vols. 145, 147, 183. London: EETS, 1913, 1916, 1930.

Fowler, Joseph T., ed. *Extracts from the Account Rolls of the Abbey of Durham.* Surtees Society, vols. 99, 100, 103. Durham: Andrews, 1898, 1899, 1901.

———. *Memorials of the Church of SS. Peter and Wilfred, Ripon.* Surtees Society, vol. 115. Durham, 1908.

Friedberg, Emil, ed. *Corpus iuris canonici.* 2 vols. Leipzig, 1879–81.

Gairdner, James, comp. *Letters and Papers, Foreign and Domestic of the Reign of Henry VIII.* Vol. 11. London: Her Majesty's Stationery Office, 1888.

Galloway, David, and John Wasson, eds., *Records of Plays and Players in Norfolk and Suffolk 1330–1642.* In *Collections 11.* Oxford: Malone Society, 1980–81.

Gerald of Wales. *The Autobiography of Giraldus Cambrensis.* Edited and translated by Harold E. Butler. London, 1937.

———. *De rebus a se gestis.* Edited by J. S. Brewer. Vol. 1 of *Opera.* Rolls Series, no. 21. London, 1861–91.

————. *Speculum ecclesie*. Edited by J. S. Brewer. Vol. 4 of *Opera*. Rolls Series, no. 21. London, 1861–91.

Gerhoh of Reichersberg. *Commentarium in Psalmos*. In PL 193: 619–1814; PL 194: 1–998.

————. *De investigatione Antichristi*. *Monumenta Germaniae Historica*. In *Libelli de Lite*, vol. 3. Hanover, 1897.

German Academic Societies, ed. *Thesaurus linguae latinae*. Leipzig: B. G. Teubner, 1900–.

Glossa ordinaria. 2 vols. In PL 113–114.

[Gnaphaeus, Gulielmus]. *The Comedy of Acolastus: Translated from the Latin of Fullonius by John Palsgrave*. Edited by P. L. Carver. Early English Text Society, o.s., vol. 202. Oxford: EETS, 1937.

Goates, Margery, ed. *Pepysian Gospel Harmony*. Early English Text Society, o.s., vol. 157. London: EETS, 1922.

Greg, W. W., ed. *Interlude of Johan the Evangelist*. Oxford: Malone Society, 1907.

————. *A New Enterlude of Godly Queene Hester Edited from the Quarto of 1561*. Materialien zur Kunde des älteren Englischen Dramas, vol. 5. Louvain: A. Uystpruyst, 1904.

————. *"Play of Robin Hood for May-Games" (ca. 1560)*. In *Collections 1*, pt. 2. Oxford: Malone Society, 1908. Pp. 125–36.

Gregory the Great. *Moralia in Job*. In PL 76: 9–782.

Grosseteste, Robert. *Epistolae*. Edited by Henry R. Luard. Rolls Series, no. 25. London, 1861.

Hall, Edward. *Hall's Chronicle*. Edited by Henry Ellis. London: J. Johnson, 1809.

————. *The Union of the Two Noble and Illustre Families of Lancestre and Yorke*. London, 1548.

Halliwell-Phillips, J. O., ed. *Letters of the Kings of England*. 2 vols. London: H. Colburn, 1848.

Heywood, John. *The Foure PP*. In *The Plays of John Heywood*. Edited by Richard Axton and Peter Happé. Cambridge, U.K.: D. S. Brewer, 1991. Pp. 111–42.

Higden, Ranulph. *Polychronicon*. Edited by Churchill Babington and J. R. Lumby. 9 vols. Rolls Series, vol. 41. London, 1885–86.

Holthausen, Ferdinand, ed. *Das Noahspiel von Newcastle on Tyne*. Göteborgs högskolas örsskrift 3, no. 3. Göteborg: Zachrisson, 1897.

Honorius of Autun. *De Gemma Animae*. In PL 172: 541–738.

Horstmann, Carl, ed. *The Early South-English Legendary*. Early English Text Society, o.s., vol. 87. London: EETS, 1887.

————. *The Northern Homily Cycle*. In *Altenglische Legenden, Neue Folge*. Heilbronn: Gebr. Henninger, 1881. Pp. 1–73.

————. *Sammlung Altenglischer Legenden*. Heilbronn: Gebr. Henninger, 1878.

————. *Yorkshire Writers: Richard Rolle of Hampole, an English Father of the Church and His Followers*. 2 vols. London: Swan Sonnenschein, 1895–96.

Hudson, Anne, ed. *Selections from English Wycliffite Writings*. Cambridge: Cambridge University Press, 1978.

Hugh of St. Cher. *Opera omnia in universum Vetus, & Novum Testamentum*. 8 vols. Venice: Nicholas Pezzana, 1732.

Hughes, Paul L., and James F. Larkin, eds. *Tudor Royal Proclamations*. 2 vols. New Haven: Yale University Press, 1964–69.

Ingram, R. W., ed. *Coventry*. Records of Early English Drama. Toronto: University of Toronto Press, 1981.

Isidore of Seville. *Isidori Hispalensis Episcopi: Etymologiarum sive Originum Libri XX*. Edited by M. W. Lindsay. 2 vols. Oxford: Clarendon Press, 1911.

Jacobus de Voragine. *The Golden Legend: Readings on the Saints*. Translated by William Granger Ryan. 2 vols. Princeton: Princeton University Press, 1993.

Jeayes, Isaac Herbert, trans. *Court Rolls of the Borough of Colchester*. Colchester, 1921.

Jerome. *In hieremiam prophetam libri sex*. Corpus Christianorum, Series Latina, vol. 74. Turnholt: Brepols, 1960.

John of Salisbury. *Frivolities of Courtiers and Footprints of Philosophers: Being a Translation of the First, Second, and Third Books and Selections From the Seventh and Eighth Books of the 'Policraticus' of John of Salisbury*. Translated by Joseph B. Pike. Minneapolis: University of Minnesota Press, 1938.

———. *Ioannis Saresberiensis episcopi Carnotensis Policratici sive De nvgis cvrialivm et vestigiis philosophorvm libri VIII*. Edited by Clement C. J. Webb. 2 vols. Oxford: Clarendon Press, 1909.

———. *The Statesman's Book of John of Salisbury; Being the Fourth, Fifth, and Sixth Books, and Selections From the Seventh and Eighth Books, of the Policraticus*. Translated by John Dickinson. New York: A. A. Knopf, 1927.

Johnston, Alexandra F., and Margaret G. Rogerson, eds. *York*. 2 vols. Records of Early English Drama. Toronto: University of Toronto Press, 1979.

Joyce, Sally L., and Evelyn S. Newlyn, eds. *Dorset / Cornwall*. Records of Early English Drama. Toronto: University of Toronto Press, 1999.

Kahrl, Stanley, ed. *Records of Plays and Players in Lincolnshire 1300–1585*. In *Collections 8*. Oxford, Malone Society, 1974.

Kempe, Margery. *The Book of Margery Kempe*. Edited by Sanford Brown Meech. Early English Text Society, vol. 212. London: EETS, 1940.

Kipling, Gordon, ed. *The Receyt of the Ladie Kateryne*. Early English Text Society, vol. 296. Oxford: EETS, 1990.

Klausner, David N., ed. *Herefordshire / Worcestershire*. Records of Early English Drama. Toronto: University of Toronto Press, 1990.

Langland, William. *Piers Plowman: The B Version*. Edited by George Kane and E. Talbot Donaldson. London: Athlone Press, 1975.

Leach, Arthur F., ed. *Beverley Town Documents*. Selden Society, vol. 14. London, 1900.

Little, A. G., ed. *Liber Exemplorum*. Aberdeen: British Society for Franciscan Studies, 1908.

Lombard, Peter. *Sententiae in IV libris distinctae*. 3d ed. 2 vols. Grottaferrata: College of St. Bonaventure, 1971, 1981.

Lumiansky, Robert M., and David Mills, eds. *The Chester Mystery Cycle*. 2 vols. Early English Text Society, s.s., vols. 3, 9. Oxford: EETS, 1974, 1986.

Lydgate, John. *Fall of Princes*. Edited by H. Bergen. 4 vols. Early English Text Society, e.s., vols. 121–24. London: EETS, 1924–27.

————. *Lydgate's Troy Book A. D. 1412–20.* Edited by H. Bergen. 4 vols. Early English Text Society, e.s., vols. 97, 103, 106, 126. London: EETS, 1906–35.

————. *The Minor Poems of John Lydgate.* Edited by Henry Noble MacCracken. 2 vols. Early English Text Society, e.s., vol. 107 and o.s., vol. 192. Oxford: EETS, 1911, 1934.

————. *Saint Albon and Saint Amphibalus.* Edited by George F. Reinecke. New York: Garland, 1985.

Machyn, Henry. *The Diary of Henry Machyn.* Edited by John G. Nichols. Camden Society, vol. 42. London, 1848.

Mannyng, Robert, of Brunne. *Handlynge Synne.* Edited by Idelle Sullens. Binghamton: Medieval and Renaissance Texts and Studies, 1983.

————. *Meditations on the Life and Passion of Christ.* Edited by Charlotte D'Evelyn. Early English Text Society, o.s., vol. 158. London: EETS, 1921.

Mapes, Walter. *The Latin Poems Commonly Attributed to Walter Mapes.* Edited by Thomas Wright. Camden Society, vol. 16. London, 1841.

Medwall, Henry. *The Plays of Henry Medwall.* Edited by Alan H. Nelson. Cambridge: D. S. Brewer, 1980.

Meredith, Peter, and Stanley J. Kahrl, eds. *The N-Town Plays: A Facsimile of British Library MS Cotton Vespasian D VIII.* Leeds Texts and Monographs. Leeds: University of Leeds,1977.

Mill, Anna J., and E. K. Chambers, eds. "Dramatic Records of the City of London: The Repertories, Journals, and Letter Books." In *Collections 2*, pt. 3. Oxford: Malone Society, 1931. Pp. 285–320.

Mirk, John. *Mirk's Festial.* Edited by Theodor Erbe. Early English Text Society, e.s., vol. 96. Oxford: EETS, 1905.

More, Sir Thomas. *The Confutation of Tyndale's Answer.* Edited by Louis A Schuster. Vol. 8 of *Complete Works.* New Haven: Yale University Press, 1973.

————. *History of Richard III.* Edited by Richard Sylvester. Vol. 2 of *Complete Works.* New Haven: Yale University Press, 1963.

Morris, Richard, ed. *Cursor Mundi.* 7 vols. Early English Text Society, o.s., vols. 57, 59, 62, 66, 68, 99, 101. Oxford: EETS, 1874–93.

Nelson, Alan H., ed. *Cambridge.* 2 vols. Records of Early English Drama. Toronto: University of Toronto Press, 1989.

Nicholas of Lyra. *Postillae perpetuae in Vetus et Novum Testamentum.* 5 vols. Rome: Conrad Sweynheym, 1471–72.

Nonius Marcellus. *Compendiosa doctrina.* Edited by L. Müller. 2 vols. Leipzig: B. G. Teubner, 1888.

Oresme, Nicholas. *Le Livre de éthiques d'Aristote.* Edited by Albert D. Menut. New York: G. E. Stechert, 1940.

Palsgrave, John. See Gnaphaeus, Guilielmus.

Paris, Matthew. *Gesta abbatum.* Edited by Henry T. Riley. 3 vols. Rolls Series, vol. 28. London, 1867–69.

PL: *Patrologia latina.* Edited by J. P. Migne. 221 vols. Paris: Garniére Press, 1844–64.

Pecock, Reginald. *The Repressor of over Much Blaming of the Clergy.* Edited by Churchill Babington. 2 vols. Rolls Series, vol. 19. London, 1860.

Pilkington, Mark C., ed. *Bristol.* Records of Early English Drama. Toronto: University of Toronto Press, 1997.

Powicke, F. M., and C. R. Cheney, eds. *Councils and Synods . . . A.D. 1205–1313.* 2 vols. Oxford: Oxford University Press, 1964.

Prynne, William. *Antiquae Constitutiones Regni Angliae sub Regibus Joanne, Henrico Tertio, et Edoardo Primo . . .* London: W. Prynne, 1672.

Rabanus Maurus. *Expositio super Jeremiam.* In PL 111: 979–90.

Ragusa, Isa, and Rosalie B. Green, trans. *Meditations on the Life of Christ.* Princeton: Princeton University Press, 1961.

Rastell, John. *A Hundred Merry Tales and Other English Jestbooks of the Fifteenth and Sixteenth Centuries.* Edited by P. M. Zall. Lincoln: University of Nebraska Press, 1963.

Riggio, Milla, ed. *The Play of Wisdom: Its Texts and Contexts.* New York: AMS Press, 1998.

Robbins, R. H., ed. *Historical Poems of the XIVth and XVth Centuries.* New York: Columbia University Press, 1959.

Robertson, Jean, and D. J. Gordon, eds. *A Calendar of Dramatic Records in the Books of the Livery Companies of London 1485–1640.* In *Collections 3.* Oxford: Malone Society, 1954.

Ross, Woodburn O., ed. *Middle English Sermons.* Early English Text Society, o.s., vol. 209. London: EETS, 1940.

Sextus Pompeius Festus. *De verborum significatu quae supercant cum Pauli epitome.* Edited by Emil Thewrewk de Ponor. Budapest: Hungarian Literary Academy, 1889.

Simmons, Thomas, and Henry Nolloth, eds. *The Lay Folks' Catechism.* Early English Text Society, o.s. 118. London: EETS, 1901.

Skeat, W. W., ed. *Pierce the Ploughmans Crede.* Early English Text Society, o.s., vol. 30. London: EETS, 1867.

Smith, Toulman, ed. *English Gilds.* Early English Text Society, o.s., vol. 40. Oxford: EETS, 1870.

Somerset, J. Alan B., ed. *Shropshire.* 2 vols. Records of Early English Drama. Toronto: University of Toronto Press, 1994.

Spector, Stephen, ed. *The N-Town Play: Cotton MS Vespasian D.8.* 2 vols. Early English Text Society, s.s., vols. 11–12. Oxford: EETS, 1991.

Stevens, Martin, and A. C. Cawley, eds. *The Towneley Plays.* Early English Text Society, s.s., vols. 13–14. Oxford: EETS, 1994.

Stokes, James, ed. *Somerset.* 2 vols. Records of Early English Drama. Toronto: University of Toronto Press, 1996.

Stow, John. *A Survey of London.* Edited by C. L. Kingsford. 2 vols. Oxford: Clarendon Press, 1908.

Tanner, Norman P., ed. *Decrees of the Ecumenical Councils.* 2 vols. London: Sheed and Ward, 1990.

Thomas Aquinas. *Opera omnia.* 25 vols. Parma: Peter Fraccadori, 1852–73. Reprint, New York: Musurgia Publishers, 1948–50.

———. *Summa theologica.* Edited and translated by the Fathers of the English Dominican Province. 20 vols. London: Burns Oates and Washbourne, 1921.

Thomas de Chobham. *Summa confessorum.* Edited by F. Broomfield. Analecta mediaevalia namurcensia, vol. 25. Louvain: Editions Nauwelaerts, 1968.

Thomas of Celano. *The First Life of St. Francis.* In *St. Francis of Assisi: Writings and*

Early Biographies. 4th rev. ed. Edited by Marion A. Habig. Chicago: Franciscan Herald Press, 1983.

Thompson, A. H., ed. *Visitations of Religious Houses in the Diocese of Lincoln.* 3 vols. Lincoln Record Society. Lincoln, 1914, 1918, 1929.

Tyndale, William. *Tyndale's Old Testament.* Translated by William Tyndale. With an introduction by David Daniell. New Haven: Yale University Press, 1992.

Varro, Marcus Terentius. *On the Latin Language.* Edited and translated by Roland G. Kent. 2 vols. Cambridge: Harvard University Press, 1938.

Wager, Lewis. *Life and Repentaunce of Marie Magdalene.* Edited by Frederic Ives Carpenter. Chicago: University of Chicago Press, 1902.

Wasson, John M., ed. *Devon.* Records of Early English Drama. Toronto: University of Toronto Press, 1986.

Weatherly, Edward, ed. *Speculum Sacerdotale.* Early English Text Society, vol. 200. Oxford: EETS, 1936.

Wilkins, D., ed. *Concilia Magnae Britanniae et Hiberniae.* 4 vols. London: R. Gosling, 1737–38.

Wilson, J. Dover, and Bertram Dobell, eds. *The Resurrection of Our Lord.* Malone Society Reprints. Oxford, 1912.

Wright, John, trans. *The Play of Antichrist.* Toronto: Pontifical Institute of Mediaeval Studies, 1967.

Wright, Thomas, ed. *A Selection of Latin Stories.* Percy Society, vol. 8. London, 1842.

———. *The Simonie.* In *Political Songs of England.* Camden Society, vol. 6. London, 1839. Pp. 323–45, 399–401.

Wyclif, John. *De novis ordinibus.* In *Polemical Works.* Edited by Rudolf Buddensieg. 2 vols. London: The Wyclif Society, 1883. 1: 323–36.

———. *The English Works of Wyclif Hitherto Unprinted.* Edited by F. D. Matthew. Early English Text Society, o.s., vol. 74. London: EETS, 1880.

Secondary Sources

Aichele, Klaus. *Das Antichristdrama des Mittelalters der Reformation und Gegenreformation.* The Hauge: Martin Nijhoff, 1974.

Allen, Judson B. *The Ethical Poetic of the Later Middle Ages.* Toronto: University of Toronto Press, 1982.

Anderson, John, and Arthur C. Cawley. "The Newcastle Play of *Noah's Ark.*" *Records of Early English Drama Newsletter* 2 (1977): 11–17.

Anglo, Sydney. *Spectacle, Pageantry, and Early Tudor Policy.* Oxford: Clarendon Press, 1969.

Ashley, Kathleen. "Sponsorship, Reflexivity and Resistance: Cultural Readings of the York Cycle Plays." In *The Performance of Middle English Culture: Essays on Chaucer and the Drama in Honor of Martin Stevens,* edited by James J. Paxson, Lawrence M. Clopper, and Sylvia Tomasch. Cambridge, U.K.: Boydell and Brewer, 1998. Pp. 9–24.

Aston, Margaret. "Lollard Women Priests?" In *Lollards and Reformers: Images and Literacy in Late Medieval Religion.* London: Hambledon Press, 1984. Pp. 49–70.

Axton, Richard. *European Drama of the Early Middle Ages.* London: Hutchinson University Library, 1974.

———. "Popular Modes in the Earliest Plays." In *Medieval Drama,* edited by Neville

Denny. Stratford-Upon-Avon Studies, vol. 16. London: Edward Arnold, 1973. Pp. 13–40.

Badir, Patricia. "Representations of the Resurrection at Beverley Minster Circa 1208: Chronicle, Play, Miracle." *Theatre Survey* 38 (1997): 9–41.

Bailey, Terence. *The Processions of Sarum and the Western Church.* Toronto: The Pontifical Institute, 1971.

Baker, Donald C. "Is *Wisdom* a 'Professional Play?'" In *The Wisdom Symposium,* edited by Milla Cozart Riggio. New York: AMS, 1986. Pp. 67–86.

Baldwin, John W. *Masters, Princes and Merchants: The Social Views of Peter the Chanter and His Circle.* 2 vols. Princeton: Princeton University Press, 1970.

Bannister, H. M. "Bishop Roger of Worcester and the Church of Keynsham, with a List of Vestments and Books Possibly Belonging to Worcester." *English Historical Review* 32 (1917): 389–93.

Barish, Jonas. *The Antitheatrical Prejudice.* Berkeley: The University of California Press, 1981.

Barnes, T. D. "Christians and the Theater." In *Roman Theater and Society: E. Togo Salmon Papers I,* edited by William J. Slater. Ann Arbor: University of Michigan Press, 1996. Pp. 161–80.

Barron, Caroline M. "The Parish Fraternities of Medieval London." In *The Church in Prereformation Society: Essays in Honour of F. R. H. Du Boulay,* edited by Caroline M. Barron and Christopher Harper-Bill. Woodbridge, U.K.: Boydell Press, 1985. Pp. 13–37.

Barron, Caroline M., and Laura Wright. "The London Middle English Guild Certificates of 1388–9." *Nottingham Medieval Studies* 39 (1995): 108–45.

Beadle, Richard. "Monk Thomas Hyngham's Hand in the Macro Manuscript." In *New Science Out of Old Books: Studies in Manuscripts and Early Printed Books in Honour of A. I. Doyle,* edited by Richard Beadle and A. J. Piper. Aldershot, Hants.: Scolar Press, 1995. Pp. 315–41.

———. "Plays and Playing at Thetford and Nearby 1498–1540." *Theatre Notebook* 32 (1978): 4–11.

———. "The York Cycle: Texts, Performances, and the Bases for Critical Enquiry." In *Medieval Literature: Texts and Interpretation,* edited by Tim Machan. Binghamton: Medieval and Renaissance Texts and Studies, 1991. Pp. 105–19.

Beadle, Richard, ed. *The Cambridge Companion to Medieval English Theatre.* Cambridge: Cambridge University Press, 1994.

Beckwith, Sarah. "Ritual, Church and Theatre: Medieval Dramas of the Sacramental Body." In *Culture and History 1350–1600: Essays on English Communities, Identities and Writing,* edited by David Aers. Detroit: Wayne State University Press, 1992. Pp. 65–89.

Bennett, Judith M. "Conviviality and Charity in Mediaeval and Early Modern England." *Past and Present* 134 (1992): 19–41.

Berger, Thomas L., and William C. Bradford Jr. *An Index of Characters in English Printed Drama to the Restoration.* Englewood, Colo.: Microcard Editions Books, 1975.

Bevington, David. *From "Mankind" to Marlowe: Growth of Structure in the Popular Drama of Tudor England.* Cambridge: Harvard University Press, 1962.

———. *Tudor Drama and Politics.* Cambridge: Harvard University Press, 1968.

Bigongiari, Dino. "Were There Theatres in the Twelfth and Thirteenth Centuries?" *Romanic Review* 37 (1946): 201–24.

Billington, Sandra. *Mock Kings in Medieval Society and Renaissance Drama*. Oxford: Clarendon Press, 1991.

Bills, Bing D. "The 'Suppression Theory' and the English Corpus Christi Plays: A Re-Examination." *Theatre Journal* 32 (1980): 157–68.

Blackstone, Mary. "A Survey and Annotated Bibliography of Records Research and Performance History Relating to Early British Drama and Minstrelsy for 1984–8." *Records of Early English Drama Newsletter* 15 (1990): 1–104.

Blamires, Alcuin. "Women and Preaching in Medieval Orthodoxy, Heresy, and Saints' Lives." *Viator* 26 (1995): 135–52.

Boas, Frederick S. *University Drama in the Tudor Age*. Oxford: Oxford University Press, 1914.

Borges, Jorge Luis. *Labyrinths: Selected Stories and Other Writings*, edited by Donald A. Yates and James E. Irby. New York: New Directions, 1964.

Boyle, Leonard E. "The Fourth Lateran Council and Manuals of Popular Theology." In *The Popular Literature of Medieval England*, edited by Thomas J. Heffernan. Knoxville: University of Tennessee Press, 1985. Pp. 30–43.

Brannen, Anne. "Parish Play Accounts in Context: Interpreting the Bassingbourn St. George Play." *Research Opportunities in Renaissance Drama* 35 (1996): 55–72.

Briscoe, Marianne. "Deserts of Desire: Reading Across the Midlands." *Fifteenth Century Studies* 13 (1988): 263–73.

———. "Some Clerical Notions of Dramatic Decorum in Late Medieval England." *Comparative Drama* 19 (1985): 1–13.

Briscoe, Marianne G., and John C. Coldewey, eds. *Contexts for Early English Drama*. Bloomington: Indiana University Press, 1989.

Cawley, A. C. "The Grotesque Feast in the *Prima Pastorum*." *Speculum* 30 (1955): 213–17.

———. "Middle English Metrical Versions of the Decalogue with Reference to the English Corpus Christi Cycles." *Leeds Studies in English*, n.s. 8 (1975): 129–145.

Cawley, A. C., Jean Forrester, and John Goodchild. "References to the Corpus Christi Play in the Wakefield Burgess Court Rolls: The Originals Rediscovered." *Leeds Studies in English*, n.s. 19 (1988): 85–104.

Cawley, A. C., et al., eds. *Medieval Drama*. Vol. 1 of *The Revels History of the Drama in English*. London, 1983.

Chambers, E. K. *The Elizabethan Stage*. 4 vols. Oxford: Clarendon Press, 1923.

———. *English Literature at the Close the Middle Ages*. Oxford History of English Literature. Vol. 2, pt. 2. Oxford: Clarendon Press, 1945.

———. *The Mediaeval Stage*. 2 vols. Oxford: Clarendon Press, 1903.

Clopper, Lawrence M. "Arnewaye, Higden and the Origin of the Chester Plays." *Records of Early English Drama Newsletter* 8 (2) (1983): 4–11.

———. "The Chester Plays: Frequency of Performance." *Theatre Survey* 14 (1973): 46–58.

———. "*Communitas*: The Play of Saints in Late Medieval and Tudor England." *Mediaevalia* 18 (1995): 81–109.

———. "The Engaged Spectator: Langland and Chaucer on Civic Spectacle and the *Theatrum.*" *Studies in the Age of Chaucer* 22 (2000): 123–47.

———. "The 1520s: Changes in Civic Drama and Ceremony." *Research Opportunities in Renaissance Drama* 31(1992): 58–61.

———. "Framing Medieval Drama: The Franciscans and English Drama." Forthcoming in *Ludus.*

———. "The History and Development of the Chester Cycle." *Modern Philology* 75 (1978): 219–46.

———. "Lay and Clerical Impact on Civic Religious Drama and Ceremony." In *Contexts for Early English Drama,* edited by Marianne G. Briscoe and John C. Coldewey. Bloomington: Indiana University Press, 1989. Pp. 102–36.

———. "*Mankind* and Its Audience." *Comparative Drama* 8 (1974–75): 347–55.

———. "*Miracula* and *The Tretise of Miraclis Pleyinge.*" *Speculum* 65 (1990): 878–905.

———. "The Principle of Selection of the Chester Old Testament Plays." *Chaucer Review* 13 (1978): 219–46.

———. "The Problem of the Clerkenwell Plays." *Comparative Drama* 34 (2000).

———. "The Rogers' Description of the Chester Plays." *Leeds Studies in English,* n.s. 7 (1974): 63–94.

———. "'*Songes of Rechelesnesse*': Langland and the Franciscans. Ann Arbor: University of Michigan Press, 1997.

———. "Why Are There So Few English Saint Plays?" *Early Theatre* 2 (1999): 107–12.

Coakley, John. "Gender and the Authority of Friars: The Significance of Holy Women for Thirteenth-Century Franciscans and Dominicans." *Church History* 60 (1991): 445–60.

Coffman, George. "The Miracle Play in England—Nomenclature." *Publications of the Modern Language Association* 31 (1916): 448–65.

———. "A Plea for the Study of the Corpus Christi Plays as Drama." *Studies in Philology* 27 (1929): 411–24.

Coldewey, John. Comment on Stanley Kahrl's "Learning About Local Control." In Dutka, *Records of Early English Drama.* Pp. 118–27.

———. "The Digby Plays and the Chelmsford Records." *Research Opportunities in Renaissance Drama* 18 (1975): 103–21.

———. "Early Essex Drama: A History of Its Rise and Fall, and a Theory Concerning the Digby Plays." Ph.D. diss. University of Colorado, 1972.

———. "English Drama in the 1520s: Six Perspectives." *Research Opportunities in Renaissance Drama* 31 (1992): 57–78.

———. "The Last Rise and Final Demise of Essex Town Drama." *Modern Language Quarterly* 36 (1975): 239–60.

———. "The Non-cycle Plays and the East Anglian Tradition." In Beadle, *Cambridge Companion.* Pp. 189–210.

———. "Plays and 'Play' in Early English Drama." *Research Opportunities in Renaissance Drama* 28 (1985): 181–88.

Coletti, Theresa. "The Design of the Digby Play of *Mary Magdalene.*" *Studies in Philology* 76 (1979): 313–33.

———. "'*Paupertas est donum dei*': Hagiography, Lay Religion, and the Economics of Salvation in the Digby *Mary Magdalene.*" Forthcoming.

Cox, John D., and David Scott Kastan, eds. *A New History of Early English Drama.* New York: Columbia University Press, 1997.

Craddock, Laurence G. "Franciscan Influences on Early English Drama." *Franciscan Studies* 10 (1950): 383–417.

Craig, Hardin. *English Religious Drama of the Middle Ages.* Oxford: Clarendon Press, 1955.

Craik, T. W. *The Tudor Interlude.* Leicester: Leicester University Press, 1967

Craun, Edwin D. *Lies, Slander, and Obscenity in Medieval English Literature: Pastoral Rhetoric and the Deviant Speaker.* Cambridge: Cambridge University Press, 1997.

Crouch, David J. F. "Paying to See the Play: The Stationholders on the Route of the York Corpus Christi Play in the Fifteenth Century." *Medieval English Theatre* 13 (1991): 64–111.

Davidson, Clifford. "British Saint Play Records: Coping with Ambiguity." *Early Theatre* 2 (1999): 97–106.

———. *Illustrations of the Stage and Acting in England to 1580.* Kalamazoo: Medieval Institute Publications, 1991.

———. "Middle English Saint Plays." In Davidson, *Saint Play.* Pp. 31–122.

———. "Saint Plays and Pageants of Medieval Britain": http://www.wmich.edu/medieval/research/edam/saint.html.

———. "Saints in Play: English Theatre and Saints' Lives." In *Saints: Studies in Medieval Hagiography,* edited by Sandro Sticca. Medieval and Renaissance Texts and Studies, vol. 141. Binghamton, 1996. Pp. 145–60.

———. *Visualizing the Moral Life: Medieval Iconography and the Macro Moralities.* New York: AMC, 1989.

———, ed. *The Saint Play in Medieval Europe.* Early Drama, Art, and Music Monograph Series, vol. 8. Kalamazoo: Medieval Institute Publications, 1986.

Davis, Nicholas. "Allusions to Medieval Drama in Britain (3): A Findings List." *Medieval English Theatre* 5 (1983): 83–86.

———. "Allusions to Medieval Drama in Britain (4): Interludes." *Medieval English Theatre* 6 (1984): 61–91.

———. "Another View of the *Tretise of Miraclis Playinge.*" *Medieval English Theatre* 4 (1982): 48–55.

———. "The Meaning of the Word 'Interlude.'" *Medieval English Theatre* 6 (1984): 5–15.

———. "'The Tretise of Myraclis Pleyinge': On Milieu and Authorship." *Medieval English Theatre* 12 (1990): 124–51.

de Lubac, Henri. *Exégèse médiévale: Les quatre sens de l'écriture.* 4 vols. in 2 pts. Paris: Aubier 1959–64.

Dessen, Alan. *Shakespeare and the Late Moral Plays.* Lincoln: University of Nebraska Press, 1986.

Dixon, Mimi Still. "'Thys Body of Mary': 'Femynyte' and 'Inward Mythe' in the Digby *Mary Magdalene.*" *Mediaevalia* 18 (1995): 221–44.

Dobson, R. B., ed. *The Peasants' Revolt of 1381.* 2d ed. London: Macmillan, 1983.

Dorrell, Margaret. "Two Studies of the York Corpus Christi Play." *Leeds Studies in English,* n.s. 6 (1972): 63–111.

Duffy, Eamon. *The Stripping of the Altars: Traditional Religion in England 1400–1580.* New Haven: Yale University Press, 1992.

Dunn, E. Catherine. "Popular Devotion in the Vernacular Drama of Medieval England." *Medievalia et Humanistica,* n.s. 4 (1973): 55–68.

Dutka, JoAnna. "The Lost Dramatic Cycle of Norwich and the Grocers' Play of the Fall of Man." *Review of English Studies,* n.s. 35 (1984): 1–13.

———. "Mystery Plays at Norwich: Their Formation and Development." *Leeds Studies in English,* n.s. 10 (1978): 107–20.

Dutka, JoAnna, ed. *Records of Early English Drama: Proceedings of the First Colloquium.* Toronto: Records of Early English Drama, 1979.

Dutton, Richard. "Censorship." In Cox and Kastan, *New History.* Pp. 287–304.

Eccles, Mark. "*Ludus Coventriae:* Lincoln or Norfolk?" *Medium Aevum* 40 (1971): 135–41.

Edwards, A. S. G. "Middle English *Pageant* 'Picture.'" *Notes and Queries* 237 (1992): 25–26.

Elliott, John. "Drama at the Oxford Colleges and the Inns of Court, 1520–1534." *Research Opportunities in Renaissance Drama* 31 (1992): 64–66.

———. "Early Staging in Oxford." In Cox and Kastan, *New History.* Pp. 68–76.

———. "Plays, Players, and Playwrights in Renaissance Oxford." In *From Page to Performance: Essays in Early English Drama,* edited by John A. Alford. East Lansing: Michigan State University Press, 1995. Pp. 179–94.

Emmerson, Richard K. "Contextualizing Performance: The Reception of the Chester *Antichrist.*" *Journal of Medieval and Early Modern Studies* 29 (1999): 89–119.

———. "Eliding the 'Medieval': Renaissance 'New Historicism' and Sixteenth-Century Drama." In *The Performance of Middle English Culture: Essays on Chaucer and the Drama in Honor of Martin Stevens,* edited by James J. Paxson, Lawrence M. Clopper, and Sylvia Tomasch. Cambridge, U.K.: D. S. Brewer, 1998. Pp. 25–41.

———. "The Morality Character as Sign: A Semiotic Approach to *The Castle of Perseverance.*" *Mediaevalia* 18 (1995): 191–220.

Epp, Garrett. "The Towneley Plays and the Hazards of Cycling." *Research Opportunities in Renaissance Drama* 32 (1993): 121–50.

Erler, Mary C. "Palm Sunday Prophets and Processions and Eucharistic Controversy." *Renaissance Quarterly* 48 (1995): 58–81.

Fawtier-Jones, E. C. "Les Vies de Sainte Catherine d'Alexandrie en Ancien Française." *Romania* 56 (1930): 80–104.

Fines, John. "Heresy Trials in the Diocese of Coventry and Lichfield, 1511–12." *Journal of Ecclesiastical History* 14 (1963): 160–74.

Flanigan, C. Clifford. "The Liturgical Drama and Its Tradition: A Review of Scholarship, 1965–75." *Research Opportunities in Renaissance Drama* 18 (1975): 81–102.

———. "Medieval Latin Music-Drama." In *The Theatre of Medieval Europe: New Research in Early Drama,* edited by Eckehard Simon. Cambridge: Cambridge University Press, 1991. Pp. 21–41.

———. "The Roman Rite and the Origins of the Liturgical Drama." *University of Toronto Quarterly* 43 (1974): 263–84.

Fletcher, Alan J. "The N-Town Plays." In Beadle, *Cambridge Companion.* Pp. 163–88.

Fortman, Edmund J. *The Triune God: A Historical Study of the Doctrine of the Trinity.* Philadelphia: Westminster, 1972.

French, Katherine L., Gary G. Gibbs, and Beat A. Kümin, eds. *The Parish in English Life 1400–1600.* Manchester: Manchester University Press, 1997.

Gamer, Helena M. "Mimes, Musicians, and the Origin of the Mediaeval Religious Play." *Deutsche Beiträge zur Geistigen Überlieferung* 5 (1965): 9–28.

Gardiner, Harold C. *Mysteries' End: An Investigation of the Last Days of the Medieval Religious Stage.* New Haven: Yale University Press, 1946.

Gash, Anthony. "Carnival against Lent: The Ambivalence of Medieval Drama." In *Medieval Literature: Criticism, Ideology, and History,* edited by David Aers. New York: St. Martin's Press, 1986. Pp. 74–98.

Gatch, Milton McC. "Mysticism and Satire in the Morality of *Wisdom.*" *Philological Quarterly* 53 (1974): 342–62.

Gibson, Gail. "The Play of *Wisdom* and the Abbey of St. Edmund." *Comparative Drama* 19 (1985): 117–35. Reprinted in *The Wisdom Symposium,.* edited by Milla Cozart Riggio. New York: AMS, 1986. Pp. 39–66.

———. *The Theater of Devotion: East Anglian Drama and Society in the Late Middle Ages.* Chicago: Chicago University Press, 1989.

Gibson, James M. "'*Interludum Passionis Domini*': Parish Drama in Medieval New Romney." In *English Parish Drama,* edited by Alexandra F. Johnston and Wim Hüsken. Amsterdam: Rodopi, 1996. Pp. 137–48.

Gibson, James M., and Isobel Harvey. "A Sociological Study of the New Romney Passion Play." *Research Opportunities in Renaissance Drama* 39 (2000): 203–21.

Gransden, Antonia. *Historical Writing in England.* 2 vols. Ithaca: Cornell University Press, 1974–82.

Grant, R. *Miracle and Natural Law in Graeco-Roman and Early Christian Thought.* Amsterdam: North Holland Publishing, 1952.

———. "The Vocabulary of Miracle." In *Miracles: Cambridge Studies in Their Philosophy and History,* edited by Charles Moule. London: A. R. Mowbray, 1965. Pp. 235–38.

Grantley, Darryll. "The Source of the Digby *Mary Magdalen.*" *Notes and Queries* 229 (1984): 457–59.

Greg, W. W. "Bibliographical and Textual Problems of the English Miracle Cycles. III—Christ and the Doctors: Inter-relation of the Cycles." *The Library,* 3d. ser. 5 (1914): 280–319.

———. *A Bibliography of English Printed Drama to the Restoration.* 4 vols. London: The Bibliographical Society, 1939–59.

Hackett, M. B. *The Original Statutes of Cambridge University.* Cambridge: Cambridge University Press, 1970.

Haigh, Christopher. *English Reformations: Religion, Politics, and Society under the Tudors.* Oxford: Clarendon Press, 1993.

Happé, Peter. "The Protestant Adaptation of the Saint Play." In Davidson, *Saint Play.* Pp. 205–40.

Hardison, O. B., Jr. *Christian Rite and Christian Drama in the Middle Ages: Essays in the Origin and Early History of Modern Drama.* Baltimore: The Johns Hopkins University Press, 1965.

Harris, Jesse W. *John Bale: A Study in the Minor Literature of the Reformation.* Urbana: University of Illinois Press, 1940.

Haskins, Susan. *Mary Magdalen: Myth and Metaphor.* New York: Harcourt Brace, 1993.

Henshaw, Millett. "The Attitude of the Church toward the Stage to the End of the Middle Ages." *Medievalia et Humanistica* 4 (1952): 3–17.

Hieatt, Constance B. "A Case for *Duk Moraud* as a Play of the Miracles of the Virgin." *Mediaeval Studies* 32 (1970): 345–51.

Hill, Eugene D. "The Trinitarian Allegory of the Moral Play of *Wisdom.*" *Modern Philology* 73 (1975): 121–35.

Hilton, Rodney. *Bond Men Made Free: Medieval Peasant Movements and the English Rising of 1381.* New York: Viking Press, 1973.

Hoskins, W. G. "English Provincial Towns in the Early Sixteenth Century." In *Provincial England: Essays in Social and Economic History.* London: Macmillan, 1963; reprint, 1965. Pp. 65–85.

———. *Local History in England.* 2d ed. London: Longmans, 1972.

Hudson, Anne. "Lollardy: The English Heresy?" In *Lollards and Their Books.* London: Hambledon Press, 1985. Pp. 141–63.

———. *The Premature Reformation: Wycliffite Texts and Lollard History.* Oxford: Clarendon Press, 1988.

Hudson, Anne, and H. L. Spencer. "Old Author, New Work: The Sermons of MS Longleat 4." *Medium Aevum* 53 (1984): 220–38.

Hughes, Jonathan. *Pastors and Visionaries: Religion and Secular Life in Late Medieval Yorkshire.* Woodbridge, Suffolk: Boydell Press, 1988.

Hunningher, Benjamin. *The Origin of the Theater.* New York: Hill and Wang, 1955.

Hutton, Ronald. *The Rise and Fall of Merry England: The Ritual Year 1400–1700.* Oxford: Oxford University Press, 1994.

Ingram, Reginald W. "1579 and the Decline of Civic Religious Drama in Coventry." In *The Elizabethan Theatre VII,* edited by G. R. Hibbard. Port Credit, Ont.: 1982. Pp. 114–28.

———. "'Pleyng geire accustumed belongyng & necessarie': Guild Records and Pageant Production at Coventry." In Dutka, *Records of Early English Drama.* Pp. 60–92.

———. "'To find the players and all that longeth thereto': Notes on the Production of Medieval Drama in Coventry." In *The Elizabethan Theatre V,* edited by G. R. Hibbard. Hamden, Conn.: Archon, 1975. Pp. 17–44.

James, Mervyn. "Ritual, Drama and Social Body in the Late Medieval English Town." *Past and Present* 98 (1983): 3–29.

Jeffrey, David. "English Saints' Plays." In *Medieval Drama,* edited by Neville Denny. London: Edward Arnold, 1973. Pp. 69–89.

Johnston, Alexandra. "The Plays of the Religious Guilds of York: The Creed Play and the Pater Noster Play." *Speculum* 50 (1975): 55–90.

———. "The Procession and Play of Corpus Christi in York after 1426." *Leeds Studies in English,* n. s. 7 (1974): 55–62.

————. "The Robin Hood of the Records." In *Playing Robin Hood: The Legend as Performance in Five Centuries,* edited by Lois Potter. Newark: University of Delaware Press, 1998. Pp. 27–44.

————. "Summer Festivals in the Thames Valley Counties." In *Custom, Culture and Community in the Later Middle Ages: A Symposium,* edited by Thomas Pettit and Leif Síndergaard. Odense: Odense University Press, 1994. Pp. 37–56.

————. "What If No Texts Survived? External Evidence for Early English Drama." In Briscoe and Coldewey, *Contexts for Early English Drama.* Pp. 1–19.

————. "What Revels Are in Hand?" Dramatic Activities Sponsored by the Parishes of the Thames Valley." In *English Parish Drama,* edited by Alexandra Johnston and Wim Hüsken. Amsterdam: Rodopi, 1996. Pp. 95–104.

————. "*Wisdom* and the Records: Is There a Moral?" In *The Wisdom Symposium,* edited by Milla Cozart Riggio. New York: AMS, 1986. Pp. 87–102.

Johnston, Alexandra, and Sally-Beth MacLean. "Reformation and Resistance in Thames/Severn Parishes: The Dramatic Witness." In *The Parish in English Life,* edited by Beat Kümin, Gary B. Gibbs, and Katherine French. Manchester: Manchester University Press, 1997. Pp. 178–200.

Jolliffe, P. S. *A Check-List of Middle English Prose Writings of Spiritual Guidance.* Toronto: Pontifical Institute of Mediaeval Studies, 1974.

Jones, Douglas. *The Church in Chester: 1300–1540.* Chetham Society, 3d ser., vol. 7. Manchester, 1957.

Jones, Joseph R. "Isidore and the Theatre." In *Drama and the Middle Ages: Comparative and Cultural Essays.* 2d ser. Edited by Clifford Davidson and John H. Stroupe. New York: AMS Press, 1993. Pp. 1–23.

————. "The *Song of Songs* as a Drama in the Commentators from Origen to the Twelfth Century." In *Drama and the Classical Heritage: Comparative and Critical Essays,* edited by Clifford Davidson, Rand Johnson, and John H. Stroupe. New York: AMS Press, 1993. Pp. 29–51.

Jones, Leslie, and C. R. Morey. *The Miniatures of the Manuscripts of Terence Prior to the Thirteenth Century.* 2 vols. Princeton: Princeton University Press, 1930–31.

Justice, Steven. *Writing and Rebellion: England in 1381.* Berkeley: University of California Press, 1994.

Kahrl, Stanley. "Learning about Local Control." In Dutka, *Records of Early English Drama.* Pp. 101–18.

————. "Medieval Drama in Louth." *Research Opportunities in Renaissance Drama* 10 (1967): 129–33.

Keene, Derek. *Survey of Medieval Winchester.* 2 pts. Winchester Studies, vol. 2. Oxford: Oxford University Press, 1985.

Keller, Otto. *Lateinische Volksetymologie und Verwandtes.* Leipzig: B. G. Teubner, 1891.

Kelley, Michael R. *Flamboyant Drama: A Study of* The Castle of Perseverance, Mankind, *and* Wisdom. Carbondale: Southern Illinois University Press, 1979.

Kelly, Henry Ansgar. *Ideas and Forms of Tragedy from Aristotle to the Middle Ages.* Cambridge: Cambridge University Press, 1993.

Kendall, Ritchie D. *The Drama of Dissent: The Radical Poetics of Nonconformity, 1380–1590.* Chapel Hill: University of North Carolina Press, 1986.

Ker, N. R. *Medieval Libraries of Great Britain: A List of Surviving Books.* 2d ed. London: Royal Historical Society, 1964.

King, Pamela. "Morality Plays." In Beadle, *Cambridge Companion.* Pp. 240–64.

Kipling, Gordon. *Enter the King: Theatre, Liturgy, and Ritual in the Medieval Civic Triumph.* Oxford: Oxford University Press, 1997.

Kline, Daniel T. "Structure, Characterization, and the New Community in Four Plays of Jesus and the Doctors." *Comparative Drama* 26 (1992–93): 344–57.

Knowles, David, and R. Neville Hadcock. *Medieval Religious Houses: England and Wales.* London: Longmans, 1953.

Kolve, V. A. *The Play Called Corpus Christi.* London: Edward Arnold, 1966.

Lancashire, Ian. *Dramatic Texts and Records of Britain: A Chronological Topography to 1558.* Toronto: University of Toronto Press, 1984.

———. "Annotated Bibliography of Printed Records of Early British Drama and Minstrelsy for 1978–79." *Records of Early English Drama Newsletter* 5 (1980): 1–34.

———. "Annotated Bibliography of Printed Records of Early British Drama and Minstrelsy for 1980–81." *Records of Early English Drama Newsletter* 7 (1982): 1–40.

———. "Annotated Bibliography of Printed Records of Early British Drama and Minstrelsy for 1982–83." *Records of Early English Drama Newsletter* 9 (1984): 1–56.

———. "History of a Transition: Review Article." *Medieval and Renaissance Drama in England* 3 (1986): 277–88.

Latham, R. E. *Revised Medieval Latin Word-List from British and Irish Sources.* London: British Academy, 1965.

Leach, Arthur F. "Some English Plays and Players, 1220–1548." In *An English Miscellany Presented to Dr. Furnivall in Honour of His Seventy-Fifth Birthday.* Oxford: Clarendon Press, 1901. Pp. 205–34.

Lekai, Louis J. *The Cistercians: Ideals and Reality.* Kent, Ohio: Kent State University Press, 1977.

Lepow, Lauren. *Enacting the Sacrament: Counter-Lollardy in the Towneley Cycle.* Rutherford, N.J.: Fairleigh Dickinson University Press, 1990.

Lewis, Charlton T., and Charles Short. *A Latin Dictionary.* Oxford: Clarendon Press, 1966.

Lindenbaum, Sheila. "Ceremony and Oligarchy: The London Midsummer Watch." In *City and Spectacle in Medieval Europe,* edited by Barbara A. Hanawalt and Kathryn L. Reyerson. Minneapolis: University of Minnesota Press, 1994. Pp. 171–88.

———. "Entertainment in English Monasteries." *Fifteenth Century Studies* 13 (1988): 411–21.

———. "The Smithfield Tournament of 1390." *Journal of Medieval and Renaissance Studies* 20 (1990): 1–20.

Loomis, Roger Sherman. "Some Evidence for Secular Theatres in the Twelfth and Thirteenth Centuries." *Theatre Annual* 3 (1945): 33–43.

Loomis, Roger Sherman, and Gustave Cohen, "Were There Theatres in the Twelfth and Thirteenth Centuries?" *Speculum* 20 (1945): 92–98.

Lumiansky, Robert M., and David Mills. *The Chester Mystery Cycle: Essays and Documents*. Chapel Hill: University of North Carolina Press, 1983.

Luxton, Imogen. "The Reformation and Popular Culture." In *Church and Society in England: Henry VIII to James I*, edited by Felicity Heal and Rosemary O'Day. Hamden, Conn.: Shoestring Press, 1977. Pp. 57–77.

MacLean, Sally-Beth. "Festive Liturgy and the Dramatic Connection: A Study of Thames Valley Parishes." *Medieval and Renaissance Drama in England* 8 (1996): 49–62.

———. "Hocktide: A Reassessment of a Popular Pre-Reformation Festival." In *Festive Drama*, edited by Meg Twycross. Cambridge, U.K.: D. S. Brewer, 1996. Pp. 233–41.

———. "King Games and Robin Hood: Play and Profit at Kingston upon Thames." *Research Opportunities in Renaissance Drama* 29 (1986–87): 85–94.

———. "Marian Devotion in Post-Reformation Chester: Implications of the Smiths' 'Purification' Play." In *The Middle Ages in the North-West: Papers Presented at an International Conference Sponsored Jointly by the Centres of Medieval Studies of the Universities of Liverpool and Toronto*, edited by Tom Scott and Pat Starkey. Oxford: Leopard's Head Press, 1995. Pp. 237–55.

———. "Saints on Stage: An Analytical Survey of Dramatic Records in the West of England." *Early Theatre* 2 (1999): 45–62.

Manly, John M. "The Miracle Play in Mediaeval England." *Essays by Divers Hands. Transactions of the Royal Society of Literature of the United Kingdom*, n.s. 7 (1927): 133–53.

Mann, David. "The Roman Mime and Medieval Theatre." *Theatre Notebook* 46 (1992): 136–44.

Marshall, John. "'Her virgynes, as many as a man wylle': Dance and Provenance in Three Late Medieval Plays *Wisdom/The Killing of the Children/The Conversion of St Paul*." *Leeds Studies in English* 25 (1994): 111–48.

———. "O 3e Souverens Þat Sytt and 3e Brothern Þat Stond Ryght Wppe': Addressing the Audience of *Mankind*." *European Medieval Drama* 1 (1997): 189–202.

Marshall, Mary H. "*Theatre* in the Middle Ages: Evidence from Dictionaries and Glosses." *Symposium* 4 (1950): 1–39, 366–89.

McConica, James K. *English Humanists and Reformation Politics under Henry VIII and Edward VI*. Oxford: Clarendon Press, 1965.

McFarlane, K. B. *The Nobility of Later Medieval England*. Oxford: Clarendon Press, 1973.

———. "'Bastard Feudalism.'" In *England in the Fifteenth Century: Collected Essays*. London: Hambledon Press, 1981. Pp. 23–43.

McKinnell, John. "Drama and Ceremony in the Last Years of Durham Cathedral Priory." *Medieval English Theatre* 10 (1988): 91–111.

———. "Staging the Digby *Mary Magdalen*." *Medieval English Theatre* 6 (1984): 127–52.

McRee, Benjamin R. "Unity or Division? The Social Meaning of Guild Ceremony in Urban Communities." In *City and Spectacle in Medieval Europe*, edited by Barbara A. Hanawalt and Kathryn L. Reyerson. Minneapolis: University of Minnesota Press, 1994. Pp. 189–207.

Meredith, Peter. "John Clerke's Hand in the York Register." *Leeds Studies in English,* n.s. 12 (1981): 245–71.

———. "Manuscript, Scribe, and Performance: Further Looks at the N. Town Manuscript." In *Regionalism in Late Medieval Manuscripts and Texts: Essays Celebrating the Publication of "A Linguistic Atlas of Late Mediaeval England,"* edited by Felicity Riddy. Cambridge, U.K.: D. S. Brewer, 1991. Pp. 109–28.

———. "*Mary Magdalen* at Durham." *Medieval English Theatre* 4 (1982): 66–70.

———. "The Professional Travelling Players of the Fifteenth Century: Myth or Reality?" *European Medieval Drama* 2 (1998): 21–34.

———. "Scribes, Texts, and Performance." In *Aspects of Early English Drama,* edited by Paula Neuss. Cambridge, U.K.: D. S. Brewer, 1983. Pp. 13–29.

Meyers, Walter E. "Typology and the Audience of the English Cycle Plays." In *Typology and English Medieval Literature,* edited by Hugh T. Keenan. New York: AMS Press, 1992. Pp. 261–73.

MED: *Middle English Dictionary.* Edited by Hans Kurath et al. Ann Arbor: University of Michigan Press, 1956–.

Mills, A. D. "A Corpus Christi Play and Other Dramatic Activities in Sixteenth-Century Sherborne, Dorset." In *Collections 9.* Oxford: Malone Society, 1977. Pp. 1–15.

Mills, David. *Recycling the Cycle: The City of Chester and Its Whitsun Plays.* Studies in Early English Drama, vol. 4. Toronto: University of Toronto Press, 1998.

———. " 'The Towneley Plays' or 'The Towneley Cycle.' " *Leeds Studies in English,* n.s. 17 (1986): 95–104.

———. "*Tretise of Miraclis Pleyinge.*" In Cawley, *Revels History 1.* Pp. 83–91.

Milner, Susannah. "Flesh and Food: The Function of Female Asceticism in the Digby *Mary Magdalene.*" *Philological Quarterly* 73 (1994): 385–401.

Minnis, A. J. *Medieval Theory of Authorship.* London: Scolar Press, 1984.

Minnis, A. J., and A. B. Scott, eds. *Medieval Literary Theory and Criticism c.1100–c.1375: The Commentary Tradition.* Oxford: Clarendon Press, 1988.

Moore, Bruce. "The Banns in Medieval English Drama." *Leeds Studies in English* 24 (1993): 91–122.

Nelson, Alan H. "Drama in the 1520s: Cambridge University." *Research Opportunities in Renaissance Drama* 31 (1992): 64–68.

———. *Medieval English Stage: Corpus Christi Pageants and Plays.* Chicago: University of Chicago Press, 1974.

———. "Principles of Processional Staging: York Cycle." *Modern Philology* 67 (1970): 303–20.

Neumann, Bernd. *Geistliches Schauspiel im Zeugnis der Zeit: Zur Aufführung mittelalterlicher religiöser Dramen im deutschen Sprachgebiet.* 2 vols. Munich: Artemis Verlag, 1987.

New Catholic Enclopedia. 15 vols. New York: McGraw-Hill, 1967.

Nicoll, Allardyce. *Masks, Mimes, and Miracles: Studies in the Popular Theatre.* New York: Harcourt, Brace, 1931.

Nissé, Ruth. "Reversing Discipline: The *Tretise of Miraclis Pleyinge,* Lollard Exegesis, and the Failure of Representation." *Yearbook of Langland Studies* 11 (1997): 163–94.

Norland, Howard B. *Drama in Early Tudor Britain: 1485–1558*. Lincoln: University of Nebraska Press, 1995.

Ogilvy, J. D. A. "*Mimi, Scurrae, Histriones:* Entertainers of the Early Middle Ages." *Speculum* 38 (1963): 603–19.

Olson, Glending. *Literature as Recreation in the Later Middle Ages*. Ithaca: Cornell University Press, 1982.

———. "Plays as Play: A Medieval Ethical Theory of Performance and the Intellectual Context of the *Tretise of Miraclis Pleyinge*." *Viator* 26 (1995): 195–221.

Orme, Nicholas. *Education and Society in Medieval and Renaissance England*. London: Hambledon Press, 1989.

Owst, G. R. *Literature and Pulpit in Medieval England*. Oxford: Basil Blackwell, 1933.

Palliser, D. M. *Tudor York*. Oxford: Oxford University Press, 1979.

Palmer, Barbara D. "Early English Northern Entertainment: Patterns and Peculiarities." *Research Opportunities in Renaissance Drama* 34 (1995): 167–82.

———. "'Towneley Plays' or 'Wakefield Cycle' Revisited." *Comparative Drama* 21 (1988): 318–48.

Parker, Roscoe E. "Some Records of the 'Somyr Play.'" In *Studies in Honor of John C. Hodges and Alwin Thaler*, edited by Richard Davis and John Lievsay. Tennessee Studies in Literature, special no. Knoxville: University of Tennessee Press, 1961. Pp. 19–26.

Parry, P. H. "On the Continuity of English Civic Pageantry: A Study of John Lydgate and the Tudor Pageant." *Forum for Modern Language Studies* 15 (1979): 222–36.

Pearsall, Derek. *John Lydgate*. London: Routledge and Kegan Paul, 1970.

Pederson, Steven I. *The Tournament Tradition and Staging The Castle of Perseverance*. Theatre and Dramatic Studies, vol. 38. Ann Arbor: UMI Research Press, 1987.

Pelikan, Jaroslav. *The Christian Tradition: A History of the Development of Doctrine*. 5 vols. Chicago: University of Chicago Press, 1971–89.

Pendleton, Thomas A. "Mystery's Addenda: Secular Drama in Late Sixteenth-century Coventry." *Mediaevalia* 18 (1995): 341–65.

Phythian-Adams, Charles. "Ceremony and the Citizen: The Communal Year at Coventry 1450–1550." In *Crisis and Order in English Towns 1500–1700: Essays in Urban History*, edited by Peter Clark and Paul Slack. London: Routledge and Kegan Paul, 1972. Pp. 57–85.

Pilkinton, Mark C. "Pageants in Bristol." *Records of Early English Drama Newsletter* 13 (1988): 8–11.

Potter, Robert. *The English Morality Play: Origins, History and Influence of a Dramatic Tradition*. London: Routledge and Kegan Paul, 1975.

Raby, F. J. E. *A History of Secular Latin Poetry in the Middle Ages*. 2 vols. Oxford: Clarendon Press, 1934.

Rastall, Richard. "Minstrels and Minstrelsy in Household Account Books." In Dutka, *Records of Early English Drama*. Pp. 3–25.

———. "Music in the Cycle." In Lumiansky and Mills, *Chester Mystery Cycle*. Pp. 111–64.

Richardson, H. G. "Dives et Pauper." *Notes and Queries*, ser. 11, no. 4 (1911): 321–23.

Riggio, Milla. "The Allegory of Feudal Acquisition in *The Castle of Perseverance*." In

Allegory, Myth, and Symbol, edited by Morton W. Bloomfield. Cambridge: Harvard University Press, 1981. Pp. 187–208.

Robbins, R. H. "A Dramatic Fragment from a Caesar Augustus Play." *Anglia* 72 (1954): 31–34.

Rose, Martial, ed. *The Wakefield Mystery Plays.* New York: Anchor Books, 1963.

Rubin, Miri. *Corpus Christi: The Eucharist in Late Medieval Culture.* Cambridge: Cambridge University Press, 1991.

Rutledge, Paul. "Steracles in Norfolk." *Records of Early English Drama Newsletter* 20 (1995): 15–16.

Salter, F. M. *Mediaeval Drama in Chester.* Toronto: University of Toronto Press, 1955.

Sanders, Norman, et al., eds. *The Revels History of Drama in English, Volume II: 1500–1575.* London: Methuen, 1980.

Schiller, Gertrud. *Iconography of Christian Art.* Translated by Janet Seligman. 2 vols. London: Lund Humphries, 1971–72.

Schmitt, Natalie Crohn. "The Idea of a Person in Medieval Morality Plays." *Comparative Drama* 12 (1978): 23–34.

———. "Was There a Medieval Theater in the Round? A Re-examination of the Evidence." *Theatre Notebook* 23 (1968–69): 130–42; (1969–70): 18–25.

Schnusenberg, Christine Catharina. *The Relationship Between the Church and the Theatre Exemplified by Selected Writings of the Church Fathers and by Liturgical Texts Until Amalarius of Metz—775–852 A.D.* Lanham, New York: University Press of America, 1988.

Severs, J. Burke, et al., eds. *Manual of the Writings in Middle English 1050–1500.* 9 vols. to date. Hamden, Conn.: Connecticut Academy of Arts and Sciences, 1967–.

Sheingorn, Pamela. *The Easter Sepulchre in England.* Early Drama, Art, and Music Reference Series, vol. 5. Kalamazoo: Medieval Institute Publications, 1987.

STC: *Short-Title Catalogue of Books Printed in England, Scotland, and Ireland, 1475–1640, A.* Edited by A. W. Pollard and G. R. Redgrave. 2d ed. London: 1976.

Simon, Eckehard, ed. *The Theatre of Medieval Europe: New Research in Early Drama.* Cambridge: Cambridge University Press, 1991.

Smart, Walter K. *Some English and Latin Sources and Parallels for the Morality of Wisdom.* Menasha, Wis.: George Banter, 1912.

Somerset, J. A. B. "Local Drama and Playing Places at Shrewsbury: New Findings from the Borough Records." *Medieval and Renaissance Drama in England* 2 (1985): 1–30.

Southern, Richard W. *The Medieval Theatre in the Round: A Study of the Staging of 'The Castle of Perseverance' and Related Matters.* London: Faber, 1957.

Spector, Stephen. "The Provenance of the N-Town Codex." *The Library,* 6th ser. 1 (1979): 25–33.

Spencer, H. Leith. *English Preaching in the Late Middle Ages.* Oxford: Clarendon Press, 1993.

Spivack, Bernard. *Shakespeare and the Allegory of Evil: The History of a Metaphor in Relation to His Major Villains.* New York: Columbia University Press, 1958.

Sponsler, Claire. "The Culture of the Spectator: Conformity and Resistance to Medieval Performances." *Theatre Journal* 44 (1992): 15–29.

WORKS CITED

Stacpoole, Albertic, et al., eds. *The Noble City of York*. York: Cerialis Press, 1972.

Staines, David. "The English Mystery Cycles." In Simon, *Theatre of Medieval Europe*. Pp. 80–96.

Stallybrass, Peter, and Allon White. *The Politics and Poetics of Transgression*. Ithaca: Cornell University Press, 1986.

Stein, Paulus. *Furstenwaldensis: ΤΕΡΑΣ*. Marburg dissertation. Berlin: G. Schade, 1909.

Stevens, Martin. *Four Middle English Mystery Cycles: Textual, Contextual, and Critical Interpretations*. Princeton: Princeton University Press, 1987.

———. "Herod as Carnival King in the Medieval Biblical Drama." *Mediaevalia* 18 (1995): 43–66.

———. "The Missing Parts of the Towneley Cycle." *Speculum* 45 (1970): 254–65.

———. "Postscript." *Leeds Studies in English*, n.s. 6 (1972): 113–15.

———. "The Staging of the Wakefield Plays." *Research Opportunities in Rennaissance Drama* 11 (1968): 115–28.

———. "The Towneley Plays Manuscript (HM 1): *Compilatio* and *Ordinatio*." *Text* 5 (1991): 157–73.

———. "The York Cycle: From Procession to Play." *Leeds Studies in English*, n.s. 6 (1972): 37–61.

Stratman, Carl J., *Bibliography of Medieval Drama*. 2d ed. rev. 2 vols. New York: Frederick Ungar, 1972.

Streitberger, W. R. *Court Revels 1485–1559*. Studies in Early English Drama, vol. 3. Toronto: University of Toronto Press, 1994.

———. "The Development of Henry VIII's Revels Establishment." *Medieval English Theatre* 7 (1985): 83–100.

Surtees, Robert. *The History and Antiquities of the County Palatine of Durham*. 4 vols. London: J. Nichols and Son, 1816–40.

Theiner, Paul. "The Medieval Terence." In *The Learned and Lewed: Studies in Chaucer and Medieval Literature*, edited by Larry D. Benson. Cambridge: Harvard University Press, 1974. Pp. 231–47.

Thompson, A. Hamilton. *The English Clergy and Their Organization in the Later Middle Ages*. Oxford: Clarendon Press, 1947.

Thomson, John A. F. *The Later Lollards, 1414–1520*. Oxford: Oxford University Press, 1965.

Tillott, P. M., ed. *A History of Yorkshire: The City of York*. Victoria History of the Counties of England. London, 1961.

Tittler, Robert. "Henry Hardware's Moment and the Puritan Attack on Drama." *Early Theatre* 1 (1998): 39–54.

———. "The Incorporation of Boroughs, 1540–1558." *History* 62 (204) (1977): 24–42.

Travis, Peter W. *Dramatic Design in the Chester Cycle*. Chicago: University of Chicago Press, 1982.

Turner, Victor. *The Ritual Process: Structure and Anti-structure*. Chicago: Aldine, 1969.

Tuve, Rosamond. *Allegorical Imagery: Some Mediaeval Books and Their Posterity*. Princeton: Princeton University Press, 1966.

Twycross, Meg. "*Mary Magdalen* at Durham." *Medieval English Theatre* 4 (1982): 63–66.

———. "'Places to Hear the Plays': Pageant Stations at York, 1398–1572." *Records of Early English Drama Newsletter* 4 (2) (1978): 10–33.

Twycross, Meg, and Sarah Carpenter. "Masks in Medieval English Theatre: The Mystery Plays." *Medieval English Theatre* 3 (1981): 7–44, 69–113.

Tydeman, William. *The Theatre in the Middle Ages.* Cambridge: Cambridge University Press, 1978.

van Dyke, Carolyn. *The Fiction of Truth: Structures of Meaning in Narrative and Dramatic Allegory.* Ithaca: Cornell University Press, 1985.

Velz, John W. "Sovereignty in the Digby *Mary Magdalene*." *Comparative Drama* 2 (1968): 32–43.

Viller, Marcel, et al., eds. *Dictionnaire de spiritualité ascétique et mystique, doctrine et histoire.* Paris: Beauchesne, 1937–.

Walker, Greg. *Plays of Persuasion: Drama and Politics at the Court of Henry VIII.* Cambridge: Cambridge University Press, 1991.

———. *The Politics of Performance in Early Renaissance Drama.* Cambridge: Cambridge University Press, 1998.

Wasson, John. "Corpus Christi Plays and Pageants at Ipswich." *Research Opportunities in Renaissance Drama* 19 (1976): 99–108.

———. "The English Church as Theatrical Space." In Cox and Kastan, *New History.* Pp. 25–37.

———. "The Morality Play: Ancestor of Elizabethan Drama?" In *The Drama in the Middle Ages: Comparative and Critical Essays,* edited by Clifford Davidson, C. J. Gianakaris, and John H. Stroupe. New York: AMS, 1982. Pp. 316–27.

———. "The *St. George* and *Robin Hood* Plays in Devon." *Mediaeval English Theatre* 2 (1980): 66–69.

Weimann, Robert. *Shakespeare and the Popular Tradition in the Theater: Studies in the Social Dimension of Dramatic Form and Function.* Edited by Robert Schwartz. Baltimore: The Johns Hopkins University Press, 1978.

Wenzel, Siegfried. "An Early Reference to a Corpus Christi Play." *Modern Philology* 74 (1977): 390–94.

———. "*Somer Game* and Sermon References to a Corpus Christi Play." *Modern Philology* 86 (1989): 274–81.

Westfall, Suzanne. *Patrons and Performance: Early Tudor Household Revels.* Oxford: Clarendon Press, 1990.

Westlake, H. F. *The Parish Gilds of Mediaeval England.* London: Society for Promoting Christian Knowledge, 1919.

White, Eileen. "'Bryngyng Forth of Saynt George': The St. George Celebrations in York." *Medieval English Theatre* 3 (1981): 114–21.

———. "Places for Hearing the Corpus Christi Play in York." *Medieval English Theatre* 9 (1987): 23–63.

White, Paul Whitfield. *Theatre and Reformation: Protestantism, Patronage, and Playing in Tudor England.* Cambridge: Cambridge University Press, 1993.

Whitman, Jon. *Allegory: The Dynamics of an Ancient and Medieval Technique.* Cambridge: Harvard University Press, 1987.

Wickham, Glynne. *Early English Stages, 1300–1660.* 3 vols. London: Routledge and Kegan Paul, 1959–81.

Wiles, David. *The Early Plays of Robin Hood.* Cambridge, U.K.: D. S. Brewer, 1981.

Williams, Arnold. *The Characterization of Pilate in the Towneley Plays.* East Lansing: Michigan State College Press, 1950.

———. "Typology and the Cycle Plays: Some Criteria." *Speculum* 43 (1968): 677–84.

Wilson, F. P. *The English Drama 1485–1585.* Oxford: Clarendon Press, 1969.

Wittig, Joseph S. "'Piers Plowman' B, Passus IX–XII: Elements in the Design of the Inward Journey." *Traditio* 28 (1972): 212–13.

Womack, Peter. "Imagining Communities: Theatres and the English Nation in the Sixteenth Century." In *Culture and History 1350–1600: Essays on English Communities, Identities and Writing,* edited by David Aers. Detroit: Wayne State University Press, 1992. Pp. 91–145.

Woolf, Rosemary. *The English Mystery Plays.* Berkeley: University of California Press, 1972.

Woozley, A. D. "Universals." In *The Encyclopedia of Philosophy,* edited by Paul Edwards. 8 vols. New York and London: Macmillan, 1967. 8:194–206.

Wright, Steven K. "Is the Ashmole Fragment a Remnant of a Middle English Saint Play?" *Neophilologus* 75 (1991): 139–49.

Wyatt, Diana. "Performance and Ceremonial in Beverley before 1642." Ph.D. diss. University of York, 1983.

Young, Abigail A. "Minstrels and Minstrelsy: Household Retainers or Instrumentalists?" *Records of Early English Drama Newsletter* 20 (1995): 11–17.

———. "Plays and Players: The Latin Terms for Performance." *Records of Early English Drama Newsletter* 9 (2) (1984): 56–62; 10 (1) (1985): 9–16.

Young, Karl. *The Drama of the Medieval Church.* 2 vols. Oxford: Clarendon Press, 1933.

❦ I N D E X ❧